Further Afield
Pages 102–119

Old Delhi
Pages 92–101

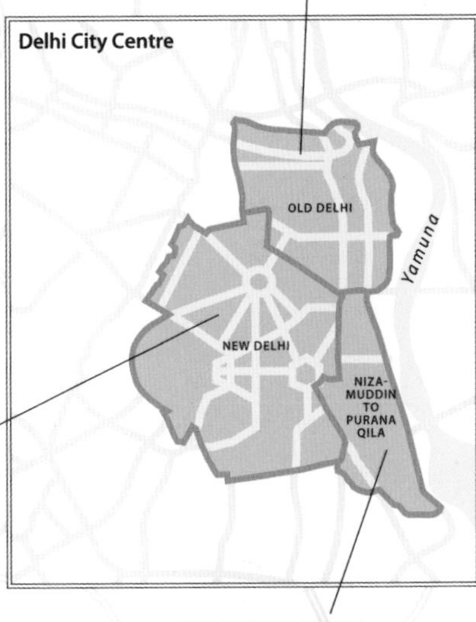

New Delhi
Pages 70–83

Nizamuddin to Purana Qila
Pages 84–91

EYEWITNESS TRAVEL

DELHI
AGRA & JAIPUR

DELHI
AGRA & JAIPUR

Main Contributors **Anuradha Chaturvedi**
Dharmendar Kanwar & Ranjana Sengupta

LONDON, NEW YORK,
MELBOURNE, MUNICH AND DELHI
www.dk.com

Project Editor Aruna Ghose
Art Editor Alpana Khare
Editors Ira Pande, Madhulita Mohapatra, Razia Grover
Designers Anand Naorem, Benu Joshi, Mugdha Sethi
Cartography Uma Bhattacharya
Picture Editor Radhika Singh

Main Contributors
Anuradha Chaturvedi, Dharmendar Kanwar, Partho Datta,
Premola Ghose, Ranjana Sengupta, Subhadra Sengupta

Photographers
Aditya Patankar, Amit Pashricha, Dinesh Khanna,
Fredrick & Laurence Arvidsson, Ram Rahman

Illustrators
Ajay Sethi, Ampersand, Ashok Sukumaran, Avinash,
Dipankar Bhattacharya, Gautam Trivedi, Mark Warner

Printed and bound in China

First American Edition, 2000

Reprinted with revisions 2001, 2003, 2007, 2010, 2013, 2015

17 18 19 10 9 8 7 6 5 4 3

Published in the United States by
Dorling Kindersley Limited, 345 Hudson Street,
New York, New York 10014

ISSN 1542-1554

ISBN 978-1-4654-2825-7

Floors are referred to throughout in accordance with American usage; ie the "first floor" is the floor at ground level.

MIX
Paper from
responsible sources
FSC™ C018179

The information in this DK Eyewitness Travel Guide is checked regularly.
Every effort has been made to ensure that this book is as up-to-date as possible at the time of going to press. Some details, however, such as telephone numbers, opening hours, prices, gallery hanging arrangements and travel information are liable to change. The publishers cannot accept responsibility for any consequences arising from the use of this book, nor for any material on third party websites, and cannot guarantee that any website address in this book will be a suitable source of travel information. We value the views and suggestions of our readers very highly. Please write to: Publisher, DK Eyewitness Travel Guides, Dorling Kindersley, 80 Strand, London, WC2R 0RL, UK, or email: travelguides@dk.com.

Front cover main image: Hawa Mahal, or the "Palace of Winds", in Jaipur

◀ Camels crossing the river by the Taj Mahal, Agra

A gathering at a village square in Rajasthan

Contents

Ganesha, the elephant-headed god of wisdom

Introducing Delhi, Agra & Jaipur

Delhi Area by Area

Beyond Delhi Area by Area

Embroidered slippers

Travellers' Needs

A contemporary inlaid-marble platter

Survival Guide

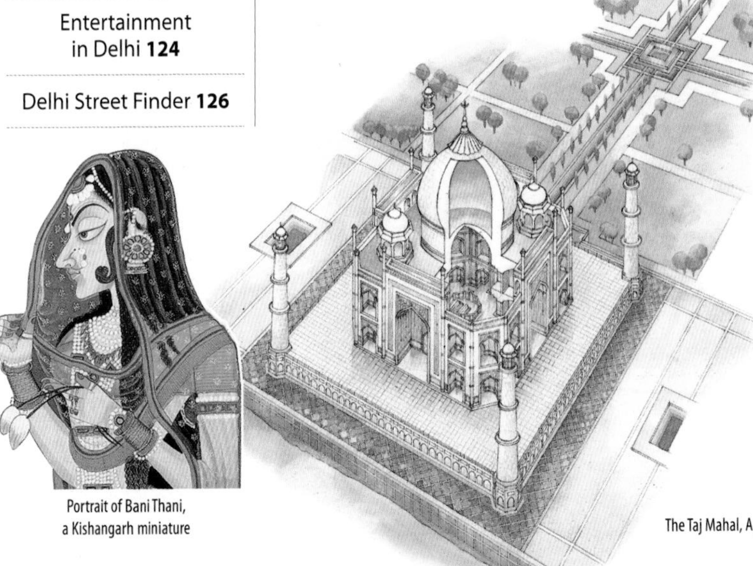

Portrait of Bani Thani, a Kishangarh miniature

The Taj Mahal, Agra

HOW TO USE THIS GUIDE

This guide helps you to get the most from your visit to the region. It provides both detailed practical information and expert recommendations. *Introducing Delhi, Agra and Jaipur* maps the region and sets it in its historical and cultural context. The three regional sections, plus *Delhi,* describe important sights, using maps, photographs and illustrations. Features cover topics from music and dance to food and festivals. Restaurant and hotel recommendations can be found in *Travellers' Needs*. The *Survival Guide* has tips on everything from transport to using the telephone, and the *Glossary* explains Indian terms and words.

Delhi

The city is divided into areas, each with its own chapter. A last chapter, *Further Afield,* covers peripheral sights. All sights are numbered and plotted on the chapter's area map. Each sight is presented in numerical order within the chapter, making it easy to locate.

All pages relating to Delhi have red thumb tabs.

Sights at a Glance lists the chapter's sights by category: Mosques and Tombs, Museums and Galleries, Streets and Gardens, Historic Sites, Monuments and Markets.

A locator map shows where you are in relation to other areas of the city centre.

1 Area Map

For easy reference, sights are numbered and located on a map. City centre sights are also marked on the Delhi Street Finder map *(pages 126–35).*

Stars indicate the sights that no visitor should miss.

2 Street-by-Street Map

This gives a bird's-eye view of the key areas in each chapter.

A suggested route for a walk is shown in red.

3 Detailed information

The sights in Delhi are described individually. Useful addresses, telephone numbers, opening hours and other practical information are also provided. The key to the symbols used is on the back flap of the book.

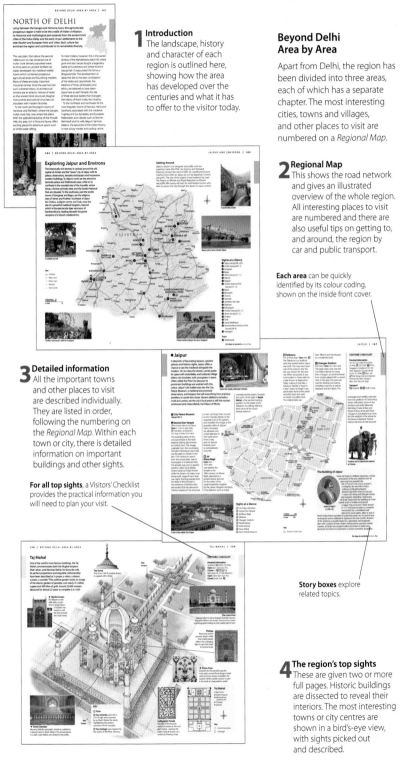

1 Introduction
The landscape, history and character of each region is outlined here, showing how the area has developed over the centuries and what it has to offer to the visitor today.

Beyond Delhi Area by Area

Apart from Delhi, the region has been divided into three areas, each of which has a separate chapter. The most interesting cities, towns and villages, and other places to visit are numbered on a *Regional Map*.

2 Regional Map
This shows the road network and gives an illustrated overview of the whole region. All interesting places to visit are numbered and there are also useful tips on getting to, and around, the region by car and public transport.

Each area can be quickly identified by its colour coding, shown on the inside front cover.

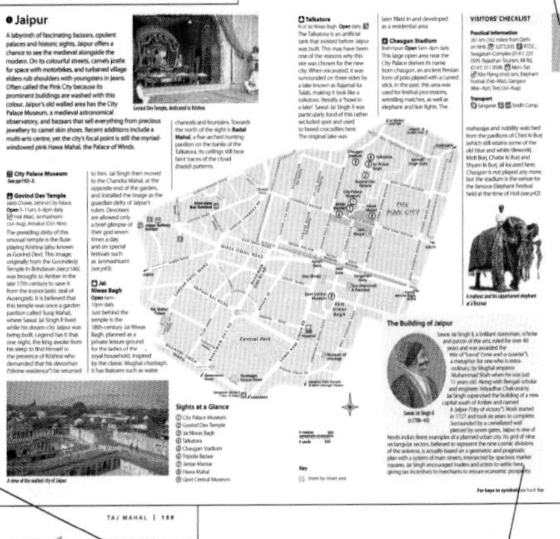

3 Detailed information
All the important towns and other places to visit are described individually. They are listed in order, following the numbering on the *Regional Map*. Within each town or city, there is detailed information on important buildings and other sights.

For all top sights, a Visitors' Checklist provides the practical information you will need to plan your visit.

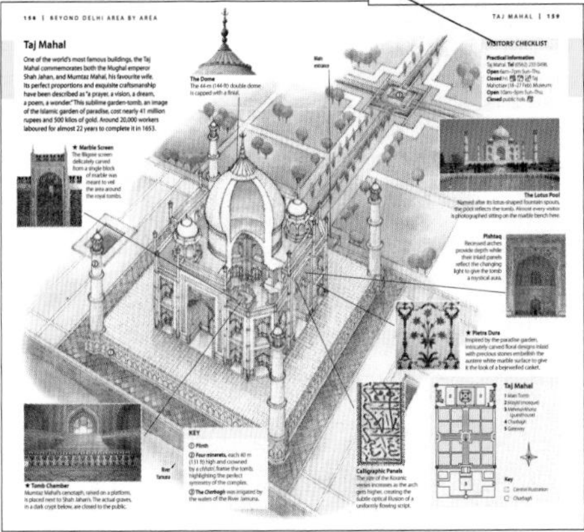

Story boxes explore related topics.

4 The region's top sights
These are given two or more full pages. Historic buildings are dissected to reveal their interiors. The most interesting towns or city centres are shown in a bird's-eye view, with sights picked out and described.

INTRODUCING DELHI AGRA & JAIPUR

GREAT DAYS IN DELHI, AGRA & JAIPUR

Known as the Golden Triangle, this circuit has a bewildering array of things to do and see. The cities offer a fascinating window into the culture, heritage and heart of India, including the best Mughal architecture, amazing cuisines and exquisite art and handicrafts. These itineraries will help you plan your stay without missing out on any of the essential experiences. There are two- and three-day tours that outline the main attractions. The price guides include cost of travel, food and admission fees. Pick, combine and follow your favourite tours.

The main gateway to Humayun's Tomb, Delhi

A Family Day Out in Delhi

Family of 4 allow at least ₹5,000

- **Visit the Rail Museum and Nehru Planetarium**
- **Shop at the Santushti Shopping Complex**
- **Explore Humayun's Tomb**

Morning

Start the day by viewing vintage trains at the **Rail Museum** *(see p108)*. A toy train takes visitors around and, on some days, the old Patiala State Steam Monorail is steamed up as well. A must-see is the *Fairy Queen*, manufactured in 1855 and listed in the *Guinness Book of Records* as the world's oldest working locomotive. Next, visit the **Nehru Memorial Museum and Library** *(see p82)*, once the official residence of India's first prime minister, Pandit Jawaharlal Nehru, and now a museum. Within its grounds is the **Nehru Planetarium** *(see p82)*. A dome-shaped screen and a sky theatre hold live and taped shows on astronomy, with a Carl Zeiss Spaceflight master projector to view the sky. You can also see the historic module, Soyuz T-10, which carried Rakesh Sharma, India's first astronaut, to space in 1984.

Afternoon

Take a lunch break at Basil and Thyme at the nearby **Santushti Shopping Complex** *(p122)*, where some of the city's best boutiques provide a tempting distraction. After a delicious meal and bit of shopping, head for **Humayun's Tomb** *(see p87)*. Set in the centre of a stylised garden, India's first great Mughal garden tomb is a tranquil place. Pause to examine the fine trellis-work of the stone screens. The lawns provide space for children to run around and enjoy themselves after a morning spent indoors.

Museums and Shopping in Delhi

Two Adults allow at least ₹5,000

- **Take a short historical walk to the National Museum**
- **Enjoy an al fresco lunch at Lodi Gardens**
- **Discover the Crafts Museum and the fine shops in Khan Market**

Morning

Start the day with a walk down majestic **Rajpath** *(see p75)*, New Delhi's main ceremonial street, to **India Gate** *(see p75)*. The lawns here are a great vantage point to view the magnificent sweep of Lutyens's capital complex. A brisk walk to Janpath will bring you to the **National Museum** *(see pp76–9)*. Highlights include objects from the Indus Valley Civilization, miniature paintings and the Indo-Chinese Buddhist art sections.

India Gate, surrounded by lawns, a pleasant picnic spot

◀ Miniature painting of a Rajput prince, surrounded by female attendants in a garden pavilion

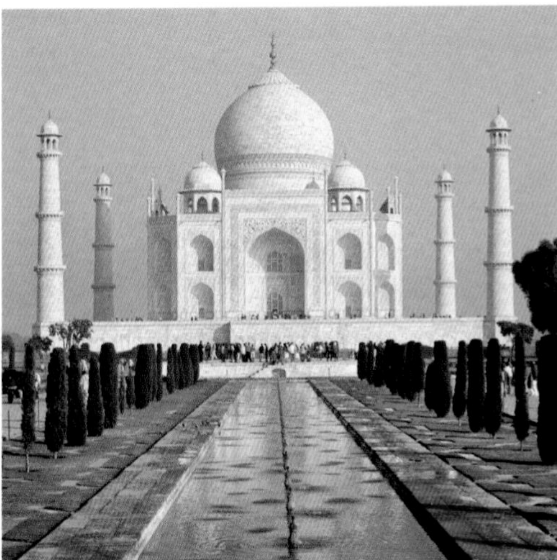

Taj Mahal at sunrise, a sublime experience

A short taxi ride from here will bring you to **Lodi Gardens** *(see p83)* for a delicious al fresco lunch at **Lodi Garden Restaurant** *(see p250)*.

Afternoon

After lunch, visit the **Crafts Museum** *(see pp90–91)*, to see an unusual art collection. Open courtyards with shady trees provide good resting places for children and the elderly. End your day at lively **Khan Market** *(see p83)*, exploring the excellent bookshops, boutiques and cafés to be found there.

A Day in Agra

Two Adults allow at least ₹5,000

- **View the sunrise over the Taj Mahal**
- **Discover the glories of the Itmad-ud-Daulah Tomb**
- **Say goodbye to the Taj, Shah Jahan style**

Morning

Try and reach Agra the evening before so that you can watch the sun rise over the **Taj Mahal** *(see pp158–9)* – the changing colours of the marble make for an unforgettable experience. It is also the best time of the day to visit the Taj as the afternoon sun heats the marble and makes it difficult to walk barefoot (mandatory here). Nothing can top this experience, so break off for lunch to recover your breath.

Afternoon

Head for **Itmad-ud-Daulah's Tomb** *(see pp162–3)* to see the superb *pietra dura* interiors and the delicate marble screens, that almost rival those of the Taj. The last lap of the day must belong to historic **Agra Fort** *(see p154)*. Shah Jahan was imprisoned by his son in the fort's Musamman Burj. He spent his last days gazing lovingly at the Taj, across the river. You can stand at the same window to say your final goodbye to the Taj.

A Day in Jaipur

Two Adults allow at least ₹8,000

- **Take an elephant ride to the dramatic Rajput fort-palace of Amber**
- **Palace-hop in Jaipur**
- **Grab lunch at a heritage hotel**
- **Visit a traditional Indian bazaar**

Morning

Begin your day with a trip to the dramatic 16th-century hill fort of **Amber** *(see pp204–5)*. An elephant ride takes you to the complex, with courtyards, private gardens and pillared apartments. Back in Jaipur, a city of palaces, start palace-hopping by first going to the **City Palace** *(see pp192–3)*, a part of which still houses the erstwhile royal family. Close by is the **Jantar Mantar** *(see pp196–7)*, still used to calculate astronomical events. Finally, visit **Hawa Mahal** *(see p190)*, a whimsical façade of windows and quite unlike any other palace.

Afternoon

A leisurely lunch at the **Rambagh Palace Hotel** *(see p199)* comes with all the trappings of a royal feast, including splendidly attired waiters. However, don't miss out on an afternoon of shopping at the lively bazaars around **Bari Chaupar** *(see pp188–9)* for brightly printed textiles, hand-made paper and silver jewellery. Also check out Johari Bazaar's jewellery shops, showcasing the famous *kundan* and precious stone work.

Elephants waiting for visitors outside Amber Fort, Jaipur

Exhibits at the National Gallery of Modern Art

Three Days in Delhi

Two Adults allow at least ₹5,000

- **View the antiquities at the National Museum**
- **Watch the Son et Lumière at the Red Fort**
- **Climb to the top of the Qutb Minar**
- **Explore Hauz Khas Village**
- **Experience Bollywood at the Kingdom of Dreams**

Day 1

Morning Begin the day with a stroll around **India Gate** *(p75)*. Designed by the British architect Edwin Lutyens, the monument commemorates the Indian soldiers who died during World War I. From here, take a walk along **Rajpath** *(p75)*, the city's main ceremonial street, towards the parliament buildings. Next, visit the nearby **National Museum** *(pp76–9)*, which has a great collection of historic antiquities on display. For a more contemporary perspective of India, pop into the **National Gallery of Modern Art** *(p75)*. Don't miss out on the gallery's stunning journey through Indian art, titled *In the Seeds of Time*, which includes works by eminent artists such as Amrita Shergill and Jamini Roy.

Afternoon Take a cycle rickshaw tour of **Chandni Chowk** *(94–7)*, and explore the network of streets that take you to the heart of Old Delhi. Catch a glimpse of the beautiful Naughara street, which is lined with old, brightly-painted *havelis* (mansions). On your way, stop by the *jalebiwalla* for a taste of traditional sweets in Chandni Chowk. Then, visit the peaceful **Jami Masjid** *(p96)*, one of Shah Jahan's finest architectural wonders. Afterwards, head out of Chandni Chowk to the **Red Fort** *(pp98–9)*, where you can wrap up your Old Delhi adventure with a sound-and-light show. Visit nearby **Connaught Place** *(p80)* for dinner – there are plenty of options, varying from the more traditional to fusion, Asian and European. The pretty colonnaded streets make for a good walk after dinner.

The Jami Masjid, one of Delhi's largest mosques

Day 2

Morning Spend your morning at the **Qutb Minar** *(pp116–17)*. Visit the complex early, before the tourists arrive, and enjoy a peaceful stroll around the ancient monuments. The most prominent feature of the complex is the stunning, five-storeyed Victory Tower. The tower was built with materials from ransacked Hindu temples, and the architecture reflects a fascinating cross of Hindu and Islamic styles. If you have time, visit the nearby village of **Mehrauli** *(p117)*, which has an array of beautiful monuments as well.

Afternoon Head north towards **Hauz Khas** *(p110)*. Here you can enjoy lunch at one of the unconventional eateries in **Hauz Khas Village** *(p242)*, a bustling neighbourhood, popular with designers and artists, but also one that houses the ruins of the oldest *madarsa* (university) in New Delhi. After lunch, take a stroll in the lovely Deer Park. The Delhi Art Gallery, which has a great collection of contemporary art, is located here as well.

There are many private galleries, boutiques, coffee shops and tea rooms around the area. If you browse through the eccentric stores, you can find vintage Bollywood movie posters, funky souvenirs and classic *kurtas* (Indian shirts). Later, take a short drive to the **Baha'i House of Worship** *(p119)*, better known as the Lotus temple. Completed in 1986, the temple is shaped like a lotus, and designed in a contemporary fashion. The Baha'i faith emphasizes on monotheism, and is dedicated to the spiritual unity of all races, religions and castes. Devote the evening to the **Lodi Gardens** *(p83)*, a popular sunset spot. This green oasis is usually crowded with people, walking and running, during all hours of the day. There are several monuments within the park that can be explored, such as the tomb of Sikander Lodi. Have dinner at the **Lodi Garden Restaurant** *(p250)*, or head to the nearby **Khan Market** *(p83)* for drinks, dinner and some retail therapy.

Day 3
Morning Start with a trip to the **National Rail Museum** *(pp108–9)*, which offers insight into India's extensive rail network. Tour the area on the toy train, which takes you around the park. Next, head to **Dilli Haat** *(p109)*, which is themed like a village market and features artisans from all over the country. There is much to buy in this market – from a variety of handicrafts to shawls, jewellery, lamps, and much more. The market offers hassle free shopping. Sample food from states as diverse as Kashmir and Goa. The Rajasthani stall has particularly good *kulfi* (ice cream) and delicious *kejsangri* (desert beans).

Bara Gumbad or the "big dome" at the Lodi Gardens

Afternoon After lunch, make a quick visit to **Humayan's Tomb** *(p87)*. This majestic mausoleum belongs to the second Mughal emperor, Humayun, and is an architectural marvel of the period. Afterwards, catch the Delhi metro to Gurgaon. Get off at the IFFCO metro station for a Bollywood-style show at the Kingdom of Dreams (book tickets for the show in advance). Described as the carnival of India, this all-singing and dancing ensemble gives insight into India's other great love – cinema. The interior of the Kingdom of Dreams complex offers a glimpse of every region in India. From Goan architecture, with its vividly-painted buildings, to ornate sculptures reminiscent of Khajuraho in Madhya Pradesh, the auditorium is a sight to behold. You can sample traditional foods from every region – buttermilk from Himachal Pradesh, delicious snacks from Gujarat, and spicy *vindaloo* (curry) from Goa.

To extend your trip...
Take a four-hour drive from Delhi to **Alwar** *(pp210–11)*, a city that offers a totally different experience of the region. There are plenty of majestic fort hotels with commanding views and fabulous suites. The **City Palace** *(p210)*, built in the 18th century, gives visitors a view of beautiful Rajput architecture. The Vinai Vilas Mahal within the palace has stunning, ornate balconies and intricate stone carvings. The **City Palace Museum** *(p210)* has a fine collection of Indian miniature paintings. Enjoy the view of the countryside around this elegant property.

Colourful handicrafts on display at the Dilli Haat

Two Days in Agra

Two Adults allow at least ₹8,000

- **Discover the history of the Taj Mahal**
- **Take a boat ride near the Agra Fort**
- **Travel to the ancient city of Fatehpur Sikri**
- **Visit the renowned tomb of Akbar in Sikandra**

The beautifully carved sandstone pillars of the palace of Fatehpur Sikri

Day 1

Morning The best time to visit the **Taj Mahal** *(pp158–61)* is early in the morning. It is ideal to arrive an evening prior to your visit, and get a timely start the next day. Famously described by Rabindranath Tagore as "a solitary tear suspended on the cheek of time", the Taj is a magnificent sight to behold at dawn. Explore the chambers and the gardens. The calligraphic panels and the jewelled marble patterns are exquisite. Unwind over lunch at nearby **Dasprakash** *(p254)*.

Afternoon Spend the afternoon exploring the incredible red arches of **Agra Fort** *(p154)*. Located across the Yamuna River, the fort has an arrangement of halls, galleries and courtyards, and the Taj Mahal can be viewed from almost everywhere. There is much to learn and see here – from the emperor Shah Jahan's private mosque, **Mina Masjid** *(p154)*, and the grape garden, **Anguri Bagh** *(p154)*, to the fish palace, **Machchhi Bhawan** *(p154)* and the **Musamman Burj** *(p154)*, the tower where Shah Jahan was later imprisoned. It is also possible to take a boat along the river for splendid views of the Taj.

Day 2

Morning Start off with a short drive from Agra to the deserted city of **Fatehpur Sikri** *(pp174–7)*. Built by Akbar in 1571, it served as his capital for 14 years. However, the lack of an adequate supply of water led to its eventual abandonment. The city has since been restored and today, it is an enchanting sight. Visit the **Buland Darwaza** *(p177)*, and the marvellous **Tomb of Sheikh Salim Chishti** *(p177)*, where many passersby tie knots of thread and make wishes. Get an early start to avoid the crowds.

Afternoon Akbar himself is buried at **Sikandra** *(p164)*, a small village on the outskirts of Agra. His tomb is a marvellous symmetrical structure, set in a beautiful garden, and the room has wonderful acoustics. Make sure you experiment with sound in the burial chamber, and ask your guide for more information on the use of these acoustics. End the day with a walk through the **bazaars** *(pp259–61)* of Agra, where you can shop for nick-nacks. To enjoy good food and live instrumental music, have dinner at **Esphahan** *(p254)* at the Oberoi Amarvilas.

To extend your trip...
The **Keoladeo Ghana National Park** *(p172–3)* is a great stopover between Agra and Jaipur. Ride a bicycle through the bird sanctuary, or take a walk in the park. Travel further to **Mathura** *(p165)*, and discover the Krishna temples.

Akbar's tomb at Sikandra, Agra

Two Days in Jaipur

Two Adults allow at least ₹6,000

- **Explore the collections at the City Palace Museum**
- **See the detailed *jali* work at Hawa Mahal**
- **Ride an elephant up to Amber Fort**
- **View the sunset from the fort of Nahargarh**

The ornamental entrance to Chandra Mahal at the Jaipur City Palace

Day 1

Morning Located in the heart of Jaipur is the **City Palace** *(pp192–5)*, which today houses an impressive collection of textiles, weaponry and miniature Mughal paintings. Visit the museum to appreciate the grand blend of Rajput and Mughal architecture, the role of the maharaja, and the rich heritage of the area. At the **Chandra Mahal** *(p194)*, have a look at the delicate marble work and floral depictions, embedded with precious stones. Enjoy a traditional Rajasthani lunch at MI Road.

Afternoon Head north to **Hawa Mahal** *(p190)*, the elegant "Palace of Winds" in the Old City. The palace has an intricately-designed façade, with lovely *jali* work (ornately-carved stone lattice) on the windows. The initial purpose of these carvings was to allow the women of the harem to watch the parades without being seen. Next, explore the twisting bazaars around the palace. Taste the local *kachoris* (round balls of dough, stuffed with lentils and spices), and *lassi* (whipped yoghurt shake) at the popular *lassiwala*. Visitors will find a lane dedicated to wedding paraphernalia, a jewellery market, numerous shops that sell cloth, and almost everything else imaginable. There are a few charming old *havelis* scattered within the walled city as well. In the evening, make your way to **Chokhi Dhani** *(p256)* for a typical village experience in Jaipur. This quaint, themed village offers puppet shows, head massages, and rides on camels and elephants. Enjoy a delicious traditional dinner while seated on rustic mats.

Day 2

Morning Begin the day with a tour of **Amber Fort** *(pp204–6)*, one of the most exquisite fort palaces in Rajasthan. The fort is a short drive from Jaipur, and visitors usually take an elephant ride up the steep climb to the complex. Check out the ornate glass palace, **Sheesh Mahal** *(p206)*, and the captivating temple of goddess Kali, the **Shila Devi Temple** *(p206)*. The views across the valley are incredible, and there are a few boutiques within the fort where visitors can do a little shopping. Later, walk to the nearby Anokhi Museum of Handblock Print, where you can discover the rich history of craftsmanship and handblock printing in India. Grab a cup of coffee while you view the exhibits. Those further interested in the textile traditions of the city can visit **Sanganer** *(p208)*, a bustling Jaipur suburb, and **Bagru** *(p208)*, a village that specializes in traditional textile printing.

Afternoon After lunch, head to the famous **Jantar Mantar** *(p196–7)*, the largest ancient observatory in Jaipur, with 16 monumental instruments installed to calculate the changes of season and time. The observatory was built by the well-known astronomer Sawai Jai Singh II, who believed that predictions would be more accurate if the size of each instrument was bigger. Wind up the day with a visit to the fort of **Nahargarh** *(p202)*, where you can catch the sunset, along with wonderous views of Jaipur. There is a little restaurant within the walls of the fort, where visitors can enjoy a meal.

To extend your trip...
Travel north of Jaipur to **Shekhawati** *(pp216–17)*, famous for its painted *havelis*. Located close to each other, the small towns of **Mandawa** *(p217)*, **Nawalgarh** *(p217)* and **Sikar** *(p217)* have beautiful restored forts with murals, which attract many visitors. Many of these fort-palaces have been converted into hotels, and are a wonderful way to experience the heritage. Do not forget to visit the beautiful **Ranthambhore National Park** *(pp228–9)*, where you may even be able to view the elusive Bengal tiger. Book in advance.

Panoramic view of the splendid Amber Fort, Jaipur

Putting Delhi, Agra & Jaipur on the Map

The Delhi, Agra and Jaipur region lies in the heart of North India. It covers an area of about 114, 000 sq km (44, 000 sq miles) and has a population of over 23 million. Delhi is the capital of India, while Jaipur is the capital of Rajasthan. Agra is a major district headquarters in the state of Uttar Pradesh. Both Delhi and Jaipur have international airports, while Agra is serviced by domestic flights. The region also has good road and railway connections, with Agra about three hours and Jaipur about four by train from Delhi.

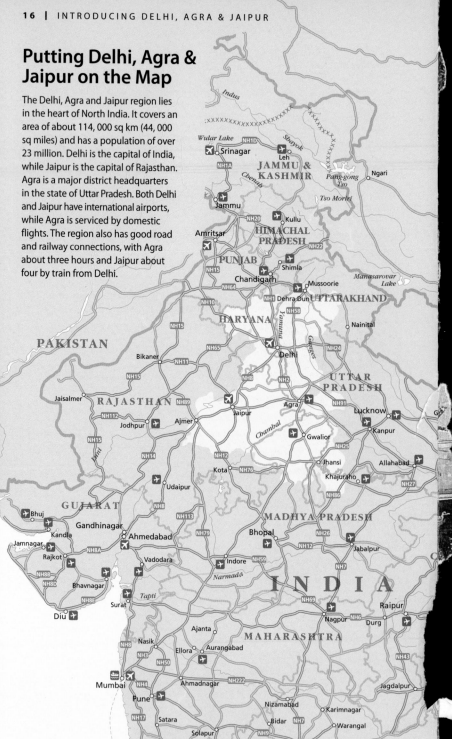

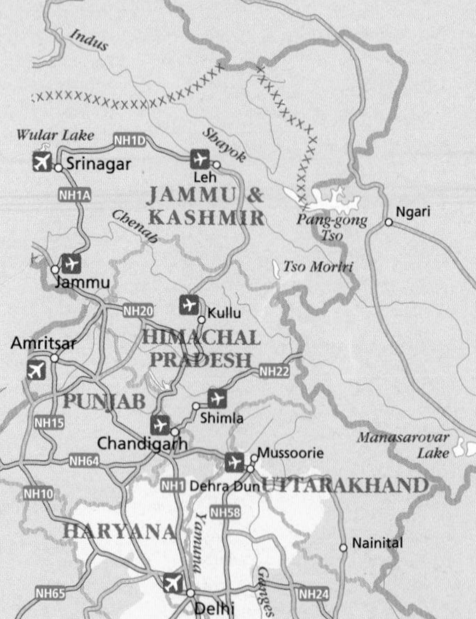

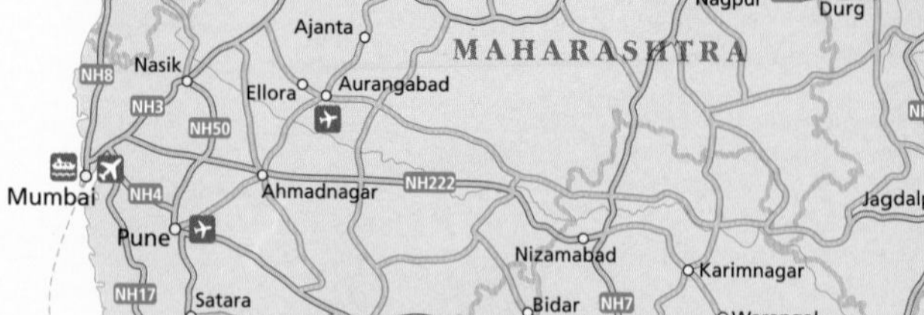

For keys to symbols *see back flap*

The external boundaries of India as shown on this map are neither correct nor authentic.

Delhi City Centre and Greater Delhi

Some of Delhi's most impressive buildings can be seen in this area. The sights described in this book are grouped within three areas, each of which can be explored by foot. Vijay Chowk is the vantage point for the grand sweep of Raj buildings grouped on Raisina Hill. To the north, the magnificent Jami Masjid, with its busy hive of lanes, was once the heart of the Mughal empire and is still the focus of Old Delhi. The past and present mingle here and yet preserve their own space and identity. To the east, the medieval quarter around the *dargah* of the Sufi Nizamuddin Auliya leads along Mathura Road to the ruined Purana Qila. This ancient site has interesting origins, going back to a distant mythological past.

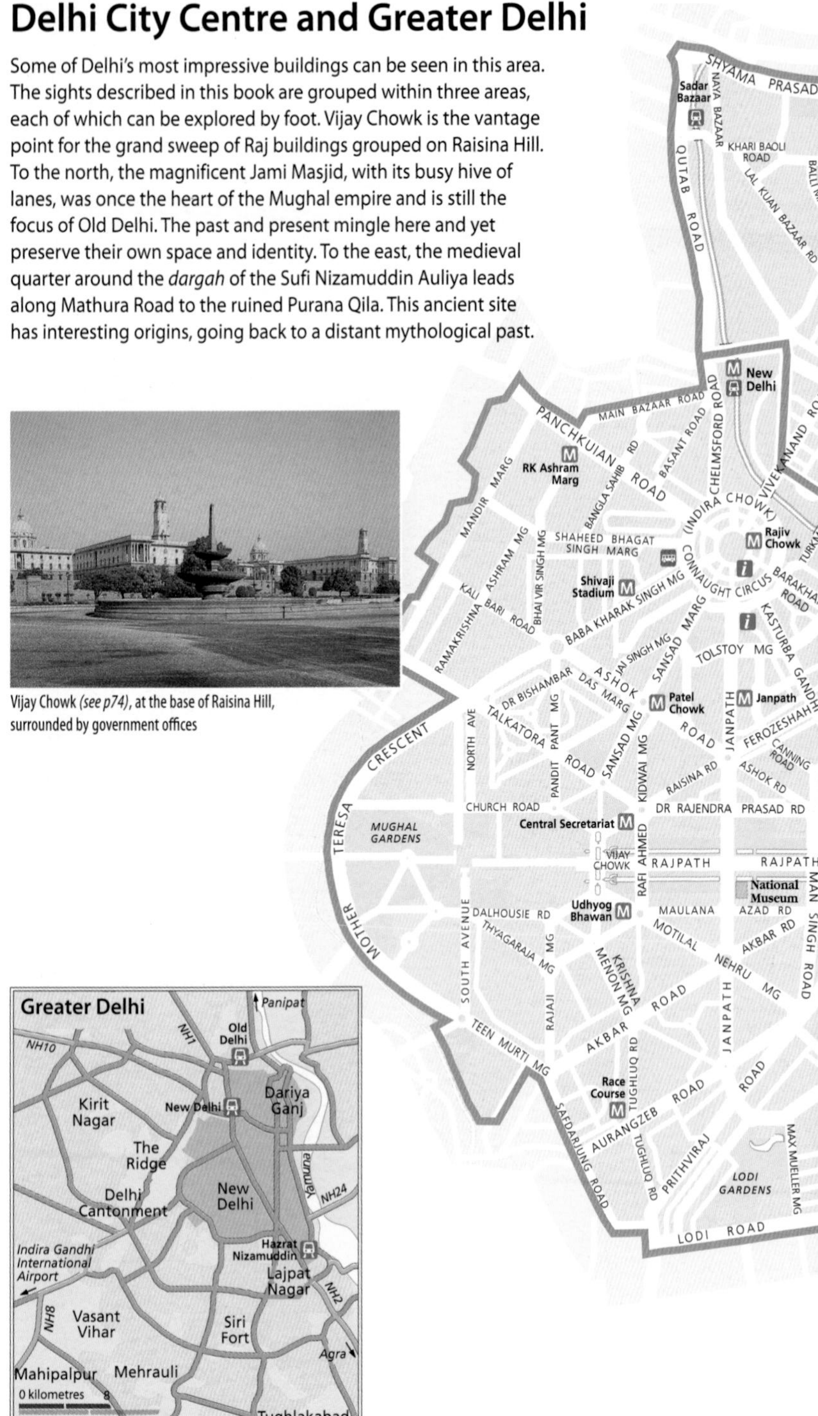

Vijay Chowk *(see p74)*, at the base of Raisina Hill, surrounded by government offices

For keys to symbols *see back flap*

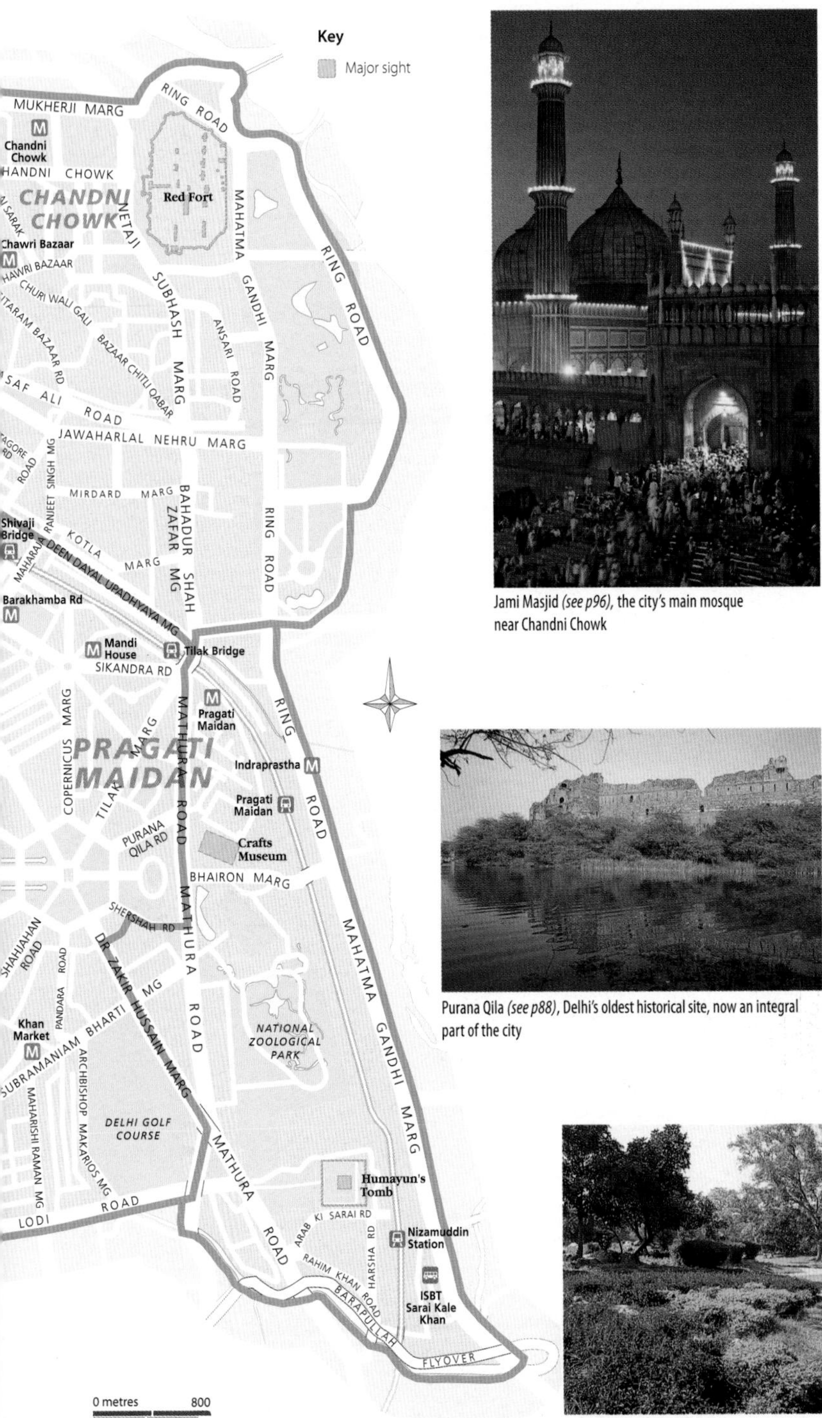

Jami Masjid *(see p96)*, the city's main mosque near Chandni Chowk

Purana Qila *(see p88)*, Delhi's oldest historical site, now an integral part of the city

Buddha Jayanti Park *(see p108)*, created on the Ridge in northwest Delhi

A PORTRAIT OF DELHI, AGRA & JAIPUR

The Delhi, Agra and Jaipur region lies at the geographical heart of North India. Its strategic location along the north-south and east-west routes has given it a focal position in Indian history and many great empires have been ruled from here. What we see today is a dynamic blend of the old and the new, a proudly traditional social structure within a modern liberalized economy.

This landlocked region is enclosed by mountains to the north, the desert and the forested Aravallis to the west. To the east are the agriculturally rich riverine plains, with vast fields of sugarcane, wheat, mustard and lentils. Southwards, these flat plains dramatically metamorphose into the earth pillars of the Chambal ravines, a rugged landscape once inhabited by fierce bandits. Invaders, entering the sub-continent from the mountain passes of the northwestern frontiers, conquered this region centuries ago and made it their home.

The Legacy of the Past

The earliest civilization in this region was the Harappan culture in the second millennium BC. However, it was the Aryan settlements in the next millennium that provided the region with its philosophical moorings, epic literature, such as the *Ramayana* and *Mahabharata,* and its early Hindu kingdoms. In the first and second centuries, the area was the centre of a Buddhist empire when the Kushana emperors who ruled from Taxila (now in Pakistan) made Mathura their second capital. After the decline of the great Hindu and Buddhist empires, powerful Rajput rulers seized control of parts of North India. Many of the magnificent forts from which their feudal kingdoms were ruled can still be seen today.

Religion has always been the cultural link between the epochs,

Men in colourful turbans at the village square

◀ A group of musicians at the Diwan-i-Khas in Jaipur's City Palace

Cenotaphs of the Bharatpur kings at Kusum Sarovar near Brindavan

and by the 13th century, Hinduism had been influenced by the Bhakti Movement which stressed the need for a personal god. This resulted in the Krishna cult, centred around Mathura and Brindavan – places associated with the youth of this popular god. Even as the Bhakti Movement flourished, invaders from Afghanistan and Central Asia conquered the north. Delhi, and later Agra, became the capitals of the Muslim sultans. The cross-fertilization of indigenous and Islamic cultures bred a unique hybrid that influenced art, architecture, music and cuisine, reaching its zenith with the Mughals.

The 19th century saw the decline of the Mughal empire and the growing power of the British East India Company. In 1858, the East India Company's territories in India were transferred to the British Crown, and the country settled down to a 90-year span of Pax Britannica. The legacy of the British Raj lives on in modern India's administrative and educational systems, and English is today the common language of communication between India's different linguistic regions and states.

Open-air classes at a village school near Neemrana

In 1947, British rule came to an end and India became an independent nation. Since then, the country has faced the challenge of building industries, and tackling the social problems of illiteracy, poverty and the caste system. As the population of India raced towards one billion, these problems became more pressing. So, in the 1990s, India adopted an open-market economy, adding yet another dimension of change to a land that is constantly on the move.

People and Culture

The capital of India, New Delhi, is known as a city of migrants. After the violent Partition of India and Pakistan in 1947, millions of people, mainly from West Punjab, flocked here in search of a new life. Since then, there has been a continuing influx of people from all over India. The second most populous city in the world after Tokyo, Delhi has doubled its population since 1990 to 25 million. The majority of its citizens have settled here primarily for economic reasons – the average wage here is twice that of the country as a whole.

This mega-city nevertheless retains a small-town friendliness in its different neighbourhoods. Life still centres around the family, even though the joint family system is breaking down here, as is the case in all big Indian cities. Beyond the family is the larger world of the regional community which plays a significant role in the city's social and cultural life. Diaspora groups very often come together for auspicious occasions such as marriages or festivals, with which the Indian calendar is punctuated. Its mixed population has made Delhi a resolutely cosmopolitan city where Hindus, Muslims, Christians and Sikhs live side by side. Yet, each community has retained its distinct cultural identity, and the city is less a melting pot than a *thali* (plate) whose offerings may either be savoured singularly or in interesting combinations.

Bullock carts transporting rural goods

A fashion model

Different levels of development are evident in Delhi, Agra and Jaipur. But in all three cities, with the liberalized economy bringing in a sudden flood of consumer goods, and cable television channels beaming foreign cultures into their homes, the lifestyles and expectations of the people are rapidly changing.

What makes the region so interesting is that contrasts often exist here in perfect harmony – a bullock cart plods placidly beside the latest luxury car; weather forecasts are made both by satellite imaging and astrological calculations; and jeans-clad youngsters eating pizza in fast food joints are just as much at ease in a sari or *dhoti*, sitting cross-legged on the floor at home, to participate in traditional ceremonies or rituals.

A religious procession in Jaipur moving along in traditional splendour

Landscape and Wildlife

The Delhi, Agra and Jaipur region lies at the heart of northern India and covers a wide ecological zone, flanked by the Himalayas to the north and the ravines of the River Chambal to the south. To the west are the Aravalli mountain range and the Thar Desert, and to the east stretch the riverine plains watered by the Yamuna and the Chambal. Forests once covered much of this area but, with growing urbanization, have now been reduced to a few pockets around the national parks. These are the habitats of many prized species, like the endangered tiger.

Indian Trees

The region's rich variety of trees has local species as well as some of recent import. Some are sacred, others are valued for their healing qualities.

Banyan leaves

Sub-Himalayan Region

The Indian pine *(chir)* and *sal (Shorea robusta)* once formed thick forests that covered this area, but few remain today. However, there are still areas with sufficient forest cover to support a varied wildlife.

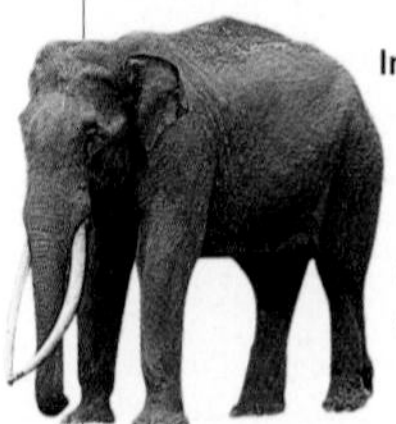

Indian elephants are smaller than the African species and are found on the lower Himalayan slopes. These gentle, intelligent animals are easy to train and domesticate.

Cheetal, the graceful Indian spotted deer, moves in herds in the grassland areas.

Monkeys of two types, the rhesus and the langur, thrive here.

Dry Deciduous Forests

This ecological zone covers the arid and semi-arid tracts along the Aravallis. The mixed vegetation of scrub and deciduous trees comprises acacias, cassia and *dhak (Butea monosperma)*, cacti and wild grasses.

Sambar, India's largest deer, is crowned with impressive antlers.

Tiger, the national animal, is now a protected species. Loss of forest cover today has brought it to the brink of extinction.

Crested serpent eagle, with its underwing pattern of black and white bands, is a large raptor often seen in the Ranthambhore forests.

Ashoka *(Saraca indica)*, one of India's five sacred trees, is extolled in Indian literature.

Pipal *(Ficus religiosa)*, a hardy tree that grows anywhere, is also the sacred Bodhi tree under which the Buddha attained enlightenment in Bodh Gaya.

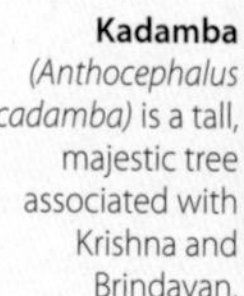

Neem *(Azadirachta indica)*. This large, shade-giving tree has an extraordinary range of medicinal, antiseptic and disinfectant properties.

Kadamba *(Anthocephalus cadamba)* is a tall, majestic tree associated with Krishna and Brindavan.

Wetlands

In the southwest are shallow inland lakes, marshes and swamps that have been formed from subterranean artesian wells. This is the habitat of otters and a wide variety of resident and migratory birds who feed on fish and aquatic plants.

Painted stork, with its black and pink plumage, keeps its long beak immersed in water, probing the sediment at the bottom for food.

Darter or snake bird boasts dark, glossy plumage. Large flocks can be found in marshy areas, spearing fish with their sharp beaks and then swallowing them.

Riverine Areas

These lie to the south and east along the Yamuna and Chambal rivers. The southern area is marked by desolate ravines, formed by erosion and covered with tufts of wiry grass, but to the east the rich alluvial plains form a thriving agricultural belt. The rivers support a rich aquatic wildlife.

Gharial *(Gavialis gangeticus)* is a species of crocodile found in the Ganges and its tributaries. It is named after the pitcher-like *(ghara)* hump on its long, lean snout.

King cobra is the world's largest venomous snake. This lethal reptile has a characteristic mark on its hood and is considered to be one of Shiva's sacred creatures.

Religions

India is a mosaic of different religions, varying from the ancient animistic beliefs of the tribal communities to the rigid orthodoxies of the Hindu caste system. The majority of India's population are Hindus, while around 138 million (13 per cent) are Muslims. Several other religions, such as Sikhism, Buddhism, Jainism, Zoroastrianism, Judaism and Christianity, also flourish. Jawaharlal Nehru *(see p82)* saw a unity in this diversity, and the Constitution of India declares it to be a secular republic, where the state has no official religion and all faiths can be freely practised.

Hinduism

The bedrock of Hinduism constitutes the four *Vedas* and the *Upanishads,* which are a holistic compilation of knowledge, philosophy and ethics. Yet, Hinduism is not a religion of written precepts, but a way of life that has evolved organically over the past 5,000 years.

In practice, Hindus worship a huge pantheon of gods and goddesses *(see pp28–9)*. Socially, they can be divided into four castes – the upper caste Brahmins (priests), the Kshatriyas (warriors), the Vaishyas (merchants and traders), and the lowest caste, Sudras (workers). The caste system envisioned society as an organic whole with each part or caste performing a vital function.

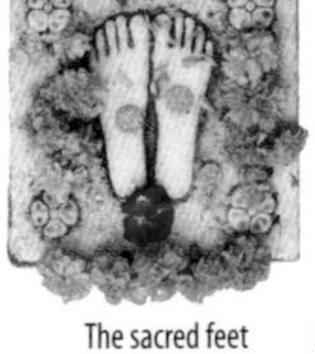

The sacred feet of Vishnu

The traditional family structure was that of a joint family presided over by its patriarch. This is now fast disappearing in urban areas. Yet, *sanskara*, traditional values, are still instilled into children, and complicated rites mark each stage of orthodox Hindu life. There is also an aspect of Hinduism which shuns idol-worship, and prefers to concentrate on larger philosophical issues. Sadhus, who wear saffron to indicate their retreat from the material world, are its most visible practitioners. They hold a most respected position in Hindu society.

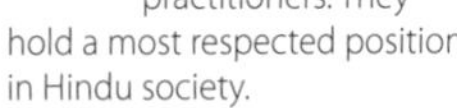

Islam

Islam was introduced into Western India in the 8th century by Arab traders, but it gained prominence in the north only after the 12th century, when it was declared the state religion under the medieval Muslim rulers.

A sufi mystic on a carpet outside a *dargah* (shrine)

Today, Muslims are India's second largest religious community, despite a large exodus to Pakistan after the traumatic Partition of 1947 *(see pp62–3)*. Muslims can be broadly divided into two sects, the Sunnis and the Shias. The latter believe that Prophet Mohammed's cousin Ali and his descendents are the true *imams*. Traditional Muslim education, based on the Koran, is still imparted by the clergy in *madrasas* near mosques, which are central to the entire community. In India, the Friday public prayers, led by the local imam, are only open to men, and nearly all Muslim places of worship follow strict rules of segregation.

Sufism is a less orthodox mystic Islamic order. Its teachings emphasize direct experience of god, and Sufis believe that mystical ecstasy can be attained even through music and dance. Sufi saints like Nizamuddin Auliya *(see p86)* attracted many converts from Hinduism, and the fusion of the two religious traditions led to a flowering of poetry, music and art.

Pundits dressed in saffron clothes, conducting *yagnas*

Sikhism

Sikhism is a reformist religion founded by Guru Nanak in the 15th century. Eschewing idol worship, rituals and the caste system, it believes in a formless god. The Sikh, with his characteristic turban, is easy to identify. He is supposed to abide by the five "k"s': *kesh* (long hair), *kachha* (underpants), *kirpan* (small sword), *kangha* (comb) and *kara* (bracelet). The Sikhs follow the teachings of ten gurus that are contained in their holy book, the *Adi Granth,* kept in the Golden Temple at Amritsar (Punjab).

Religious persecution by the later Mughals led the tenth guru, Gobind Singh, to reorganize the community in 1699 as a military order called the Khalsa, based on the principles of *sangat* (congregation), *simran* (meditation), *kirtan* (hymn singing), *langar* and *pangat* (sharing and partaking of food in a common kitchen).

Sikh priest reciting verses from the *Adi Granth* in the Golden Temple, Amritsar

Christianity

The rise of Christianity in this region dates to the late 15th century when Catholic missionaries travelled to India in the wake of Portuguese traders. About this time, Christian Armenian communities also settled in Mughal India, procuring a licence to trade. There is evidence that the Mughal

Church services are often conducted in local dialects

emperor Akbar *(see pp56–7)* invited Jesuit priests to religious discussions held in Fatehpur Sikri *(see pp174–5)*. With the coming of the East India Company, Protestant missionaries spread across the country, setting up educational institutions and hospitals in the 18th and 19th centuries. Many are still run by dedicated workers. They also involved themselves with reform movements and influenced the government to take measures against practices such as sati *(see p52)*. Marriages between Indians and the Europeans who came led to the birth of the Anglo-Indian community. During the Raj *(see pp60–61)*, the railways and many of the subordinate civil services were run by them.

Indian Christians believe that the apostle St Thomas brought the religion to South India in the 1st century AD. Today, church services have been Indianized to a large extent by absorbing some dialects, practices and rituals to make it easier for local worshippers to follow them.

Other Religions

Apart from these four major groups, India has other smaller though distinct religious communities. **Buddhists** are followers of Gautam Buddha who lived and preached the gospel of non-violence and peace. From India, Buddhism spread to other countries in Asia but, ironically, it has now nearly vanished in the land of its birth. The 14th Dalai Lama, the spiritual leader of the Tibetan Buddhists, now lives in India with his followers in exile and is a widely respected figure. **Jains**, the followers of Mahavira, are a pacific and non-violent community who respect life in every form, and observe rigid fasts and self-denial. They are divided into the Svetambaras (dressed in white) and the Digambaras (who shun clothing). The **Parsis** are followers of Zoroaster and came from Persia between the 8th and the 9th century. A small community, they have nevertheless played a significant role in Indian industry and are known for their philanthropy. The first **Jews** came to India in about 562 BC and now live mainly in Mumbai and Cochin.

A golden Buddha statue

Jain nuns cover their mouths to avoid swallowing insects, in respect of all life forms

The Pantheon of Gods and Goddesses

The great pantheon of Hindu gods and goddesses is a bewildering array, ranging from anthropomorphic symbols and shapes to exotic half-human, half-animal forms. Each god has a personal *vahana* (vehicle) and symbols of power. Although community worship takes place in temples, especially on festivals, for most Hindus, the home with its own shrine and personal deities is where the daily *puja* (prayer) is conducted.

Lakshmi, the goddess of wealth, is also the consort of Vishnu. Her *vahana* is an owl.

Saraswati, the goddess of learning and music, is the consort of Brahma and has a swan as her *vahana*. Seated on a lotus, with a garland of white flowers, she is seen as the embodiment of purity.

Shesh Nag is the hundred-headed leviathan on whose coils Vishnu reclines.

Narada, the sage, accompanies Vishnu.

Ganesha, remover of obstacles.

Hanuman, the monkey god, is a faithful attendant of Lord Rama.

Vishnu, the Preserver, floats on Kshirsagar (the sacred ocean), the source of all life.

Religious Symbols

Kamal ("lotus") is a Vaishnavite symbol for purity.

Chakra ("wheel") is a universal symbol of the wheel of life.

Om, a symbol of the primal sound, is recited to start all religious ceremonies.

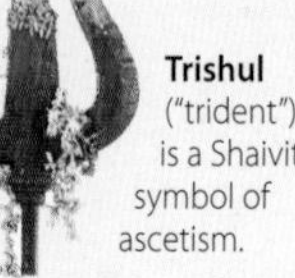

Trishul ("trident") is a Shaivite symbol of ascetism.

Shankh ("conch shell") is a Vaishnavite symbol of the life-giving ocean.

Ganesha, the elephant-headed son of Shiva, is invoked at the start of any auspicious task.

Hanuman the monkey god *(see p201)*, is invoked by those in need of courage and fortitude.

Rama *(right)*, the epitome of virtue, was Vishnu's seventh *avatara* (incarnation), and **Krishna** *(left)*, the embodiment of love, was the eighth. Vishnu is said to assume these *avataras* to save the world from destruction. The last *avatara*, Kalki, will fashion a new world when this one reaches the end of its time.

Brahma sits on a lotus attached to Vishnu's navel.

Shiva lives atop Mount Kailash. The River Ganges flows from his matted locks.

Nandi, the bull, is Shiva's vehicle and is always present at Shiva temples.

Garuda, the half eagle, is Vishnu's vehicle on his travels through the cosmos.

The Holy Trinity

A popular calendar art depiction of the Holy Trinity, that comprises Brahma the Creator, Vishnu the Preserver, and Shiva the Destroyer. Vishnu mediates between Brahma and Shiva to preserve life. The world was created when the ocean was churned by the gods and demons (see p49) *to extract the divine nectar (amrit). The present age (Kaliyuga) is only one stage of the unending cycle of life.*

Parvati lives in the Himalayan hills with Shiva. This gentle daughter of the mountains is worshipped in many forms, which collectively represent the Devi (goddess) cult.

Durga rides a tiger with her deadly arsenal of weapons and destroys evil, in the form of the buffalo-demon Mahishasura. She is the fierce persona of the gentle Parvati.

Kali, wearing a garland of skulls, rampages through creation, annihilating evil. Along with Durga, she is the patron goddess of many Rajput clans who lived by the sword.

Architecture: A Brief History

In North India, monumental architecture followed historical and political change. The wide variety of styles that emerged were executed in a distinctly "Indian" way, influenced by climate and local building traditions. Sadly, few buildings before the 12th century survived the ravages of time, war and climate, but the region is rich in medieval remains, of which the Taj Mahal is the centrepiece. An interesting feature is the mingling of Hindu and Islamic styles, which blends the sensuous beauty of temple sculpture with the austere grandeur of Islamic architecture. Gardens, fountains, screened arches and shaded interiors are some features used for keeping buildings cool.

Carved niche at Agra Fort

Early Indian Architecture (Up to 12th Century)

The temple was the social and economic focus of a town. Early Hindu temples, built on a square base, follow sacred building rules. The deity lies within the sanctum, and the outer surface is profusely decorated.

Carved frieze on *shikhara*

The shikhara is a pointed arch over the sanctum.
Garbhagriha, the womb-like inner sanctum sanctorum.

The mandapa is a hall in front of the sanctum.

Piled stone blocks raise the temple's height

The entrance is spanned by a square stone lintel, carved with sacred images.

Teli ka Mandir (9th century) at Gwalior *(see p178)* is a rare example of a North Indian temple of that time.

Sultanate Architecture (13th to 15th Centuries)

A sandstone and marble panel

Techniques for constructing true arches and domes were learnt by Indian masons from the Muslims after the 12th century. Mortar, another significant technology transfer, made it possible to build high structures. Hindu carving skills added a new element to the Islamic architectural lexicon.

Detail of a geometric panel

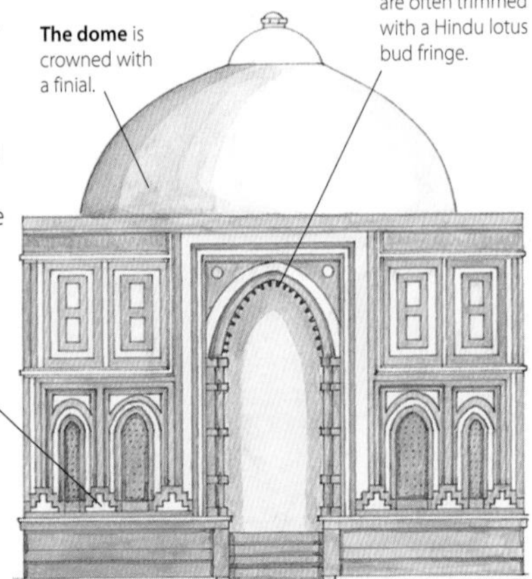

The dome is crowned with a finial.
Islamic arches are often trimmed with a Hindu lotus bud fringe.
Geometric ornamentation is an Islamic feature.

Alai Darwaza (c.1311) in Delhi, with one of the oldest surviving domes, is one of the gems of early Islamic architecture *(see p116)*.

Mughal Architecture (16th to Late 18th Centuries)

Mughal buildings awe the viewer and assert the exalted status of their imperial patron. Whether built of red sandstone or marble, symmetry, grandeur and landscaping are some common features. Inlay work, decorative *jaalis* and cusped arches give these buildings an ethereal grace that offsets their massive size.

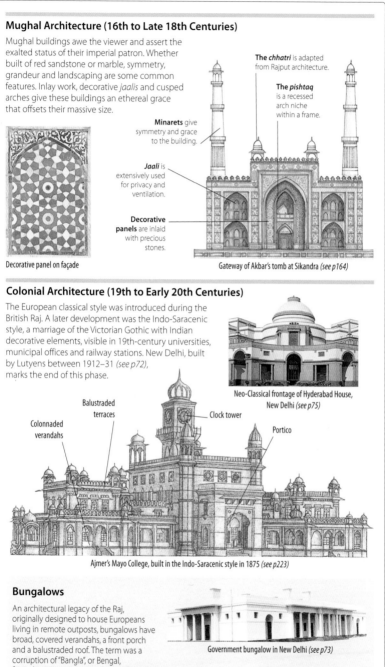

Decorative panel on façade

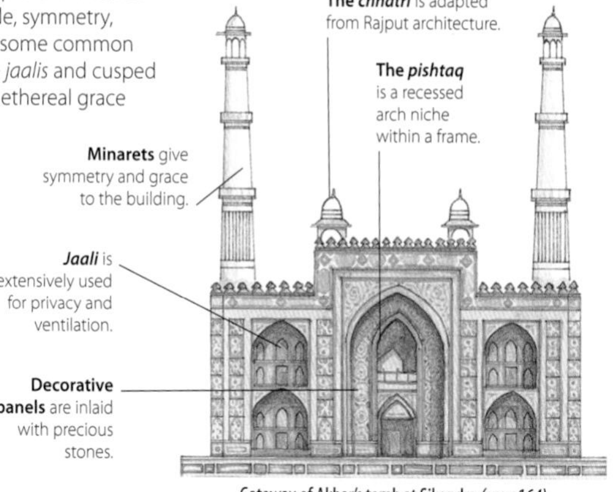
The *chhatri* is adapted from Rajput architecture.
The *pishtaq* is a recessed arch niche within a frame.
Minarets give symmetry and grace to the building.
Jaali is extensively used for privacy and ventilation.
Decorative panels are inlaid with precious stones.

Gateway of Akbar's tomb at Sikandra *(see p164)*

Colonial Architecture (19th to Early 20th Centuries)

The European classical style was introduced during the British Raj. A later development was the Indo-Saracenic style, a marriage of the Victorian Gothic with Indian decorative elements, visible in 19th-century universities, municipal offices and railway stations. New Delhi, built by Lutyens between 1912–31 *(see p72)*, marks the end of this phase.

Neo-Classical frontage of Hyderabad House, New Delhi *(see p75)*

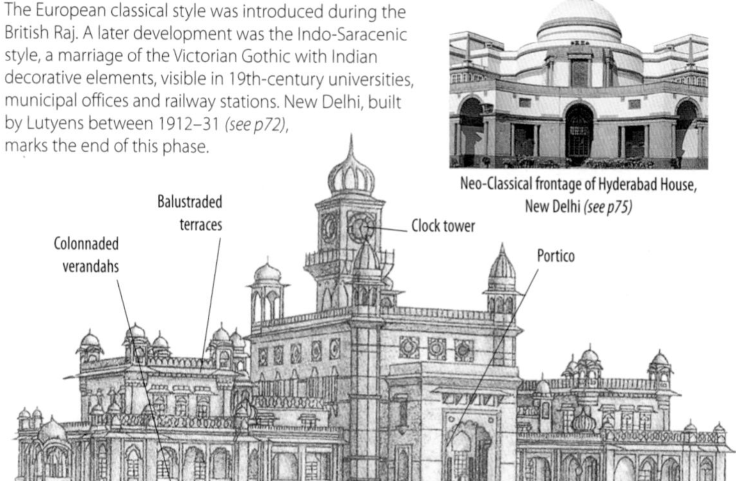
Balustraded terraces
Colonnaded verandahs
Clock tower
Portico

Ajmer's Mayo College, built in the Indo-Saracenic style in 1875 *(see p223)*

Bungalows

Government bungalow in New Delhi *(see p73)*

An architectural legacy of the Raj, originally designed to house Europeans living in remote outposts, bungalows have broad, covered verandahs, a front porch and a balustraded roof. The term was a corruption of "Bangla", or Bengal, for its basic structure was derived from the indigenous Bengali rural hut. Until 1947, few bungalows outside towns had running water or electricity but their high ceilings and shaded interiors kept them dark and cool in summer. However, when Herbert Baker *(see p72)* designed a bungalow for New Delhi's mandarins, its unhappy occupants christened his airless edifice "Baker's Oven".

Architectural Styles

Some of India's finest forts and palaces lie in this region. Forts often served both as defensive buildings and as self-sufficient walled cities, built along natural outcrops or near rivers. Palaces were either part of a fort complex, or individual royal residences with public and private spaces separated by gardens and courtyards. Later, during the Raj, fortified palaces gave way to stately mansions inspired by European models. The beautiful garden tombs, of which the Taj is the most famous example, were a Mughal innovation. In contrast to these are rural houses that blend into the landscape. These eco-friendly structures, based on indigenous building skills, are well insulated, and both cheap and easy to build.

Forts

Most Mughal forts, built of red sandstone with marble trimmings, contained a city complex with private and public areas and were seats of imperial power. Rajput forts, like Amber *(see pp204–5)* and Gwalior *(see p178)*, on the other hand, follow a different plan and their solid bastions were built primarily for self-defence.

Ramparts have pierced holes for cannons.

The *burj* acted as a watchtower.

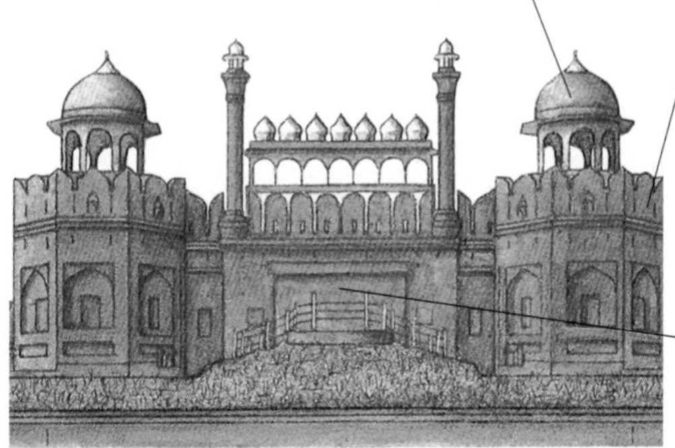

Foundation inscription from the Red Fort

Lahore Gate is named after the direction it faced.

Red Fort at Delhi *(see pp98–9)*

Palaces

Some of the region's most spectacular palaces date to the 19th century in a style that imitated English stately homes. The older, medieval palaces nestle within forts and had separate quarters for men *(mardana)* and women *(zenana)* with landscaped gardens and private mosques or temples.

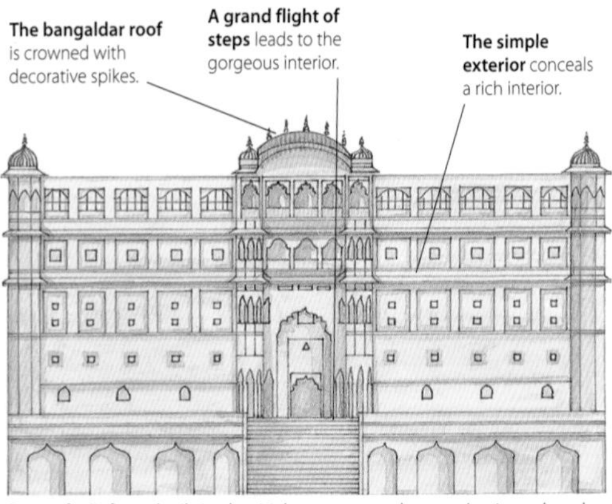

The bangaldar roof is crowned with decorative spikes.

A grand flight of steps leads to the gorgeous interior.

The simple exterior conceals a rich interior.

Samode Palace, built in the 19th century and now a heritage hotel *(see pp236–7)*, has fabulously gilded and mirrored rooms. It is built in the traditional design but has period furniture rather than the usual cushions and floor coverings used in older palaces.

Detail from a mirrored room

The Garden Tomb

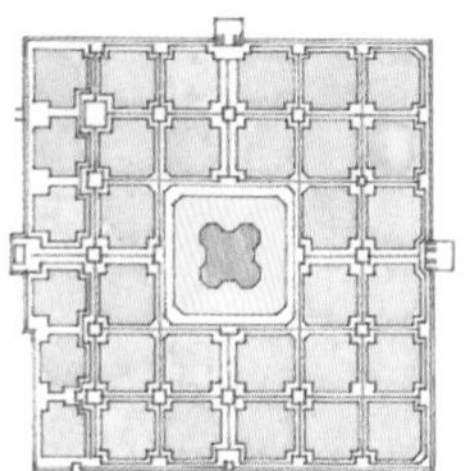

The *charbagh* *(see p171)* is a terraced garden that surrounds the tomb to give its austere lines a soft focus. The Taj Mahal, set at the edge of one, is the most famous example of this style.

The dome surmounts the central space.

Arched cloisters lead to the crypt.

Humayun's tomb *(see p87)* is one of the earliest Mughal garden tombs, which were set on a raised plinth within a *charbagh*. Other features include a private mosque and crypts for other royal graves.

Traditional Houses

Indian villagers usually live in simple houses made of local material, often mud and thatch. They have cool, shaded interiors and are brightly decorated on the outside. Building materials come from the land and are renewed annually at Diwali *(see p41)*.

Mud walls are reinforced with straw and cowdung.

Thatched roofs keep the interiors cool and shaded.

Ritual paintings brighten mud walls.

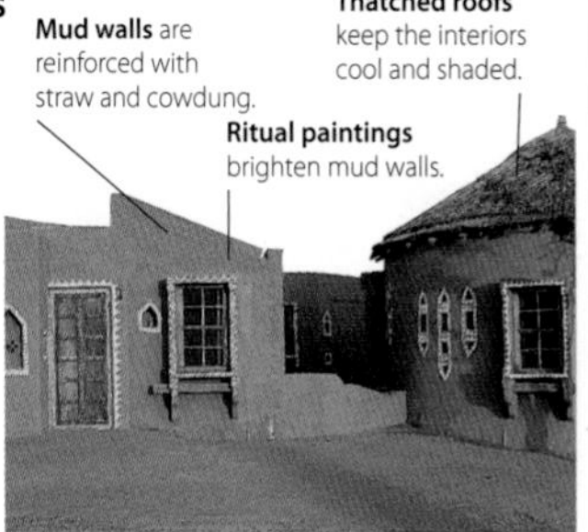

A rural Indian house at Mandawa *(see p217)*

Havelis

The *haveli*, a multi-storeyed mansion for wealthy merchant families, was usually built around one or more courtyards which formed a focal point for the domestic activity of the joint family. Shekhawati's painted *havelis (see pp216–17)* are examples of this architectural style.

The terrace gave an airy overview of the surroundings.

Covered verandahs separated living areas into smaller private units.

Haveli of the Bhartiya family, Shekhawati region

Glossary of Terms

Baoli Underground stepwell, such as Ugrasen's Baoli *(see p80)*.

Burj Residential or fortificatory tower; also bastion.

Chajja Overhanging eaves or cornices to protect buildings from the sun and rain.

Chhatri

Chhatri Open square or octagonal pavilion, literally an umbrella.

Diwan-i-Aam Hall of Public Audience.

Diwan-i-Khas Hall of Private Audience.

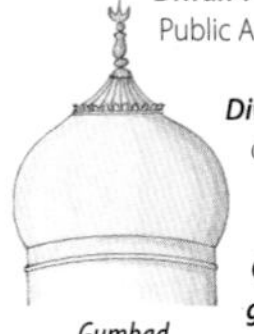

Gumbad

Gumbad/ gumbaz Dome, often crowned with a finial; the term is also used for a mausoleum.

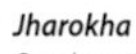

Jharokha Overhanging oriel window supported on brackets; some were used for the official appearances of the ruler.

Jharokha

Masjid Mosque.

Mihrab Arched niche facing Mecca in a mosque.

Minar Free-standing tower such as the Qutb Minar *(see p116)*.

Mohalla Quarter of town inhabited by members of one caste.

Namazgah Space near mosque for celebration of major Muslim festivals.

Minar

Qila Castle, fortress, citadel.

Sheesh Mahal Chamber profusely decorated with mirror mosaic; glass palace.

Stambha Stately pillar, post or column.

Stupa Tumulus, burial or reliquary mound.

Stambha

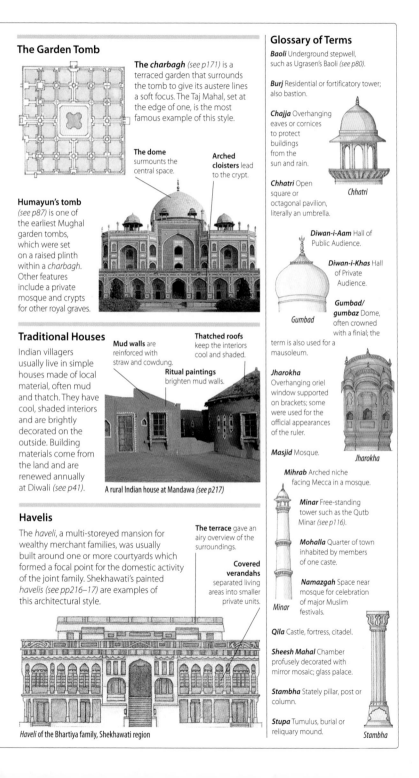

Music, Dance and Theatre

India's performing arts are simultaneously modes of worship and a joyous celebration of life. Music and dance originated in the temples, gradually acquiring a secular, more sensuous character as royal patrons founded individual schools *(gharanas)*. Two prominent classical forms in this region are Kathak and Hindustani music. The artiste creates a mood *(rasa)* which invites the audience to participate in it so as to make the performance a mutually shared experience.

Qawwalis* and *bhajans are devotional songs that go back to medieval Sufi and Bhakti cults. Sung intensely to arouse mystical ecstasy, they celebrate the power of divine love.

Raslila, a folk variation of Kathak, narrates the life of Lord Krishna. Traditionally, the Ramlila *(below)* and the Raslila featured young boys.

Hands are used in stylized mudras, symbolic movements that follow the *Natya Shastra*, a classic treatise on the performing arts.

Lehenga, a long skirt worn over tight pyjamas, accentuates the swirling movement of the dancer.

Ramlila enacts the story of the epic *Ramayana* in a cycle of ten episodic folk plays during the Dussehra festival *(see p41)*.

Hindustani Music

The origins of Hindustani music date to about 3000 BC and the *Sama Veda (see p311)*. The *raga* (melodic mode) and *tala* (rhythmic cycle) are the foundation of Indian classical music, of which the Dhrupad and the Khayal are two major vocal styles. Indian classical music has no formal notational score, giving artistes a wide scope to elaborate the mood of a *raga*, each with its own set of notes. To preserve individuality, knowledge was passed down orally from teacher to pupil through schools called *gharanas*. The Gwalior *gharana (see p178)* is said to be the oldest one in the region.

Late Pandit Ravi Shankar, one of India's foremost sitar players, introduced classical music to the West.

Amjad Ali Khan belongs to a famous family of *sarod* players, who developed the *rabab*, a medieval lute from Central Asia, to its present form.

Nine *rasas* (moods) are mentioned in the 4th-century treatise *Natya Shastra*. From the erotic, comic and pathetic to the odious, marvellous and quiescent, *rasa* covers every mood and expression, whether in music or painting. This 17th-century *Ragamala* painting *(see pp36–7)* depicts the mood of the morning *Raga Todi*.

Nautch Girl was the pejorative title given to dancing girls in the 19th century when Kathak became mere entertainment.

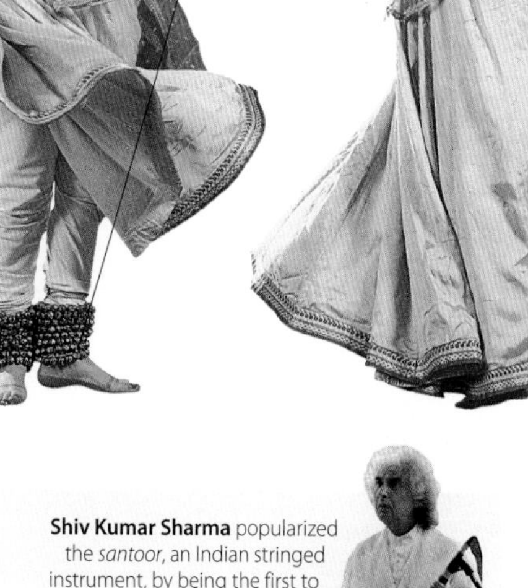

Rapid body movements keep time with the beat of the accompanying percussionist.

Ghungroos are brass bells that aid the rhythmic beat. Foot stamping controls and varies their sound.

Gorgeous jewellery and the colour red on the hands and feet make the intricacies of the dance easy to see.

Kathak

This North Indian classical dance form, which received lavish patronage in the court of Jaipur, derives from the epic tales (kathas) *narrated by balladeers. A typical Kathak performance is a blend of complex footwork and facial expressions* (abhinaya) *to enact an episode, often from Krishna's life.*

Shiv Kumar Sharma popularized the *santoor*, an Indian stringed instrument, by being the first to use it to play classical music.

Zakir Hussain plays the *tabla*, a pair of drums that provide percussion to most music and dance performances.

Contemporary theatre draws on classical Sanskrit and folk drama (above). Avant-garde street plays are popular with fringe and protest theatre groups. The National School of Drama *(see p124)* often produces Indian adaptations of classics, such as King Lear and Macbeth.

Painting

Two distinct schools of painting, Rajput and Mughal, emerged in 16th-century North India. The meteoric growth and popularity of miniature painting was due to the introduction of paper as well as the lavish patronage of Muslim and Rajput rulers. The Mughals encouraged Persian miniature painters to settle in India where they came into contact with indigenous traditions. A fusion of the two styles under the rulers Akbar, Jahangir and Shah Jahan led to a burst of artistic activity when court painters, such as Mansur, produced folios of birds, flowers, royal portraits and illustrated manuscripts. As Mughal patronage declined in the 18th century, other regional centres of art developed in North India.

Jain palm leaf manuscripts, such as this piece (c.1439), use bright primary colours. Their large-eyed human figures and narrative depiction of themes influenced early Rajput art.

Early Mughal paintings were pictorial narratives of historical events and literary texts. This leaf from a 16th-century *Babur Nama* shows Babur crossing the River Son. Mughal landscapes are rendered realistically, unlike the more romantic Rajput allegories.

Monsters symbolize the threats to Krishna at birth.

Space is divided into units, each dealing with a separate episode of the story.

Rajput paintings are known for their bright colours and stylized figures. Classical texts and religious figures are recurrent subjects, such as this 18th-century page from the Rasikapriya romance of the Bundi School.

Ragamalas are sets of paintings, strung like a garland, that depict the mood of individual *ragas* *(see p34)*. This 17th-century *Ragini Dev-Gandhari*, an early morning *raga*, has dainty figures, and the delicate floral border that was a hallmark of Mughal paintings.

Pahari painting emerged from the hill *(pahari)* states of the western Himalayas, where many artists went in search of work after the decline of Mughal patronage. Raja Sansar Chand of Kangra, a patron of this style, can be seen in this late 18th-century Pahari painting.

The Company School flourished in the colonial period. This portrait of King Edward VII and Queen Alexandra, attired in Indian clothes and ornaments, was painted by a local artist as a specially commissioned work.

Nature is depicted in metaphorical terms, as in the snake-like ripples of lightning.
Narrative progression shows the growth of Krishna from infancy to boyhood.
Human faces are drawn in profile and space lacks perspective.
Colours and pigments were extracted from precious stones and plants.

Rajput Miniatures

Rajput ateliers were named after their patron courts (see p219)*, each with a distinctive style, such as this 18th-century Mewar miniature,* Krshna Revealing his Divinity as Visnu to his Parents. *Rajput paintings have a narrative theme – a court episode or a mythological tale. Unlike Mughal paintings, their treatment of space and the natural world is poetic rather than realisitic and evokes a musical mood or* rasa (see p34). Baramasa *(cycle of seasons) and* Ragamala *(garland of* ragas*) paintings are famous examples of this romantic style.*

Contemporary Indian Art

A nationalist poet, musician, philosopher and educationalist, Rabindranath Tagore (d.1941) pioneered the 19th-century Bengal Renaissance art movement, which was a step towards the modernist impulse in Indian art. He drew heavily on the rich mythic content of folk art. Later, Amrita Shergill (d.1941) brought a European style to Indian themes and scenes. Contemporary Indian art evolved from the work of these and other seminal artists. Yet it retained an Indian identity even when experimenting with fashionable European styles. Modern Indian artists have taken inspiration from Tantric symbols, mythology and miniature paintings to produce a vibrant art style which has tried to retain the richness of its folk and classical art forms even as they work with different media and materials.

Head Study, Rabindranath Tagore

Indian Design

Indian design has evolved out of a very close bond between the artist and his craft, in which the skill of the hand is regarded as a sacred gift, passed down from father to son in an unbroken line. This has ensured a design tradition that is both a living art form as well as a means of fulfilling the everyday needs of the community, be they sacred or functional. Freely enriched by the traditions of other races and cultures, India's artistic heritage is renowned throughout the world for its vibrancy and creativity.

Geometric designs, or *rangolis*, form the base of traditional decoration.

Mud and thatch are regarded as sacred media, being the gift of Mother Earth.

The rounded shape of the pot has not changed since 2500 BC.

Pottery has a 5,000-year-old history *(see pp48–9)* making it one of the world's oldest skills. The potter's wheel produces cheap, eco-friendly objects of daily use.

The wheel or *chakra* is regarded as a symbol of the eternal circle of life and death.

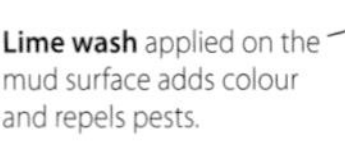

Lime wash applied on the mud surface adds colour and repels pests.

The living space is embellished with surface decorations ranging from relief carvings to mirror-work. Whether a mud hut or palace, the Indian home is the origin of most forms of art.

Colour

The colours of Indian design are taken from nature, with names to match. The five shades of white are lyrically compared to the clouds when the rain is spent, the August moon, conch shell, jasmine flower and the surf of the sea. Indigo, madder and turmeric are valued for their dyes, and the crushed flowers of the flame of the forest *(Butea monosperma)* yield a soft yellow colour still used in rural India for playing Holi *(see p40)*. Each colour has a ritual significance as well: red is auspicious, celebratory and associated with weddings and festivals, saffron symbolizes renunciation, yellow is worn during the spring festival of Vasant, and green in the monsoon. The Indian dyer *(right)* uses plants and roots for extracting colour.

A dyer at work

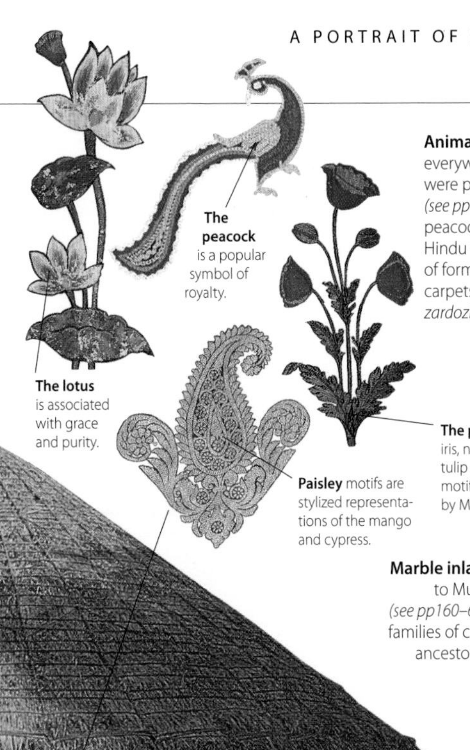

Animal and flower motifs can be seen everywhere. The most elegant floral patterns were perfected in Mughal and Rajput painting *(see pp36–7)*, while the popular lotus and peacock motifs are inherent to Buddhist and Hindu temple iconography. Worked in a variety of forms these motifs are most visible in textiles, carpets, painting, jewellery, ceramics and *zardozi (see p157)*.

The peacock is a popular symbol of royalty.

The lotus is associated with grace and purity.

Paisley motifs are stylized representations of the mango and cypress.

The poppy, the iris, narcissus and tulip are textile motifs inspired by Mughal art.

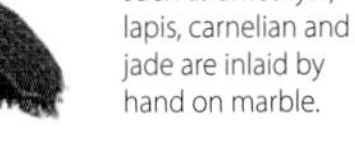

Marble inlay can be traced to Mughal *pietra dura (see pp160–61)*. Agra still has families of craftsmen whose ancestors worked at the Mughal court.

Precious stones such as amethyst, lapis, carnelian and jade are inlaid by hand on marble.

Floral patterns, inspired by the Islamic paradise garden concept, are common.

Home and Family

The earliest art objects were those needed for everyday life. Emerging from the home and its daily rituals, the shape and form of articles was based on religious symbols which ensured their survival down the ages. With time, sophisticated materials and techniques learnt from royal courts enhanced design consciousness, resulting in a more exclusive range of decorative art.

Wall paintings are often inspired by nature.

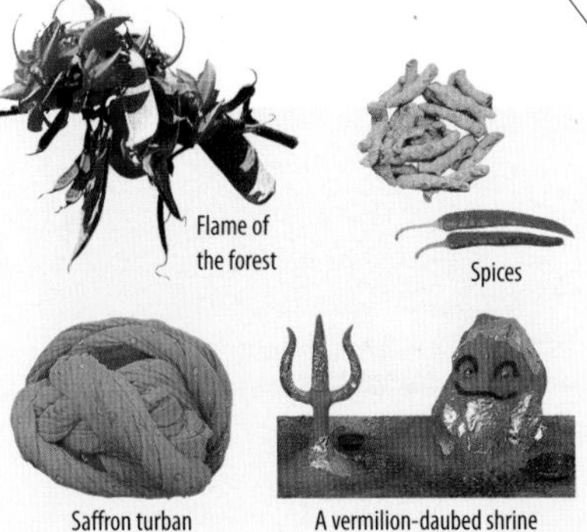

Flame of the forest

Spices

Saffron turban

A vermilion-daubed shrine

Form and function are equally important in Indian design, endowing even everyday utility objects with beauty. As architectural skills developed over the centuries, basic forms and materials became more sophisticated. This graceful trellised stone window is an example of this change.

Festivals in India

Indians love celebrations. Festivals are both religious and social events, where ritual fasting and joyful feasting often go hand in hand. Hindu festivals usually follow the lunar calendar and both the full moon *(purnima)* and the new moon *(pradosh)* are considered auspicious. Some fairs and festivities are connected to the pantheon of gods and goddesses, others to ancient pastoral, fertility or martial rites. Muslim festivals, too, are determined by the new moon. This means that the dates of festivals vary from year to year.

Shishir (Jan–Mar)

This is the most auspicious period in the Indian calendar. **Lohri** and **Makar Sankranti** follow one another in early January. The former is observed mainly by Punjabis as the height of winter, and the latter, confined to Jaipur, marks the movement of the sun from the equator to the Tropic of Capricorn. The wind usually changes direction on this day and colourful kites fill the sky. **Vasant Panchami**, towards the end of January, is said to be the first day of spring. Shia Muslims also observe **Muharram**, a ten-day period of mourning for the martyrdom of the Prophet's grandson, Hazrat Imam Hussain, at Karbala (Iraq). On the tenth and final day, impressive processions of *tazias* (replicas of his tomb) are taken out and young boys and men, dressed in black, flagellate themselves in a frenzy of religious fervour. The occurence of this festival varies, depending on the beginning of the lunar calendar.

A child enjoying the festivities of Holi

In February, devotees of Shiva observe **Shivaratri**, or the night of his celestial wedding to Parvati. **Holi**, one of the most important Hindu festivals in this region, takes place on a full-moon night, and is celebrated as the end of winter, usually in March. On the eve of Holi, bonfires are lit and an effigy of the demon Holika is burnt to signify the triumph of good over evil. The next day, people swarm the streets, sprinkling coloured water and powder *(gulal)* on each other. This lively festival was especially dear to Lord Krishna.

Vasant (Mar–May)

The Hindu year begins with Vasant (spring). Nine days of fasting *(navaratris)* precede the birth of Rama *(see p29)* on **Ramnavami**. During this period, most households prepare special vegetarian foods, which are cooked in *ghee* (clarified butter) without garlic or onions.

Muslims celebrate **Milad-ul-Nabi**, the birthday of the Prophet in March. The pastoral festival of **Baisakhi** on 13 April heralds the harvest season in North India, and is celebrated with singing and dancing. Later in the month comes **Shitala Ashtami**, a Rajasthani folk festival to commemorate Shitala Devi, goddess of smallpox and a manifestation of Durga. A religious fair that is attended by many villagers is held at the Chaksu temple *(see p226)*. Christians celebrate **Good Friday**, to commemorate the crucifixion of Christ, and **Easter**, the resurrection of Christ, at this time as well.

Grishma (May–Jun)

As the heat intensifies, the festival season comes to a halt. The most sacred

Holi celebrations in the villages of Brajbhumi, near Mathura

of Buddhist festivals, **Buddha Jayanti** or **Buddha Purnima** is celebrated *(see p42)*.

Varsha (Jul–Sep)

With the monsoon comes **Janmashtami**, the birth of Lord Krishna on a moonless night. Celebrations reach their peak at midnight, while the day is given to fasting.

The **Urs**, one of the biggest Muslim fairs in the subcontinent, takes place in Ajmer. It is held over 13 days at the *dargah* of the great Sufi saint Moinuddin Chishti *(see pp224–5)*. **Onam** heralds the harvest season in Kerala, and falls between August and September.

Ganesh Chaturthi is a 10-day event in honour of the birth of Lord Ganesha. It is marked by ceremonious processions of Ganesha's idols.

Painting of Dussehra effigies that will later be set alight

Sharad (Sep–Oct)

This season of festivals begins with **Dussehra**. For ten days, *Ramlilas (see p34)* are held and fairs organized to celebrate the legend of Rama. These dramatize episodes from the *Ramayana*: the exile of Rama, his brother Lakshman and wife Sita. Her abduction by the demon-king Ravana of Lanka and the epic battle for her rescue glorifies the monkey god, Hanuman, who helped Rama defeat Ravana and return in triumph to Ayodhya. Huge effigies of Ravana, his brother and his son are stuffed with fireworks to be set alight on the last day, Vijaya Dashami. Dussehra is preceded by the *navaratri* fasts. Bengalis celebrate this period as **Durga Puja**, when grand marquees *(pandals)* are erected over images of the goddess Durga.

Muslim pilgrims gathered at the Urs in Ajmer

In October, **Id-ul-Fitr** marks the end of Ramadan or Ramzan, the month of fasting for Muslims, commemorating the period when the Prophet received the message of the Koran from Allah. The actual day of celebration varies according to the sighting of the new moon. A special *namaaz* is held at Delhi's Jami Masjid. This festival is also called Mithi (sweet) Id, as *sewian*, a delicacy made with sweetened vermicelli, is prepared in celebration.

Hemant (Nov–Jan)

The onset of the winter season ushers in cool days and a large number of festivals. **Diwali**, or the festival of lights, marks Rama's joyous entry into Ayodhya when the town was lit with lamps to greet him. It also heralds the Hindu New Year when old accounts are closed. Hindus believe that Lakshmi, the goddess of wealth, visits her devotees on that night, so houses are painted, sweets exchanged, and a profusion of *melas* encourages wild spending on homes and clothes.

A variety of Diwali crackers are available at pavement stalls during the festival

Bhai Duj, two days later, is a family festival in honour of brothers, who give gifts to their sisters.

Another festival soon after Diwali is **Govardhan Puja** or Annakut, celebrated in both Rajasthan and Mathura. It commemorates the day Lord Krishna lifted the Govardhan hillock on his little finger to protect the area from a deluge sent by an irate Indra, the god of rain. On the full moon after Diwali, Sikhs celebrate **Guru Purab**, the birthday of Guru Nanak, the founder of Sikhism. In Rajasthan, the **Pushkar Fair** *(see pp220–21)* attracts throngs of tourists as well as pilgrims and herdsmen. **Christmas** and New Year, now national festivals, are celebrated with flair all over the country. At this time, restaurants fill and brightly-lit streets bustle with throngs of busy shoppers.

A parrot-shaped paper kite

DELHI, AGRA & JAIPUR THROUGH THE YEAR

Three definite seasons, the summer, monsoon and winter, with a brief but glorious spring and autumn, span the year in the region. The calendar is filled with festivals and fairs celebrated by each of the diverse religious or local communities. Some follow the changing seasons and mark pastoral occasions, while others celebrate anniversaries and events of national importance such as the Republic Day *(see p75)*. Most cultural shows are held during the winter.

Summer (Mar–Jun)

From mid-March until June the North Indian plains experience a hot and dry summer. The temperatures in March and April can be mild and variable, but by May and June the heat builds up to a crescendo with the mercury rising up to 46° C (114° F). This is a signal for many residents to move to the Himalayan hill stations. Those who stay back remain indoors and only venture out after sunset. Most festivities, too, come to a halt at this point.

Holi *(Mar)*. This exuberant festival of colour marks the end of winter. In and around Brindavan *(see p166)*, Holi celebrations last two weeks.

Elephant Festival *(Mar)*, Jaipur. Around Holi, 60 decorated elephants parade through the streets bearing revellers who throw colour at one another. Elephant polo matches are also held at Chaugan Stadium.

Nauchandi Mela *(Mar)*, Meerut. Held around the shrine of a Muslim saint and a temple, this fair has come to symbolize Hindu-Muslim unity. Its origins date to the late-17th century when local leaders decided to merge festivities held concurrently at both shrines. Today, this is more a fun-filled carnival than a religious event *(see p87)*. **Jahan e Khusrau** *(Mar)*, Delhi. The three-day international Sufi music festival is one of the city's most eagerly awaited events. Performances are held at Humayun's tomb. **ITC Sangeet Sammelan** *(Mar)*, Delhi (sometimes held in Calcutta). This important Hindustani classical music event, sponsored by a major Indian industrial house, attracts music-lovers from far and wide.

Gangaur Festival *(Mar/Apr)*, Jaipur. For 18 days, new brides and young girls worship Gauri, one of the manifestations of Parvati, the consort of Shiva. Bejewelled images of the goddess are carried through the city, escorted by bullock-drawn chariots, bands of musicians and women singing hymns. **Shankarlal Sangeet Sammelan** *(Mar)*, Delhi. This is the capital's oldest classical vocal and instrumental music festival.

Baisakhi *(13 Apr)*. On this day Gobind Singh, the last Sikh guru, founded the Khalsa, the "Holy Army of the Pure". Gala processions, dancing and feasting mark the occasion. It also signals the onset of summer and the start of the harvest season.

Urs *(Apr)*, Delhi. For three days devotees of the Sufi saint Nizamuddin Auliya *(see p86)* celebrate his birth anniversary with night-long *qawwalis* and a funfair. **Buddha Jayanti** *(May)*, Delhi. The Buddha's birth, his attaining enlightenment, and his death all fell on the full moon of the fourth lunar month. Prayer meetings are held at Delhi's Buddha Jayanti Park. **National Film Festival** *(Jul)*, Delhi. During this two-week-long

Procession of Buddhist lamas on Buddha Jayanti

Elephant Festival

Average Daily Hours of Sunshine

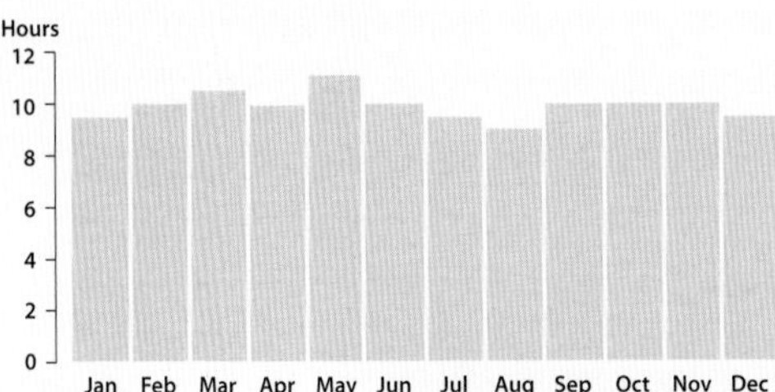

Sunshine Chart
Ranging from balmy to fiercely hot, North India has sunshine through the year. To those unaccustomed to tropical weather, even the winter afternoons of this region may be uncomfortably warm. Sun hats, dark glasses, sunblock and several glasses a day of mineral water are highly recommended.

festival, regional films from India, that have won awards and acclaim, are screened at the large Siri Fort Auditorium.
Summer Theatre Festival *(May/Jun)*, Delhi. A theatre festival is organized by the National School of Drama.

Monsoon (Jul–Aug)

July, August and most of September are hot and humid with intermittent showers. All newspapers eagerly report the progress of the southwest monsoon and though rainfall is scanty in the region, this season is celebrated for its magical transformation of the earth.
Mango Festival *(early Jul)*, Delhi. Held at the peak of the mango season, over 1,000 varieties of delicious mangoes grown in North India are on view at the Talkatora Stadium.

Shehnai player at Teej

Teej *(Aug)*, Jaipur. Young girls, dressed in green, sing songs and play on specially erected swings. This joyous event venerates Parvati, the goddess of marital harmony. It also heralds the advent of the much awaited monsoon.
Independence Day *(15 Aug)*. This is a national holiday, commemorating India's freedom from British rule in 1947. The Prime Minister addresses the nation from the ramparts of the historic Red Fort in Delhi.

Popular belief maintains that a dancing peacock heralds the much-awaited monsoon

Raksha Bandhan *(full moon in Aug)*. Young girls tie sacred threads *(rakhis)* on their brothers' wrists as a token of love, and receive in exchange gifts and a promise of everlasting protection.
Janmashtami *(Aug)*. Krishna's birth is celebrated all over India. In Brindavan, *Raslilas* are performed, and in Delhi, there are shows of *Krishna Katha*, a dance-drama on the Krishna story.

Public gathering for the Prime Minister's speech on Independence Day, Red Fort

National Holidays

Republic Day (26 Jan)
Independence Day (15 Aug)
Gandhi Jayanti (2 Oct)

Public Holidays

Shivaratri (Feb)
Holi (Mar)
Id-ul-Zuha (Mar)
Good Friday (Apr)
Baisakhi (13 April)
Ramnavami (Apr)
Mahavir Jayanti (Apr/May)
Buddha Jayanti (May)
Milad-ul-Nabi (May/Jun)
Janmashtami (Aug)
Dussehra (Oct)
Diwali (Oct/Nov)
Guru Purab (Nov)
Christmas (25 Dec)

Average Monthly Rainfall

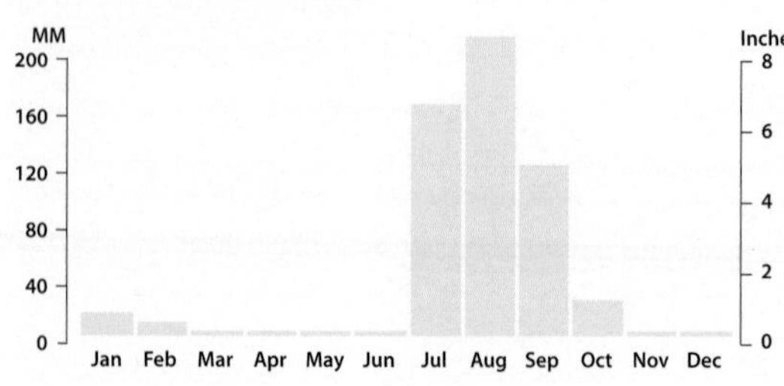

Rainfall Chart
Apart from local showers, this region receives its rain mostly during the south-west monsoon, which lasts from July to September. The landscape turns lush green but the humidity, sometimes as high as 90 per cent, makes this the wrong season for travelling in the plains of North India.

Winter (Oct–Feb)

This is the perfect season when the monsoon has cleared the dust haze and the days begin to grow cooler. The onset of winter also marks the sowing of winter crops such as mustard. The chill in the air is at its worst between mid-December and mid-January, and though temperatures often fall below 3° C (37° F), the days are sunny. Spring is the main season for weddings, parades, picnics, polo and cricket matches, flower shows and various other cultural events.

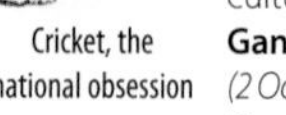

Cricket, the national obsession

Gandhi Jayanti *(2 Oct)*. Mahatma Gandhi's birth-day is widely celebrated as a national holiday.

Phoolwalon ki Sair *(early Oct)*, Delhi. A colourful procession of floral banners and fans from the Jogmaya Temple and the Sufi shrine of Qutbuddin Bakhtiyar Kaki culminates at Jahaz Mahal in Mehrauli *(see pp114–15)*. Music and poetry recitations *(mushairas)* are also held.

The IIC Experience *(mid Oct)*, Delhi. Organized by the India International Centre, the festival celebrates world music, dance, theatre, film, literature and special cuisine.

Qutb Festival *(Oct)*, Delhi. A feast of Indian classical music and dance, organized by Delhi Tourism, is held against the dramatic backdrop of the Qutb Minar.

Dussehra *(Oct)*. A nine-day festival enacting episodes from the *Ramayana* depicting Rama's battle against Ravana. The tenth day, Vijaya Dashami, celebrates Rama's defeat of Ravana, and huge effigies of the demon-king, his brother and son are burnt. In Delhi, the Shriram Bharatiya Kala Kendra's month-long dance-drama encapsulates the much-loved epic.

Diwali *(Oct/Nov)*. Oil lamps illuminate each home to commemorate Rama's return to Ayodhya after 14 years of exile. Sweets are exchanged and fire-crackers are lit in exuberant celebration. During this period every locality holds Diwali *melas*.

Parampara Festival *(Nov)*, Delhi and Hyderabad. A cultural event for lovers of classical music and dance involving some of the country's leading artistes.

Pushkar Fair *(Nov)*, Pushkar. Asia's largest camel and cattle fair takes place in this pilgrim town *(see pp220–21)*.

India International Trade Fair *(14–21 Nov)*, Delhi. Pragati Maidan hosts this event for Indian industry, exhibiting goods manufactured locally and abroad. Cultural events are also held in the grounds.

Balloon Mela *(Nov)*, Delhi. A large number of brightly lined hot-air balloons dot the sky.

A hot-air balloon at the Balloon Mela

Tansen Festival *(Nov)*, Gwalior. Classical singers pay homage to the famous Indian musician, Tansen, Mughal emperor Akbar's favourite court musician.

Chrysanthemum Show *(1st week Dec)*, Delhi. The YWCA organizes a display of exquisite blooms.

Kathak Utsav *(Dec)*, Delhi. Exponents of this North Indian dance form enthrall audiences with their artistry.

The Prithvi Theatre Festival *(Dec)*, Delhi. Mumbai-based group, formed in memory of Prithviraj Kapoor, hosts a theatre fest in collaboration with Max Mueller Bhavan and the National School of Drama.

Christmas *(25 Dec)*. A public holiday, Christmas is celebrated all over and is an occasion for everyone to shop, feast and party.

New Year's Eve *(31 Dec)*. All hotels and clubs organize New Year's Eve balls.

Lohri *(13 Jan)*. Bonfires are lit amidst song and dance to mark the height of winter.

Cars displayed at the India International Trade Fair

Average Monthly Temperature

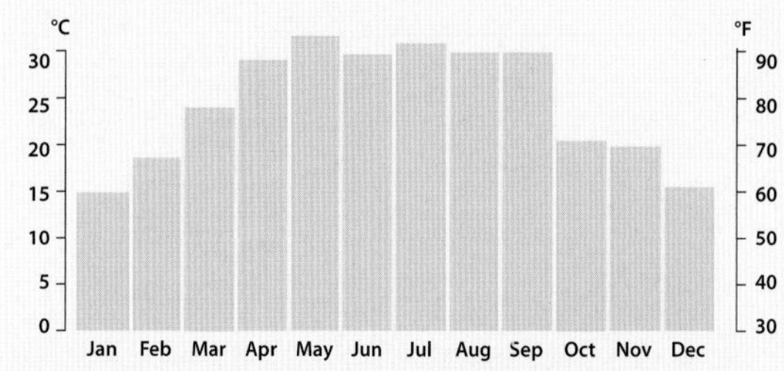

Temperature Chart
This region is hot and dry throughout the year, barring October to February. The mercury begins to rise from March, and by May heat wave conditions prevail with hot and dusty gusts of the *loo* winds. By the end of June, however, dark clouds signal the onset of the monsoon.

Bagpipers at the Beating Retreat ceremony

Makar Sankranti *(14 Jan)*, Jaipur. Kites are flown to celebrate the return of the sun from the equator to the Tropic of Capricorn.
Jaipur Literature Festival *(mid Jan)* Jaipur. Originally, a part of the Jaipur Heritage International Festival, it is considered to be the biggest literature festival in Asia.
Republic Day *(26 Jan)*. A national holiday. Pomp and pageantry mark India's birth as an independent republic. In Delhi, a colourful military parade is held at Rajpath.
Beating Retreat *(29 Jan)*, Delhi. A moving ceremony that recalls the end of the day's battle when armies retreated to their camps. There is a grand display of regimental bands performing against the spectacular back-drop of North and South Blocks. As the sun sets, a bugle sounds the retreat, fireworks are lit and fairylights outline the buildings.
Surajkund Crafts Mela *(1–14 Feb)*, Surajkund. This handicrafts fair is held at an 11th-century historic site on the outskirts of the capital.
International Yoga Week *(Feb–Mar)*, Rishikesh. On the banks of the Ganges, scholars and students from all over the world participate in yoga classes and seminars.
Vintage Car Rally *(Feb)*, Delhi. *The Statesman* newspaper organizes this event when vintage cars, or the "grand old ladies", are flagged off from Statesman House to embark on a 20-km (12-mile) journey. Their owners often dress up in period costumes.
Vasant Panchami *(Feb)*. A spring festival when crops ripen and nature is in full bloom. People wear yellow and worship Saraswati.
Taj Mahotsav *(18–27 Feb)*, Agra. A ten-day cultural fiesta of music and dance in the vicinity of the Taj Mahal. The event showcases India's vibrant arts, crafts and cuisines.
Shivaratri *(Feb)*. Night-long celebrations mark the wedding of Shiva on the 14th day of a lunar fortnight. Offerings are made to Shiva, and an all-day fasting ritual is followed.
Kathak Bindadin Mahotsav *(Feb)*, Delhi. A five-day dance festival organized by the Kathak Kendra.
Dhrupad Festival *(Feb)*, Delhi. Leading exponents of this ancient musical tradition present a series of recitals.

Vintage cars prove their mettle on an uphill road outside Delhi

THE HISTORY OF DELHI, AGRA & JAIPUR

North Indian society sprang from the wide plains of the Indus and Ganges rivers, sites of continuous human settlement since about 2500 BC, when a sophisticated urban culture flourished along the Indus Valley. After 600 BC, powerful empires such as the Mauryas, Kushanas and Guptas presided over the rise of Buddhism and Hinduism, two major religions that emerged from North India.

Overland trade with Central Asia and the Far East invited conquest and settlement as well. Interestingly, India is a derivative of "Indoi", a Greek word given to people who lived across the River Sindhu, or Indus. From 1500 BC on, North India was home to immigrants. These included the Aryans, Greeks and Parthians, Scythians, Huns and Mongols.

An important development took place in AD 1192 when Muhammad Ghori displaced the Rajputs from Delhi to found the first major Islamic kingdom in the region. Later, with the coming of the Mughals in 1526, North India underwent a process of social and political change that lasted nearly 300 years, as a vibrant Indo-Islamic cultural fusion took place. Imperial centralization under the Mughals brought peace and prosperity in its wake, while art and architecture scaled new heights of excellence.

The rise of the British East India Company in the 18th century, after the decline of the Mughals, was the start of 200 years of British rule in India. The colonial period, which also marks the political unification of the subcontinent, ended in 1947 when India became independent. Today a mature democracy, India is trying to tackle poverty and illiteracy with economic and political reform in this rapidly expanding nation.

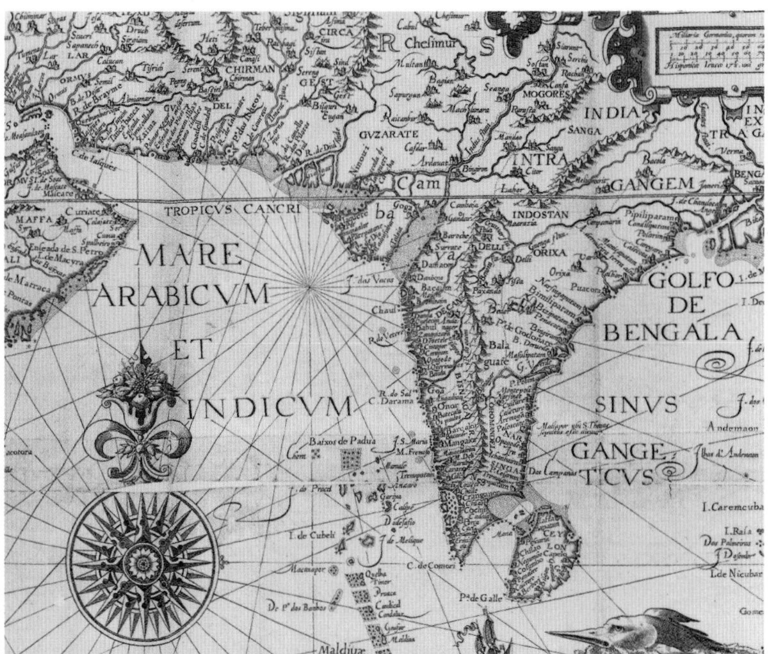

A 16th-century Portuguese map of India, locating trading bases in the county

◀ Royal procession, a mid-19th-century mural in the Moti Mahal, Gwalior

Early Civilizations

Indian civilization first flourished between 2500 and 1500 BC in the Harappan settlements along the River Indus. These sophisticated urban settlements, with an underground drainage system and well laid out streets, were spread over an area much larger than either ancient Egypt or Mesopotamia. The reasons for the decline of this early civilization are still unclear, but by 1500 BC, the Aryans, who had entered India through the passes of the Hindu Kush, had settled down in northwest India. Sacred texts such as the *Rig Veda* record aspects of their culture. By 600 BC, with the gradual adoption of widespread crop cultivation, several new urban sites had emerged in the Ganges Valley. Many of these were capitals of independent kingdoms, and some cities of that age, such as Mathura, Patna and Varanasi, still exist.

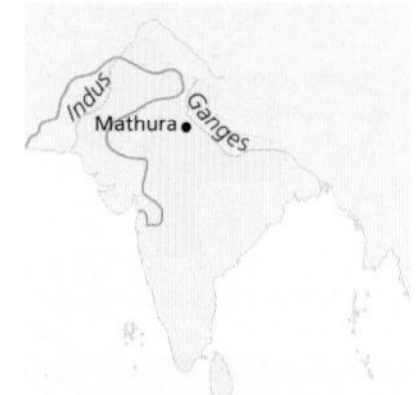

Early Civilizations

— Extent of Indus Valley Civilization

▢ Extent of Aryan settlements

Copper Harpoon (c.1500 BC)
Copper and bronze implements for farming and hunting were used in the Indo-Gangetic valley.

Burial urn from a Harappan site.

Indus Seal (Tree)
Over 2,000 steatite seals have been found in the Indus Valley, each with an emblem and a script that has still not been fully deciphered.

Platter (c.800 BC)
A Painted Grey Ware platter from the Ganges Valley area. Austere and functional, such objects were made of baked clay.

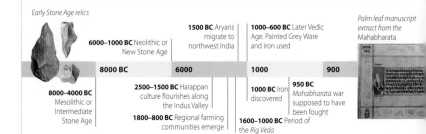

Early Stone Age relics

8000 BC | 6000 | 1000 | 900

8000–4000 BC Mesolithic or Intermediate Stone Age

6000–1000 BC Neolithic or New Stone Age

2500–1500 BC Harappan culture flourishes along the Indus Valley

1800–800 BC Regional farming communities emerge

1600–1000 BC Period of the *Rig Veda*

1500 BC Aryans migrate to northwest India

1000 BC Iron discovered

1000–600 BC Later Vedic Age. Painted Grey Ware and iron used

950 BC *Mahabharata* war supposed to have been fought

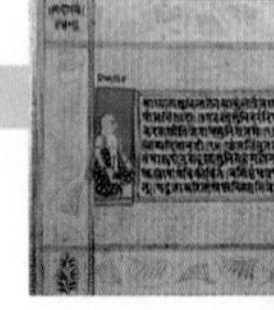

Palm leaf manuscript extract from the Mahabharata

Beliefs and Ideas
Sacred Rig Vedic hymns, composed by the Aryans in praise of Nature and various gods, were later absorbed into Hinduism. Several Hindu gods and rituals, even the caste system *(see p26)*, can be traced to Aryan beliefs.

Where to See Harappan Artifacts

The finest collection of Indus Valley artifacts, arranged chronologically, is in New Delhi's National Museum *(see pp 76–9)*. Some archaeological finds, especially Painted Grey Ware from the site of Indraprastha mentioned in the epic *Mahabharata*, are lodged in a small museum in Delhi's Purana Qila itself *(see p88)*. The state museums at Kurukshetra *(see p144)* and Mathura *(see p165)* have a good collection of statues and archaeological finds excavated from this region.

Harappan dice at the National Museum

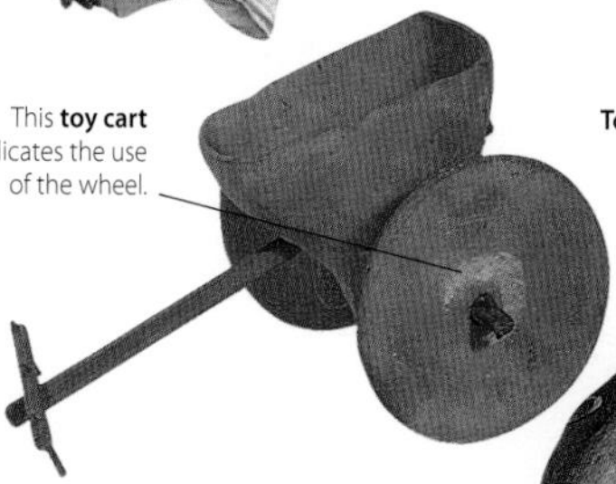

This **toy cart** indicates the use of the wheel.

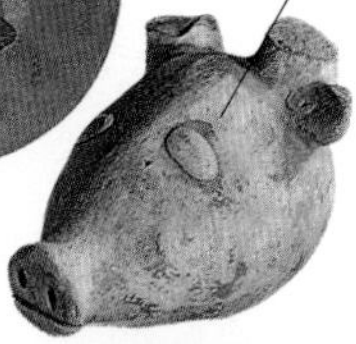

Toy animals testify to the Harappan artisan's skill.

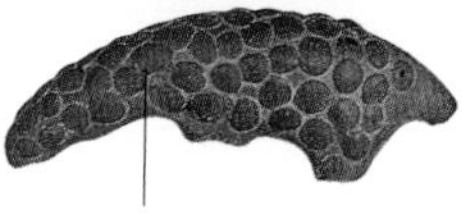

Baked clay was used by the Harappans to shape various objects such as this anteater.

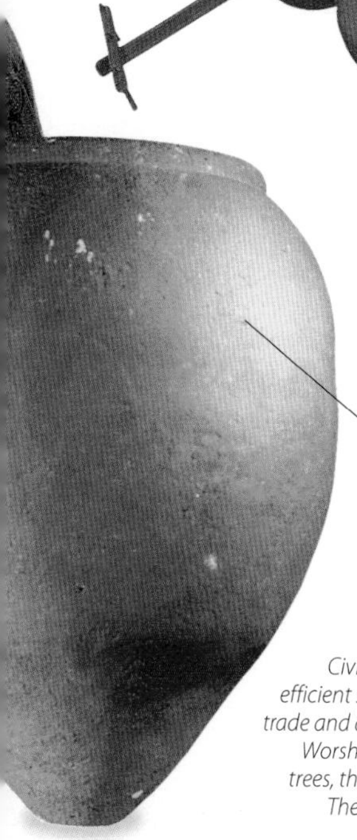

Grain was stored in wide-mouthed jars.

Harappan Culture

The Indus Valley (or Harappan) Civilization (2500–1500 BC) had an efficient system of government based on trade and a thriving agricultural economy. Worshippers of a mother goddess and trees, they used water for ritual practice. These Harappan artifacts are in the National Museum.

The Origin of Life
An 18th-century painting depicting the popular Hindu myth that life was created when the divine nectar *(amrit)*, hidden in the Ocean of Milk, was won by the gods from the demons *(see p29)*.

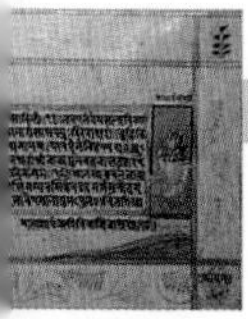

600 BC Rise of cities such as Mathura and Varanasi in the Ganges Valley

486 BC Death of the Buddha

468 BC Mahavira, founder of Jainism, dies

327–325 BC Alexander the Great in India

315 BC Megasthenes, Greek ambassador to India, writes social treatise, *Indika*

600 | 500 | 400 | 300

491–461 BC Reign of Ajatshatru, King of Magadha

424–321 BC Nanda dynasty

321 BC Accession of Chandragupta, founder of the Mauryan dynasty

600 BC *Upanishads*, early philosophical texts

Indo-Greek coins

Ancient Empires

Under the Mauryan Emperor Ashoka, North India saw its first large-scale empire. Contact with Central Asia, which began around 200 BC, determined crucial political alliances after the Mauryas, and by the 1st century AD, the Kushanas from Central Asia had an empire that extended as far as the Ganges Valley. This period also saw the rise and spread of Buddhism. In the 4th century, the Gupta kings presided over the flowering of classical Sanskrit at the hands of writers such as Kalidasa. The emergence of the Holy Trinity *(see pp28–9)* and temple worship also date from the Gupta Age.

Early Empires

- Mauryan Empire
- Kushana Empire
- Gupta Empire

Buddhism
A peaceful, non-violent religion, its message of tolerance and social equality won Buddhism many followers, among them the Mauryan emperor Ashoka. Its rise had a profound impact on social, political and cultural life.

Speckled red sandstone was extensively used in Mathura art.

The human form, sensuously carved, has expressive lines. The gold ornaments and elaborate hair styles of the figures reflect the court fashions of the age.

Ashokan Edict
(3rd century BC)
Considered valuable historical records, such rock edicts, installed throughout his kingdom, proclaim Ashoka's ethical code *(dhamma)* as well as important events.

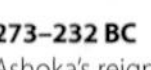

273–232 BC Ashoka's reign

261 BC Battle of Kalinga leads Ashoka to embrace Buddhism

180–165 BC Foundation of Indo-Greek empire by Demetrius

80 BC Maues, Shaka king in northwest India

AD 78–110 Reign of Kushana king Kanishka; Fourth Buddhist Council held in Kashmir

2nd-century Buddhist begging bowl

200 BC | 100 BC | AD 1 | AD 100 | 200

185 BC Accession of Sungas in Magadha

165–130 BC Menander I, Indo-Greek king, rules over the northwest

AD 20–46 Gondophernes, Indo-Parthian king in Taxila; St Thomas comes to South India

150 Rudradaman, the Sha king in West India; first Sar inscription on imperishab material dates from his rei

Mauryan sculpture

Kanishka (AD 78–144)
This famous Kushana king came from Central Asia (as the boots and cloak of his headless statue reveal) to control a large part of North India. Another great patron of Buddhism, his reign presided over its spread to China, Central Asia and Afghanistan, along the famous Silk Route.

Where to See Ancient Art

The Government Museum, Mathura *(see p165)* and the National Museum, New Delhi *(see pp76–9)* have fine collections of Mauryan, Kushana, Gupta and Sunga sculptures. The Northern Ridge *(see p107)* and Feroze Shah Kotla *(see p101)* have well-preserved Ashokan pillars.

Sunga pillar, National Museum

Yakshas* and *yakshis, male and female nature spirits, as well as the foliage behind them, represent fertility and an abundance of life. Their presence highlights the mood of revelery and fecundity.

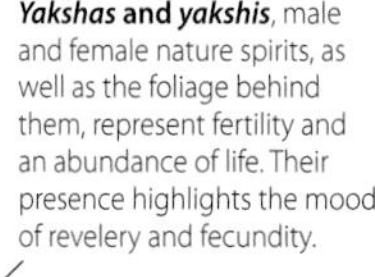

Greek features like curly hair and sharp noses distinguish Gandhara sculpture.

Vasantasena, a courtesan, slumped in a drunken state, is helped to her feet.

Gandhara Sculpture
After the 1st century AD, a distinct Hellenistic style first emerged in Gandhara in the northwest. The Buddha was now depicted in a sublime human form, rather than through symbols such as the lotus and *chakra*, with expressions that recall classical Greek sculpture.

Mathura School of Art

Between the 1 st and 6th centuries AD, a renowned school of art flourished at Mathura (see p165). *Statues of Jain, Buddhist and Hindu divinities, with remarkably expressive faces, were produced along with secular art such as this dramatic 2nd-century Kushana panel,* The Drunken Courtesan.

300–399 *Ramayana, Mahabharata* compiled. *Bhagavad Gita* written

319–20 Accession of Chandragupta I, and establishment of the Gupta dynasty

335 Accession of Samudragupta

375–415 Reign of Chandragupta II

399–414 Chinese traveller Fa Hsien in India

Iron pillar

476 Birth of Aryabhatta, the astronomer

Gold coin of Samudragupta

500–527 Hun control over North India

606–47 Harsha's reign

630–44 Hiuen Tsang, a Chinese Buddhist scholar, travels in India

712 Arab conquest of Sind

300 | 400 | 500 | 600 | 700

18th-century painting of the 4th-century Gupta erotic treatise, Kamasutra

Rajput Dynasties

Rajput clans rose to prominence in North India from the late 7th century. Claiming a high caste warrior status *(kshatriya)*, they traced their lineage to the sun and moon to firmly establish their legitimacy, and ruled over North, West and Central India. After losing Delhi and Kannauj to the Muslims, they confined their activities to the western region, now Rajasthan, where rival clans fought for supremacy. Widely renowned for their loyalty and valour, most Rajput clans were welcomed as allies by Mughal rulers.

Locator Map

Extent of Rajput Kingdoms

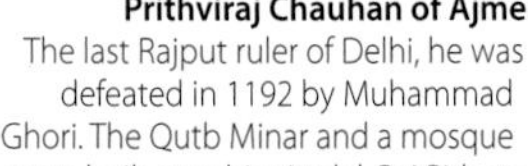

Prithviraj Chauhan of Ajmer
The last Rajput ruler of Delhi, he was defeated in 1192 by Muhammad Ghori. The Qutb Minar and a mosque were built over his citadel, Rai Pithora.

Turbans indicate the home, region and status of a person.

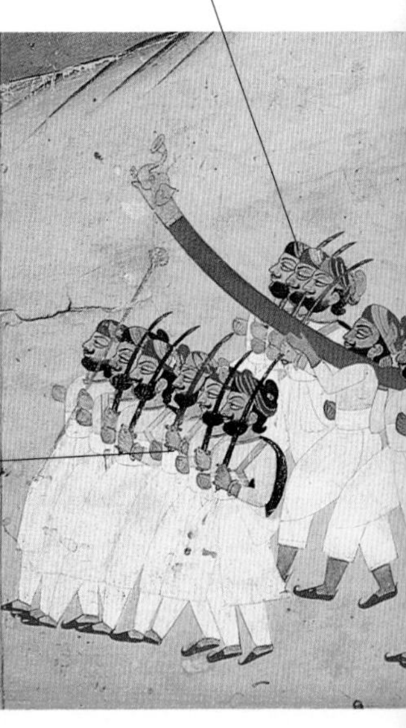

Pageantry was a vital part of the Rajput concept of kingship.

Sacred Beliefs
Rajput kings were patrons of Hinduism and worshipped martial gods such as Hanuman *(see p201)* and Shakti. They were also prolific builders of beautiful temples.

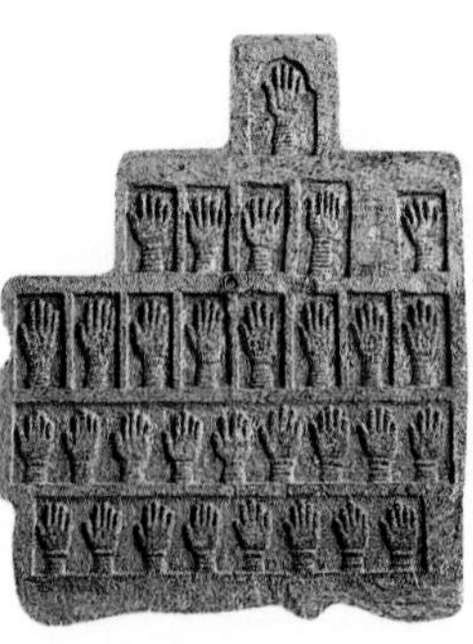

Sati Sites
Hand imprints mark the sites where women immolated themselves by jumping into their husband's funeral pyre. This cruel practice, called *sati*, was made illegal in 1829.

736 Dhilika (Delhi) is founded by the Rajput Tomaras

760 The Palas rule over Bengal and Bihar

800–1036 The Gurjara-Pratiharas rule over Kannauj

750 — **775** — **800**

800 Shankaracharya, the Hindu philosopher, challenges Buddhism and Jainism

11th-century copper plate inscriptions of a Rajput king, Raja Chachuka

A Rajput court dress

Rajput Art
Rajput rulers were great patrons of architecture and painting. This unusual 18th-century miniature from Jaipur shows Rajput women playing polo *(see p199)*.

Man Singh I of Amber
This loyal Mughal ally, one of the "nine jewels" *(navaratna)* of Akbar's court, was among the first Rajputs to befriend the Mughals. Such alliances paved the way for peace in North India and a fusion of Hindu and Islamic cultures, especially in architecture.

Palanquins, such as this fanciful one, were carried by a retinue of clansmen during ceremonial processions.

The ruler epitomizes the best of Rajput chivalry and valour.

Weapons are an essential part of a Rajput's attire.

A Royal Procession

Rajput princes enjoyed a divine status in the eyes of their clan. Rajputana, literally the land of princes, once had some 21 kingdoms ruled by rival clans which included the Sisodias of Mewar, Kachhawahas of Amber and Jaipur, Rathors of Marwar and Bikaner, Haras of Kota and Bundi, Chauhans of Ajmer, and Bhattis of Jaisalmer.

Where to See Rajput India

Amber *(see pp204–5)* and the jungle fort at Ranthambhore *(see pp228–9)* are some famous Rajput forts in this region. The museum inside the City Palace, Jaipur *(see pp192–3)* and Alwar *(see p210)* display private collections. The National Museum, New Delhi, also has a wide display of Rajput miniature paintings *(see pp36–7)*, sculpture and jewellery.

Amber Fort *(see pp204–5)*

883–1026 The Hindu Shahis rule over Kabul and the Punjab

973–1192 The Chahamanas of Sakambhari rule over Ajmer, Rajasthan

974–1238 The Solankis rule Anhilwad in Gujarat

875 | 900 | 925 | 950 | 975

916–1202 The Chandellas rule over Bundelkhand and build the Khajuraho temples in Central India

Phad, *a Rajput folk painting*

974–1233 The Paramars rule Dhar in Central India

10th-century Khajuraho temple

The Delhi Sultans

The fabulous wealth of India attracted Arab traders and raiders, such as Mahmud of Ghazni. A slave general of Muhammad Ghori, called Qutbuddin Aibak, established himself in North India and founded the Mamluk (Slave) Dynasty. Followed by the Khiljis, Tughlaqs, Sayyids and Lodis, these Muslim rulers, called the Sultans of Delhi, established an empire that survived into the early 16th century and changed the cultural and urban milieu of much of the subcontinent by introducing new technologies and customs.

Coming of Islam

— Empire of Mamluks (1236)

Empire of Tughlaqs (1335)

Illustrated Koran (17th century)
The noble Islamic art of calligraphy was introduced by Muslim rulers and used to embellish royal decrees, manuscripts and copies of the Koran, as well as buildings.

Ceramic Tiles
Jamali Kamali *(see p115)* has fine examples of this Islamic art.

Qutbuddin Aibak built the first storey of the Qutb Minar and a mosque to proclaim his victory over the Rajputs.

Quwwat-ul-Islam, which means "Might of Islam", was the first congregational mosque in Delhi.

Madrasa and tomb of Alauddin Khilji

Persian Wheel
The water wheel came in the wake of Muslim rule. Its simple technology is still used in rural areas to draw underground water for irrigation.

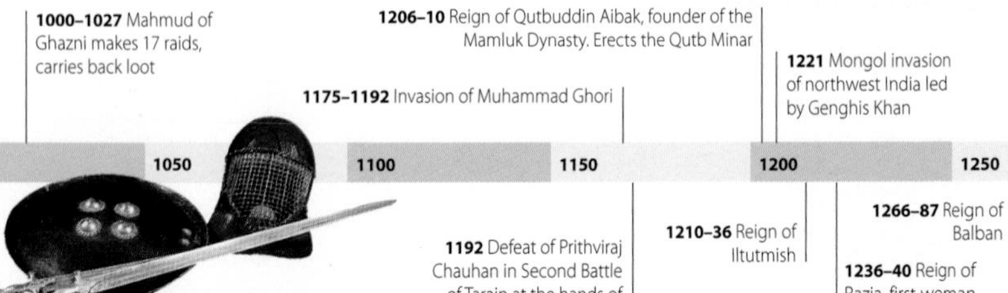

Sultanate weaponry

1000–1027 Mahmud of Ghazni makes 17 raids, carries back loot

1175–1192 Invasion of Muhammad Ghori

1192 Defeat of Prithviraj Chauhan in Second Battle of Tarain at the hands of Muhammad Ghori

1206–10 Reign of Qutbuddin Aibak, founder of the Mamluk Dynasty. Erects the Qutb Minar

1210–36 Reign of Iltutmish

1221 Mongol invasion of northwest India led by Genghis Khan

1236–40 Reign of Razia, first woman ruler of Delhi

1266–87 Reign of Balban

Feroze Shah Tughlaq added the topmost storeys in 1368.

Iltutmish, Qutbuddin's successor, built the second and third storeys.

Alai Darwaza was built by Alauddin Khilji in 1311.

Nizamuddin Auliya
Mystic sages called Sufis were among the immigrants from Central Asia. This 17th-century miniature shows Nizamuddin Auliya *(see p86)* with the poet Amir Khusrau. Together, they raised metaphysical love, poetry and music to the level of divine worship.

Where to See the Delhi Sultanate

The Mehrauli area *(see pp114–17)*, Hauz Khas *(see p110)*, Tughlaqabad *(see p118)*, Feroze Shah Kotla *(see p101)*, Purana Qila *(see p88)* and Lodi Gardens *(see p83)* show the various architectural styles of the Sultanate. The National Museum *(see pp76–9)* has a fine collection of artifacts dating to this period.

Begumpuri Masjid *(see p113)*

Music
Amir Khusrau, poet and musician, is said to have introduced the multi-stringed sitar and the raga style to North Indian music.

The Qutb Minar

In 1193, Qutbuddin Aibak built the Qutb Minar (see p116) *and a mosque to announce the advent of the Muslim sultans. This 19th-century lithograph shows a part of the Qutb complex that was built over the remains of an earlier Rajput citadel at Mehrauli* (see pp114–15).

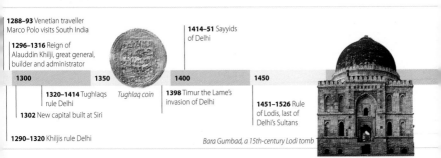

1288–93 Venetian traveller Marco Polo visits South India

1290–1320 Khiljis rule Delhi

1296–1316 Reign of Alauddin Khilji, great general, builder and administrator

1302 New capital built at Siri

1320–1414 Tughlaqs rule Delhi

Tughlaq coin

1398 Timur the Lame's invasion of Delhi

1414–51 Sayyids of Delhi

1451–1526 Rule of Lodis, last of Delhi's Sultans

1300 | 1350 | 1400 | 1450

Bara Gumbad, a 15th-century Lodi tomb

The Great Mughals

The Mughals, like the Ottomans of Turkey, the Safavids of Iran and the Tudors of England, were one of the greatest medieval dynasties. For over 200 years they held firm political control over the subcontinent, establishing a stable administrative system and a rich pluralistic culture blending the best of Hindu and Islamic traditions. Great patrons of art and architecture, they also encouraged the translation of Sanskrit texts into Persian. Markets and cities flourished under them, making India famous.

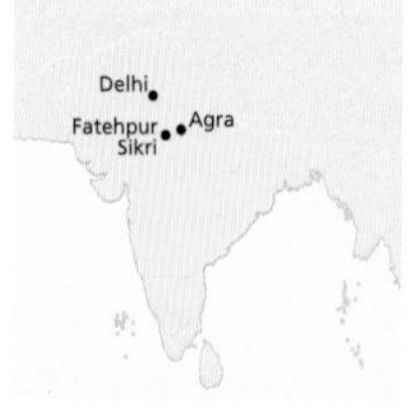

Mughal Empire

Mughal Empire at the end of the 17th century

Buland Darwaza at Fatehpur Sikri
Erected to celebrate Akbar's victory over Gujarat in 1572–3, Buland Darwaza *(see p177)* is part of the great Mughal architectural legacy that still dominates the region.

Hierarchy of nobles depended on the rank given by the emperor.

Rajput princes were often loyal Mughal supporters. Shah Jahan's grandmother was a Rajput princess.

Mughal Art
A ruby-studded ceremonial gold spoon, Jahangir's jade wine cup, a gold enamelled glass hookah base and Mughal miniature paintings *(see pp36–7)* offer vivid glimpses of the Mughals' extravagant patronage of art.

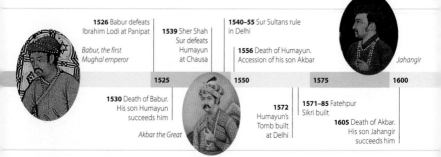

Babur, the first Mughal emperor

1526 Babur defeats Ibrahim Lodi at Panipat

1530 Death of Babur. His son Humayun succeeds him

1539 Sher Shah Sur defeats Humayun at Chausa

Akbar the Great

1540–55 Sur Sultans rule in Delhi

1556 Death of Humayun. Accession of his son Akbar

1572 Humayun's Tomb built at Delhi

1571–85 Fatehpur Sikri built

Jahangir

1605 Death of Akbar. His son Jahangir succeeds him

1525 | 1550 | 1575 | 1600

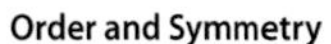

Order and Symmetry
The "taming of the land" that took place under the Mughals, whether it was their landscaped gardens or their system of justice and revenue settlement, was founded on this dual principle.

Where to See Mughal India

Fatehpur Sikri *(see pp174–6)* and the Taj Mahal *(see pp158–61)* are among the finest examples of Mughal architecture in this region. The area around Delhi's Red Fort *(see pp98–9)* also has several Mughal relics. Important collections of Mughal art, manuscripts, coins, jewellery, costumes and armoury are housed in both the National Museum, Delhi *(see pp76–9)* and the City Palace Museum, Jaipur *(see pp192–3)*.

Mughal necklace

Shah Jahan with his son in the foreground receiving a gift from a noble.

Diwan-i-Khas was used for special audience with the emperor and his advisors.

Court robes and turbans indicated status and religion.

A railing separated the imperial circle from lower state officials.

Military Organization
All senior administrators *(mansabdars)* maintained an armed retinue *(sawars)* and rank *(zat)* determined salary.

Shah Jahan's Court

The splendour of the Mughal court is illustrated in this 17th-century painting of Shah Jahan among his nobles, grouped in strict hierarchical order round the throne. Mughal emperors, seated in an elevated alcove, used glittering court rituals to display their supreme political position as they took stock of the state affairs from their officials.

1627 Accession of Shah Jahan

1628 Tomb of Itimad-ud-Daulah built by Nur Jahan at Agra

1638–48 Shah Jahan builds new capital at Shahjahanabad, Delhi

1652 Taj Mahal completed

1659 Aurangzeb crowned emperor

1707 Death of Aurangzeb, the last Great Mughal

1625 | 1650 | 1675 | 1700 | 1725

The Taj Mahal

Aurangzeb

European Traders, Colonizers and Mercenaries

Crippled by the sack of Delhi in 1739 by Nadir Shah of Persia, Mughal power declined rapidly. This was exploited by petty rulers, European mercenaries, and the British East India Company, set up in the 1690s to trade in spices and cotton. Its commercial success led to the rise of the Company as a political power, which ushered in some social reforms and new power equations. Yet, the social instability engendered by the Company's unpopular trade and political practices erupted in the Indian Mutiny or Great Revolt of 1857.

The Indian Mutiny of 1857

- Areas where British administration was disputed
- Site of major revolt in 1857

The Decline of the Mughals
Nadir Shah's plunder of Delhi *(see p96)* was the signal for the rise of the Jats and Marathas. Suraj Mal Jat *(see p170)* filled Bharatpur Fort, seen above, with looted Mughal treasures.

British officer killing a rebel leader at Fatehpur.

Sepoys mutinied against animal grease on bullets as it violated religious taboos.

Indian rebels led by disgruntled princes ultimately lost the war.

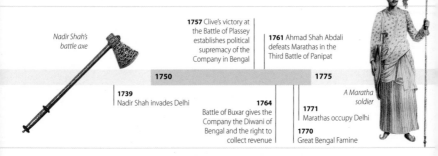

Economic Exploitation
A 19th-century lithograph shows the impoverishment of cotton ginners as cheap English mill-made cloth flooded the Indian market.

Nadir Shah's battle axe

A Maratha soldier

1739 Nadir Shah invades Delhi

1750

1757 Clive's victory at the Battle of Plassey establishes political supremacy of the Company in Bengal

1761 Ahmad Shah Abdali defeats Marathas in the Third Battle of Panipat

1764 Battle of Buxar gives the Company the Diwani of Bengal and the right to collect revenue

1770 Great Bengal Famine

1771 Marathas occupy Delhi

1775

A Nabob and his Concubines
A corruption of *nawab*, this name described officials who made huge fortunes from the East India Company's cotton and spice trade in India. Many adopted the feudal lifestyles of the Indian princes as this 19th-century painting shows.

Indian Sepoys
The Company's commercial interests were protected by its military establishment, which employed Indian foot soldiers called sepoys.

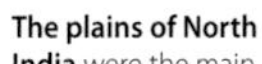

The plains of North India were the main battle areas.

Palanquins transported rebel princes and gentlefolk to the scene of battle.

Sepoys Rebelling at Fatehpoor

This lithograph of a pitched battle during the Mutiny show sepoys and Indian leaders being tackled by the Company's troops. The Indian Mutiny or Great Revolt of 1857 was seen as India's first war of independence from colonial rule by some nationalists as it shook the foundation of the East India Company's rule in India.

Where to See European India

Sardhana *(see p146)* has a cathedral built by Begum Samroo, the Indian wife of Walter Reinhardt, a European mercenary. Meerut's church, where the first shots of the sepoy mutiny were fired, survives in mint condition *(see p146)*. The cantonments in Meerut and Agra, the Agra cemetery *(see p156)* and St James's Church in Delhi *(see p105)* are other sites that go back to the time of the Indian Mutiny.

Sardhana Cathedral *(see p146)*

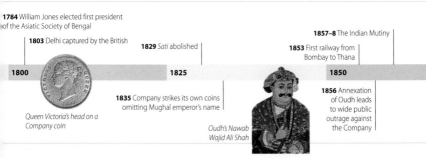

1784 William Jones elected first president of the Asiatic Society of Bengal

1803 Delhi captured by the British

1800

Queen Victoria's head on a Company coin

1829 *Sati* abolished

1825

1835 Company strikes its own coins omitting Mughal emperor's name

Oudh's Nawab Wajid Ali Shah

1853 First railway from Bombay to Thana

1857–8 The Indian Mutiny

1850

1856 Annexation of Oudh leads to wide public outrage against the Company

Pax Britannica

The foundation of British rule, or the Raj, was laid only after the Indian Mutiny, which truly revealed the unpopularity of the East India Company. An Act of Parliament in 1858 brought its rule to a close and its Indian territories became part of Britain's empire. India was now ruled directly by the Crown through a viceroy. Though the Raj was unabashedly Victorian and conservative, and its *raison d'être* was economic profit and political control, its abiding legacy was the political unification of the subcontinent, and the introduction of modern Western education, a centralized civil administration and judicial system, along with a wide network of railways and postal services.

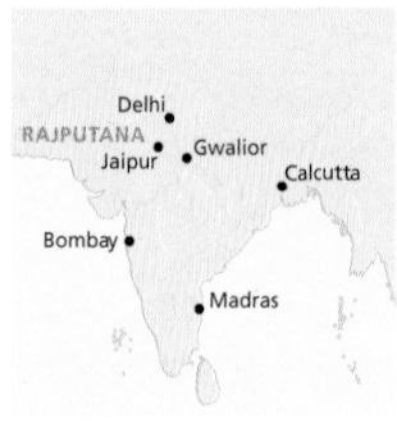

British India

British territory, 1858

The Steel Frame
Some 2,000 British officers ruled over a subcontinent of 300 million people. The paternalistic civil service brought order and justice even to remote outposts.

Indian attendants in viceregal livery re-enact a Mughal procession.

Northern Gate of the Jami Masjid.

Memsahib with her Tailor
Despite the climate, the English clung to their own dress styles. Children were sent "home" to study, and a large Indian staff enabled a luxurious lifestyle.

Lord Canning, the first Viceroy

1858 Victoria proclaims Lord Canning first Viceroy of India

1859 Withdrawal of Doctrine of Lapse, a major cause of the 1857 revolt

1861 Indian Council Act

1865 Telegraphic communication is established with Europe

Lord Dalhousie, author of the notorious Doctrine of Lapse (see p311)

1875

1876 Victoria proclaims herself Empress of India

1877 Lytton's Delhi Durbar

A Sahib Travelling
A vast rail network was set up by the British to facilitate commerce and travel. This lithograph of first-class travel, a privilege of "whites only", is from the 19th century.

Raj Cuisine
While kebabs, curry and rice became a part of British culinary preference, Westernized Indians took to drinking tea and nibbling biscuits. An early 20th-century biscuit tin label reflects this exchange of tastes.

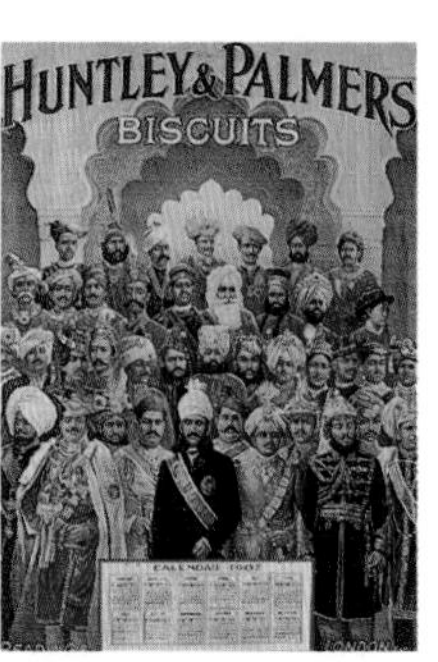

Caparisoned elephants carry the new rulers.

Crowds line the streets to see the grand spectacle.

Where to See British India

Raisina Hill and the surrounding area *(see pp72–3)*, Agra's St John's College *(see p156)*, and Mayo College *(see p223)* in Ajmer are examples of colonial architecture. Delhi's Coronation Memorial *(see p107)* and the University area *(see p107)* are other sites with a Raj connection.

Detail of India Gate *(see p75)*

The Durbar, 1903

This painting of Curzon's Delhi Durbar (1903), held to celebrate the coronation of Edward VII, shows a procession winding through the historic streets of Delhi. Held periodically, such assemblies announced both the grandeur and the political might of British rule in India.

1878 Vernacular Press Act

1885 Indian National Congress founded

1878–80 Second Anglo-Afghan War

1883–4 Ilbert Bill controversy

Lord Curzon, Viceroy 1899–1905

1899 Lord Curzon becomes Viceroy

1900

1905 Partition of Bengal by Lord Curzon causes national outrage

1904 Ancient Monuments Preservation Act

The Freedom Movement

The founding of the Indian National Congress in 1885 gave Indians a platform from which to demand freedom from foreign rule. Their ideology was provided by Gandhi, whose message of non-violence and economic self-reliance gave them moral confidence, and united castes and communities under a common cause. At first the movement for freedom was ruthlessly suppressed, but by the 1930s it became too large for the British to handle. Finally, weakened by World War II and under growing international pressure, England granted India formal independence in 1947.

Freedom Movement

• Major towns associated with the Freedom Movement

Round Table Conference (1931) The British tried to work out a settlement with Gandhi, accompanied by formidable campaigner and poet, Sarojini Naidu.

Khadi, homespun cloth, was worn as a statement of patriotism.

Huge crowds turned out to register their support. Gandhi united castes and communities as never before.

The police dogged public assemblies, often brutally beating the audience.

The Cellular Jail, Andaman Islands Hundreds of freedom fighters were shipped here by the British. Many were hanged, some died of diseases such as malaria. Now a national monument, the jail's is known as Kala Pani ("black waters"), a name recalling its dark past.

Rabindranath Tagore

1906 Muslim League formed at Dacca

1907 Congress splits at Surat between the moderates and extremists

1908 Tilak, a prominent nationalist, sentenced to six years transportation on charges of sedition

1910

1913 Rabindranath Tagore wins the Nobel Prize for Literature

1914 Canada refuses Indians aboard the ship *Kamagata Maru* permission to land

1915 Home Rule League started by Annie Besant

1917 Gandhi takes up the cause of indigo farmers at Champaran, Bihar

1919 Police fires at unarmed crowd at Jallianwala Bagh in Amritsar, Punjab

1920 Non-cooperation Movement launched by Gandhi

1920

New Delhi
New Delhi was declared the Raj's capital in 1911. This early photo shows Parliament House, then the Legislative Assembly building.

Where to See the Freedom Movement

The National Archives *(see p75)* and the Gandhi Smriti *(see p82)* have a permanent exhibition on the Freedom Movement. Panels on this theme are also displayed at the Jawahar Pavilion in Pragati Maidan *(see p89)*. Teen Murti House *(see p82)* offers a view of Nehru's life.

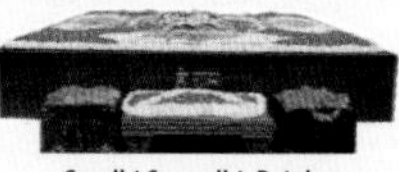

Gandhi Samadhi, Rajghat *(see p101)*

Nehru and Jinnah
Prominent lawyers who joined Gandhi's national movement, they enjoyed an iconic status in India and Pakistan after Independence.

Gandhi delivered his powerful message of freedom at public meetings.

The Partition (1947)
A huge displacement of people across the borders took place at the division of the subcontinent into India and Pakistan, leading to an eruption of violent communal riots.

Mahatma Gandhi

Called Mahatma ("great spirit"), MK Gandhi returned to India from South Africa in 1915 as a protest against apartheid. He travelled across the subcontinent, launching a moral crusade that encouraged non-violent Civil Disobedience against colonial rule.

1930–32 Gandhi leads the Dandi Salt March and Civil Disobedience Movement

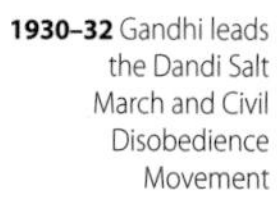

Subhash Chandra Bose and members of the Indian National Army

1930

1940

1939 Resignation of the Congress Ministers

1940 Muslim League adopts the Pakistan Resolution

1942 Quit India Movement

1947 India attains Independence

1948 Assassination of Mahatma Gandhi

Bungalow designed for a new capital at Delhi in the 1930s

Nehru is sworn in as the first Prime Minister by Lord Mountbatten

India Today

India celebrated 68 years of independence in 2015. Nehru, the first prime minister, laid the foundations for a modern nation state with a democratic, secular polity, a strong industrial base and a planned economy, with non-alignment as the keystone of its foreign policy. India's 1.2 billion people speak 22 languages, and though many of them are illiterate and unemployed, a vigorous and free press and electoral system ensure that their interests and rights are safeguarded and well represented. The three major national political parties are the Congress, the Aam Aadmi Party (Common Man's Party), and the more right-wing Bharatiya Janata Party (Indian People's Party).

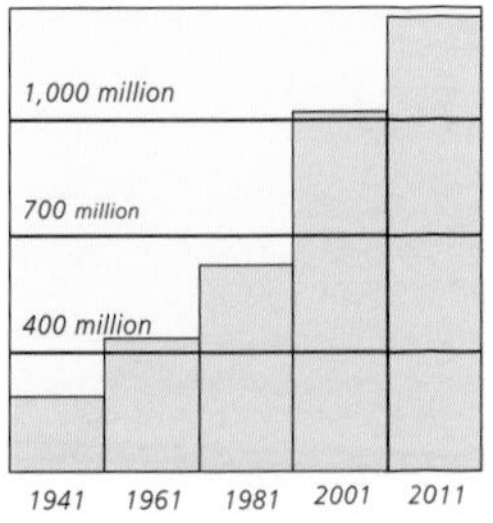

Population Figures

Growth of population

Rural India More than half the country's population lives in its villages. An adult literacy programme is under way to educate the disadvantaged, particularly women.

New Delhi was built between 1911 and 1933 by Lutyens and Baker.

The Indian flag is a tricolour of saffron, white and green, with a *chakra* (wheel) in the centre.

The Nehru Family Jawaharlal Nehru is seen here with his daughter Indira Gandhi (who was not related to Mahatma Gandhi), and her son Rajiv Gandhi. All three were prime ministers of India. Rajiv's Italian-born widow, Sonia, now heads the Congress Party.

1950 India becomes a Republic

1952 First General Election

1953 Mount Everest scaled by Hillary and Tenzing

1955 Bandung Conference on Non-Alignment

1960

1962 India-China War

1964 Death of Jawaharlal Nehru, first prime minister

1965

1965 War with Pakistan

1966 Indira Gandhi becomes prime minister

1970

1971 War with Pakistan, birth of Bangladesh

1974 First nuclear test, Pokhran

1975

1975 Indira Gandhi declares the unpopular Emergency

1977 Janata Party, the first non-Congress coalition, takes power

1980

1980 Indira Gandhi returns as prime minister

1982 India sends scientific team to Antarctica

1984 Indira Gandhi assassinated. Her son Rajiv Gandhi succeeds her as prime minister

1985

Industrial Development
Nehru, the architect of the country's industrial base, hailed factories as the new temples of modern India. India is now a major industrial power with a huge workforce of skilled workers.

Cricket
Introduced by the British, this game is now a national obsession. Recently retired Sachin Tendulkar, the "little master", is regarded by many as the greatest batsman since Donald Bradman.

The Indian Army is one of the largest in the world.

South Block and its twin, North Block, were designed to flank Raisina Hill.

The Republic Day Parade

A magnificent parade on 26 January celebrates the day when India became a republic in 1950. A colourful flypast, folk dances and floats display its pluralistic society, and the president, as head of the republic, takes the salute at Rajpath.

Protest Rallies
India's vibrant democracy expresses itself through popular protest *(dharna)* in which women figure prominently. The Narmada Bachao activists, seen here, have mobilized women and displaced tribal people against the World Bank-funded Narmada Dam.

Contemporary Literature
India has a rich writing tradition in all languages. *The White Tiger*, written by Aravind Adiga *(right)*, won the Man Booker Prize in 2008. *The Lives of Others*, by Neel Mukherjee, was shortlisted for the Man Booker in 2014, as was *The Lowland*, by Jhumpa Lahiri, the year before.

A woman casts her vote

1990 VP Singh becomes prime minister; announcement of reservation for backward classes

1991 Rajiv Gandhi assassinated; New Liberalization Policy under Prime Minister Narasimha Rao

1992 Destruction of Babri Masjid in the state of Uttar Pradesh leads to communal riots

1998 The right-wing Bharatiya Janta Party (BJP) comes to power for the first time; AB Vajpayee becomes prime minister

1999 Conflict with Pakistan over Kashmir at Kargil; 13th General Elections re-elect a BJP-led government

2001 Earthquake in Gujarat

2004 Manmohan Singh elected prime minister; UPA government in power

2007 Prathiba Patil elected as first female president of India

2010 Delhi hosts the Commonwealth Games

2014 BJP's Narendra Modi sworn in as India's 15th Prime Minister

1990 | 1995 | 2000 | 2005 | 2010 | 2015 | 2020

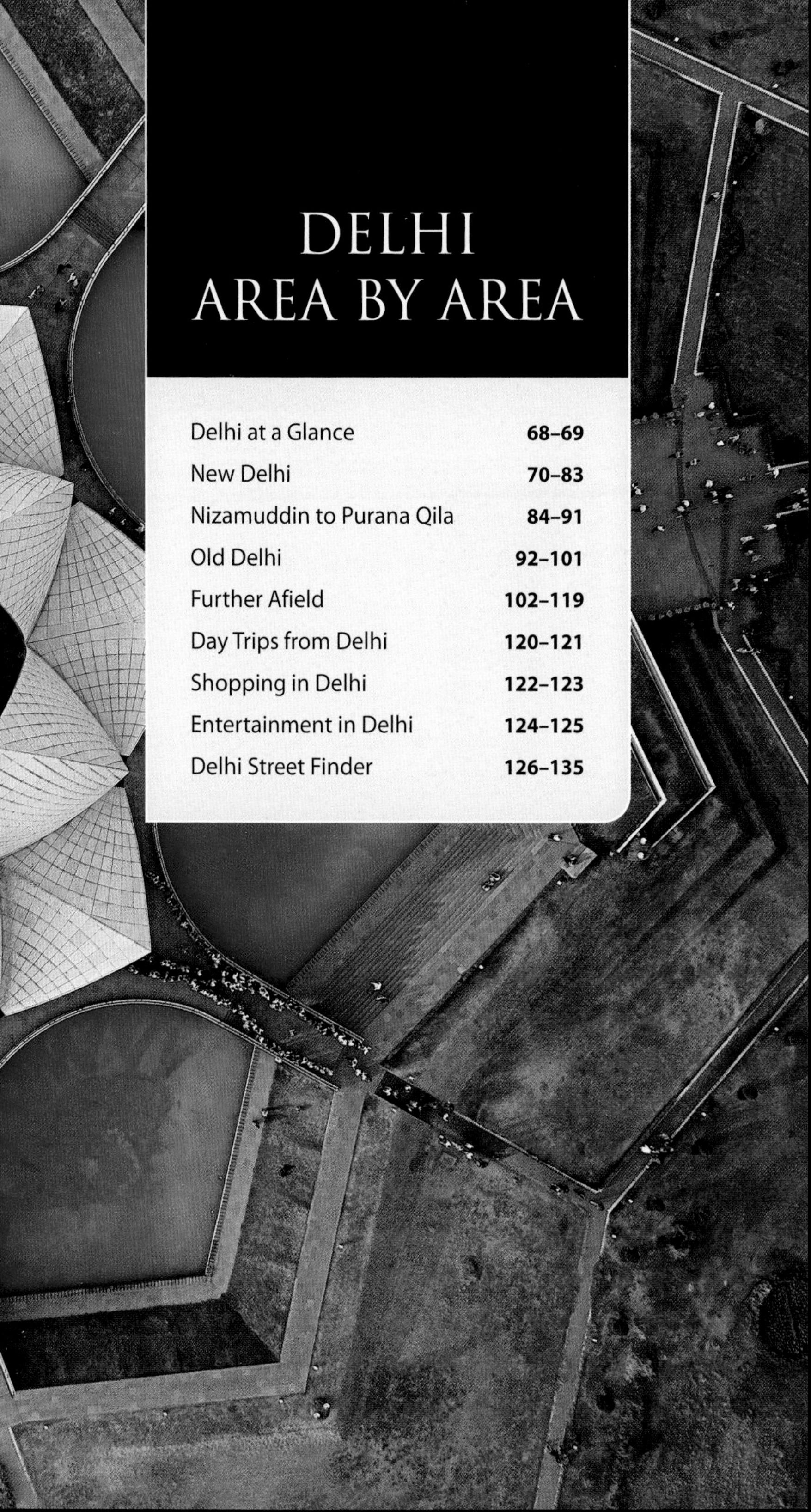

DELHI AREA BY AREA

Delhi at a Glance

Situated along the Yamuna river, Delhi was built by the British in the 1930s and is the youngest of several historic cities that have occupied this site. Now a noisy and chaotic metropolis of 25 million people and a mélange of shanty settlements and smart colonies, it is still dotted with the remains of its interesting past. There are museums and art galleries with impressive collections, and its shops offer a tempting array of handicrafts. Delhi is a major cultural centre of the country with music, dance and art events held throughout the year.

The Jami Masjid *(see p96)* is the largest congregational mosque in Asia with lively bazaars in the surrounding lanes.

Connaught Place *(see p80)*, was built in the 1930s as the business centre of New Delhi, in concentric circles round a central park. Its stately colonnaded corridors contain shops and offices.

Rashtrapati Bhavan *(see p74)* is the official residence of the President of India. Called Viceroy's House in colonial times, it was designed by Edwin Lutyens and occupies the crest of Raisina Hill. Its forecourt is the venue for colourful state pageantry.

The National Museum *(see pp76–9)* houses the most comprehensive collection of antiquities in the country. This 2nd-century Sunga panel of a grieving woman is part of a stunning section on sculpture from various periods and places.

CHANDNI CHC
QUTAB ROAD
OLD DELH
(See pp92–101)
ASAF ALI RO
PANCHKUIAN ROAD
CHELMSFORD ROAD
VIVEKANAND ROAD
BABA KHARAK SINGH MG
SANSAD MARG
KASTURBA GANDHI MG
ASHOK ROAD
NEW DELHI
(See pp70–83)
TALKATORA ROAD
CRESCENT
COPERNICUS MARG
TERESA
DR RAJENDRA PRASAD RD
RAJPATH
MOTHER
MOTILAL NEHRU MG
SHAHJAHAN ROAD
TEEN MURTI MG
AKBAR ROAD
JANPATH
AURANGZEB ROAD
ROAD
PRITHVIRAJ
LODI ROAD
LO

◀ The beautiful 27-petalled Lotus Temple, better known as the Baha'i House of Worship

Red Fort *(see pp98–9)*, an impressive fort-palace built by Shah Jahan, was the seat of Mughal power. After the Indian Mutiny of 1857, the British converted it into a garrison and it was stripped of many precious treasures.

The Crafts Museum *(see pp90–91)* complex offers an insight into India's cultural, craft and rural traditions. The museum exhibits textiles, folk art and objects of everyday use in terracotta, metal and wood.

Humayun's Tomb *(see p87)* is where the second Mughal emperor Humayun is buried. This garden tomb with its imposing double dome is considered by many to be the first great Mughal mausoleum in this region.

अमर
जवान

NEW DELHI

The British built New Delhi, between 1911 and 1931, to be the showcase of the Empire. On Independence, this grand imperial capital became the official and bureaucratic centre of the new Indian nation. Today, the former Viceroy's House is the president's residence, and ministers and civil servants live nearby in spacious bungalows along the tree-lined avenues. Kingsway, the east-west processional avenue leading to India Gate, is now Rajpath, where every 26 January the Republic Day Parade is held *(see p75)*. The National Museum is on Janpath. To the north are Connaught Place, the Birla Mandir and the cultural complex at Mandi House. Despite strict security restrictions, New Delhi is the city's most impressive area.

Sights at a Glance

Historic Buildings, Streets and Plazas

1 Rashtrapati Bhavan
2 Vijay Chowk
4 Rajpath
6 India Gate

Churches and Temples

3 Cathedral Church of Redemption
11 Lakshmi Narayan Mandir

Museums

5 National Museum
7 National Gallery of Modern Art
13 Nehru Memorial Museum and Library
14 Gandhi Smriti

Monuments

9 Ugrasen's Baoli
12 Jantar Mantar

Gardens

15 Lodi Gardens

Shops and Markets

10 Connaught Place
16 Khan Market

Theatres and Art Galleries

8 Mandi House Complex

Restaurants *pp250–52*

1 Big Chill
2 Daniell's Tavern
3 Dhaba
4 Elan
5 Khan Chacha
6 Kwality
7 Latitude 28
8 Lodi Garden Restaurant
9 Pind Balluchi
10 Saravana Bhavan
11 Sevilla
12 Smokehouse Bar & Grill
13 Spice Route
14 The Shim Tur
15 Triveni Tea Terrace
16 Varq
17 Veda
18 Wasabi

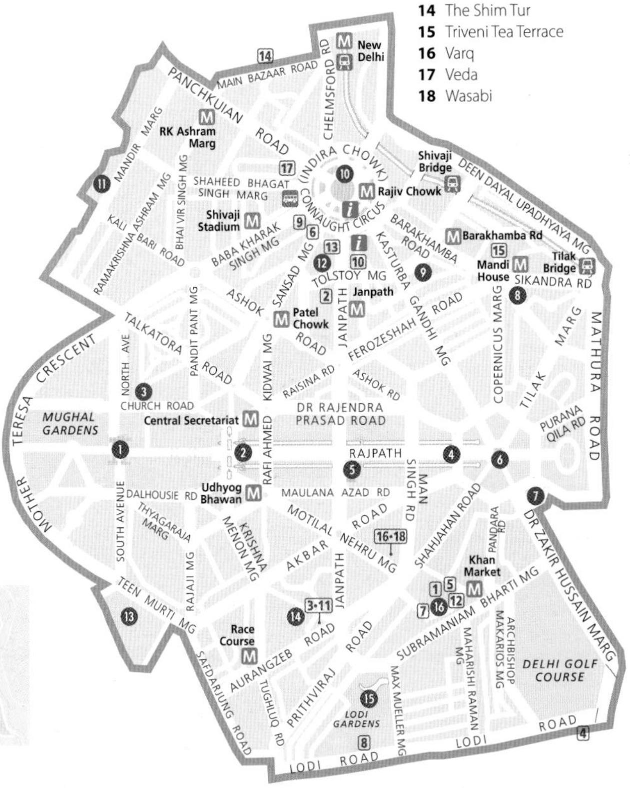

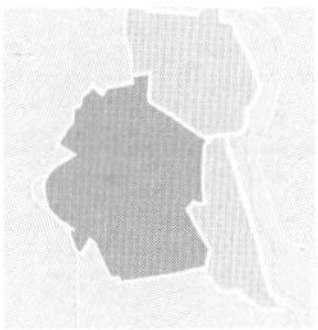

See also Street Finder maps 1, 2, 5

◀ The memorial at India Gate, bedecked with flowers on Navy Day

Street-by-Street: Around Vijay Chowk

The barren, treeless grounds around Raisina Hill were selected as the site of the new capital city. Now a well-guarded verdant area, it houses India's president, ministers and officials, as well as its Parliament and ministries. Imperial hierarchical conventions, both spatial and political, laid down by the British are still followed, so that even today, Indian ministers and officials live in spacious bungalows on broad tree-shaded avenues around Rashtrapati Bhavan where no high-rise buildings are allowed. From Vijay Chowk, Lutyens's grand central vista lies ahead – large trees and fountains line the lawns of Rajpath up to India Gate, the Canopy and the National Stadium at the far end.

2 ★ Vijay Chowk
A pair of red sandstone obelisk-shaped fountains flank this forecourt that overlooks a grand vista.

Sansad Bhavan is also known as Parliament House.

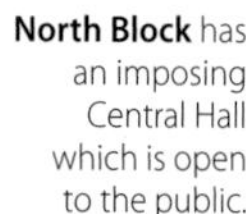

North Block has an imposing Central Hall which is open to the public.

DALHOUSIE ROAD

THYAGARAJ MARG

The Iron Gates
Copied from a pair Lutyens saw in Chiswick, England, these are held by highly ornamental sandstone gateposts. Rashtrapati Bhavan lies to the west of them.

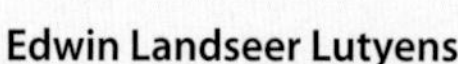

Edwin Landseer Lutyens

Building the Secretariats on rocky scrubland

Architect Edwin Landseer Lutyens (1869–1944), President of the Royal Academy from 1938 to 1944, was commissioned to design India's new capital in 1911. With Herbert Baker, his colleague, it took him 20 years to build the city in a unique style that combined Western Classicism with Indian decorative motifs. The result is classical in form and English in manner with Neo-Mughal gardens and grand vistas meeting at verdant roundabouts. Delayed by World War I and quarrels between Baker and Lutyens, spiralling costs met by Indian revenues led Mahatma Gandhi to term it a "white elephant". Ironically, the British lived here for only 16 years.

★ South Block
The Prime Minister's Office and the Defence Ministry are located within this block, a high security zone.

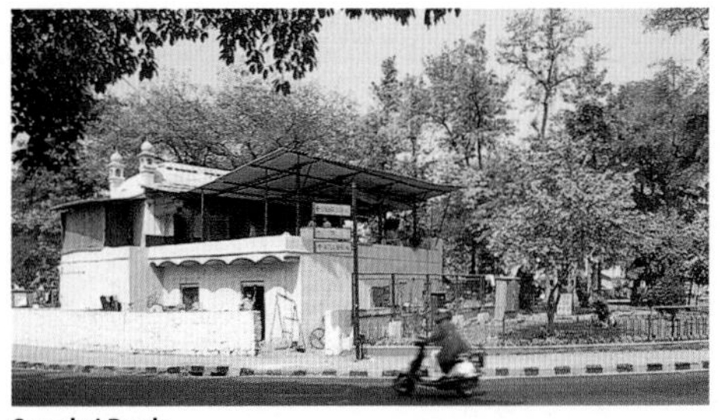

Sunehri Bagh
This gently curving street leads to a picturesque roundabout with a simple 18th-century mosque built by a *pir* called Sayyid Sahib. Shady trees are a standard feature of all Lutyens's avenues.

OLD DELHI
NEW DELHI
NIZA MUDDIN TO PURANA QILA

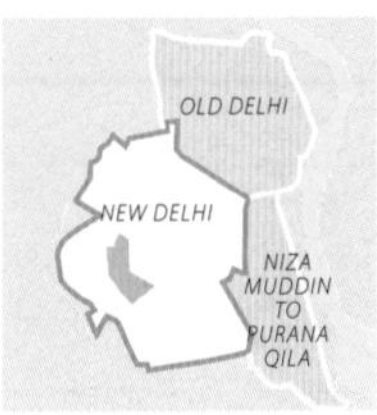

Locator Map
See Street Finder map 4

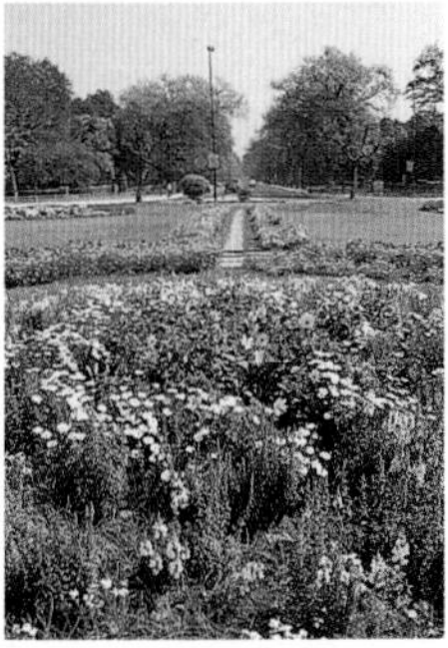

Roundabout
Beautifully landscaped road intersections are a haven for workers during lunch.

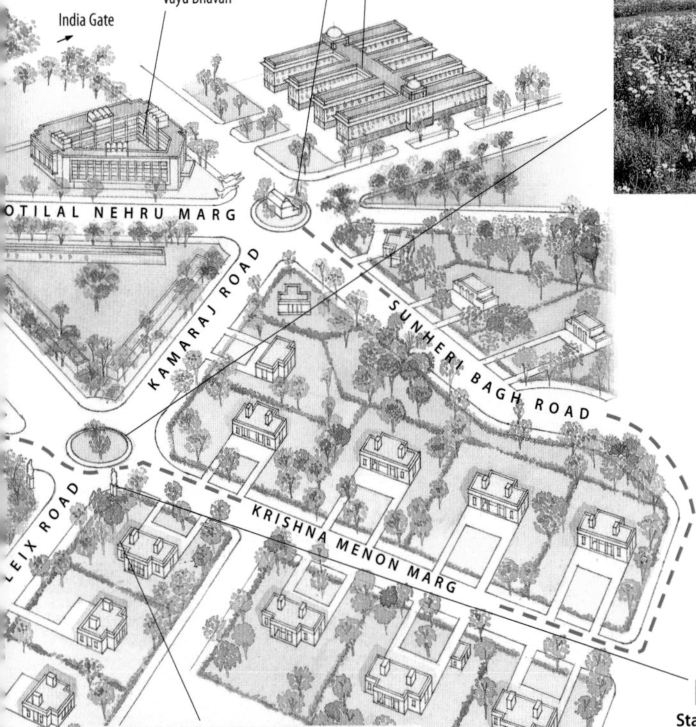

India Gate
Vayu Bhavan
Udyog Bhavan
OTILAL NEHRU MARG
KAMARAJ ROAD
SUNHERI BAGH ROAD
KRISHNA MENON MARG
LEIX ROAD

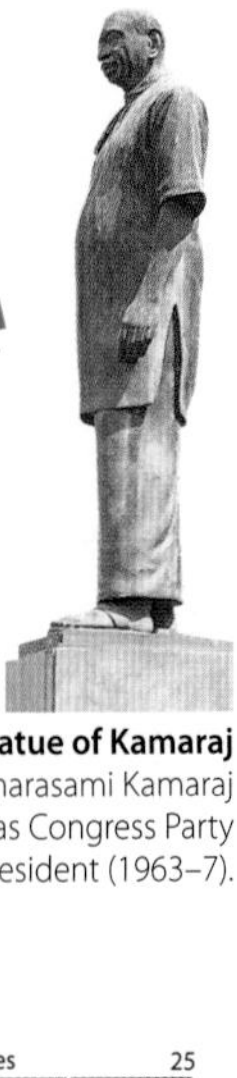

Statue of Kamaraj
Kumarasami Kamaraj was Congress Party President (1963–7).

★ Bungalow-lined Avenues
Strict building bylaws preserve the original architecture of the colonial bungalows in the tree-lined avenues of this area.

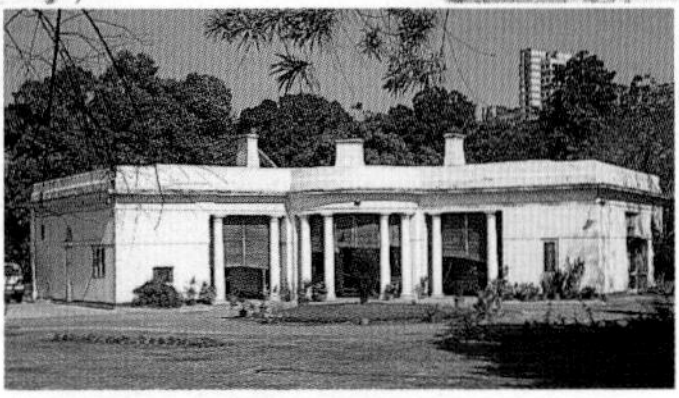

0 metres 25

0 yards 25

Key

— Suggested route

Rashtrapati Bhavan seen through Lutyens's ornate iron gates

❶ Rashtrapati Bhavan

Map 4 E2. **Tel** (011) 2301 5321. **Open** 9am–4pm Fri–Sun. **Closed** Mon–Thu. phone or book online to visit. **presidentofindia.nic.in**. Change of Guard Ceremony: **Tel** (011) 2301 3287. Apr–Oct: 8am; Nov–Mar: 10am Sat only. Kitchen Museum: **Tel** (011) 2301 2960. **Open** As for tour. Mughal Gardens: **Open** Feb–Mar. **Closed** Mon.

Designed by Edwin Lutyens *(see p72)* to be the focal point of New Delhi during British rule, the house built for the viceroy, which is today the President of India's official residence, stands at the crest of Raisina Hill. This 20th-century architectural masterpiece covers an area of 4.5 acres (2 ha). The cupola of its copper and sandstone dome rises 55 m (180 ft). Within are courtyards, banqueting halls, state apartments and private living quarters. The *pièce de résistance* is the Durbar Hall, where all important Indian state and ceremonial occasions are held. Situated beneath the dome and forming the centre-piece of the "H"-shaped building, this circular hall was originally the Throne Room and contains the two gold and crimson thrones Lutyens designed for the vice-roy and vicereine. The **Kitchen Museum** showcases items used to cook, serve and dine at the Rashtrapati Bhavan, through the pre- and post-Independence periods.

To the west of the grounds are the formal **Mughal Gardens** with water-courses and fountains built on three levels, ending with Lutyens' "butterfly garden".

Jaipur Column, Rashtrapati Bhavan

❷ Vijay Chowk

Map 4 F2. N Block: **Open** 9am–6pm Mon–Fri. Sansad Bhavan: **Open** 11am–5pm Tue–Sat. Visit is subject to Parliament not being in session.

The area where Rajpath meets Raisina Hill, known as Vijay Chowk, was planned as a commanding approach to the Viceroy's House. This is where the unforgettable "Beating Retreat" ceremony takes place each year on 29 January *(see p45)*.

Rising impressively from the levelled top of Raisina Hill are the two virtually identical **Secretariat** buildings, designed by Herbert Baker and known as the North and South Blocks. These long classical edifices house the Home and Finance ministries and the Ministry of Foreign Affairs. The stately Central Hall of the North Block (to the left, if facing Vijay Chowk) is open to the public.

Sited to the north of Vijay Chowk, Baker's circular **Sansad Bhavan** (Parliament House) was a later addition following the Montagu-Chelmsford Reforms of 1919, to house the Legislative Assembly. The Constitution of India was drafted here in the early days of Independence. Today, both the Rajya Sabha (Upper House) and the Lok Sabha (House of the People) meet here when Parliament is in session. The Lok Sabha's often boisterous debates take place in the Central Hall.

Sansad Bhavan (Parliament House), where the Constitution of India was drafted

❸ Cathedral Church of the Redemption

1 Church Rd, North Avenue. **Map** 4 E1. **Tel** (011) 2309 4229. **Open** 8am–noon; 4–6pm daily.

Henry Alexander Medd (1892–1977), the architect of this magnificent church, was inspired by Palladio's church of Il Redentore in Venice, from which it also derives its name. Consecrated in 1931, the cathedral formed an integral element of the plan for the imperial capital complex, and was built as the main Anglican church for senior British officials in New Delhi. Today, it is the diocese of the Bishop of the Church of Northern India. Among the many memorial tablets inside the church, there is one in honour of its architect.

The Neo-Classical Cathedral Church of the Redemption

❹ Rajpath

Map 5 A2. National Archives: **Tel** (011) 2338 4797. **Open** 9:30am–6:30pm Mon–Sat. **Closed** Sun & public hols. Indira Gandhi National Centre for the Arts: **Tel** (011) 2338 8105. **Open** 9:30am–5:30pm Mon–Fri.

This 3-km- (2-mile-) long avenue, used for parades and lined with canals and fountains along its lovely lawns, is very popular with Delhi residents on steamy summer evenings.

The **National Archives**, situated at the intersection with Janpath, houses a major collection of state records and private papers. Opposite is the **Indira Gandhi National Centre for the Arts** (IGNCA), with an archive of rare manuscripts. It holds many national and international exhibitions and symposia.

❺ National Museum

See pp76–9.

❻ India Gate

Map 5 B2.

At the eastern end of Rajpath, the 9-m (30-ft) wide India Gate was built to commemorate the Indian and British soldiers who died in World War I and those who fell in battle in the North-West Frontier Province and the Third Afghan War. An eternal flame burns in memory of unknown soldiers who died in the 1971 Indo-Pakistan war. Facing India Gate is the sandstone canopy where King George V's statue was installed after his death in 1936. The statue is now at Coronation Park *(see p107)*. Around India Gate are the stately homes of erstwhile Indian princes, including Hyderabad House where official state banquets are held, and Jaipur, Bikaner, Patiala and Baroda Houses.

India Gate

❼ National Gallery of Modern Art

Jaipur House, Dr Zakir Hussain Marg, near India Gate. **Map** 5 C2. **Tel** (011) 2338 4640/2835. **Open** 10am–5pm Tue–Sun. **Closed** Mon & public hols. **W** **ngmaindia.gov.in**

Jaipur House, the former residence of the Jaipur maharajas, is one of India's largest museums of modern art. Its vast collection includes graphics, paintings and sculptures dating from the mid-19th century to the present day. The galleries display works of British landscape painters such as the Daniells, and Indian artists such as the Tagores, Jamini Roy, Amrita Shergill and Raja Ravi Varma. Works of contemporary artists such as MF Husain, Ram Kumar, KG Subramanyam and Anjolie Ela Menon are also seen here. Reproductions of paintings are sold at the gallery shop.

Republic Day Parade

Indians love parades and ever since 1950, when India became a republic, the Republic Day parade on 26 January has always attracted large crowds despite the often chilly weather. The president, the prime minister and other dignitaries watch as soldiers in dashing uniforms from the many regiments and squadrons of the Army, Navy and Air Force march smartly past. Brightly dressed schoolchildren, civil defence services personnel and others quick-step down the grand vistas of Rajpath to the rousing percussion of military bands. Most popular are the Camel Corps and the inventive floats representing each state of the country. A ceremonial fly-past by the Indian Air Force signals the end of the parade.

Republic Day Parade

❺ National Museum

Five millennia of Indian history can be explored at the National Museum, with a collection of more than 200,000 pieces of Indian art. The nucleus collection of about 1,000 artifacts was sent to London in the winter of 1948–9 for an exhibition at the Royal Academy. After its return, it was housed in the Durbar Hall of Rashtrapati Bhavan until the present building was complete in 1960. The collection of Indus Valley relics and Central Asian treasures from the Silk Route is considered among the finest in the world. Some sections of the museum are undergoing renovation and exhibits may not be on display.

★ Dara Shikoh's Marriage Procession
An 18th-century Mughal miniature painting in gold and natural pigments.

★ Nataraja
This 12th-century Chola statue of the cosmic dance of Lord Shiva is the centrepiece of the museum's South Indian bronzes.

The Coins and Indian Scripts Gallery has on display an impressive collection of coins and the evolution of the Indian script.

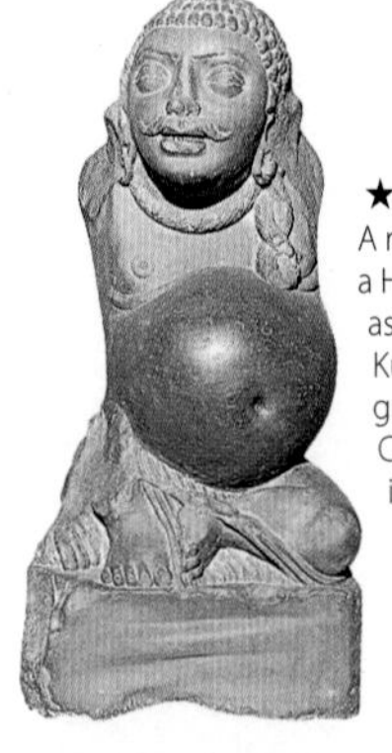

★ Kubera
A rare example of a Hindu god shown as a 2nd-century Kushana (*see pp50–51*) grandee with marked Central Asian features is among a large collection of Mathura Art.

The Serindian Collection

Silk painting, 7th–8th century

Almost 700 years after the Silk Route fell into disuse, Sir Aurel Stein, a British archaeologist, led a series of expeditions (1900–16) to uncover its treasures. On view at the National Museum, Stein's Central Asian collection of the artifacts he found in the Taklamakan Desert has silk paintings, Buddhist manuscripts and valuable records of life along this ancient trade route.

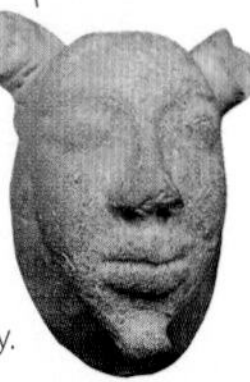

Terracotta Mask
This unusual human mask made of terracotta dates back to 2700 BC, and was unearthed in Mohenjodaro in the early 20th century.

VISITORS' CHECKLIST

Practical Information
Janpath, Rajpath Rd Area, Central Secretariat. **Map** 5 A2. **Tel** (011) 2379 2775. **Open** 10am–5pm Tue–Sun. **Closed** Mon & public hols. extra charges. 11:30am, 2:30pm, 4pm. Film shows, lectures, presentations and special exhibitions. **nationalmuseumindia.gov.in**

Transport
Central Secretariat, Udyog Bhawan. 501, 521, 522, 526, 531, 580, 615.

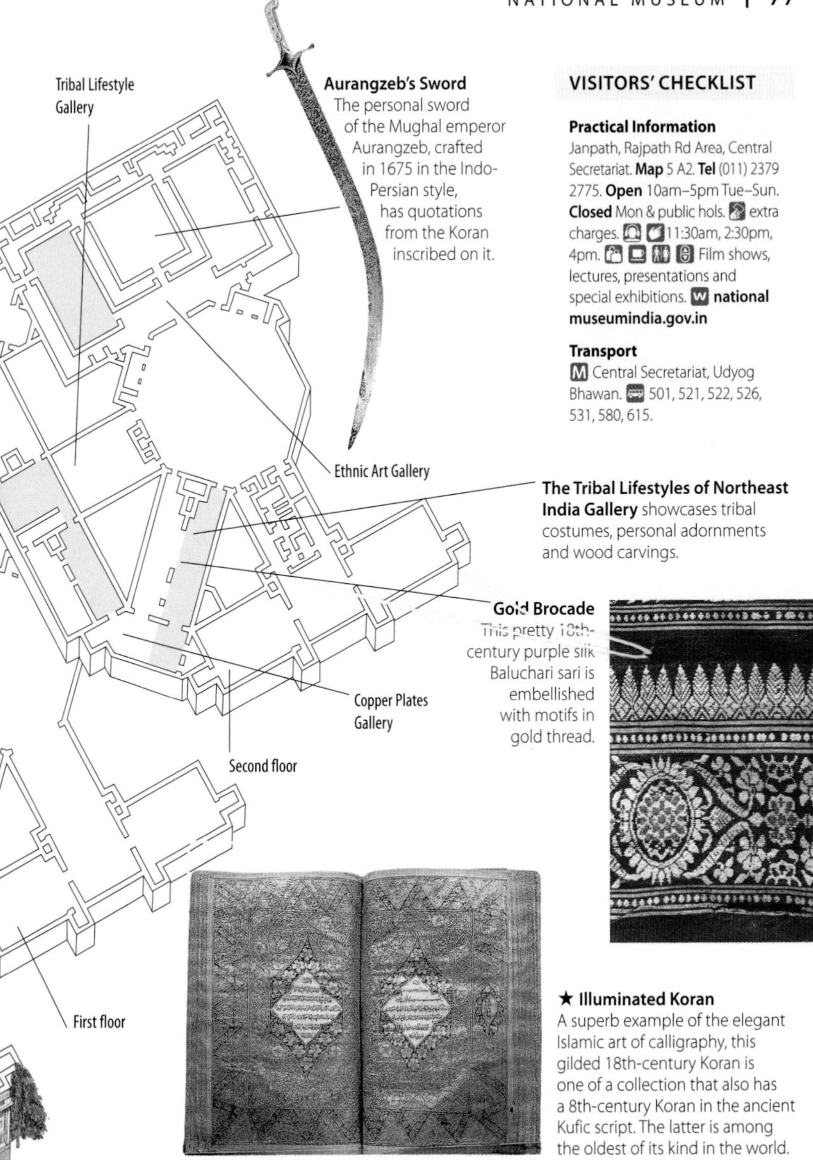

Aurangzeb's Sword
The personal sword of the Mughal emperor Aurangzeb, crafted in 1675 in the Indo-Persian style, has quotations from the Koran inscribed on it.

The Tribal Lifestyles of Northeast India Gallery showcases tribal costumes, personal adornments and wood carvings.

Gold Brocade
This pretty 18th-century purple silk Baluchari sari is embellished with motifs in gold thread.

★ Illuminated Koran
A superb example of the elegant Islamic art of calligraphy, this gilded 18th-century Koran is one of a collection that also has a 8th-century Koran in the ancient Kufic script. The latter is among the oldest of its kind in the world.

Key to Floorplan

- Ancient & Medieval Sculptures
- Chola Bronzes, Jewellery, Wood Carving
- Buddhist Art, Decorative Art
- Central Asian Antiquities, Indian Manuscripts and Coins, Wall Paintings
- Early Man
- Pre-Columbian and Western Art
- Ajanta Paintings, Thanjavur Paintings, Indian Miniature Paintings
- Textiles, Arms and Armour, Musical Instruments

Gallery Guide

The collection is displayed on three floors, grouped according to theme, epoch and style. The central foyer itself has a display of sculptures from various parts of the country. The museum also has a library and auditorium where film shows and lectures are regularly held. Information on these is published in the newspapers, and material regarding catalogues and souvenirs can be found at the ticket office in the foyer. The display is changed from time to time for variety, and special exhibitions are also held.

Exploring the National Museum Collection

Spread over three floors radiating from an octagonal courtyard, the museum has 30 galleries (some closed for renovation or devoted to temporary exhibitions). The impressive collection includes sculpture, paintings, jewellery, decorative arts and textiles. These represent the finest examples of each style and period from all over the country.

Indus Valley Culture

Excavations in the 1920s at Harappa and Mohenjodaro (now in Pakistan) revealed the remains of a sophisticated urban culture that existed between 2500–1500 BC along the Indus Valley *(see pp48–9)*. The museum's collection of relics from these sites is among the finest in the world. Although the Indus copper and bronze instruments are less opulent than the later Mesopotamian and Egyptian ones, other items, such as the figure of a dancing girl and a headless female torso, show enormous artistic skill.

Also on display are soapstone seals, used perhaps by merchants and officials, whose pictographic script remains undeciphered. Particularly notable is the display of Harappan pottery which ranges from functional items such as pots to charming toys, beads, necklaces and weights.

Ancient and Medieval Sculpture

Six galleries on the ground floor trace the growth of Indian sculpture over 1,500 years. Among the earliest pieces is a rare terracotta fertility goddess from Mathura dating to the 3rd century BC. From Amaravati in Andhra Pradesh (1st century AD), is a superb sculpted panel depicting its now vanished reliquary mound *(stupa)*. The 2nd-century AD Kushana frieze of Vasantasena, an inebriated courtesan *(see pp50–51)*, is an amusing comment on court life, while the splendid collection of Gandhara art, with its marked Hellenistic style, shows the evolution of the human form in North Indian sculpture after the 1st century. Its delicately draped statues are the first representations of the Buddha in human form. After the great stone-carved Hindu temples and images of the Gupta period (3rd–5th centuries), regional styles emerged in the south and the east. Successive galleries trace sculptural developments of the Pallava, Chalukya and the Hoysala dynasties.

2nd-century Jain votive plaque from Mathura

Bronzes

Indian bronzes, executed through the *cire perdue* or "lost wax" process as an alternative to stone temple sculptures, developed in South India under the Chola and Pallava dynasties. Idols made of bronze, an alloy of eight metals with copper as the base, were less weighty than stone and could either be worshipped at home or taken out for festive processions. The gallery's collection covers 600 years (5th–11th centuries). The pride of place belongs to a 10th-century Chola Nataraja, the name given to the Lord of Dance, Shiva. This shows him dancing the Chaturatandava, a classic representation of his cosmic dance of life and death. The circle of flames that surrounds the dancer represents the entire cosmos.

Devi, 15th-century bronze

Another 11th-century Chola bronze, *Kaliyamardan Krishna*, is a superb study of the balance and poise of the young Lord Krishna as he dances on the hood of the five-headed serpent, Kaliya, holding his tail in triumph.

Manuscripts and Wall Paintings

Among the wealth of rare manuscripts in the museum are the *Bustan-e-sadi* (1502), one of the few dated and illustrated manuscripts of pre-Mughal India. Leaves from the 16th-century *Babur Nama*, a biography of the first Mughal emperor, illustrate the style of early Mughal painting. A *Rig Veda Samita* (1514) and a beautiful 18th-century cloth scroll of the *Bhagvat Purana* are also part of this collection.

Also on display is an unparalleled *Hunting Scene* (c.1810) from the Kota School of Painting, salvaged from the Jhala Jhalim Singh Haveli in Kota, Rajasthan.

Decorative Arts

The immense variety of India's decorative arts fills two adjoining galleries. Even everyday objects, such as a 19th-century silver rosewater sprinkler from Delhi, or a hookah base enamelled in blue and green from 18th-century Rajasthan have individual flourishes.

Court patronage ensured that artists fashioned innumerable *objets d'art* to delight royal whims. Thus, floral arabesques adorn a 17th-century Mughal *degcha* (cooking pot). Daintily carved ivory statues and artifacts and elegant Hyderabad *bidri* ware, delicately inlaid with silver, are also on display.

An 18th-century *bidri ware* jewel box

Indian Miniatures

Over 350 paintings from a large collection of 18,000 are on display in the new miniature gallery. There are some Mughal masterpieces from the Jahangir and Shah Jahan period, including the famous *Jahangir Holding the Picture of Madonna* (c.1620) and *Camel Fight* (c.1615–20). Insightful portraits of the Mughal rulers Babur, Jahangir, Shah Jahan, and other court personalities such as Tansen, the legendary court musician of Akbar's time, bring Mughal history to life.

Also on view are a selection of *Ragamala* series depicting the mood of each *raga*. The Rajasthani miniatures illustrate Hindu mythological themes, particularly the devotional love between Krishna and Radha. The Kishangarh paintings, *Boat of Love* and *Radha and Krishna*, both mid-18th century, bring lyricism and beauty to this

Durga Killing Demon Raktabija, Malwa, c.1640

timeless relationship. There are also hunting scenes from Kota where the depiction of nature is real and vibrant. Court painters at Mewar produced detailed depictions of a variety of royal pursuits ranging from court activities to recreation and leisure.

Basholi paintings with their bold and intense colours, and delicate portraits from Guler are part of the large collection of Pahari paintings from the northern hill states. Deccani art from Hyderabad, a fusion of the Islamic idiom with indigenous styles, produced masterpieces such as *A Picnic Party* (early 18th century). Also on display are later provincial schools that developed after the Mughals, as well as Company art, produced for the British from the mid-18th century.

Central Asian Antiquities

Sir Aurel Stein's collection of treasures *(see p76)* discovered from the legendary Silk Route in Chinese Turkestan comprises this invaluable section. Included are paintings on silk (3rd century) and a 10th-century caravan scene on paper from Dun-huang in China that re-create the romance of those times. Fragments of another fabulous silk painting, *Ladies in a Garden*, from Astana, show lovely-looking women in elaborate coiffures with impressive gold filigree pins, lounging among blossoms.

Textiles, Arms and Armour, Musical Instruments

The textile collection displays a selection of Indian weaving techniques, including the world famous gold and silk brocades of Varanasi from the Mughal period; *ikat* and tie-and-dye from Andhra Pradesh and Gujarat; and 19th-century *kantha* embroidery from Bengal in intricate hemstitch. Also worth noting is a hand-embroidered *rumal* from Golconda dating to 1640.

The Arms and Armour Gallery has the 18th-century painted rhinohide shield of the Rajput king, Maharana Sangram Singh.

The Musical Instruments Gallery has some artifacts that are over 200 years old, including an ivory inlaid *tanpura* (a stringed instrument) from the 18th century. The core collection was donated by Sharan Rani, a famous *sarod* player.

An intricately-woven, 17th-century jamawar shawl

8 Mandi House Complex

Map 2 D5. Triveni Kala Sangam: 205 Tansen Marg. **Tel** (011) 2371 8833. **Open** 9:30am–5pm Mon–Sat. **Closed** public hols. Rabindra Bhavan: 35 Ferozeshah Rd. **Tel** (011) 2338 6626. Kamani Auditorium: Copernicus Marg. **Tel** (011) 4350 3351. Sri Ram Centre: Safdar Hashmi Marg. **Tel** (011) 2371 4307. National School of Drama: 1 Bhagwan Das Rd. **Tel** (011) 2338 9402. For Tickets: see Entertainment: *pp124–5*.

Mandi House, once the palace of the ruler of a small principality in Himachal Pradesh and today the offices of the state-owned television centre, lends its name to this cultural complex encircling a roundabout.

Triveni Kala Sangam's various art galleries hold regular contemporary art exhibitions. A pleasant open-air auditorium here stages dance and theatre performances. Well-known artistes and writers can often be glimpsed in the popular café, and there is also a bookshop specializing in Indian arts publications.

The state-sponsored arts complex, **Rabindra Bhavan**, houses the three national academies of literature (Sahitya Akademi), fine arts and sculpture (Lalit Kala Akademi), and the performing arts (Sangeet Natak Akademi) in separate wings. All have libraries and display galleries which also sell reproductions and postcards. The Lalit Kala is the site of the international Triennale exhibition in which painters and sculptors from more than 30 countries participate. Exhibitions of photography, graphics and ceramics are also held here.

Kamani Auditorium, the **Sri Ram Centre** and the **National School of Drama** host theatrical, classical music and dance events in their auditorium. The latter two have their own repertory companies which stage plays in many regional languages.

The historic stepwell, Ugrasen ki Baoli, located in the heart of New Delhi

9 Ugrasen ki Baoli

Off Hailey Rd, Vakil Lane, Connaught Place. **Map** 2 D5.

This stepwell *(see p33)* is reached by turning left on Hailey Road into a narrow lane without a sign-post just before the Consulate General of Malta. A little way along on the right are the remains of an old stone wall; the *baoli* is behind it and can be entered through a narrow buttressed gateway, usually locked, but the *chowkidar* will open the gate. With 103 red-stone steps and a series of arches supported by columns, this is one of Delhi's finest stepwells. Its architectural features suggest a 15th-century date, though popular myth holds that it was built in the 14th century by Raja Ugrasen, an ancestor of the mercantile Aggarwal community, to provide water and shelter for travellers.

Mirror-work skirts on sale at Janpath, Connaught Place

10 Connaught Place

Map 1 C4. Shops: **Open** 10:30am–9pm Mon–Sat (timings for individual shops may vary). **Closed** Sun & public hols.

Robert Tor Russell, one of New Delhi's architects, designed this imperial plaza named after the Duke of Connaught, an uncle of King George V. Noble Palladian archways and stuccoed colonnades deliberately recalled the very English terraces of Cheltenham and Bath; and when the first shops raised their shutters in 1931, they had names such as "Empire Stores" to distinguish them from the local shops selling Indian goods in shopping areas like Gole Market and Chandni Chowk. Today there are as many offices as shops in the central circle, officially renamed Rajiv Chowk. (The outer circle is now Indira Chowk.) The shops are an eclectic mix of travel agencies, banks, outlets for several leading international brands and the ubiquitous gift kiosks. Though Connaught Place has, in recent years, lost out to other local markets, its shaded arcades offer a pleasant atmosphere to stroll in and to browse through the pavement book stalls. There are many restaurants also located here, as well as a number of cinema halls. The central lawns, earlier a venue for street theatre,

Connaught Place, the British-built shopping complex in New Delhi

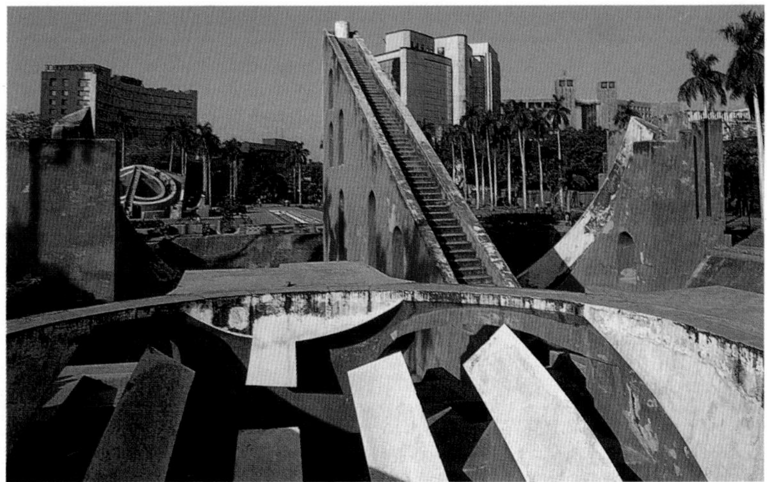

The brick and plaster astronomical instruments in Jantar Mantar

shoe-shine boys and self-styled "ear cleaners", have made way for the Delhi Metro. The popular Central Park features an amphitheatre, 21 fountains and flowered lawns. Nearby popular shopping centres include the state emporia at **Baba Kharak Singh Marg** and the stalls along Janpath.

⓫ Lakshmi Narayan Mandir

Near Gole Market, Mandir Marg, Connaught Place. **Map** 1 A4.

The prominent industrialist GD Birla built this temple dedicated to Lakshmi Narayan in 1938. Mahatma Gandhi attended its first *puja* as this was among the country's first temples that had no caste restrictions. Popularly known as Birla Mandir, it is a fairly typical example of contemporary Indian temple architecture.

Approached by a flight of marble stairs, the main shrine has images of Vishnu and his consort, Lakshmi. It is surmounted by ochre and maroon *shikharas* (temple towers). Subsidiary shrines dedicated to Radha-Krishna, Hanuman, Shiva and Durga *(see pp28–9)* are set around the courtyard. On the walls are quotations from Hindu scriptures, often with English translations. They are also decorated with paintings from the *Mahabharata (see p145)* and *Ramayana (see p41)*.

Surrounded by a peaceful park with a pleasant marble pavilion on one side and a large *dharamshala* (resthouse) on the other, this popular temple is a good place to visit as it is spotlessly clean and very well-maintained.

The popular Lakshmi Narayan Mandir

⓬ Jantar Mantar

Parliament Street, Connaught Place. **Map** 1 C5. **Open** 6am–5pm daily. **Tel** (011) 2336 5358.

Sawai Jai Singh II of Jaipur built this observatory in 1724 when commissioned by the then Mughal emperor Muhammad Shah. A keen astronomer, the maharaja felt that the existing instruments were not accurate enough to calculate the eclipses and planetary positions required to set the timings of his *pujas* and other sacred rituals. He erected new observatories here, and in four other towns, including Jaipur *(see pp196–7)* with instruments that were sufficiently large and fixed to the site to be both exact and not prone to vibration. The instruments are the Samrat Yantra, a right-angled triangle whose hypotenuse is parallel to the earth's axis. This is, in fact, a gigantic sundial, and there are two brick quadrants on either side which measure its shadow. The others are the Jai Prakash Yantra, Jai Singh's invention, which, among other functions, verifies the time of the spring equinox; the Ram Yantra which reads the altitude of the sun; and the Misra Yantra, a group of instruments for a variety of purposes. Today, the observatory lies obsolete, in the centre of a pleasant park, surrounded by high-rises.

The Nehru Memorial Museum and Library at Teen Murti Bhavan

⓭ Nehru Memorial Museum and Library

Teen Murti Marg. **Map** 4 E3. **Tel** (011) 2301 7587. Museum: **Open** 9am–6:30pm Tue–Sun. **Closed** public hols. Nehru Planetarium: **Tel** (011) 2301 4504/2994. Shows: 11:30am, 1:30pm, 3pm, 4pm. **Closed** Mon & public hols.

Jawaharlal Nehru lived in this house, then called Teen Murti Bhavan, while he was India's first prime minister (1947–64). On his death, the house was converted into a national memorial comprising a **Museum** and a library for research scholars.

Originally the residence of the Commander-in-Chief of British Forces in India and located directly south of Rashtrapati Bhavan, the house was designed by Robert Tor Russell, the architect of Connaught Place and the Eastern and Western Courts on Janpath. Its design follows the established Lutyens-style classicism with a teak-panelled interior and vaulted reception rooms. Nehru's bedroom and study, still exactly as he left them, are an austere centre in a grand house. Especially interesting are the bookshelves containing Nehru's large private collection, an eclectic mix of English classics, Left Book Club editions and treatises on the Cold War.

This home has a special place in modern Indian history as it once housed not just the incumbent prime minister, but two future ones as well: his daughter, Indira Gandhi, and grandson, Rajiv. Both mother and son were assassinated *(see pp64–5)*.

The extensive grounds are home to the **Nehru Planetarium** and the square, three-arched **Kushak Mahal**, a 14th-century hunting lodge built by the Tughlaq sultan, Feroze Shah *(see p101)*.

On the roundabout, in front of the house, is the memorial known as Teen Murti ("three statues"), dedicated to the men of the Indian regiments who died in World War I. It was from this landmark that the house derived its name.

Teen Murti memorial, built in memory of the lives lost during World War I

⓮ Gandhi Smriti

5, Tees January Marg. **Map** 4 F3. **Tel** (011) 2301 2843/1480. **Open** 10am–5pm Tue–Sun. **Closed** Mon & public hols.

On 30 January 1948, at 11am, Nathuram Godse assassinated Mahatma Gandhi as he was going to his daily prayer meeting in the gardens of this house, once the residence of the Birla family *(see p81)*. A simple sandstone pillar marks the spot.

Now a museum commemorating Gandhi's life and final hours, Gandhi Smriti offers an ambience reflecting Gandhi's philosophy of lofty political principles wand down to earth common sense. A series of appealing dioramas, made up of dolls in glass cabinets, tell the story of his eventful life through such defining moments as bidding farewell to his parents while going to England and the death of Kasturba, his beloved wife. The rooms where he used to stay when in Delhi are memorably austere and convey a sense of his history. In the garden, footsteps cast in red sandstone lead to the site of his final martyrdom.

The museum complex has shops selling inexpensive editions of Gandhi's writings as well as items made from khadi, the simple homespun cloth he always wore, and which became one of the important symbols of the Freedom Movement *(see pp62–3)*.

15 Lodi Gardens

Map 5 A4. **Open** sunrise–sunset daily.

Lodi Gardens, located in the heart of residential New Delhi, was built at the behest of Lady Willingdon, the Vicereine, in 1936. Although it was originally the site of two villages, the inhabitants shifted elsewhere, and lawns and pathways were laid out around the tombs belonging to the 15th-century Sayyid and Lodi dynasties. Inside, the bridge called **Athpula**, literally "eight piers", near the entrance on South End Road, is said to date from the 17th century. To the west of it are the ramparts of the **tomb of Sikandar Lodi** (r.1489–1517) which enclose an octagonal tomb at the centre of some rather overgrown gardens. Inside it, traces of turquoise tilework and calligraphy are just about visible.

To the south of Sikandar Lodi's Tomb are the **Bara Gumbad** ("big dome") and **Sheesh Gumbad** ("glazed dome"). The names of the nobles buried within have long been forgotten, but the Bara Gumbad is an imposing structure with an attached mosque built in 1494, and a *mehmankhana* (guesthouse). The Sheesh Gumbad derives its name from the glazed turquoise tiles that still cling to its outer walls along with blue calligraphic panels. Recent research claims that this is Bahlol Lodi's tomb. The **tomb of Muhammad Shah** (r.1434–44), the third ruler of the Sayyid dynasty, is said to be the oldest in the garden. The dome of this octagonal structure is surrounded by *chhatris*, and *jaalis* once filled the spaces between the pillars. The graves inside are said to be those of the sultan himself and some of the most favoured nobles of his court.

Today, with its tree-lined pathways and well-kept lawns and flower beds, the park acts as a "green lung" for the people of Delhi. It is one of the city's most picturesque parks and a favourite haunt of joggers, yoga-enthusiasts and families who come here to picnic on weekends. Vendors selling balloons, ice-creams and snacks from handcarts are popular with children.

Muhammad Shah's Tomb

16 Khan Market

Subramaniam Bharti Marg. **Map** 5 B3. Shops: **Open** 10:30am–8pm Mon–Sat. **Closed** Sun.

This market was built in the early 1940s to serve the needs of the British forces living in the hurriedly constructed barracks at Lodi Estate. Its name, Khan Market, is in honour of the prominent Pathan nationalist and social reformer, Dr Khan Sahib, the brother of Khan Abdul Gaffar Khan, the "Frontier Gandhi". Both men were revered for their role in the struggle for independence among the warlike tribes of the North-West Frontier Province (now in Pakistan).

This popular market is much frequented by Indians and foreigners alike. There is a wide range of Indian and Western merchandise on offer here, from crockery, cakes and dog leashes to boutiques selling exquisite jewellery and designer clothes. There are also traditional sari shops, as well as Anokhi *(see p122)*, selling blockprinted linen and garments in both Western and Indian styles.

There are a number of excellent places to buy shoes, as well as good bookshops – Bahri & Sons, Full Circle and Faqir Chand's, one of the oldest shops in the market. Its other charming features are the groceries and the colourful flower shops. A number of cafés such as Coffee Bean & Tea Leaf, Café Turtle and Market Café are located here for shoppers in search of a quick snack, as well as Delhi's popular delicatessen, Sugar & Spice.

Athpula, the 17th-century bridge near the entrance to Lodi Gardens on South End Road

NIZAMUDDIN TO PURANA QILA

The Nizamuddin area, named after the famous 14th-century Sufi saint, Nizamuddin Auliya, is bisected by Mathura Road and has a clearly visible split personality. East Nizamuddin is the quieter half, with Humayun's Tomb *(see p87)* resting peacefully at the centre of a Persian garden. West Nizamuddin, the old Muslim quarter around the saint's *dargah*, is a lively *basti* which still retains its medieval character. This important pilgrim centre also has the graves of famous poets such as Amir Khusrau and Mirza Ghalib, as well as the tombs of Jahanara, the daughter of Emperor Shah Jahan, and the dilettante Muhammad Shah Rangila, a later Mughal emperor. In this neighbourhood, the medieval and modern co-exist harmoniously. Busy Mathura Road swirls past the Subz Burj tomb with its blue-tiled dome, today a traffic island. Humayun's Tomb and the Sundar Horticulture Nursery are to the west. Further north is the up-market residential colony of Sundar Nagar with antique shops, Delhi Zoo and Purana Qila, the "old fort" *(see p88)*. The crumbling battlements of the fort overlook the Crafts Museum, the small shrine of Matka Pir, a Sufi saint, and the exhibition grounds of Pragati Maidan. To the east stands the Khair-ul-Manazil Mosque, built by Maham Anga in the mid-16th century.

Sights at a Glance

Historic Site

1 Nizamuddin Complex

Tomb

2 *Humayun's Tomb p87*

Monuments

3 Purana Qila

4 Khair-ul-Manazil Mosque

Museums

5 *Crafts Museum pp90–91*

Exhibition Grounds

6 Pragati Maidan

Restaurants *p251*

1 Three Sixty Degree

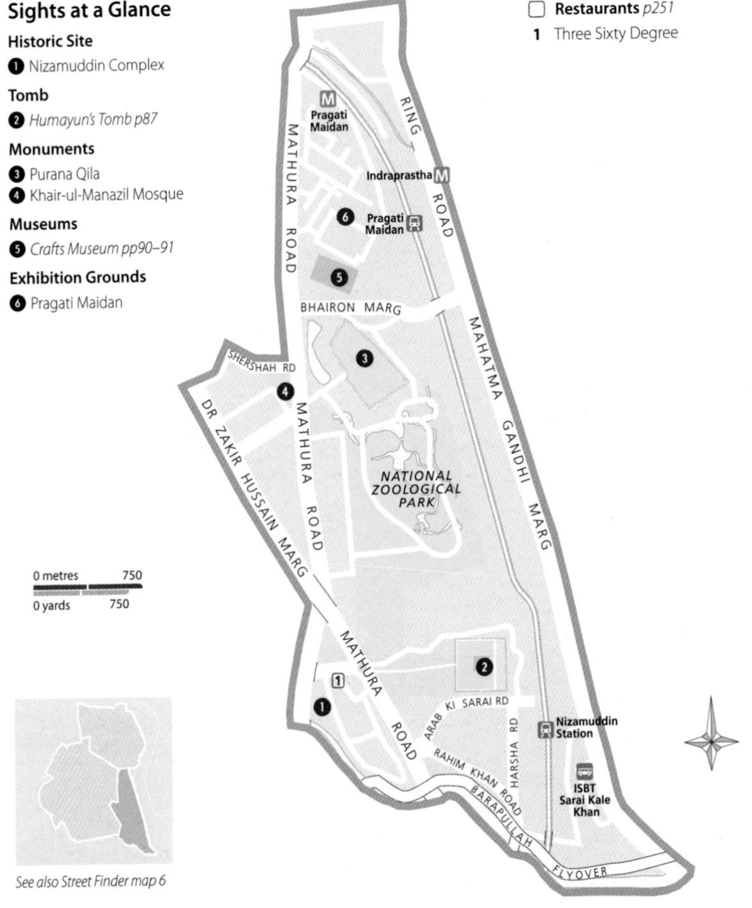

See also Street Finder map 6

◀ A group of women praying at the Nizamuddin Dargah, Delhi

❶ Nizamuddin Complex

Old Nizamuddin Bazaar, Nizamuddin East. **Map** 6 D5. Dargah: **Open** daily. Qawwali: 6:30pm Thu. Urs (Apr).

This medieval settlement, or *basti*, is named after Sheikh Hazrat Nizamuddin Auliya, whose grave and hospice are located here. Nizamuddin belonged to a fraternity of Sufi mystics, the Chishtiyas *(see p311)*, respected for their austerity, piety and disdain for politics and material desires. His daily assemblies drew both the rich and the poor, who believed that he was a "friend of God" and so a master who would intercede on their behalf on Judgement Day. Nizamuddin died in 1325 but his disciples call him a *zinda pir*, a living spirit, who heeds their pleas and alleviates their misery.

The Urs *(see p42)* is held on the anniversary of his birth and death, and celebrated by his disciples with *qawwalis* and offerings of *chadors*.

Colourful stalls lining the alley leading to Nizamuddin's *dargah*

Congregational area at the *dargah* of Hazrat Nizamuddin Auliya

A winding alley leads to the saint's grave. It is crowded with mendicants and lined with stalls selling flowers and *chadors*, polychrome clocks and prints of Mecca. The main congregational area is a marble pavilion (rebuilt in 1562) where, every Thursday evening, devotees sing songs of worship composed by the celebrated Persian poet, Amir Khusrau (1253–1325). Women are denied entry beyond the outer verandah but may peer through *jaalis* into the small, dark chamber where the saint's grave lies draped with a rose petal-strewn cloth and where imams continuously recite verses from the Koran. The complex also contains the graves of several eminent disciples, such as Jahanara Begum and Amir Khusrau.

Tomb of the famous poet Mirza Ghalib

Across the western side of the open courtyard is the red sandstone Jama't Khana Mosque, built in 1325. To its north is a *baoli* (stepwell), secretly excavated while Tughlaqabad *(see p118)* was being built because Ghiyasuddin Tughlaq had banned all building activities elsewhere. Legend has it that labourers worked here at night with the help of lamps lit, not by oil, but water blessed by Nasiruddin, Nizamuddin's successor *(see p112)*. The mid-16th-century tomb of Atgah Khan, Akbar's minister and the husband of one of his wet nurses, who was murdered by Adham Khan *(see p117)*, is to the north. An open marble pavilion, the Chaunsath Khamba ("64 pillars"), is close by. Just outside is an enclosure containing the simple grave of Mirza Ghalib (1797–1869). One of the greatest poets of his time, Ghalib wrote in both Urdu and Persian, and his verses are still recited today. Nearby is the Ghalib Academy, a repository of paintings and manuscripts.

Always crowded, the *basti* preserves with miraculous serenity, the legend of this *pir*, who was called "a king without throne or crown, with kings in need of the dust of his feet" by his disciple, Amir Khusrau.

Nizamuddin Complex

In this historic necropolis, many of the *pir's* disciples, such as Amir Khusrau and Jahanara Begum, Shah Jahan's favourite daughter, are buried close to their master. Jahanara's epitaph echoes her master's teachings: "Let naught cover my grave save the green grass, for grass well suffices as a covering for the grave of the lowly".

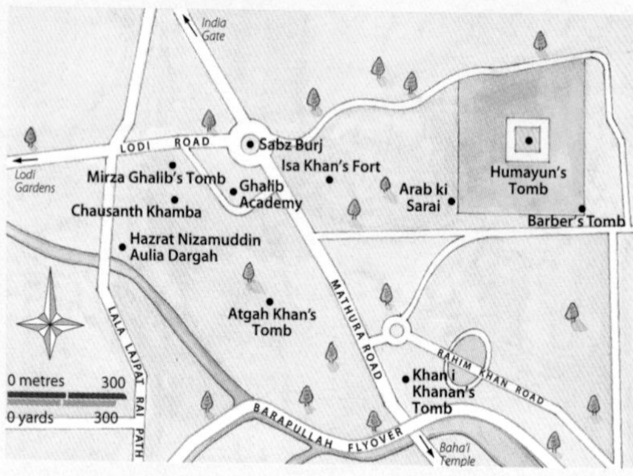

❷ Humayun's Tomb

Humayun, the second Mughal emperor *(see p88)*, is buried in this tomb, the first great example of a Mughal garden tomb and inspiration for several later monuments, such as the incomparable Taj Mahal. Built in 1565 by the Persian architect Mirak Mirza Ghiyas, it was commissioned by Humayun's senior widow, Haji Begum. Often called "a dormitory of the House of Timur", the graves of its chambers include Humayun's wives and Dara Shikoh, Shah Jahan's scholarly son. Also in the complex are the Afsarwala Tomb, the octagonal tomb and mosque of Isa Khan, a noble at Sher Shah's court, and the tomb of Humayun's favourite barber. The Arab ki Sarai housed the Persian masons who built the tomb.

VISITORS' CHECKLIST

Practical Information
Off Mathura Rd. **Map** 6 D4. **Tel** (011) 2435 5275. **Open** sunrise–sunset daily. extra charges.

Transport
M JLN Stadium.

The tomb as seen from the entrance

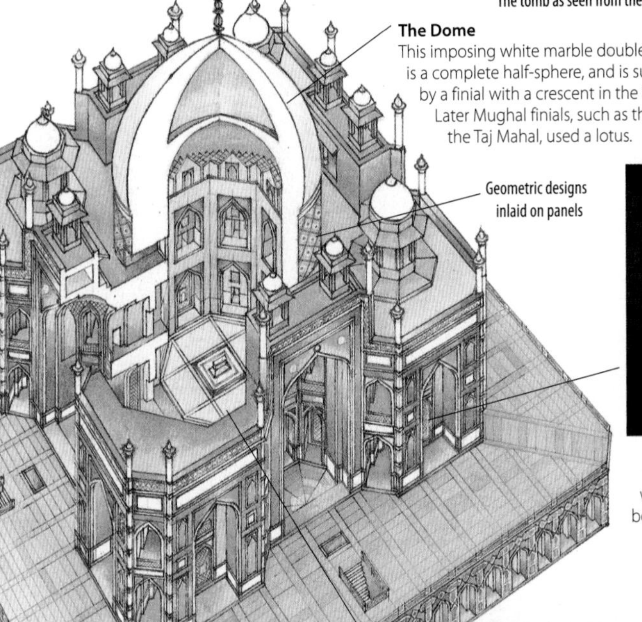

The Dome
This imposing white marble double dome is a complete half-sphere, and is surmounted by a finial with a crescent in the Persian style. Later Mughal finials, such as the one at the Taj Mahal, used a lotus.

Geometric designs inlaid on panels

Jaalis
Such fine trellis work in stone later became a signature Mughal feature.

The Tomb Chamber
The plain white marble sarcophagus stands on a simple black and white marble platform. The grave itself lies in the rather dark, bat-filled basement below.

The imposing plinth is decorated with red sandstone arches and consists of multiple chambers, a departure from the single chamber of previous tombs.

❸ Purana Qila

Mathura Rd, near Delhi Zoo. **Map** 6 D2. **Tel** (011) 2435 4260. Ⓜ Pragati Maidan. **Open** sunrise–sunset daily. Museum: **Tel** (011) 2435 5387. **Open** 10am–5pm Sat–Thu. **Closed** Fri. Organized by Delhi Heritage Walks, call 92125 34868 for more information.

Purana Qila, literally "old fort", stands on an ancient mound. Excavations near its eastern wall reveal that the site has been continuously occupied since 1000 BC. It is also believed to be the place where Indraprastha, the Pandava capital mentioned in the epic, the *Mahabharata (see p145)*, once stood. It was here that Humayun, the second Mughal emperor, began to construct his city, Dinpanah ("Asylum of Faith"), just four years after his father Babur established the Mughal dynasty in 1526 *(see pp56–7)*. However, his reign was short-lived and, in 1540, he was dispossessed of his kingdom by the ambitious Afghan chieftain, Sher Shah Suri (r.1540–45). When Sher Shah took possession of the citadel, he strengthened its fortifications, added several new structures and renamed it Shergarh. After his death, his successors were defeated by Humayun who recaptured his domains in 1555. Today, of the many palaces, barracks and houses that once existed, only Sher Shah's mosque and the building said to be Humayun's library remain.

The Yamuna once flowed on the fort's eastern side and formed a natural moat: a small lake to the west facing busy Mathura Road is all that remains today. The present fort entrance, an imposing red sandstone gate on the western wall called the **Bara Darwaza**, is one of the three principal gates of Shergarh. Its double-storeyed façade, surmounted by *chhatris* and approached by a steep ramp, still displays traces of tiles and carved foliage. **Humayun's Gate**, on the southern wall, has an inscription bearing Sher Shah's name and the date 950 AH (1543–4). To the north, the **Taliqi Darwaza** (the so-called "forbidden gate") has carved reliefs, and across the road is the red sandstone **Lal Darwaza**, or Sher Shah Gate, one of the entrances to the township that grew around the fort.

The fort of Purana Qila and its lake, where visitors paddle boat

The single-domed **Qila-i-Kuhna Mosque**, built by Sher Shah in 1541, is an excellent example of a pre-Mughal design. Its prayer hall inside has five elegant arched niches or *mihrabs* set in its western wall. Marble in shades of red, white and slate is used for the calligraphic inscriptions and marks a transition from Lodi to Mughal architecture. A second storey provided space for female courtiers to pray, while the arched doorway on the left wall, framed by ornate *jharokhas*, was reserved for members of the royal family.

The **Sher Mandal** stands to the south of the mosque. This double-storeyed octagonal tower of red sandstone was built by Sher Shah and was used as a library by Humayun after he recaptured the fort. The tower is topped by an octagonal *chhatri*, supported by eight pillars and decorated with white marble. Inside, there are remnants of the decorative plasterwork and traces of the stone shelving where, presumably, the emperor's books were placed. This was also the tragic spot where, on 24 January 1556, on hearing the muezzin's call, the devout Humayun hurried to kneel on the stairs, missed his footing and tumbled to his death. His tomb can be seen from the southern gate. Purana Qila flourished as the sixth city of Delhi *(see p111)* and traces of walls still stand in the area. There is a small **Museum** at the entrance displaying items excavated from the site.

Chhatri with decorative tilework

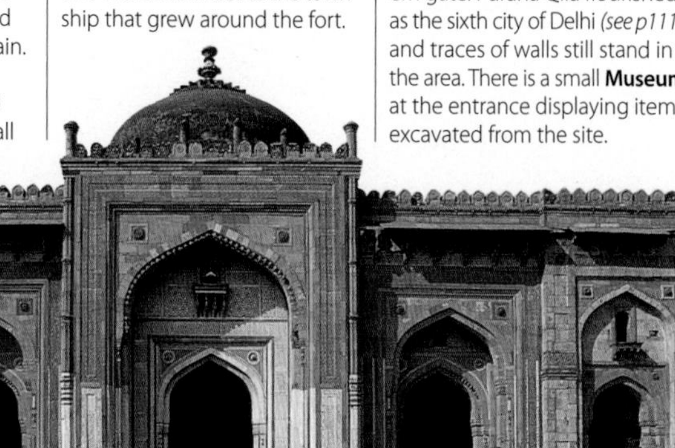

Sher Shah's mosque at Purana Qila

The single dome surmounting the prayer hall at Khair-ul-Manazil

❹ Khair-ul-Manazil

Mathura Rd, near Purana Qila.
Map 5 C2. **Open** sunrise–sunset.

This mosque, "the most auspicious of houses", was constructed in 1561 by Akbar's influential wet nurse, Maham Anga, and a courtier, Shiha-bu'd-Din Ahmed Khan. An imposing, double-storeyed red sandstone gateway leads into a large courtyard ringed by cloisters, two storeys high, one of which was used as a *madrasa*. The prayer hall with its five-arched openings is topped by a single dome. Above the central archway, a marble inscription mentions Maham Anga's and Shiha-bu'd-Din's names. Inside, the central mihrab is decorated with bands of blue and green calligraphy. Maham Anga is buried in Mehrauli with her son, Adham Khan *(see p117)*, who was executed by Akbar.

❺ Crafts Museum

See pp90–91.

❻ Pragati Maidan

Mathura Rd. **Map** 6 D1. **Tel** (011) 2337 1540. **Fax** (011) 2337 1492/3. **Open** 10am–5:30pm daily.
National Science Centre: **Tel** (011) 2337 1893. **Open** 10am–5pm daily.

India's largest exhibition centre, covering nearly 150 acres (61 ha), Pragati Maidan is the venue for numerous exhibitions and trade fairs organized by the India Trade Promotion Organization. The work of some of India's most eminent architects can be seen here. Raj Rewal has designed the Hall of Nations and Industries while the World Trade Centre is by Joseph Allen Stein. Among other notable buildings are those by Charles Correa, Achyut Kanvinde and Satish Grover. All the Indian states have pavilions spread across the fair's extensive grounds, linked by 16 km (10 miles) of roads.

A large number of exhibitions are held here throughout the year and cover products ranging from arts and crafts, textiles, electronics, jewellery and automobiles to photography, mining equipment and food products. Every year the World Book Fair and the India International Trade Fair *(see p44)* are held, drawing a great deal of international interest. Both fairs are extremely popular with local people as well as overseas visitors. The **National Science Centre** *(see p267)* is located within the grounds of Pragati Maidan. It puts on shows for children as well as adults.

A view of the Pragati Maidan complex, designed by Raj Rewal

Matka Pir

Rows of *matkas* (earthenware pots) line the entrance to the shrine of Matka Pir, a Sufi saint. According to legend, a man and his wife came to the saint to seek his help for the birth of a son. Being poor, they could only offer a humble pot of *dal* and jaggery. The saint asked them to place the pot in the courtyard and leave the rest to God. A year later, their wish fulfilled, they returned with another pot, a tradition that has continued since then. The *dargah* stands on a ridge overlooking Mathura Road, with nearby shops selling *matkas*, roasted grams, jaggery and *dal*. The biryani served here is famous – the chefs trace their origins to the Delhi Sultanate era. The saint's powers still attract many pilgrims.

The shrine of the Sufi saint, Matka Pir

5 Crafts Museum

For centuries, Indian craftsmen, such as potters and weavers, masons and carvers, have created a range of objects for everyday use that are both beautiful and practical. A unique project was started in 1956 to promote indigenous artisans by displaying their work in one place, and by the early 1980s, over 20,000 objects had been collected. This was the core around which grew India's first Crafts Museum.

Wooden ritual mask of Bhima

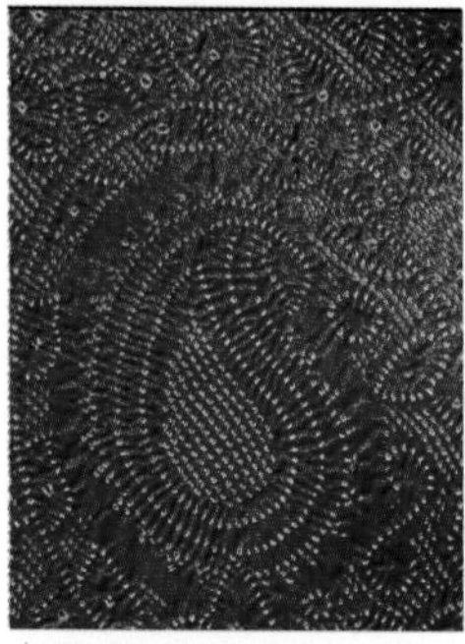

★ Bandhini Odhni
This exquisite veil is the work of the Khatri community in Bhuj, Gujarat. In tie-and-dye *(bandhini)*, grains are used to set the pattern. Threads are tied around them and the cloth dyed in different colours.

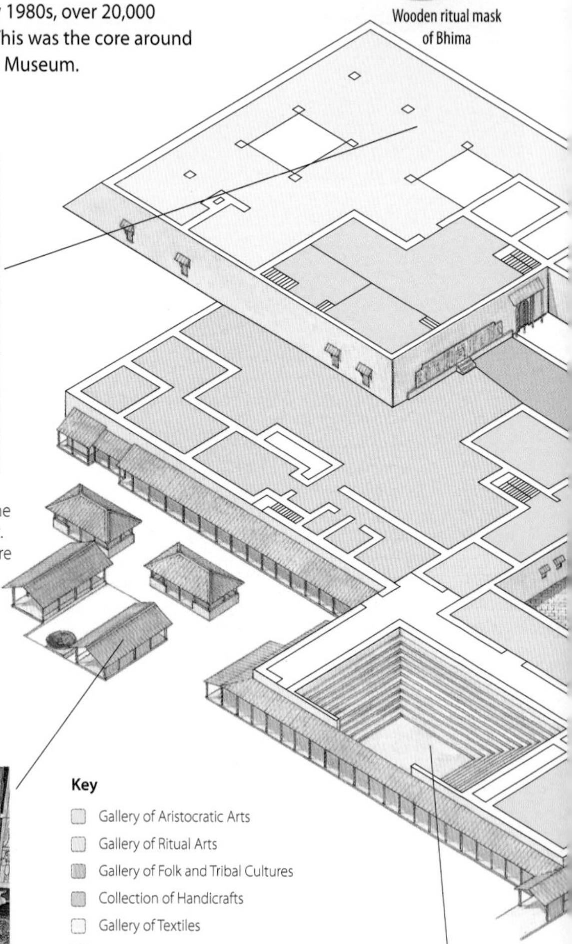

Saranga Amphitheatre

Key

- Gallery of Aristocratic Arts
- Gallery of Ritual Arts
- Gallery of Folk and Tribal Cultures
- Collection of Handicrafts
- Gallery of Textiles
- Administration Block
- Temporary Exhibition Gallery
- Visual Store

Crafts Demonstration Area
Artisans from all over India set up workshops each month (barring the monsoon) to display their skill to visitors.

Gallery Guide

The museum's display is spread over two floors of the complex, divided into separate areas by courtyards that also double up as exhibition spaces. A large open area is designated for live art displays by visiting artisans each month, except during the rainy season.

Mukhalinga
A rare, late 19th-century brass and silver phallic image (*linga*) with a human face (*mukha*).

VISITORS' CHECKLIST

Practical Information
Bhairon Marg, Pragati Maidan.
Map 6 D2. **Tel** (011) 2337 1887.
Open 10am–5pm Tue–Sun.
Closed Mon, public hols.
Crafts demonstration: **Open** 10am–6pm daily. **Closed** Jul–Sep.
W nationalcraftsmuseum.nic.in

★ Charakku
These enormous, circular vessels are cast of an alloy known as bell metal. They are still used in Kerala for wedding feasts or at temples for making *payasam* (a type of rice pudding) for devotees during festivals.

Kalamkari panel
This traditional hand-painted textile from Andhra Pradesh depicts a female deity with 12 arms.

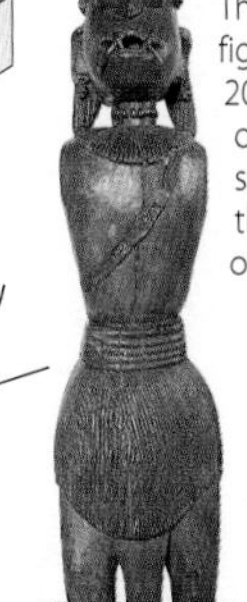

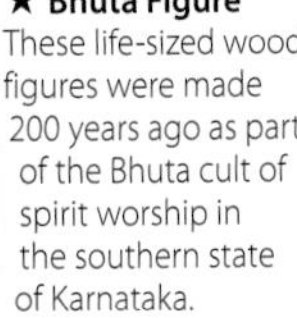

★ Bhuta Figure
These life-sized wooden figures were made 200 years ago as part of the Bhuta cult of spirit worship in the southern state of Karnataka.

Library

Entrance

Jain shrine
This 18th-century wooden shrine from Gujarat once belonged to a wealthy Shvetambara Jain family. It features elaborate wood carvings of elephants, celestial musicians and the Goddess Laxmi.

Lota, Crafts Museum Shop
Located on the premises of the Crafts Museum, the shop sells a wide selection of fine Indian folk crafts and textiles.

OLD DELHI

What is known as Old Delhi today was originally the Mughal capital of Shahjahanabad, built by Shah Jahan when he moved the imperial court from Agra to Delhi. Construction began in 1638, and ten years later the Red Fort, Jami Masjid, Chandni Chowk and the surrounding residential and mercantile quarters were ready for occupation.

The city was surrounded by a rubble wall pierced by 14 gates of which three – Delhi, Turkman and Ajmeri – survive. An elegant, mannered lifestyle flourished, enriched by the courtiers and merchants, artists and poets who lived in the lanes and quarters, called *galis* and *katras*, of the walled city. In 1739, the Persian freebooter Nadir Shah came to plunder the city of Shahjahanabad and left a bleeding ruin behind him. The final deathblow was, however, dealt when the British troops moved into the Red Fort after the Mutiny of 1857, turning it into a military garrison, while a railway line cut the walled city in half. Yet, the spirit of the place has survived all these vicissitudes and its busy *galis* continue to support a vibrant life. Modernity has brought a new urgency to the pace of the traditional traders who still live and operate from here.

Sights at a Glance

Mosques

1 Jami Masjid
6 Zinat-ul Masjid

Historic Streets and Sites

2 Chandni Chowk
4 Ajmeri Gate
5 Turkman Gate

Monuments

3 *Red Fort pp98–9*
8 Feroze Shah Kotla

Memorial

7 Rajghat

Restaurants *p251*

1 Chor Bizarre
2 Karim's

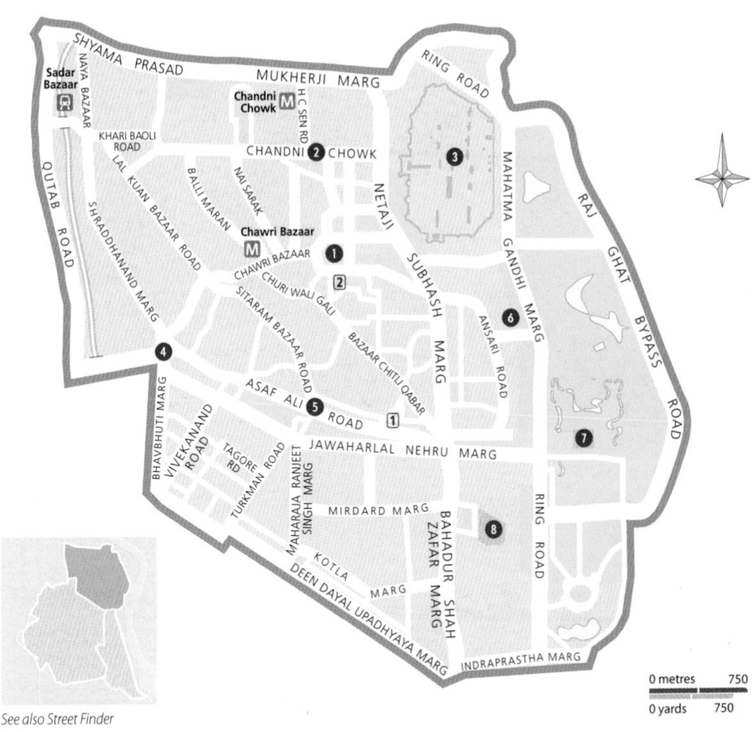

See also Street Finder maps 1, 2

Street-by-Street: Chandni Chowk

Now a busy commercial centre, Chandni Chowk was once a grand processional thoroughfare that led from the Red Fort to Jami Masjid. When it was laid out in 1648 by Jahanara Begum, Shah Jahan's favourite daughter, a canal ran down the centre of the tree-lined stately avenue. Chandni Chowk, or the "silvery, moonlit square", was then lined with merchants' shops and the grand residences or *havelis* of noblemen and merchants.

Sisganj Gurudwara
Guru Tegh Bahadur, the ninth Sikh guru, was beheaded at this site. The *gurudwara* marks the site of his martyrdom.

Sunehri Masjid
The "Golden Mosque", with three gilt domes, was built in 1722. On 22 March 1739, Nadir Shah stood on its roof to watch the massacre of Delhi's citizens.

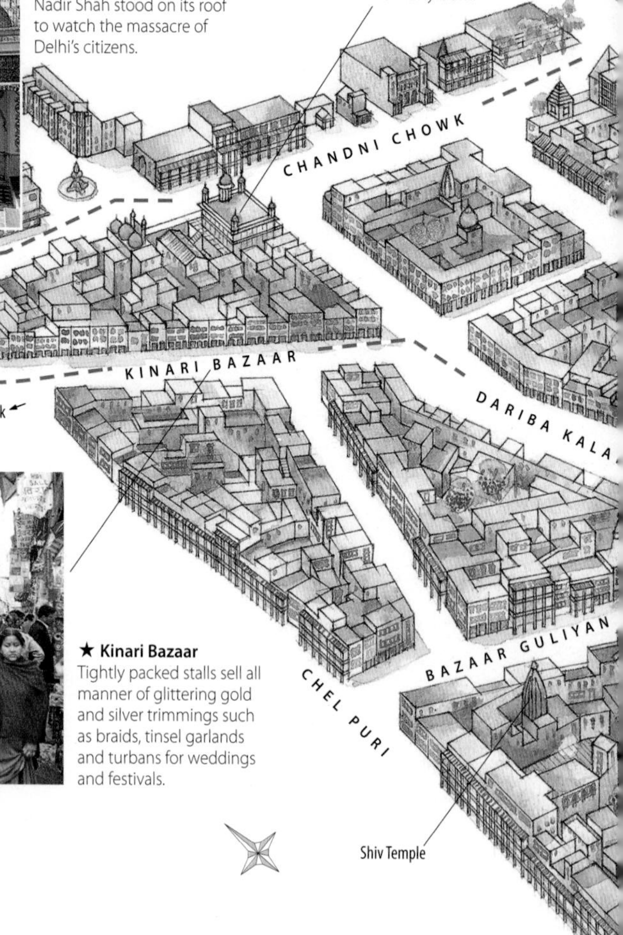

CHANDNI CHOWK

Fatehpuri Masjid (built in 1650)

KINARI BAZAAR

Nai Sarak

DARIBA KALAN

★ Kinari Bazaar
Tightly packed stalls sell all manner of glittering gold and silver trimmings such as braids, tinsel garlands and turbans for weddings and festivals.

BAZAAR GULIYAN

CHEL PURI

Shiv Temple

Karim's
Tucked away in a lane to the south of Jami Masjid is Delhi's most authentic Mughlai eatery *(see p251)*. Named after a legendary 19th-century chef, the restaurant is now run by his descendants.

Key

— Suggested route

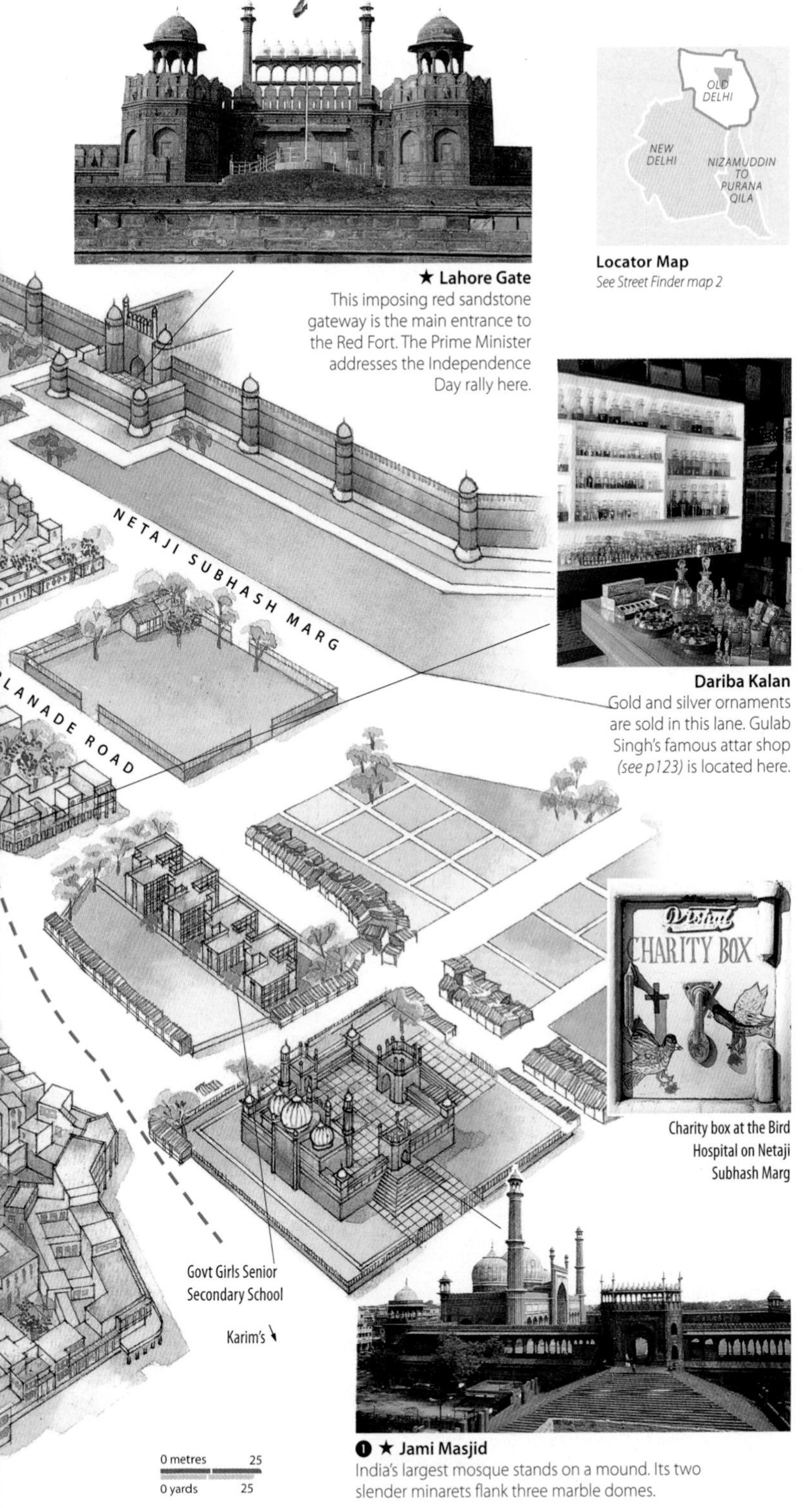

Locator Map
See Street Finder map 2

★ Lahore Gate
This imposing red sandstone gateway is the main entrance to the Red Fort. The Prime Minister addresses the Independence Day rally here.

Dariba Kalan
Gold and silver ornaments are sold in this lane. Gulab Singh's famous attar shop *(see p123)* is located here.

Charity box at the Bird Hospital on Netaji Subhash Marg

❶ ★ Jami Masjid
India's largest mosque stands on a mound. Its two slender minarets flank three marble domes.

Jami Masjid, built by Shah Jahan, the largest mosque in India

❶ Jami Masjid

Off Netaji Subhash Marg. **Map** 2 E2. Ⓜ Chawri Bazaar. **Open** 7am–12pm & 1:30–6:30pm daily. **Closed** for non-Muslims during prayer time & after 5pm. Extra charges for photography.

This grand mosque, built in 1656 by the Emperor Shah Jahan on a natural rocky outcrop, took six years and 5,000 workmen to construct at the cost of nearly a million rupees. A magnificent flight of red sandstone steps leads to the great arched entrances where, in Aurangzeb's time, horses were sold and jugglers performed. Today, sweet-sellers, shoe-minders and beggars mill around here. The huge 28 m (300 ft) square courtyard accommodates up to 20,000 people at prayer times, especially during Friday prayers and on Id, when it looks like a sea of worshippers. Next to the ablution tank in the centre is the *dikka* platform where, before loudspeakers took over, a second prayer leader echoed the imam's words and actions for worshippers too far from the pulpit.

Three imposing black and white marble domes surmount the enormous prayer hall, and two minarets frame the great central arch. From the top of the southern minaret, a steep climb of 20 minutes, there are remarkable views of the roof-line of Old Delhi giving way to the high-rises of New Delhi. Women require a male escort to enter the minaret.

❷ Chandni Chowk

Map 2 D2. Ⓜ Chandni Chowk.

Once Shahjahanabad's most elegant boulevard, this wide avenue extending from the Red Fort to Fatehpuri Masjid, is still the heart of Old Delhi, where both religious activity and commerce mix happily together. All along its length are shrines sacred to various communities. The first is the Digamber Jain Mandir. Next to it is the Bird Hospital for sick and wounded birds. Loud chants, clanging bells and calls of vendors selling flowers and vermilion powder surround the Gauri Shankar Mandir, dedicated to Shiva and Parvati, which has a *linga* said to be 800 years old. Still further, close to the Sisganj Gurudwara, is the Kotwali (police station), the scene of British reprisal after 1857 *(see p59)*. Nearly a century before, another gruesome spectacle took place nearby when one afternoon in 1739, the Persian chieftain Nadir Shah stood on the roof of the Sunehri Masjid and watched his men kill nearly 30,000 of Delhi's citizens. The actual Moonlit Square (Chandni Chowk) is the open space in front of the very British Town Hall, now the Hardayal Library. Just behind it is the Mahatma Gandhi Park, which was called Begum Bagh in Mughal times. Further down, and commanding the end of this charming quarter, stands the Fatehpuri Masjid, constructed in 1650 by Fatehpuri Begum, one of Emperor Shah Jahan's wives. Nearby are the spice markets of Khari Baoli.

Swami Shraddhanand's statue, Chandni Chowk

Chandni Chowk, a vibrant centre of commerce and religious activity

Bazaars of Old Delhi

Old Delhi's bazaars are legendary. An English visitor to these bazaars, over a hundred years ago, wrote in praise of the "Cashmere shawls, gold and silver embroidery, jewellery, enamels and carpets" to be found here. Today, the great wholesale *katras* of Chandni Chowk and Jami Masjid still retain that souk-like quality. Their narrow streets are lined with shops whose goods spill out onto the pavement; and shopping still means vigorous bargaining for a bewildering array of goods.

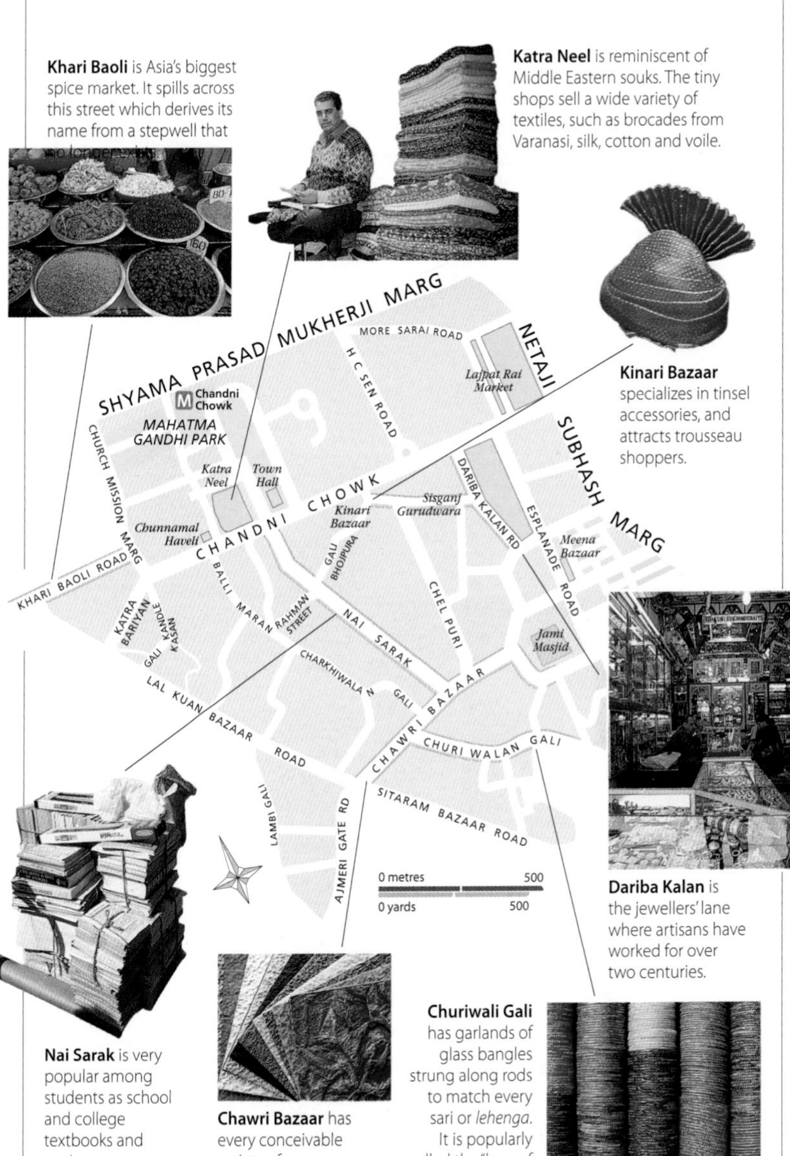

Khari Baoli is Asia's biggest spice market. It spills across this street which derives its name from a stepwell that no longer exists.

Katra Neel is reminiscent of Middle Eastern souks. The tiny shops sell a wide variety of textiles, such as brocades from Varanasi, silk, cotton and voile.

Kinari Bazaar specializes in tinsel accessories, and attracts trousseau shoppers.

Dariba Kalan is the jewellers' lane where artisans have worked for over two centuries.

Nai Sarak is very popular among students as school and college textbooks and stationery are sold on this street.

Chawri Bazaar has every conceivable variety of paper, sold here by weight.

Churiwali Gali has garlands of glass bangles strung along rods to match every sari or *lehenga*. It is popularly called the "lane of bangle-sellers".

❸ Red Fort

Red sandstone battlements give this imperial citadel its name, Red Fort (Lal Qila). Commissioned by Shah Jahan in 1639, it took nine years to build and was the seat of Mughal power until 1857, when the last emperor, Bahadur Shah Zafar, was dethroned and exiled. Lahore Gate, one of the fort's six gateways, leads on to the covered bazaar of Chatta Chowk, where brocades and jewels were once sold. Beyond this lies the Naqqar Khana, from where musicians played three times a day.

Detail of a Gilded Pillar
The Mughal love of opulence is visible in the lavish use of marble and gold in the fort.

Moti Masjid
Named after the pearly sheen of its marble, the tiny "pearl mosque" was added by Emperor Aurangzeb in 1659.

★ *Hamams*
The royal bath has three enclosures. The first provided hot vapour baths, the second sprayed rose-scented water through sculpted fountains, and the third contained cold water.

★ Diwan-i-Aam
The emperor gave daily audiences to all his subjects in this 60-pillared hall. The intricately carved throne canopy stands on a platform, while the low marble bench was for the chief minister *(wazir)*.

★ Diwan-i-Khas
The legendary Peacock Throne, one of Shah Jahan's seven jewelled thrones, was housed in this exclusive pavilion where the emperor met his most trusted nobles. The walls and pillars were once inlaid with gems and the ceiling was of silver inlaid with precious stones.

VISITORS' CHECKLIST

Practical Information
Netaji Subhash Marg, Chandni Chowk. **Map** 2 D2. **Tel** (011) 2327 7705. **Open** 6am–7pm daily. Son et Lumière: Feb–Apr & Sep–Oct: 8:30pm; May–Aug: 9pm; Nov–Jan: 7:30pm. **Closed** Mon. Museum: **Open** 10am–5pm Tue–Sun.

Khas Mahal
The royal apartments were divided by the "Stream of Paradise". The emperor's prayer room (Tasbih Khana) was flanked by his sleeping chamber (Khwabgah) and sitting room (Baithak). This overlooked the Yamuna river and led to a balcony where he appeared before his subjects at sunrise.

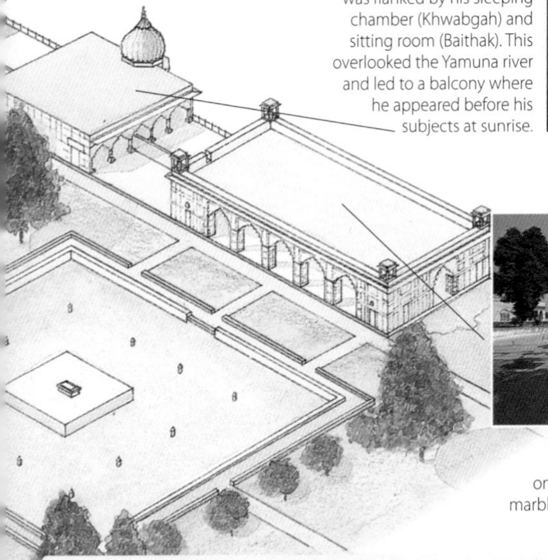

Rang Mahal
Inside these gilded chambers, once exclusively for women, is an inlaid marble fountain shaped like an open lotus.

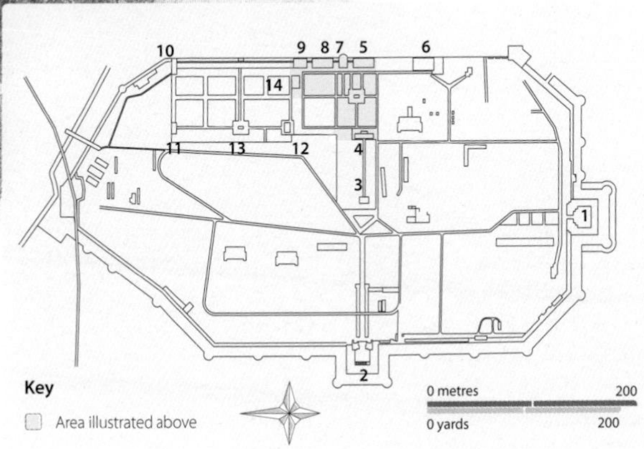

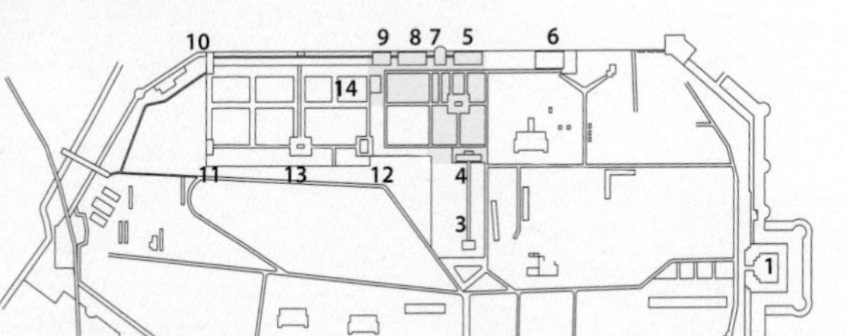

The Red Fort

1 Delhi Gate
2 Lahore Gate
3 Naqqar Khana
4 Diwan-i-Aam
5 Rang Mahal
6 Moti Mahal
7 Khas Mahal
8 Diwan-i-Khas
9 *Hamams*
10 Shah Burj (Tower)
11 Sawan (Pavilion)
12 Bhadon (Pavilion)
13 Zafar Mahal
14 Moti Masjid

Key
Area illustrated above

0 metres 200
0 yards 200

❹ Ajmeri Gate

Ajmeri Gate Rd. Ⓜ New Delhi. **Map** 1 C3.

This is one of the 14 gates that once encircled Shahjahanabad. Having survived more than 300 years, it stands in the midst of the city's congested commercial centre. Diagonally opposite Ajmeri Gate is **Ghazi-ud-Din's Tomb** and **Madrasa**. Ghazi-ud-Din Khan was an eminent courtier during the reign of the sixth Mughal emperor Aurangzeb, and his son, Mir Qamar-ud-Din, established the dynasty that were to rule the southern state of Hyderabad until Independence in 1947.

The imposing, red sandstone *madrasa* has several arcades and a mosque on its western side. Founded in the late 17th century, this was at one time Delhi's foremost *madrasa* and after 1824 came to be known as the Anglo-Arabic School. English classes were held here, and British teachers also introduced mathematics and science texts to students, which were then translated into Urdu. Ghazi-ud-Din's grave is in a marble enclosure at the mosque's southern end. Athough this complex is surrounded by today's urban congestion, it still performs the noble function it was meant to. The three-domed mosque is in regular use and students crisscross the courtyard, while striped towels hang from the hostel balconies where glorious silks may once have billowed. Until recently, the esteemed Delhi College, now the Zakir Husain College, was also located on the premises.

Ghazi-ud-Din's *madrasa*, built in the late 17th century

A cycle-rickshaw from Ajmeri Gate will take you past tiny shops to the teeming lanes of Lal Kuan Bazaar where the **Zinat Mahal** is situated. Built in 1846, this was the eponymous home of the favourite wife of the last Mughal emperor Bahadur Shah Zafar. Today, it houses a school, lawyers' offices and shops. The original façade was wonderfully carved and arcaded with an oriel window. The beautiful verse by Bahadur Shah Zafar that was inscribed over the arched gateway can still be seen.

❺ Turkman Gate

Asaf Ali Rd. **Map** 2 D3. Ⓜ New Delhi.

The solid, square-shaped, red sandstone Turkman Gate stands in splendid isolation among the modern high-rise buildings of busy Asaf Ali Road. It marked the southern boundary of Shahjahanabad and was named after a Muslim *pir*, Hazrat Shah Turkman Bayabani, whose 13th-century tomb and *dargah* stand to the east. The serpentine lanes behind the gateway are home to two medieval monuments. **Kalan Masjid** ("black mosque"), in the Bulbulekhan area, was built in 1387 by Khan-i-Jahan Junan Shah, Feroze Shah Tughlaq's prime minister. This is one of the seven mosques he built in Delhi; the others are at Khirkee and Begumpuri *(see p113)*. A short walk away lies what is believed to be the **grave of Sultana Razia** Delhi's only medieval woman ruler *(see pp54–5)*. Her brief reign was bedevilled by revolts and she was killed at Karnal in 1240 while fleeing from Delhi. Her plain rubble-stone grave lies open to the sky in a cramped enclosure amidst houses and shops. The atelier of the last practising craftsman of Delhi's blue pottery, Hazarilal, is situated in the congested alleys of Hauz Suiwalan, located behind Turkman Gate.

Auto-rickshaws parked outside the Mughal Turkman Gate

❻ Zinat-ul Masjid

Ansari Rd, Daryaganj. **Map** 2 F3. Ⓜ Kashmiri Gate. **Open** 10am–5pm daily.

This mosque was built in 1707 by Princess Zinat-un-Nissa Begum, one of Emperor Aurangzeb's daughters. The gracefully proportioned red sandstone mosque has a spacious courtyard built over a series of basement rooms. Its seven-arched prayer hall is surmounted by three domes, with alternating stripes of black and white marble. The locals who worship here have a more lyrical name for it, the Ghata ("Cloud") Mosque, because its striped domes simulate the monsoon sky.

Zinat-ul Masjid, also known as the Ghata or "Cloud" Mosque

Rajghat, cremation ground of Mahatma Gandhi

❼ Rajghat

Mahatma Gandhi Rd. **Map** 2 F3. **Open** 6am–7pm daily. Prayer meetings: 5pm Fri. National Gandhi Museum: **Tel** (011) 2331 0168. **Open** 9:30am–5:30pm Tue–Sun. **Closed** Mon & public hols. Film shows: 4–5pm Sat & Sun.

Rajghat, India's most revered symbol of nationalism, is the site of Mahatma Gandhi's cremation. A sombre black granite platform inscribed with his last words *Hey Ram* ("Oh God") now stands here. The only splash of colour comes from the garlands of orange marigolds draped over it. Devotees sing *bhajans* and the steady beat of the *dholak* lends the scene a dolorous melancholy. All visiting heads of state are taken to this *samadhi* ("memorial") to lay wreaths in memory of the "Father of the Nation". On Gandhi's birthday (2 Oct) and death anniversary (30 Jan), the nation's leaders gather here for prayer meetings. Just across the road is the **Gandhi National Museum**, crammed with memorabilia connected with Gandhi's life, including his letters and diaries. A framed plaque on the stairs explains his simple philosophy: "Non-violence is the pitting of one's whole soul against the will of the tyrant… it is then possible for a single individual to defy the might of an unjust empire."

❽ Feroze Shah Kotla

Bahadur Shah Zafar Marg. **Map** 2 F4.

Only some ramparts and ruined structures remain of Feroze Shah Kotla, the palace complex of Ferozabad, Delhi's fifth city erected by that indefatigable builder, Feroze Shah Tughlaq *(see p111)*. Entry is from the gate next to the Indian Express Building. Towards the very end of the walled enclosure stand the partial ruins of the Jami Masjid. Roofless, with only the rear wall still extant, this was at one time Delhi's largest mosque where as legend says, Timur the Lame, the Mongol conqueror who sacked Delhi in 1398, came to say his Friday prayers. Next to the Jami Masjid is a rubble pyramidal structure topped by one of the Mauryan emperor Ashoka's polished stone pillars *(see pp50–51)*, brought from the Punjab and installed here in 1356 by Feroze Shah. It was from the inscriptions on this pillar that James Prinsep, the Oriental linguist, deciphered the Brahmi script, a forerunner of the modern Devanagari, in 1837.

Khuni Darwaza (the "bloodstained gate"), opposite the Indian Express Building, was built by Sher Shah Sur as one of the gates to his city *(see p88)*. This was where Lieutenant Hodson shot Bahadur Shah Zafar's sons after the Mutiny of 1857 was quashed. Across the road is Delhi's main cricket stadium, named after the palace complex, where world-class test matches are held.

The Ashokan Pillar at Feroze Shah Kotla

FURTHER AFIELD

There is much to see and explore beyond the city centre. An undulating wooded area, the Ridge, sweeps across Delhi from the southwest to the north. The north contains the university campus and Civil Lines, an orderly civilian enclave created by the British, and the west houses the army Cantonment. South Delhi, juxtaposed between the old cities of Siri, Jahanpanah and Tughlaqabad, is a more recent addition, with many affluent suburbs, smart residential colonies, shops, cinemas and restaurants. Further south, the historic Mehrauli Archaeological Park encompasses 19th-century hunting lodges, tombs, pavilions and the towering Qutb Minar. This picturesque area was the site of Delhi's first city, Qila Rai Pithora, built around Lal Kot, a Tomar Rajput fortress.

Sights at a Glance

Historic Buildings and Sites

2 Old Delhi GPO
5 Civil Lines
8 Delhi University
10 Delhi Cantonment
15 Hauz Khas
16 Siri Fort
17 Chiragh Delhi
18 Khirkee
19 Jahanpanah
20 *Mehrauli Archaeological Park pp114–17*
23 Tughlaqabad

Temples, Churches and Mosques

1 St James's Church
14 Moth ki Masjid
24 Kalkaji Temple
25 Baha'i House of Worship

Cemeteries

3 Nicholson Cemetery

Parks and Gardens

4 Qudsia Gardens
7 Northern Ridge
9 The Ridge

Monuments

6 Coronation Memorial

Museums

11 National Rail Museum
21 Sanskriti

Tombs

12 Safdarjung's Tomb
22 Sultan Ghari

Markets

13 Dilli Haat

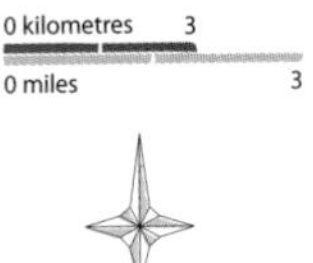

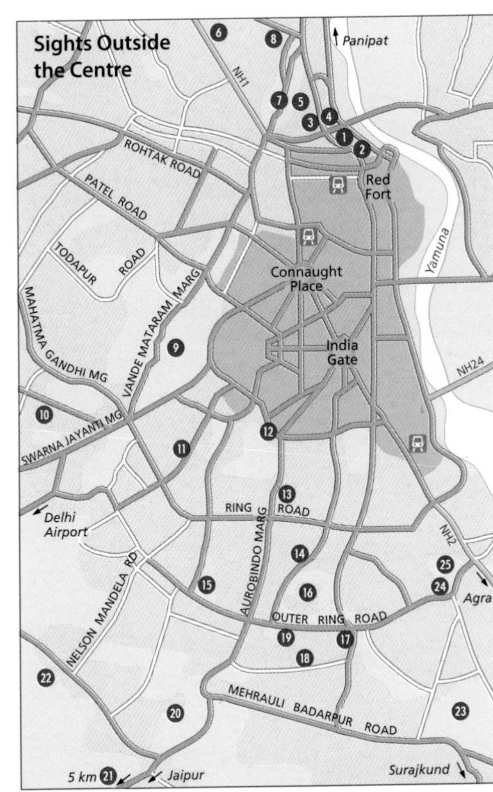

Key

Delhi city centre
Highway
Major road
Minor road

◄ The 4th-century iron pillar at the Qutub Complex, Mehrauli

For keys to symbols *see back flap*

Street-by-Street: Around Kashmiri Gate

Delhi's Kashmiri Gate area resonates with memories of the mutiny of 1857. Many of the dramatic events between the months of May and September took place on the short stretch between Kashmiri Gate and the Old Delhi General Post Office (GPO). In the 1920s, this was also a favourite watering hole of the British residents living in nearby Civil Lines. Then the street was lined with smart shops and restaurants, few of which survive now.

Shop Façades
The grand old shops are now shabby and derelict.

★ Kashmiri Gate
The Mughals used to set off from this gate to spend the summer in Kashmir. In 1857, it was the scene of a bitter battle and a plaque on the western side honours "the engineers and miners who died while clearing the gate for British forces on September 14, 1857".

Fakr-ul-Masjid
The domes and minarets of this small mosque rise above the rows of shops and offices along this busy street. Local residents come here to worship every Friday.

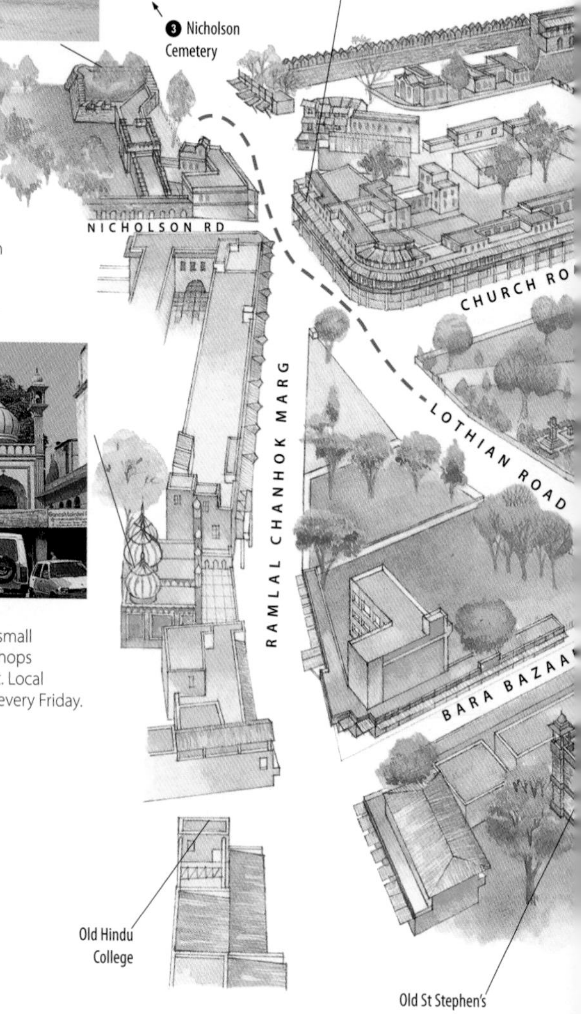

❸ Nicholson Cemetery

NICHOLSON RD

CHURCH RO

LOTHIAN ROAD

RAMLAL CHANHOK MARG

BARA BAZAA

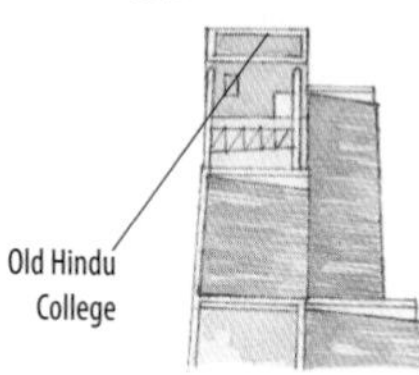

Old Hindu College

Old St Stephen's College

Key

 Suggested route

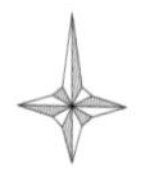

0 metres 50

0 yards 50

1 ★ St James's Church
Delhi's oldest and most historic church, consecrated in 1836, is an impressive edifice, painted yellow and white.

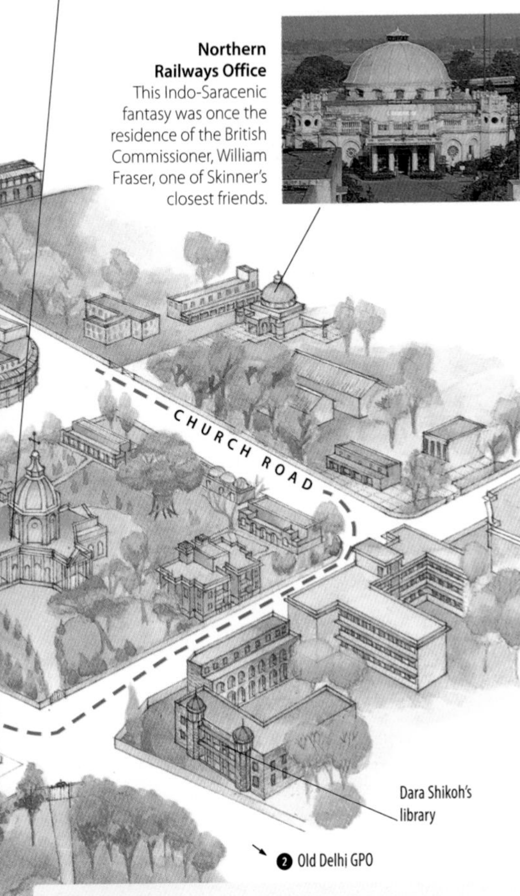
Northern Railways Office
This Indo-Saracenic fantasy was once the residence of the British Commissioner, William Fraser, one of Skinner's closest friends.
CHURCH ROAD
Dara Shikoh's library
2 Old Delhi GPO

James Skinner

One of the Empire's most swashbuckling adventurers, Skinner was the son of a Scotsman and a Rajput. Rejected by the British Army because of his mixed parentage, he raised his own cavalry regiment, Skinner's Horse, whose flamboyant yellow uniforms gave rise to the name Yellow Boys. His troops fought with distinction and are still part of the Indian Army. On his death he was honoured as a Commander of the Order of the Bath. His descendants still live on an estate in Mussoorie, Uttar Pradesh.

James Skinner (1778–1841)

1 St James's Church

Lothian Rd, Mori Gate. M Kashmiri Gate. **Open** 8am–noon; 2–5pm daily. Services: 9am Sun.

A tablet in the church founded by Colonel James Skinner explains: "This church is erected at the sole expense of Colonel James Skinner" in fulfilment of a vow made on the battlefield. Built at the cost of Rs 80,000, the church (now the oldest in Delhi) is in the shape of a Greek cross, surmounted by an imposing eight-leafed dome. The two stained-glass windows were installed in the 1860s. Skinner died at Hansi *(see p144)*. A marble tablet, in front of the altar, marks his simple grave.

The imposing Old Delhi General Post Office

2 Old Delhi GPO

Netaji Subhash Marg, Priyadarshini Colony, Lothian Rd. M Kashmiri Gate. **Open** 10am–6pm Mon–Fri (until 5pm Sat). **Closed** Sun.

To the south of Kashmiri Gate is the Old Delhi General Post Office, an old fashioned establishment caught in a time warp. This stucco-fronted colonial edifice is significant because it faces a traffic island on which stand two structures dating to the Indian Mutiny of 1857. The Telegraph Memorial is a memorial obelisk dedicated to the officers of the Telegraph Department. The inscription on it honours the telegraph operators, Brendish and Pilkington, who flashed news of the Indian Mutiny to the British garrison at Ambala. Nearby lies the ruined British Magazine. It was blown up by a Captain Willoughby on 11 May 1857 to prevent it from falling into the hands of the rebelling sepoys.

Graves at Nicholson Cemetery

❸ Nicholson Cemetery

Club Rd, Lala Hardev Sahai Marg, Civil Lines. Ⓜ Kashmiri Gate. **Open** 6am–6pm daily.

In the renovated walled cemetery named after him, surrounded by traffic and overlooked by the Inter State Bus Terminus (ISBT), lies the flamboyant Brigadier General John Nicholson, the British commander. The head-stone on his grave, which is to the right of the entrance, records that he "led the assault on Delhi but fell mortally wounded and died 3rd September 1857, aged 35". The surrounding graves belong to others like him who died at the time of the Indian Mutiny, between 10 May and 30 September 1857. The saddest are the tiny graves of children, such as the headless angel mourning over Alfred and Ida Scott's little daughter: "We gave her back to bloom in heaven".

To enter the cemetery, knock on the gate and the *chowkidar* will open it. There are no entrance charges, but a small tip (10–20 rupees) to the *chowkidar* and a donation to the Church of North India will be welcome. Monkeys are rampant in the cemetery and are dangerous if teased.

❹ Qudsia Gardens

Railway Colony, Shamnath Marg, Civil Lines. Ⓜ Kashmiri Gate. **Open** sunrise–sunset daily.

Qudsia Begum, the dancing girl who became the wife of Emperor Muhammad Shah (r.1719–48), laid out these gardens in around 1748, and although the Inter State Bus Terminus and the Tourist Park now occupy much of the original site, the imposing gateway still stands. The rest of the present park is more modern with a children's playground and a rather formidable statue of the great Rajput king, Maharana Pratap. North of the gardens is the children's home run by Mother Teresa's Missionaries of Charity, where abandoned children are cared for.

❺ Civil Lines

Bounded by Shamnath Marg and Mahatma Gandhi Marg. Ⓜ Civil Lines.

Old Delhi's Civil Lines were inhabited by the British civilian population while the Cantonment *(see p108)* was the military enclave. They lived in spacious bungalows, shopped at the Exchange Stores, dined at Maidens Hotel and worshipped at St James's Church. The old "temporary" Secretariat (built in 1912) is also located here on Mahatma Gandhi Marg. This long white building with its two towers, where the former Legislative Assembly once sat, also housed the offices of the Delhi Administration at one time. When the British moved into New Delhi, established Indian professional and merchant families settled here. Several old bungalows have been redeveloped as modern blocks of flats, yet some areas, such as Rajpur Road, still retain their essential colonial character.

To the east of Civil Lines, near the Delhi-Chandigarh bypass, is Metcalfe House, a sprawling mansion built in the 1830s by Sir Thomas Metcalfe, Delhi's eccentric British Resident from 1835–53. This house, once the hub of British social life, can be seen from the highway. It is now owned by the Defence Ministry and not open to the public.

White-plastered façade of the Oberoi Maidens Hotel in the Civil Lines area

Statues of former viceroys in the Coronation Durbar site

❻ Coronation Memorial

KB Hedgewar Rd, S of NH1 Bypass. **Tel** (011) 2462 9365. Ⓜ Vishwa Vidyalaya. **Open** sunrise–sunset.

This was the site of the Royal Durbar held in 1911 to proclaim the accession of George V as King Emperor of India. A red sandstone obelisk records that the King Emperor proclaimed his coronation to the "governors, princes and peoples of India" (in that order) and "received their dutiful homage". He also announced the transfer of the capital from Calcutta to Delhi and two days later laid the foundation stones for the new city *(see pp72–3)*. On 12 December 1911, more than 100,000 people thronged the site where the King Emperor and Queen Empress sat beneath a golden dome mounted on a crimson canopy. Today, the site is a flat, dusty and forlorn spot, and ranged round in a pathetic semi-circle are statues of former viceroys, evicted from their perches in the city to make way for later Indian leaders. These include Lords Hardinge and Willingdon (distinguished for their role in the construction of New Delhi). Towering over them all is the 22 m (73 ft) statue of the King Emperor himself, draped in his Durbar robes, which was removed from the canopy at India Gate *(see p75)* and installed here in the 1960s.

Coronation Memorial

❼ The Northern Ridge

Rani Jhansi Rd, Ridge Rd, Magazine Rd. **Open** sunrise–sunset.

The northern end of the Ridge is a forested park cut through by Ridge Road and Rani Jhansi Road, with the small clearing of Bara Hindu Rao in the middle. This area still resounds with memories of 1857. It was around Flagstaff Tower, to the far north, that British women and children took shelter before they were evacuated to Karnal near Panipat *(see p144)*.

The Mutiny Memorial (known locally as Ajitgarh), at the southern end, is a red sandstone Victorian Gothic spire built by the British to commemorate "the soldiers, British and native … who were killed" in 1857, and lists separately the names of those who died. At the entrance is a plaque, dated 1972, which points out: "The enemy of the inscriptions were those who fought bravely for national liberation in 1857". There are panoramic views of Old Delhi from the platform at the base of the tower. Nearby is a 3rd-century Ashokan Pillar, one of the two Feroze Shah Tughlaq *(see p101)* brought from Meerut in 1356. Faint inscriptions in Brahmi, extolling the virtues of practising *dhamma* (the Buddhist Way of Truth), are still visible. Feroze Shah also had a large hunting estate here where he built a lodge called Kushak-i-Shikar, a mosque, as well as a double-storeyed mansion, the Pir Ghaib, now in the grounds of the Hindu Rao Hospital (enter the main gate and turn right at the Cardiac Unit). The name, Pir Ghaib, derives from the tale of a resident *pir* who, one day, simply vanished *(ghaib)* while meditating at this site. A cenotaph in one of the rooms marks the spot.

Students unwind on the front lawns of St Stephen's College

❽ Delhi University

Vishwavidyalaya Marg. Ⓜ Vishwa Vidyalaya.

The university area runs parallel to the Northern Ridge, and colleges dot the vast campus. Arguably the most attractive of these is St Stephen's College, designed by Walter George in 1938. With its long corridors built in quartzite and its well-kept gardens, it has some deliberately cultivated Oxbridge associations. At one time this was one of India's premier institutions, with renowned scholars such as the historian Percival Spear on its staff. The office of the Vice Chancellor was once the guesthouse for British officials. It was here, in what is now the registrar's office, that the young Lord Louis Mountbatten proposed to, and was accepted by, Edwina Ashley. A plaque celebrates the event. They eventually became India's last viceroy and vicereine.

Image of the Buddha installed at Buddha Jayanti Park

9 The Ridge

Upper Ridge Rd. M Central Secretariat. **Open** sunrise–sunset. Buddha Jayanti Park: **Open** 5am–7pm daily.

Delhi's Ridge, the last outcrop of the Aravalli Hills extending northwards from Rajasthan, runs from southwest to northeast. The area was originally developed by Feroze Shah Tughlaq, some 600 years ago as his hunting resort. He erected many lodges, the ruins of which can still be seen here and towards the northern end of the Ridge *(see p107)*. This green belt of undulating, rocky terrain is covered by dense scrub forest consisting mainly of laburnum *(Cassia fistula)*, kikar *(Acacia arabica)* and flame of the forest *(Butea monosperma)* trees, interspersed with bright splashes of bougainvillea.

A large portion in the southwest is now the **Buddha Jayanti Park**, a peaceful, well-manicured enclave, criss-crossed with paved paths. Pipal *(Ficus religiosa)* trees abound, and on a small ornamental island is a simple sandstone pavilion shading the large gilt-covered statue of the Buddha, installed by the 14th Dalai Lama in October 1993. An inscription nearby quotes the Dalai Lama: "Human beings have the capacity to bequeathe to future generations a world that is truly human". Every May, Buddhist monks and devotees celebrate Buddha Jayanti *(see p42)* here.

10 Delhi Cantonment

Bounded by NH8, MG Rd and Sadar Bazaar Marg. M Dhaula Kuan. St Martin's Church: Church Rd. **Tel** (011) 2569 4632. Commonwealth War Graves Cemetery: Brar Square. **Tel** (011) 2569 1958. **Open** 7:45am–5pm daily.

The cantonment in Delhi was planned by John Begg and built by the Military Works Department in the 1930s. With its straight roads, neat, whitewashed walls, well-clipped hedges, parade ground and shooting-range, it epitomizes the quintessential spit and polish of the military.

Memorial tablet, Church of St Martin's

The garrison **Church of St Martin's**, probably the most original modern church in India, was designed by Lutyens's close associate, Arthur Gordon Shoosmith (1888–1974). Consecrated in 1931 and built from three and a half million bricks, it rises straight-walled with small, recessed windows and a 39 m (128 ft) tower, the lines between the bricks being the only ornamentation. Within is a stark classical interior with a plaque in honour of the architect and a haunting tablet in memory of the three children of Private Spier who died within days of each other at Abbottabad (now in Pakistan) in 1938. If the church is locked, contact the Presbyter-in-Charge who lives in the adjacent cottage.

A short distance from Dhaula Kuan Circle is the **Commonwealth War Graves Cemetery** where lie the Commonwealth soldiers and airmen who died on the Eastern Front in World War II. A monument at the entrance proudly declares: "Their Name Liveth Evermore". The graves are set in neat rows with matching headstones; only the regimental insignia and biblical texts are different. Every Remembrance Day (11 Nov), wreaths are laid at the Memorial Column, followed by a short prayer.

The War Graves Cemetery

11 National Rail Museum

Shanti Path, Chanakyapuri. M Race Course. **Tel** (011) 2688 1816. **Open** 9:30am–5:30pm Tue–Sun. **Closed** 1:30–2:30pm & public hols. extra for video and train rides.

India's railway network gives rise to astonishing statistics. It has a route length of 65,436 km (40,660 miles) and tracks that cover 115,000 km (71,458 miles). There are about 7,150 stations, 12,617 passenger trains, and 7,421 goods trains that run every day. The railways employ 1.6 million people, while 23 million passengers travel by train each day and eat 6 million meals through the journey.

This museum encapsulates the history of Indian railways. Steam locomotive enthusiasts will appreciate the collection that traces the development of the Indian railways from 1849, when the first 34 km (21 miles) of railway between Bombay (now Mumbai) and Kalyan was planned. The wealth of memorabilia on display inside includes the skull of an elephant which collided with a mail train at Golkara in 1894, and a realistic model of an 1868 first-class passenger coach with separate compartments for accompanying servants. Outside, are several retired steam locomotives built in Manchester, Glasgow and Darlington in the late 19th century, and the splendid salon that carried the Prince of Wales (later King Edward VII) on his travels during the 1876 Royal Durbar.

A "toy train" offers rides around the compound, and the shop sells model locomotives, ranging from ₹1,000 to 3,000.

⓬ Safdarjung's Tomb

Aurobindo Marg. Ⓜ Jor Bagh. **Tel** (011) 2336 3607. **Open** sunrise–sunset. extra charges for video photography.

This is the last of Delhi's garden tombs and was built in 1754 for Safdarjung, the powerful prime minister of Muhammad Shah, the emperor between 1719–48. Marble was allegedly stripped from the tomb of Abdur Rahim Khan-i-Khanan in Nizamuddin *(see p86)* to construct this rather florid example of late Mughal architecture. Approached by an ornate gateway, the top storey of which houses the Archaeological Survey of India's library, the tomb, with its exaggerated onion-shaped dome, stands in a *charbagh* cut by water channels. Its red and buff stone façade is extensively ornamented with well-preserved plaster carving, and the central chamber itself is unusually light and airy with some fine stone inlay work set into the floor.

A steam engine at the National Rail Museum

Cantonment Towns

Indian cavalry officer, pre-World War II

After the 1860s, over 170 cantonments (pronounced "cantoonment") were built on the outskirts of major towns to impress Indians with the seriousness of British military might. Each was a self-contained world, with symmetrical rows of barracks, finely graded bungalows, clubs and regimental messes, bazaars, hospitals and churches. Military hierarchies, too, were rigidly followed. Even after Independence, the military is mostly stationed in cantonment areas.

Shops selling traditional items of clothing at Dilli Haat

⓭ Dilli Haat

Laxmi Bai Nagar, Aurobindo Marg. Ⓜ INA. **Tel** (011) 462 9365. **Open** 11am–10pm daily.

This lively bazaar retains all the trappings of a traditional Indian village market, with acres of landscaped gardens, handicraft shops and regional food stalls. Everything you can imagine can be found at Dilli Haat – readymade garments, spices, bags, brass artifacts, jewellery, shawls, pottery, and much more. Diplomats, out-of-town shoppers and locals patronize this market for its reasonable prices and variety of products. Often, themed bazaars are organized during festivals, such as Teej, Diwali, or the Mango festival. The items are produced by artisans who purchase a spot in the market on a 15-day rotation basis. In the process, there is always something unique to discover here.

There are about 17 food stalls, each representing a different state in India. Run by their respective tourism authorities, the stalls offer delicious authentic dishes from distant and diverse regions, such as Tamil Nadu, Manipur and Kashmir. If you are lucky, you may even experience a state-organized cultural event, complete with puppet shows, dances, regional cuisine, paintings, and much shopping.

⓮ Moth ki Masjid

Behind South Extension, Part II.

Built in 1505 by Miyan Bhuwa, Sikander Lodi's prime minister, the design of this graceful red sandstone structure with its five-arched, three-domed prayer hall was developed further in later Mughal mosques. Over the central arch is a fine *jharokha* with traces of the original plaster decoration. The red sandstone gateway and the ornate decorations on the mosque's façade are also noteworthy. It is said that Sikander Lodi gave Miyan Bhuwa a *moth* (lentil seed) which reaped him such rich returns that he was able to endow this mosque. Sadly, he annoyed Sikander's successor, Ibrahim Lodi (r.1517–26), who had him put to death.

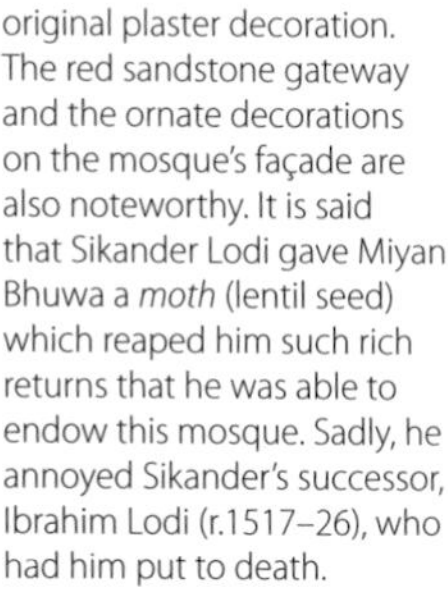

Detail of Moth ki Masjid

⓯ Hauz Khas

W of Aurobindo Marg. Ⓜ Hauz Khas.

Beyond the boutiques, art galleries and restaurants that have taken over the former village of Hauz Khas, are the medieval monuments from Feroze Shah Tughlaq's reign. In 1352, the sultan constructed a number of buildings on the banks of Hauz Khas, the large tank (now dry) excavated by Alauddin Khilji for his city of Siri *(see p112)*. Contemporary accounts claim that Feroze Shah was a prolific builder, and during his 37-year reign he constructed an astounding 40 mosques, 200 towns, 100 public baths and about 30 reservoirs.

Among the buildings here are a *madrasa*, Feroze Shah's tomb and the ruins of a small mosque at the extreme north of the complex. The double storeyed *madrasa* was built so that the tank and lower storey were at the same level, while the upper floor was at ground level. Refreshing breezes across the water must have once cooled the theological discussions held there by scholars. The low domes, colonnades and *jharokhas* relieve the severity of its façade, while plaster carvings and deep niches for books embellish the interior. The *chhatris* in the entrance forecourt are said to cover the teachers' burial mounds. The tomb of Feroze Shah lies at one end of the *madrasa*. Wine-red painted plaster calligraphy decorates the interior of the austere tomb.

The complex is best viewed in the afternoon when sunlight filters through the *jaalis* carved into the linteled archway, to cover the graves of the sultan, his sons and grandson with delicate star-shaped shadows.

East of Hauz Khas, off Aurobindo Marg, is a small rubble-built tapering structure called **Chor Minar** ("tower of thieves") with a staircase, now locked, leading to the top. This dates to the 14th-century Khilji period and its walls, pockmarked with holes, are said to have held the severed heads of thieves to deter others from crime.

Close by, to the northwest, is the **Nili Masjid** ("blue mosque"), named after the blue tiles above its *chhajja*. The inscription on the central of its three arches reveals that it was built in 1505 by one Kasumbhil, the nurse of the son of the governor of Delhi. Nearby is an Idgah, whose remaining long wall is carved with 11 mihrabs and an inscription proclaiming that it was built in 1404–5 by Iqbal Khan, a Tughlaq noble.

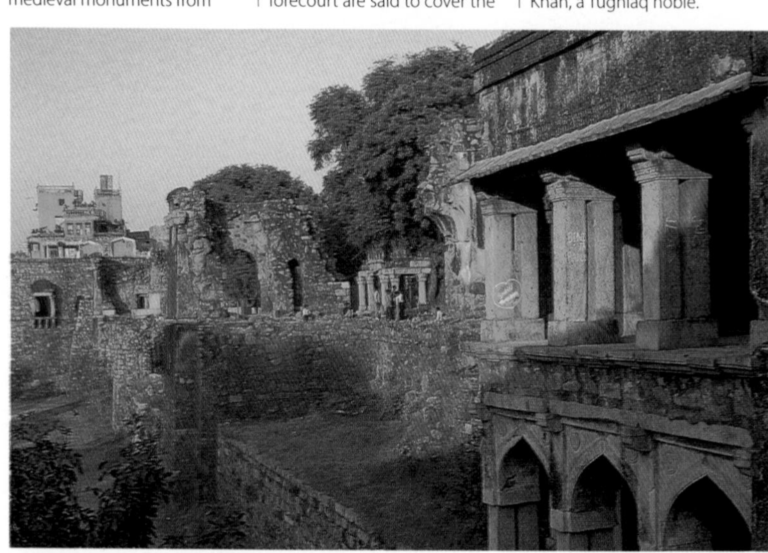

The double-storeyed *madrasa* at Hauz Khas

The Seven Cities of Delhi

Delhi's famous "seven cities" range from the 12th-century Qila Rai Pithora, built by Prithviraj Chauhan *(see p52)*, to the imperial Shahjahanabad, constructed in the 17th century. Each of these cities comprised the settlements that grew around the forts and palaces erected by powerful sultans with territorial ambitions. As the Sultanate was consolidated, the rulers moved their capitals from those defensively situated in the rocky outcrops of the Aravallis, northwards towards the open plains by the banks of the Yamuna. Today, Delhi is an amalgam of medieval citadels, palaces, tombs and mosques, and a spreading, modern concrete jungle.

Shahjahanabad was Delhi's seventh city, built between 1638 and 1649 by Shah Jahan who shifted the Mughal capital here from Agra *(see pp154–5)*.

Ferozabad, stretching north from Hauz Khas to the banks of the Yamuna, is Delhi's fifth city built by Feroze Shah Tughlaq (r.1351–88).

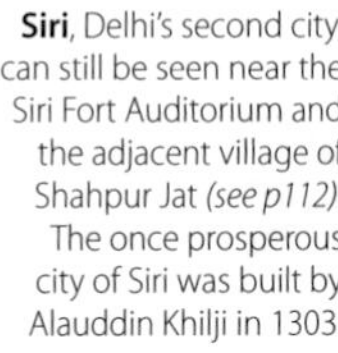

Siri, Delhi's second city, can still be seen near the Siri Fort Auditorium and the adjacent village of Shahpur Jat *(see p112)*. The once prosperous city of Siri was built by Alauddin Khilji in 1303.

Purana Qila, the citadel *(see p88)* of Delhi's sixth city, was built by Humayun. It was captured and occupied by the Afghan chieftain, Sher Shah Sur (r.1540–45) who called it Shergarh.

Jahanpanah was built by Muhammad-bin-Tughlaq (r.1325–51) as a walled enclosure to link Qila Rai Pithora and Siri. The ruined battlements of Delhi's fourth city stand near Chiragh *(see p112)*.

Qila Rai Pithora was the first of Delhi's seven cities, built by the Chauhans in about 1180. In 1192, it was captured by Qutbuddin Aibak who established his capital here *(see pp114–5)*.

Tughlaqabad, a dramatic fortress *(see p118)* on the foothills of the Aravallis, was Delhi's third city, built during Ghiyasuddin Tughlaq's four-year reign (1321–5).

Ruins of Siri, Delhi's second city built by Alauddin Khilji

⓰ Siri Fort

Asiad Village Complex, August Kranti Marg, Siri Fort Rd. Siri Fort Auditorium: **Tel** (011) 2649 3370/9397. Ⓜ Green Park.

Some crumbling ramparts are all that remain of Alauddin Khilji's 14th-century city of Siri *(see p111)*. The ruins of mosques and tombs can be found in the adjoining village of Shahpur Jat, today a shopper's paradise with many up-market boutiques, offices and a few art galleries. Siri Fort is commonly associated with the Siri Fort Auditorium which regularly hosts concerts and film festivals. It is directly adjacent to the Asian Games Village complex where there are speciality restaurants serving Indian, Chinese and Mexican cuisine.

⓱ Chiragh Delhi

Bordered by Outer Ring Rd & LB Shastri Marg. Ⓜ Green Park.

The *dargah* of the Sufi saint Nasiruddin Mahmud (died 1356), who succeeded Hazrat Nizamuddin Auliya *(see p86)* as spiritual leader of the Chishti sect, lies in the once secluded village of Chiragh Delhi. This saint, known as Raushan Chiragh-i-Dehlvi ("illuminated lamp of Delhi"), was buried here and the village that grew around his tomb was named after him. Muhammad-bin-Tughlaq, the sultan at that time, built the original village walls in the 14th century.

The shrine itself is small and should be approached on foot through the narrow, congested village lanes, past rows of tailoring establishments (including one specializing in *burqas*) and shops selling varieties of *mithai* ("sweetmeats"), *chadors*, flower garlands and other religious offerings. Some ruined *havelis*, which must have once been very beautiful, also line the street. A huge arched doorway leads to the *dargah*, a quieter and simpler shrine than that of Hazrat Nizamuddin. Shaded by trees, the tomb is set in a 12-pillared square chamber, enclosed by *jaali* screens and surmounted by a large plastered dome rising from an octagonal drum. Small domed turrets stand at the four corners. The roof inside has been embellished with fine painted plaster carvings set with mirrors, clearly a recent addition. Within the enclosure are several smaller mosques and halls, added over the years for religious discourses.

At the far end from the gateway is a partially ruined tomb that is locally claimed to be that of Bahlol Lodi (r. 1451–89), the founder of the Lodi dynasty. The *chhajja* has collapsed, but the square chamber is still surmounted by five domes, the central being the largest. The arches have engraved inscriptions.

Women devotees worshipping at Chiragh Delhi

Covered corridors with arches in the 14th-century Begumpuri Mosque, Jahanpanah

⓲ Khirkee

N of Press Enclave Marg. Ⓜ Malaviya Nagar.

The village adjacent to Chiragh Delhi is called "Khirkee" after the huge mosque built by Feroze Shah Tughlaq's prime minister, Khan-i-Jahan Junan Shah *(see p100)* in the mid-14th century. Standing today in a declivity and surrounded by village houses, is the unusual two-storeyed Khirkee ("windows") Mosque. It has a sombre fortress-like appearance with bastions on all four corners, and its severe façade is broken by rows of arched windows that are covered by portcullis-like *jaalis* which give the mosque its name. Built on a high plinth, flights of stairs lead up to imposing gateways on the north, south and east sides. The inner courtyard is partly covered, its roof supported by monolithic stone pillars, and crowned by nine sets of nine small domes. Only four courtyards remain open to the sky. This was the first example of this type of mosque design. But the division of open space by pillars was found unsuitable for large congregations, so this design was never repeated.

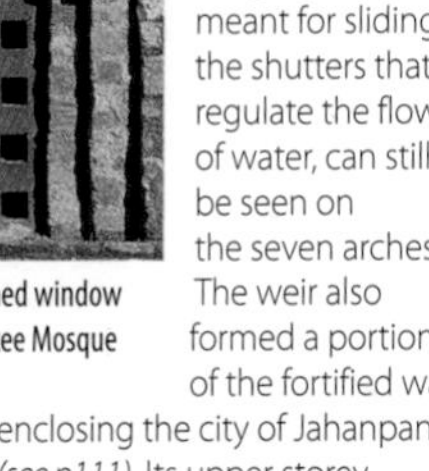
Detail of an arched window with *jaali*, Khirkee Mosque

Satpula ("seven-arches"), the dam and stone weir built by Muhammad-bin-Tughlaq in 1326, is located just down the same road. It formed part of the reservoir which was used for irrigation, and the grooves, meant for sliding the shutters that regulate the flow of water, can still be seen on the seven arches. The weir also formed a portion of the fortified wall enclosing the city of Jahanpanah *(see p111)*. Its upper storey was used as a *madrasa* during Muhammad-bin-Tughlaq's time.

The fortress-like Khirkee Mosque

⓳ Jahanpanah

S of Panchsheel Park. Ⓜ Hauz Khas.

In the heart of Jahanpanah, Muhammad-bin-Tughlaq's capital, stands **Begumpuri Mosque**, also built by Khan-i-Jahan Junan Shah. (When asking for directions, it is advisable to specifically ask for the old mosque, as a new one is located nearby.) Built on a high plinth with massive, typically Tughlaq walls, the mosque has a single imposing doorway at the head of a flight of stairs leading into the vast rectangular courtyard which is surrounded by arched cloisters, surmounted by 44 small domes. The prayer hall has 24 arched openings, the central one surmounted by a large dome. It is said that in times of need, this mosque also functioned as a treasury, granary and meeting place.

Nearby, to the north, is the palace of **Bijay Mandal**, a derelict, brooding octagonal structure rising from a high plinth. It is worth climbing the broken stone-cut stairs to the upper platform to get a sense of its size. According to the famed 14th-century Arab traveller, Ibn Batuta, it was from these very bastions that Muhammad-bin-Tughlaq held public audience and reviewed his troops. Later, in the early 16th century, the palace is believed to have been used as a residence by Sheikh Hasan Tahir, a much revered saint who visited Delhi during the reign of Sikandar Lodi. Panoramic views of the city of Delhi, extending from the Qutb Minar to Humayun's Tomb and beyond, can be seen from its upper platform.

⑳ Mehrauli Archaeological Park

Best known for the Qutb Minar, a World Heritage monument, Mehrauli was built over Rajput territories known as Lal Kot and Qila Rai Pithora. In 1193, Qutbuddin Aibak made this the centre of the Sultanate of Delhi and by the 13th century a small village, Mehrauli, had grown around the shrine of the Sufi saint, Qutb Sahib. Later, Mughal princes came to Mehrauli to hunt and some 19th-century British officials built weekend houses here, attracted by its orchards, ponds and abundant game *(shikar)*. It is still a popular weekend retreat for Delhi's rich and famous.

Dargah Qutb Sahib
This 13th-century *dargah* is still a pilgrimage point.

★ Jahaz Mahal
Venue of the Phoolwalon ki Sair *(see p44)*, this square pleasure pavilion, built during the Lodi era (1451–1526), seems to float on the Hauz-i-Shamsi tank.

KEY

① **Bagichi Masjid**

② **Jharna** (waterfall) was so-called because after the monsoon, water from the Hauz-i-Shamsi would flow over an embankment into a garden.

③ **Hauz-i-Shamsi** is a large reservoir built in 1230 by Iltutmish, who is supposed to have been guided to this site by the Prophet in a dream.

④ **Zafar Mahal** is a palace named after the *nom de plume* of the last Mughal emperor, Bahadur Shah Zafar.

⑤ **Mehrauli village**

⑥ **Dilkusha**

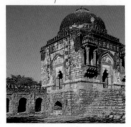

Madhi Masjid
Surrounded by bastions and a high wall, this fortress-like mosque has a large open courtyard and a three-arched, profusely ornamented prayer hall.

VISITORS' CHECKLIST

Practical Information
Anuvrat Marg, Mehrauli.
Open 8am–7pm daily.
Phoolwalon ki Sair (early Oct).

Transport
Qutb Minar.

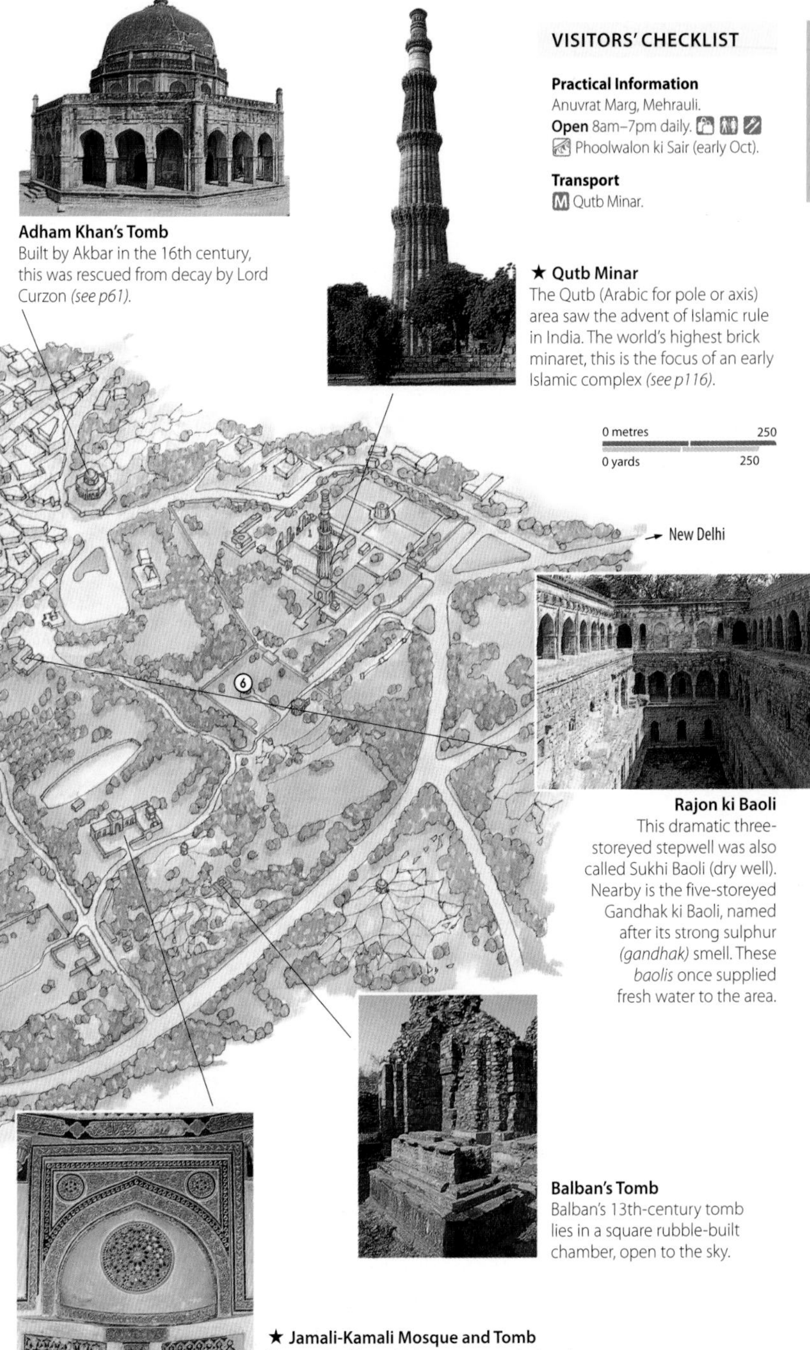

Adham Khan's Tomb
Built by Akbar in the 16th century, this was rescued from decay by Lord Curzon *(see p61)*.

★ Qutb Minar
The Qutb (Arabic for pole or axis) area saw the advent of Islamic rule in India. The world's highest brick minaret, this is the focus of an early Islamic complex *(see p116)*.

Rajon ki Baoli
This dramatic three-storeyed stepwell was also called Sukhi Baoli (dry well). Nearby is the five-storeyed Gandhak ki Baoli, named after its strong sulphur *(gandhak)* smell. These *baolis* once supplied fresh water to the area.

Balban's Tomb
Balban's 13th-century tomb lies in a square rubble-built chamber, open to the sky.

★ Jamali-Kamali Mosque and Tomb
The tomb of Jamali (the court poet during the late Lodi and early Mughal age) is inscribed with some of his verses. Its well-preserved interior has coloured tiles and richly decorated painted plasterwork. The second grave is unidentified but is widely believed to be that of his brother, Kamali.

The Qutb Complex

The Qutb Minar towers over this historic area where Qutbuddin Aibak laid the foundation of the Delhi Sultanate *(see pp54–5)*. In 1193, he built the Quwwat-ul-Islam ("the might of Islam") Mosque and the Qutb Minar to announce the advent of the Muslim sultans. Later, Iltutmish, Alauddin Khilji and Feroze Shah Tughlaq added other buildings, bringing in a new architectural style *(see p30)*. The fusion of decorative Hindu panels and Islamic domes and arches shows the mingling of two cultures.

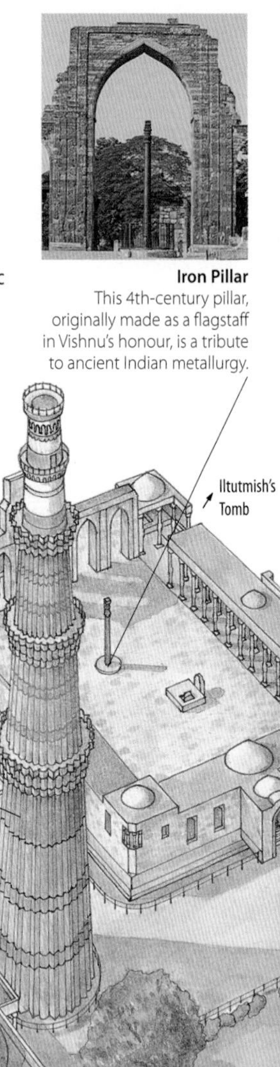

Iron Pillar
This 4th-century pillar, originally made as a flagstaff in Vishnu's honour, is a tribute to ancient Indian metallurgy.

Qutb Minar
The five-storeyed Victory Tower started by Qutbuddin Aibak was completed by his successor, Iltutmish.

Alauddin Khilji's Tomb

Iltutmish's Tomb

Carved Panels
Panels, carved with inscriptions from the Koran, embellish the gateway.

Alai Darwaza
This gateway to the complex, erected in 1311 by Alauddin Khilji, is one of the earliest buildings in India to employ the Islamic principles of arched construction *(see p30)*.

Imam Zamin's Tomb

VISITORS' CHECKLIST

Practical Information
Mehrauli, Delhi-Gurgaon Rd.
Tel (011) 2336 5358. **Open** 5:30am–7pm daily. Qutb Festival (Oct–Nov).

Transport
M Qutb Minar.

Iltutmish's Tomb
Built in 1235 by Iltutmish himself, its dome has vanished. The interior is carved with geometric and calligraphic patterns.

To Entrance

Quwwat-ul-Islam Mosque
Hindu motifs, such as tasselled ropes and bells, are clearly visible on the carved pillars of this mosque.

Dargah Qutb Sahib, shrine of the Sufi saint Qutbuddin Bakhtiyar "Kaki"

Exploring Mehrauli

Clustered round the *dargah* of Qutb Sahib, Mehrauli became a sylvan retreat for the later Mughals and top officials of the East India Company. Its medieval bazaar survives despite its recent conversion into boutiques and cafés, popular with Delhi's "smart set".

Medallion with calligraphy

Dargah Qutb Sahib

Open 4am–3pm daily.

In the heart of the Mehrauli bazaar, lies the *dargah* of a Sufi saint called Qutbuddin Bakhtiyar or "Kaki", after the small sugared cakes *(kaki)* he was fed when he fasted. It has been rebuilt several times since his death in 1235, so that today many mosques, tanks and chambers surround it, among them the lovely Moti Masjid ("pearl mosque") built in 1709. A domed marble pavilion contains his grave, which women may only view through the marble *jaalis*. A royal necropolis in the same area has the graves of some later Mughal kings, such as Bahadur Shah I (1707–12) and Akbar II (1806–37). The *dargah* and the Jogmaya Temple are the starting point for the Phoolwalon ki Sair *(see p44)*, the procession of flower-sellers which began in the 1720s as a floral tribute to the Mughal emperor. Revived by Nehru after 1947, it is now an important cultural event.

Adham Khan's Tomb

Open sunrise–sunset daily.

Near the bus terminus, at the approach to Mehrauli village, is an imposing, single-domed structure standing on a high platform. This is believed to be the last of the octagonal tombs built in Delhi and its shaded colonnades are much favoured by local youth for their siestas. Adham Khan, the son of Akbar's wet nurse, Maham Anga *(see p89)*, was considered a foster-brother of the emperor. In 1562, Adham Khan killed a rival, Atgah Khan, the husband of another wet nurse *(see p86)*. A furious Akbar ordered Adham Khan's execution, but was so moved by the death of his mother, Maham Anga, 40 days later, that he had a tomb built for both mother and son.

By far the largest building here, the tomb is locally known as the *bhulbhulaiyan* (maze) because of the narrow passages concealed within its walls. In the 1800s, the British used the tomb as a rest-house, police station and residence for minor officials.

A sunlit corridor in the tomb of Adham Khan, the son of Maham Anga

Rural huts and terracotta pots at the Sanskriti Museum

㉑ Sanskriti

Anandgram, Mehrauli-Gurgaon Rd.
Tel (011) 2652 7077. Ⓜ Arjangarh.
Open 10am–5pm Tue–Sun.
Closed Mon & public hols.

This unusual museum is set amidst beautifully landscaped spacious grounds where exhibits are displayed both in the garden and in specially constructed rural huts. The collection, too, is equally unusual. It is devoted to traditional objects of everyday use, exquisitely crafted by an unknown, unsung, rural artisan. OP Jain, whose personal collections gave birth to this museum, has donated exquisite combs, nutcrackers, lamps, foot-scrubbers and kitchenware. Terracotta objects from all over India are also on display. The pots are especially dazzling, particularly as their production techniques have not changed for centuries.

㉒ Sultan Ghari

C-9, Vasant Kunj, off Mahipalpur-Mehrauli Rd. Ⓜ Chattarpur.
Open daily.

Sultan Ghari was the first Islamic tomb to be built in Delhi and among the earliest in India. The ruler of the Slave dynasty, Iltutmish, erected this tomb in 1231 for his eldest son and heir, Nasiruddin Muhammad, who was killed in battle. Today, its fortress-like exterior appears out of place in the midst of one of Delhi's largest residential complexes, Vasant Kunj. Inside is a raised courtyard, and the tomb itself is an octagonal platform, forming the roof of the crypt *(ghar)* below. Like many monuments of this early medieval period, Sultan Ghari was constructed from pillars and stones taken from temples nearby. Fragments of these are visible in the surrounding colonnades, which may have once housed a *madrasa*. The mihrab on the west side has some fine calligraphic decoration and, interestingly, there is a marble *yonipatta*, the base of a Shiva *linga (see p311)* embedded in the floor.

The tomb, located on the road from Andheria More to Delhi Airport, is reached after turning left from the Spinal Injuries Centre and taking the next left after that.

Ghiyasuddin Tughlaq's Tomb

㉓ Tughlaqabad

Off Mehrauli-Badarpur Rd. Ⓜ Saket.
Open 5:30am–7pm daily.

This spectacular fortress, built by Ghiyasuddin Tughlaq in the 14th century *(see p111)*, was completed in just four years. The quality of its construction was influenced by building techniques in Multan where Ghiyasuddin had served as governor. It was so sturdy that the rubble-built walls clinging to the shape of the hill, survive intact all along the 6.5 km (4 mile) perimeter. To the right of the main entrance is the citadel from which rise the ruins of the Vijay Mandal ("tower of victory"). To the left is a rectangular area where arches are all that remain of a complex of palaces and halls. Beyond these, houses were once laid out in a neat grid pattern. Legend has it that when Ghiyasuddin tried to prevent the building of the *baoli* at Hazrat Nizamuddin Auliya's *dargah (see p86)*, the saint cursed him by saying that one day only jackals and the Gujjar tribe would inhabit his capital. Perhaps the saint forgot to add tourists and monkeys to that list!

A good view of the fort and of the adjoining smaller fort of Adilabad is possible from the

The crumbling ramparts of Tughlaqabad Fort

The lotus-domed Baha'i House of Worship, one of Delhi's most spectacular sights

walls. Adilabad was built by Muhammad-bin-Tughlaq (r.1325–51), who is believed to have killed his father Ghiyasuddin by contriving to have a gateway collapse on him. They are both buried in Ghiyasuddin's Tomb, joined to the Tughlaqabad Fort by a causeway that crossed the dammed waters of a lake.

The tomb was the first in India to be built with sloping walls, a design that was repeated in all subsequent Tughlaq architecture. Its severe red sandstone walls, relieved by white marble inlay, are surmounted by a white marble dome. The red sandstone *kalasha* (urn) which crowns it and the lintel spanning the arched opening, decorated with a lotus bud fringe, are both influenced by Hindu architecture.

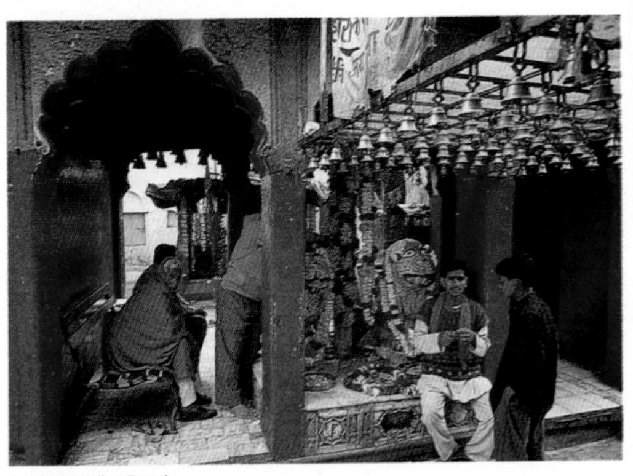

Inside the Kalkaji Temple

㉔ Kalkaji Temple

Block 9, Lotus Temple Rd, Nehru Place. M Kalkaji Mandir. **Open** 6am–10pm daily. Navaratri (Mar–Apr & Sep–Oct).

This temple is a good place to see Hinduism in bustling, popular practice. It is approached through a narrow winding alley, lined with stalls selling laminated religious prints, bangles, *sindur* (vermilion powder) and fruit, while devotional hymns blast from rival cassette stalls. The 12-domed temple, with a heavily decorated pillared pavilion, was built in the mid-18th century on an older site by Raja Kedarnath, prime minister of Emperor Akbar II. Thereafter, many contemporary additions, financed by rich merchants, have been made. The goddess Kali or Kalka, draped in silks, sits under silver umbrellas and a marble canopy. Legend has it that a farmer, on discovering that his cow regularly offered her milk to the goddess, built this temple in her name.

㉕ Baha'i House of Worship

Bahapur, Kalkaji. **Tel** (011) 2644 4029. **Open** Apr–Sep: 9am–7pm Tue–Sun; Oct–Mar: 9am–5:30pm Tue–Sun. **Closed** Mon & public hols. Prayer services: 10am, noon, 3pm & 5pm.

Just opposite the Kalkaji Temple is the Baha'i House of Worship, a world where silence and order prevails. The arresting shape of its unfurling 27-petalled white marble lotus has given it its more popular name, the Lotus Temple. The edifice, circled by nine pools and 27 acres (92 ha) of green manicured lawns, is one of Delhi's most innovative modern structures.

The Baha'i sect originated in Persia and this temple was designed by the Iranian architect, Fariborz Sahba. Construction began in 1980 and was completed in 1986. Inside, the lofty auditorium can seat 1,300 and all are welcome to meditate there and attend the daily 15-minute services. Concerts with a social message are held here often. There is an Information Centre as well, designed for those interested to learn about the faith. The temple looks spectacular after dark when the lighting gives the marble panels a luminous, ethereal quality.

Day Trips from Delhi

If you want a break from the hustle and bustle of Delhi and wish to explore the surrounding countryside, there are several interesting sights to visit, all within a 50-km (30-mile) radius of the city. The lake at Sultanpur is a haven for migratory birds in winter, and in Pataudi is a beautiful palace which belongs to its cricket-loving nawabs, now open to tourists. Surajkund, with its vast medieval reservoir, is the venue of a popular crafts fair held every February. All these excursions take about eight hours. Since they are not particularly easy to reach by public transport, it is best to hire a car and driver for the day, which can be organized by your hotel or local taxi rank and is relatively inexpensive.

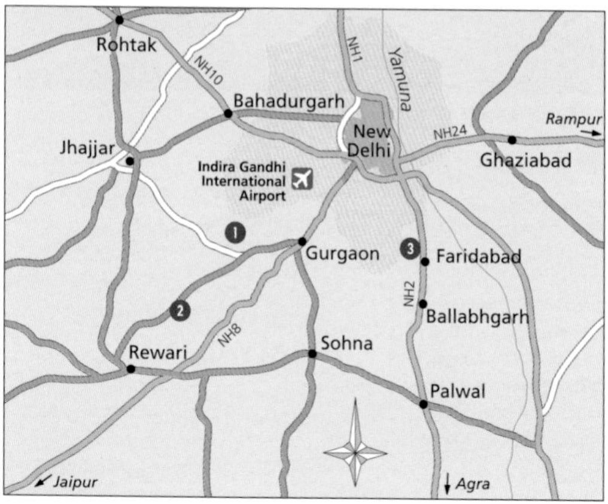

Sights at a Glance

1. Sultanpur Bird Sanctuary
2. Pataudi
3. Surajkund

Key

- City centre
- National highway
- Major road
- Minor road

0 kilometres 50

0 miles 25

❶ Sultanpur Bird Sanctuary

46 km (27 miles) W of Delhi. Haryana Tourism, Chanderlok Building, Janpath, Delhi, (011) 2332 4911. Huda City Centre. **Open** sunrise–sunset Wed–Mon. **Closed** Tue.

This sanctuary, a two-hour drive from Delhi, has been developed around a low-lying marshy area that is dry in summer, but fills up during the monsoon to form a shallow lake *(jheel)*. Sultanpur is at its best in the winter when this shallow sheet of water provides a haven for migratory birds.

Several pleasant walks, including a paved pathway which runs around the small lake, allow visitors to explore the 35-km (22-mile) area, while the many hides or *machans*, mounted on stilts, provide a good view of the birdlife on the lake. The Sarus crane, the world's tallest flying bird, breeds in the mud spits covered with reeds that rise above the waters. Often, on late winter evenings, large, noisy flocks of demoiselle cranes descend on the lake. The other birds that visit the lake include egrets, herons, kingfishers, pelicans and painted storks.

The rolling tree-shaded lawns, home to herds of friendly deer, have beautifully sited picnic spots. The sanctuary shop has a good selection of books and posters on Indian birdlife.

Sultanpur, home to a variety of deer and many migratory birds

For keys to symbols *see back flap*

❷ Pataudi

60 km (37 miles) S of Delhi. Ibrahim Kothi: Advance reservations are essential. **Tel** (011) 4666 1666.

The two-hour drive to Pataudi is a pleasant one, particularly after crossing Gurgaon when the road runs through open wheat fields and occasional villages. Pataudi, a typical North Indian town with a tangle of narrow lanes and a congested bazaar, is famous for its cricket-playing nawabs who claim descent from a 16th-century Afghan noble.

The old palace, built about 200 years ago, is now derelict, but still retains its romantic charm. The new palace, known as **Ibrahim Kothi**, was built in 1939. The elegant white, double-storeyed building, set amidst 10 acres (4 ha) of flowering gardens, has deep, pillared verandahs and is surmounted by a small dome. The well-maintained interior includes polished parquet floors, pink Venetian chandeliers and chintz furnishings. The walls are lined with portraits and sepia photographs of the present nawab's ancestors. One is of his father as a member of the famous "bodyline" English cricket team which toured Australia in the 1930s.

A section of this palace has now been refurbished and is run as a hotel; perfect for a truly royal holiday.

Elegant interior of Ibrahim Kothi

Ibrahim Kothi at Pataudi

Surajkund Crafts Mela

For two weeks in early February, Surajkund comes alive with the sounds and colours of one of India's largest arts and crafts fairs. Craftsmen and artisans from every part of the country sell their wares at a specially created village, under thatched canopies decorated with *rangoli*. Here, mirrorwork from Gujarat, painted puppets from Jaipur, fanciful bell-metal beasts from Orissa and Madhubani paintings from Bihar can be found at a wide range of prices. There are balloon sellers and food stalls to give the *mela* a carnival air, while folk dancers and musicians in colourful costumes weave in and out of the crowds. The evenings, given over to folk theatre, dance and music performances, attract huge crowds.

A performance by folk singers at the Surajkund Crafts Mela

❸ Surajkund

21 km (13 miles) S of Delhi. Haryana Tourism, Chanderlok Building, Janpath, Delhi, (011) 2332 4911.

King Surajpal of the Rajput Tomar dynasty *(see p52)*, hero of many legends, built this reservoir some time in the late 10th or early 11th century. An embankment of stone terraces was built round a pool which trapped rain water running down from the hills. A sun temple is thought to have stood on the western side. Tomar Rajputs trace their descent from the sun, hence the name: *suraj* (sun) *kund* (pool). Today, the embankment is more or less intact, though there is no trace of the temple and the pool itself is none too clean. The nearby artificial lake is picturesque and is best enjoyed from the paddle or rowing boats on hire. You might even glimpse a pale green water snake swimming alongside.

About 2 km (1.5 miles) to the west is **Anangpur Dam** built by the Tomar king, Anangpal. A rather impressive quartzite stone stucture, it blocks a narrow ravine to create an artificial lake. The dam is reached on foot, but it is an extremely brambly and rocky walk and best avoided in rainy weather.

This area is a popular picnic spot for Delhi's residents. Haryana Tourism and the Delhi Transport Corporation run special daily buses to Surajkund during the annual crafts *mela (see p45)*.

SHOPPING IN DELHI

The hallmark of shopping in Delhi is the fabulous variety of styles, merchandise and markets. Besides Connaught Place, almost every residential colony boasts a market. Old, established shops and bazaars co-exist happily with glitzy high-end boutiques and department stores, and one can buy anything from seasonal vegetables, fruits and traditional handicrafts to designer clothes and the latest imported electronic items. Be prepared to bargain where required, even a small success will make your shopping spree in Delhi a complete and satisfying experience. For practical information, see page 258.

Shops and Markets

New Delhi's main shopping centres are in Connaught Place and Janpath where the Central Cottage Industries offers an exciting and varied range of textiles, jewellery and souvenirs at fixed and reasonable prices. Indian handicrafts and handlooms are available at the state emporia on Baba Kharak Singh Marg, Dilli Haat and the Crafts Museum Shop *(see pp90–91)*. In the north is Chandni Chowk *(see p97)*, the traditional market, while to the south are Khan Market, Sundar Nagar and Santushti. The old urban villages of Hauz Khas, Shahpur Jat and Mehrauli have trendy boutiques where shoppers can explore a variety of designer clothes. The South Extension, Lajpat Nagar and Sarojini Nagar markets are popular with local shoppers. The five-star hotels, too, have shopping arcades that sell carefully-selected goods.

Silver fruit bowl

Antiques, Carpets and Shawls

Genuine antiques are rare to come by and cannot be taken out of the country unless certified by the ASI *(see p273)*. However, hotel shops, Sundar Nagar and the **Crafts Museum Shop** stock excellent reproductions of miniature paintings, woodcarving and bronzes made by artisans today. Contemporary silverware is available at **Cooke & Kelvey** and **Ravissant**. For Afghan and Kashmiri carpets and shawls, such as the paisley jamawar and pashmina, the best outlets are **Cottage Industries** and **The Carpet Cellar**.

Jewellery

Superb pieces of traditional jewellery, such as *kundan* and *meenakari*, are available at **Bharany's**. The best places for silver jewellery are Dariba Kalan, in Chandni Chowk, and Sundar Nagar market.

Brass and copper vessels and other objects on sale, Sundar Nagar market

A selection of cotton *dhurries* from Fabindia on display

Textiles and Quilts

Indian silks and cotton are famous throughout the world. Cottage Industries and the state emporia have a good selection of textiles from different parts of India. **Fabindia**, **The Shop**, **Tulsi**, **Cottons** and **Anokhi** are fine places to shop for good quality ready-made garments, linen and light cotton quilts, while **Shyam Ahuja** sells *dhurries* and linen. The best selection of designer clothes and accessories is available at **Abraham & Thakore**.

Leather

Leather goods, in particular shoes and bags, are found in most major shopping areas such as Connaught Place, Khan Market and South Extension. For quality hand-made shoes and jackets, the Chinese-owned outlets, such as **John Brothers**, still set the standards for comfort and durability. For trendier goods there is **Da Milano**, which has several branches.

Handicrafts and Gifts

Indian handicrafts are available at the state emporia, specifically **Kamala**, the Crafts Museum Shop and Dilli Haat on Aurobindro Marg. **Tibet House** has *thangkas*, carpets, woollen shawls and jackets. **The Neemrana Shop** and **Good Earth** have a good selection of gift items, such as candles, handmade paper products and artifacts in ceramics, wood and metal.

Embroidered textiles sold on Janpath

Books, Music and Newspapers

Every local market has stalls selling newspapers, magazines, CDs and bestsellers. The largest number of books and music shops are in South Extension, Khan Market and Vasant Vihar. **Tekson's Bookshop** and **Full Circle** stock a wide variety of books by international publishing houses. **Motilal Banarsidas** in Old Delhi specializes in books on Indology. Every Sunday, a bazaar selling old and second-hand books is held on the pavements of Daryaganj where it is possible to pick up interesting bargains.

Speciality Shops

In Chandni Chowk's Dariba Kalan is **Gulab Singh Johari Mal**, a marvellous old-fashioned shop where one can test Indian perfumes from lovely cutglass bottles. Herbal cosmetics by Kama and Forest Essentials are found in their outlets at Khan Market. Good Earth *(see Handicrafts and Gifts)* also sells Amritam, its own aromatheraphy brand.

Spices, dry and fresh seasonal fruit are found at INA Market while **Steak House** and the Gourmet Shoppe at The Oberoi *(see p238)* stock a wide variety of cheese, cold cuts, breads and pasteries. Indian tea, from the gardens of Assam and Darjeeling, can be found at various outlets in Khan Market and at **Aapki Pasand**.

DIRECTORY

Antiques, Carpets and Shawls

Cooke & Kelvey
3, Scindia House, India Connaught Lane, Janpath. **Map** 1 C5.
Tel (011) 2331 4095.

Cottage Industries
Jawahar Vypar Bhawan, Janpath. **Map** 1 C5.
Tel (011) 2332 0439.

Crafts Museum Shop
Pragati Maidan. **Map** 6 D2.
Tel (011) 2337 1887.

Ravissant
50–51, Commercial Complex, New Friends Colony. **Tel** (011) 2683 7278.

The Carpet Cellar
1, Anand Lok, August Kranti Marg. **Tel** (011) 4164 1777.

Jewellery

Bharany's
14, Sundar Nagar Market. **Map** 6 D3.
Tel (011) 2435 8528.

Textiles and Quilts

Abraham & Thakore
4, Nelson Mandela Marg, DLF Emporium, Vasant Kunj. **Tel** (011) 4606 0995.

Anokhi
32, Khan Market. **Map** 5 B3.
Tel (011) 2460 3423.

Cottons
N-Block Market, Greater Kailash I.
Tel (011) 4163 5108.

Fabindia
N-Block Market, Greater Kailash I.
Tel (011) 4669 3725/23.

Shyam Ahuja
Santushti. **Map** 4 E4.
Tel (011) 2467 0112.

The Shop
10, Regal Building, Sansad Marg, Connaught Place. **Map** 1 C5.
Tel (011) 2334 0971.

Tulsi
Santushti. **Map** 4 E4.
Tel (011) 2687 0339.

Leather

Da Milano
39–B, Khan Market.
Map 5 B3.
Tel (011) 4175 1755.

John Brothers
216, Competent House, F-Block, Connaught Place. **Map** 1 C4.
Tel (011) 2331 6158.

Handicrafts and Gifts

Good Earth
Santushti. **Map** 4 E4.
Tel (011) 2410 0108.

Kamala
Rajiv Gandhi Handicrafts Bhavan, Baba Kharak Singh Marg. **Map** 1 B5.
Tel (011) 6596 9600.

The Neemrana Shop
26–A, Khan Market.
Map 5 B3.
Tel (011) 4358 7183.

Tibet House
Lodi Rd. **Map** 5 B5.
Tel (011) 2461 1515.

Books, Music and Newspapers

Full Circle
Khan Market.
Map 5 B3.
Tel (011) 2465 5641.

Motilal Banarsidas
Jawahar Nagar.
Tel (011) 2385 8335.

Tekson's Bookshop
South Extension Market.
Tel (011) 4164 6505.

Speciality Shops

Aapki Pasand
15, Netaji Subhash Marg. **Map** 2 E3.
Tel (011) 2326 0373.

Gulab Singh Johri Mal
320, Dariba Kalan, Chandni Chowk.
Map 2 E2.
Tel (011) 2327 1345.

Steak House
Jor Bagh Mkt.
Tel (011) 2461 1129.

ENTERTAINMENT IN DELHI

Delhi, as the capital of India, has a rich and varied cultural life, mainly because the government has, over the last 50 years or more, consciously promoted a revival of traditional art forms. As a result, dancers, musicians and folk artistes from all over India deem it an honour to perform here before discerning audiences. Although Delhi is still a culturally conservative city, jazz, theatre and rock concerts are frequent, and there are several good bars and night clubs.

The city's cultural calendar livens up between October and March when the season is in full swing. The number of events multiply as all major festivals of music, dance, theatre and cinema are held at this time.

View of the India International Centre, New Delhi

Entertainment Guides and Tickets

All newspapers list the day's entertainment on their engagements page. Other useful sources of information on events, restaurants, sports and related activities are the weekly *Delhi Diary*, the online *Time Out Delhi* and the monthly magazine *First City*.

At several venues in the city, such as the India International Centre *(see Lectures and Discussions)*, entry is free. At others, such as the Indian Council for Cultural Relations, it is by invitation. Tickets for selected music festivals and theatre, however, are advertised and sold at certain bookshops or at the box office. A useful website is www.delhievents.com.

Music and Dance

Delhi is a fantastic place to experience the full range and richness of classical dance and music. Performances by the best exponents of the major dance styles of Bharata Natyam, Kathak, Odissi and Kathakali take place in the high season. The same is true of concerts of Hindustani and Carnatic music, the two major streams of classical music. During the season, shows are held mainly at **Siri Fort Auditorium** and **Kamani Auditorium**. **Triveni Kala Sangam** and the **India Habitat Centre** have performances all the year round. The state-run **Indian Council for Cultural Relations** also organizes shows at Azad Bhavan and the FICCI auditorium.

Colourful folk dances from all over India can be seen during the annual Trade Fair at **Pragati Maidan** *(see p89)*.

Theatre

The main theatre repertory company is the **National School of Drama** which presents plays in its own open air auditorium and at Kamani Auditorium nearby. In 1999, the company began a National Theatre Festival, to be held every May–Jun. Its performances are in Hindi and Urdu and include works by contemporary Indian and Western playwrights.

Several amateur theatre groups perform in both Hindi and English, contributing to a hectic theatre season in the winter. The main venues are **Shri Ram Centre**, Kamani, and the India Habitat Centre *(see Music and Dance)*.

Films

Delhi plays host to an international film festival which is held in January of every even year at the Siri Fort complex. Tickets can be obtained from the box office. Other film festivals, organized by the Directorate of Film Festivals, are held here as well. These are mainly regional Indian cinema and foreign films that are not usually screened on the commercial circuit. Documentary films, presenting the works of up-and-coming filmmakers, are screened at the India International Centre, **Max Mueller Bhavan** and the **British Council**. Many foreign cultural centres, like the Alliance Française and the **French Cultural Centre** also have regular film shows.

Popular Indian and foreign films are screened at the many cinema halls dotted all over the city. Among the better-equipped halls are **3C's**, **PVR Saket**, **PVR Priya**, **PVR Plaza** and **DT Cinemas**. All daily

Shubha Mudgal, a well-known classical singer

newspapers carry details of film shows. The tickets should be bought well in advance as cinema, both Indian and foreign, continues to be a major form of popular entertainment.

Exhibitions

The number of art galleries continues to grow in response to an increased interest in contemporary Indian art. Regular exhibitions present the work of painters, sculptors and photographers. Certain well known galleries such as **Art Heritage** and others located at Triveni Kala Sangam, India Habitat Centre, India International Centre and Max Mueller Bhavan are in the city centre. Others, such as **Vadehra Art Gallery**, are in South Delhi. The **National Gallery of Modern Art** *(see p75)* and the **National Museum** *(see pp76–9)* both regularly organize major exhibitions.

Lectures and Discussions

Lectures, discussions and seminars covering a wide range of subjects, such as international and current affairs, wildlife and ecology, mountaineering and Indian culture are regularly held at the **India International Centre**. These are announced in the daily newspapers and are open to all. Other venues where such programmes are held are the **Indira Gandhi National Centre for the Arts** (IGNCA), British Council and the India Habitat Centre.

Lavish interiors of Rick's bar at the Taj Mahal Hotel

Nightlife

Delhi's nightlife is particularly lively. The five-star hotels house most of the better bars and clubs, such as **Club Bar**, **Olive Bar & Restaurant, Rick's**, **Agni** and **Aura**. These are popular with the young crowd, especially on Saturday nights. **Q'Ba** offers live music on weekends.

DIRECTORY

Music and Dance

Indian Council for Cultural Relations
Azad Bhavan, IP Estate.
Map 1 C4.
Tel (011) 2337 9309.

India Habitat Centre
Lodi Rd. **Map** 5 B5.
Tel (011) 2468 2001.

Kamani Auditorium
Copernicus Marg.
Map 2 D5.
Tel (011) 4350 3351.

Pragati Maidan
Map 6 D1.
Tel (011) 2337 1540.

Siri Fort Auditorium
Asian Village Complex.
Tel (011) 2649 3370.

Triveni Kala Sangam
205, Tansen Marg.
Map 2 D5.
Tel (011) 2371 8833.

Theatre

National School of Drama
Bahawalpur House.
Map 2 E5.
Tel (011) 2338 9402.

Shri Ram Centre
Mandi House. **Map** 2 D5.
Tel (011) 2371 4307.

Films

3C's
15, Feroze Gandhi Marg, Lajpat Nagar III.
Tel (011) 2984 7846.

British Council
17, Kasturba Gandhi Marg. **Map** 1 C5.
Tel (011) 2371 0111.

DT Cinemas
Saket & Vasant Kunj.
Tel (011) 2614 0000.

French Cultural Centre
2, Aurangzeb Rd.
Map 5 A3.
Tel (011) 3041 0000.

Max Mueller Bhavan
3, Kasturba Gandhi Marg.
Map 2 D5.
Tel (011) 2347 1100.

PVR Plaza
H Block, Connaught Place.
Map 1 C4.
Tel (011) 4760 4200.

PVR Priya
61, Community Centre, Basant Lok, Vasant Vihar.
Tel (011) 4760 4300.

PVR Saket
Community Centre, Saket.
Tel (011) 4710 4000.

Exhibitions

Art Heritage
Triveni Kala Sangam.
Map 2 D5.
Tel (011) 2371 9470.

National Gallery of Modern Art
Jaipur House, Dr Zakir Hussain Marg, India Gate.
Map 5 C2.
Tel (011) 2338 4640.

National Museum
Janpath.
Map 5 A2.
Tel (011) 2379 2775.

Vadehra Art Gallery
D-178, Okhla Phase 1.
Tel (011) 6547 4005.

Lectures and Discussions

India International Centre
40, Lodi Estate, Max Mueller Marg.
Map 5 A4.
Tel (011) 2461 9431.

Indira Gandhi National Centre for the Arts
1, CV Mess, Janpath.
Map 5 A4.
Tel (011) 2338 3895.

Nightlife

Agni
The Park, Sansad Marg.
Map 1 C5.
Tel (011) 2374 3000.

Aura
Claridge's Hotel.
Map 5 A3.
Tel (011) 3955 5082.

Club Bar
The Oberoi, Dr Zakir Hussain Marg.
Map 6 D4.
Tel (011) 2436 3030.

Olive Bar & Restaurant
One Style Mile, Haveli 6, Kalka Das Marg, Mehrauli.
Tel (011) 2957 4444.

Q'Ba
E-42 & E-43, Inner Circle, Connaught Place.
Map 1 C4.
Tel (011) 4517 3333.

Rick's
Taj Mahal Hotel.
Map 5 B3.
Tel (011) 2302 6162.

DELHI POLICE
DELHI POLICE

DELHI STREET FINDER

Delhi is a confusing city to get around. New Delhi and the adjoining Nizamuddin to Purana Qila area are fairly well marked out, whereas Old Delhi is a maze of narrow lanes *(galis)* and bylanes. The city has extended far beyond the main city centre, in keeping with its burgeoning population, and the vast complexes of residential housing add to the confusion of getting around. Navigating the city's roads and streets *(margs)* is challenging. Signposts are often hard to find and most of the names have changed or are known by more than one name. Connaught Place is officially known as Rajiv Gandhi Chowk, Connaught Circus is Indira Gandhi Chowk and Sansad Marg is also known as Parliament Street. The Street Finder covers the city centre area and lists the major sights, hotels, restaurants, shops and entertainment venues. The Further Afield map is on page 103 and covers the area north, west and south of the city centre.

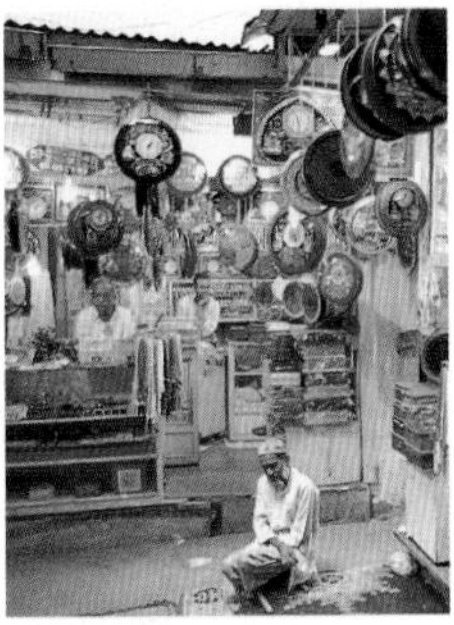

Shops at the entrance to the Dargah at Nizamuddin

Key

- Major sight
- Place of interest
- Other buildings
- Railway station
- Metro station
- Bus terminus
- Tourist information
- Hospital
- Police station
- Temple
- *Gurudwara*
- Church
- Mosque
- Tomb
- Railway line

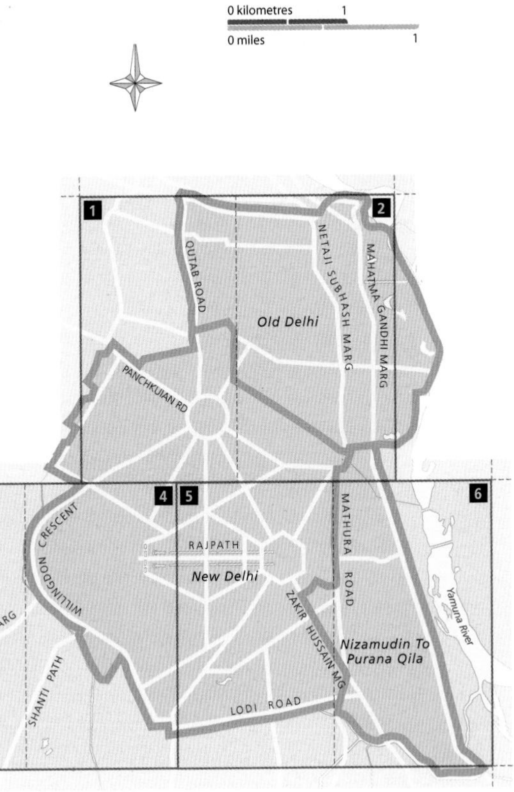

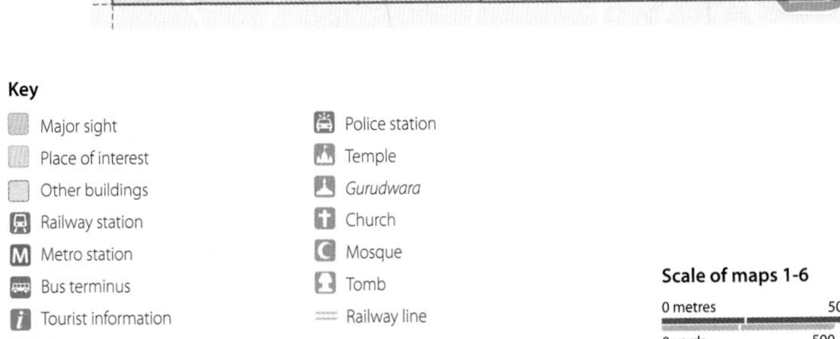

Scale of maps 1-6

0 metres 500

0 yards 500

◀ View of Rajpath from Vijay Chowk, New Delhi

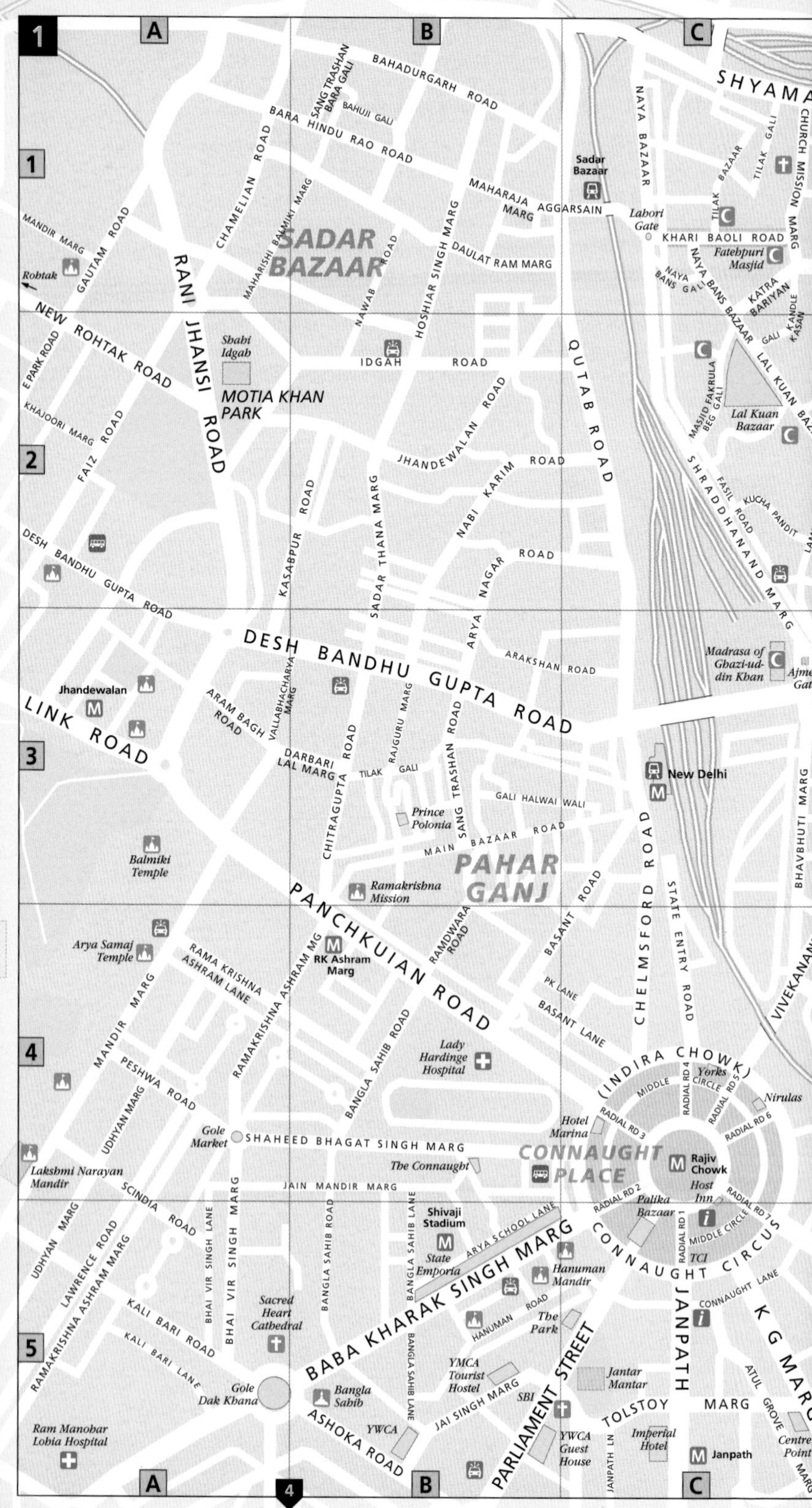
SADAR BAZAAR
MOTIA KHAN PARK
PAHAR GANJ
CONNAUGHT PLACE
Rohtak
Shahi Idgah
Sadar Bazaar
Lahori Gate
Fatehpuri Masjid
Lal Kuan Bazaar
Madrasa of Ghazi-ud-din Khan
Ajmer Gate
Jhandewalan
New Delhi
Prince Polonia
Balmiki Temple
Ramakrishna Mission
Arya Samaj Temple
RK Ashram Marg
Lady Hardinge Hospital
Yorks
Nirulas
Hotel Marina
Rajiv Chowk
Host Inn
Palika Bazaar
TCI
Gole Market
The Connaught
Lakshmi Narayan Mandir
Shivaji Stadium
State Emporia
Hanuman Mandir
The Park
Sacred Heart Cathedral
YMCA Tourist Hostel
SBI
Jantar Mantar
Gole Dak Khana
Bangla Sahib
YWCA
YWCA Guest House
Imperial Hotel
Janpath
Centre Point
Ram Manohar Lohia Hospital
DESH BANDHU GUPTA ROAD
LINK ROAD
PANCHKUIAN ROAD
RANI JHANSI ROAD
NEW ROHTAK ROAD
QUTAB ROAD
CHELMSFORD ROAD
STATE ENTRY ROAD
BABA KHARAK SINGH MARG
PARLIAMENT STREET
JANPATH
K G MARG
CONNAUGHT CIRCUS
(INDIRA CHOWK)
ASHOKA ROAD
SHAHEED BHAGAT SINGH MARG
JAIN MANDIR MARG
IDGAH ROAD
JHANDEWALAN ROAD
MAHARAJA AGGARSAIN MARG
KHARI BAOLI ROAD
SHYAMA
SHRADDHANAND MARG
ARAKSHAN ROAD
MAIN BAZAAR ROAD
BASANT ROAD
BASANT LANE
PK LANE
VIVEKANAND
BHAVBHUTI MARG
TOLSTOY MARG
CONNAUGHT LANE
MANDIR MARG
PESHWA ROAD
SCINDIA ROAD
KALI BARI ROAD
KALI BARI LANE
LAWRENCE ROAD
RAMAKRISHNA ASHRAM MARG
UDHYAN MARG
BHAI VIR SINGH MARG
BHAI VIR SINGH LANE
BANGLA SAHIB ROAD
BANGLA SAHIB LANE
ARYA SCHOOL LANE
HANUMAN ROAD
JAI SINGH MARG
JANPATH LN
ATUL GROVE
NAYA BAZAAR
CHURCH MISSION MARG
TILAK BAZAAR
TILAK GALI
BAHADURGARH ROAD
BARA HINDU RAO ROAD
SANG TRASHAN BARA GALI
BAHUJI GALI
CHAMELIAN ROAD
MAHARISHI BALMIKI MARG
NAWAB ROAD
HOSHIAR SINGH MARG
DAULAT RAM MARG
GAUTAM ROAD
MANDIR MARG
E PARK ROAD
KHAJOORI MARG
FAIZ ROAD
DESH BANDHU GUPTA ROAD
KASABPUR ROAD
SADAR THANA MARG
NABI KARIM ROAD
ARYA NAGAR ROAD
ARAM BAGH ROAD
VALLABHACHARYA MARG
DARBARI LAL MARG
CHITRAGUPTA ROAD
TILAK GALI
RAJGURU MARG
SANG TRASHAN ROAD
GALI HALWAI WALI
RAMDWARA ROAD
RAMA KRISHNA ASHRAM LANE
NAYA BANS GALI
NAYA BANS BAZAAR
KATRA BARIYAN
KANDLE KASAN
GALI
LAL KUAN BAZAAR
MASJID FAKRULA BEG GALI
FASIL ROAD
KUCHA PANDIT
MIDDLE CIRCLE
RADIAL RD 1
RADIAL RD 2
RADIAL RD 3
RADIAL RD 4
RADIAL RD 5
RADIAL RD 6
RADIAL RD 7
A
B
C
1
2
3
4
5

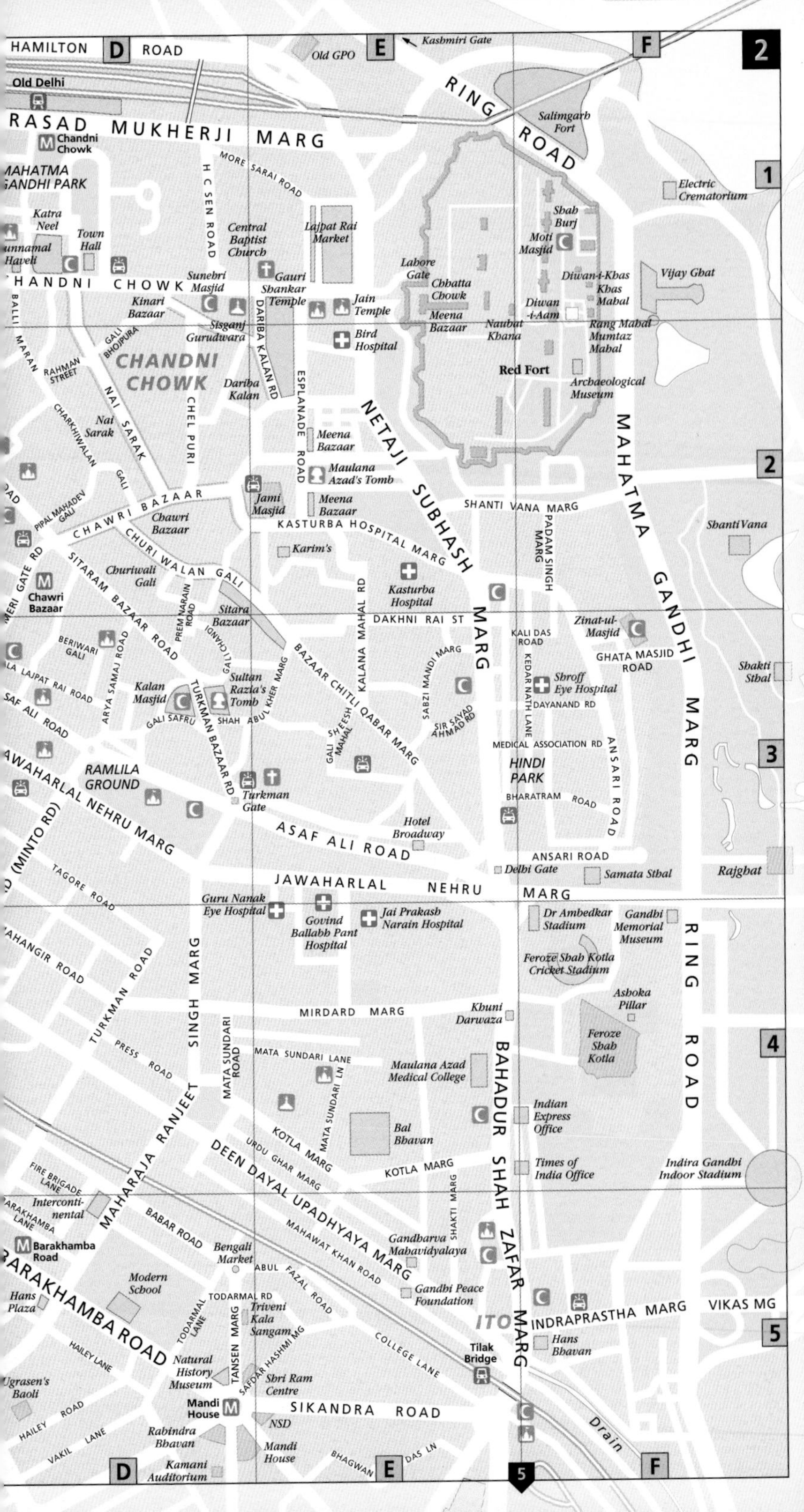

2
D
E
F
1
2
3
4
5
HAMILTON ROAD
Kashmiri Gate
Old GPO
Old Delhi
RING ROAD
Salimgarh Fort
RASAD MUKHERJI MARG
Chandni Chowk
MAHATMA GANDHI PARK
MORE SARAI ROAD
H C SEN ROAD
Electric Crematorium
Katra Neel
Town Hall
Central Baptist Church
Lajpat Rai Market
Shah Burj
Moti Masjid
Chunnamal Haveli
Lahore Gate
Gauri Shankar Temple
Chhatta Chowk
Diwan-i-Khas
Khas Mahal
Vijay Ghat
CHANDNI CHOWK
Sunehri Masjid
Kinari Bazaar
Jain Temple
Diwan -i-Aam
Meena Bazaar
Naubat Khana
Rang Mahal
Mumtaz Mahal
Sisganj Gurudwara
DARIBA KALAN RD
Bird Hospital
BALLI MARAN
GALI BHOJPURA
CHANDNI CHOWK
RAHMAN STREET
Red Fort
ESPLANADE ROAD
Archaeological Museum
Dariba Kalan
NAI SARAK
CHEL PURI
Nai Sarak
NETAJI SUBHASH MARG
MAHATMA GANDHI MARG
CHARKHIWALAN
Meena Bazaar
Maulana Azad's Tomb
GALI
Jami Masjid
Meena Bazaar
SHANTI VANA MARG
PIPAL MAHADEV GALI
CHAWRI BAZAAR
Chawri Bazaar
PADAM SINGH MARG
KASTURBA HOSPITAL MARG
Shanti Vana
CHURI WALAN GALI
Karim's
SITARAM BAZAAR ROAD
Churiwali Gali
Kasturba Hospital
Chawri Bazaar
PREM NARAIN ROAD
Sitara Bazaar
DAKHNI RAI ST
KALANA MAHAL RD
Zinat-ul-Masjid
KALI DAS ROAD
GHATA MASJID ROAD
BERIWARI GALI
ARYA SAMAJ ROAD
GALI CHANDI
BAZAAR CHITLI QABAR MARG
SABZI MANDI MARG
Shakti Sthal
LAJPAT RAI ROAD
Sultan Razia's Tomb
ABUL KHER MARG
KEDAR NATH LANE
Shroff Eye Hospital
Kalan Masjid
DAYANAND RD
ASAF ALI ROAD
GALI SAFRU
SHAH
TURKMAN BAZAAR RD
GALI SHEESH MAHAL
SIR SAYAD AHMAD RD
MEDICAL ASSOCIATION RD
ANSARI ROAD
HINDI PARK
RAMLILA GROUND
Turkman Gate
BHARATRAM ROAD
JAWAHARLAL NEHRU MARG
Hotel Broadway
ASAF ALI ROAD
ANSARI ROAD
(MINTO RD)
Delhi Gate
Samata Sthal
Rajghat
TAGORE ROAD
JAWAHARLAL NEHRU MARG
Guru Nanak Eye Hospital
Jai Prakash Narain Hospital
Dr Ambedkar Stadium
Gandhi Memorial Museum
Govind Ballabh Pant Hospital
RING ROAD
JAHANGIR ROAD
Feroze Shah Kotla Cricket Stadium
TURKMAN ROAD
Ashoka Pillar
MIRDARD MARG
Khuni Darwaza
MAHARAJA RANJEET SINGH MARG
PRESS ROAD
MATA SUNDARI ROAD
MATA SUNDARI LANE
Maulana Azad Medical College
Feroze Shah Kotla
BAHADUR SHAH ZAFAR MARG
MATA SUNDARI LN
Indian Express Office
Bal Bhavan
KOTLA MARG
DEEN DAYAL UPADHYAYA MARG
URDU GHAR MARG
KOTLA MARG
Times of India Office
Indira Gandhi Indoor Stadium
FIRE BRIGADE LANE
Interconti-nental
SHAKTI MARG
BARAKHAMBA LANE
BABAR ROAD
MAHAWAT KHAN ROAD
Gandharva Mahavidyalaya
Barakhamba Road
Bengali Market
ABUL FAZAL ROAD
BARAKHAMBA ROAD
Modern School
Gandhi Peace Foundation
Hans Plaza
TODARMAL RD
TODARMAL LANE
Triveni Kala Sangam
ITO
INDRAPRASTHA MARG
VIKAS MG
SAFDAR HASHMI MG
COLLEGE LANE
Hans Bhavan
TANSEN MARG
Natural History Museum
Tilak Bridge
HAILEY LANE
Shri Ram Centre
Ugrasen's Baoli
Mandi House
SIKANDRA ROAD
Drain
HAILEY ROAD
NSD
VAKIL LANE
Rabindra Bhavan
Mandi House
BHAGWAN DAS LN
Kamani Auditorium
5

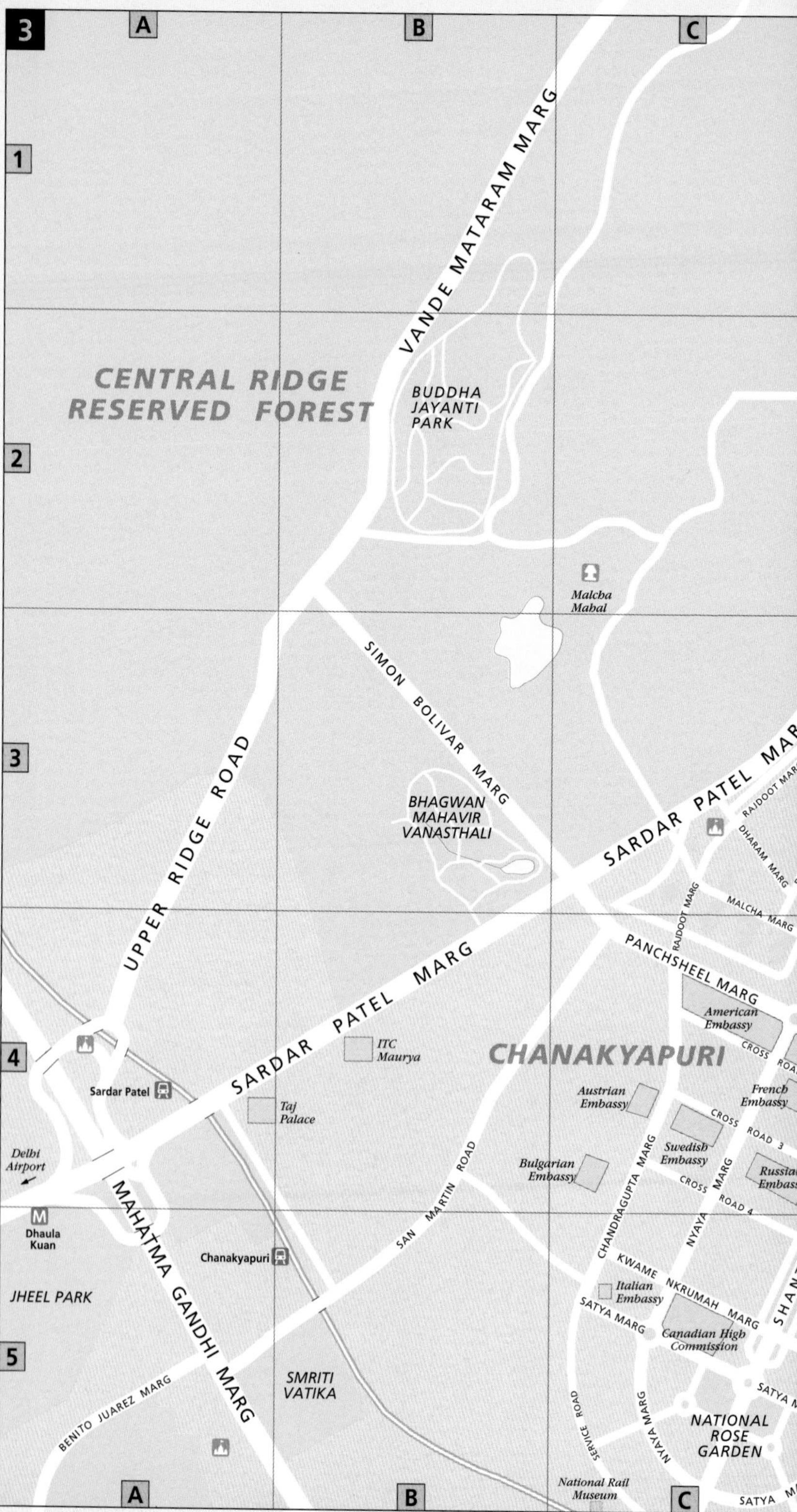

3
A
B
C
1
2
3
4
5
VANDE MATARAM MARG
CENTRAL RIDGE RESERVED FOREST
BUDDHA JAYANTI PARK
Malcha Mahal
SIMON BOLIVAR MARG
UPPER RIDGE ROAD
BHAGWAN MAHAVIR VANASTHALI
SARDAR PATEL MARG
RAJDOOT MARG
DHARAM MARG
MALCHA MARG
PANCHSHEEL MARG
American Embassy
CROSS ROAD
CHANAKYAPURI
ITC Maurya
Taj Palace
Sardar Patel
Delhi Airport
Austrian Embassy
French Embassy
CROSS ROAD 3
Swedish Embassy
Bulgarian Embassy
Russian Embassy
CROSS ROAD 4
SAN MARTIN ROAD
CHANDRAGUPTA MARG
NYAYA MARG
Dhaula Kuan
MAHATMA GANDHI MARG
Chanakyapuri
JHEEL PARK
KWAME NKRUMAH MARG
Italian Embassy
SATYA MARG
Canadian High Commission
SHANTI
BENITO JUAREZ MARG
SMRITI VATIKA
SERVICE ROAD
NATIONAL ROSE GARDEN
National Rail Museum

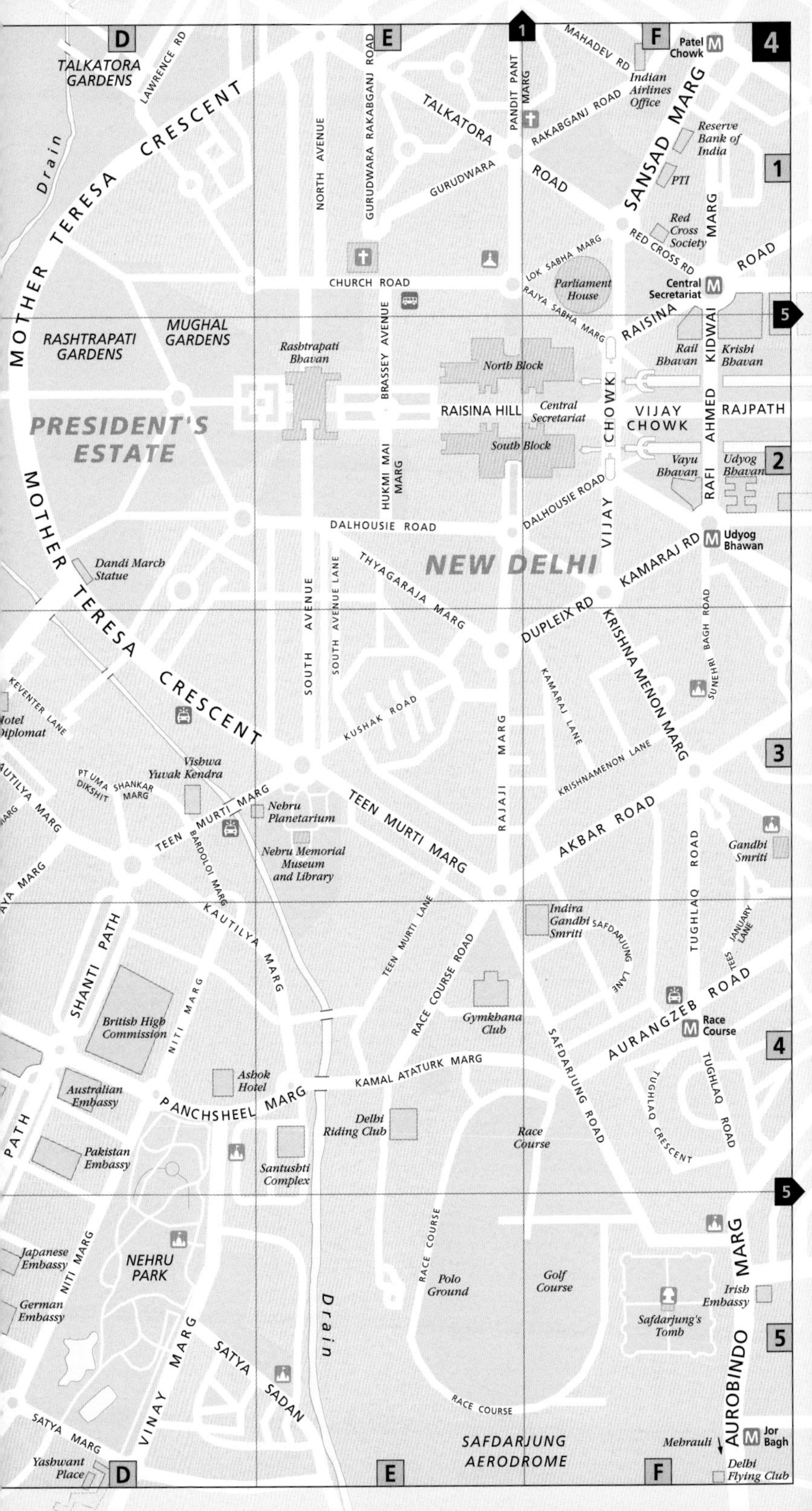

TALKATORA GARDENS
LAWRENCE RD
Drain
MOTHER TERESA CRESCENT
NORTH AVENUE
GURUDWARA RAKABGANJ ROAD
TALKATORA ROAD
PANDIT PANT MARG
RAKABGANJ ROAD
GURUDWARA
MAHADEV RD
Patel Chowk
Indian Airlines Office
SANSAD MARG
Reserve Bank of India
PTI
Red Cross Society
RED CROSS RD
LOK SABHA MARG
Parliament House
CHURCH ROAD
Central Secretariat
RAJYA SABHA MARG
RAISINA ROAD
RASHTRAPATI GARDENS
MUGHAL GARDENS
Rashtrapati Bhavan
BRASSEY AVENUE
North Block
Rail Bhavan
Krishi Bhavan
PRESIDENT'S ESTATE
RAISINA HILL
Central Secretariat
VIJAY CHOWK
RAJPATH
RAFI AHMED KIDWAI MARG
South Block
Vayu Bhavan
Udyog Bhavan
HUKMI MAI MARG
DALHOUSIE ROAD
Udyog Bhawan
NEW DELHI
KAMARAJ RD
Dandi March Statue
THYAGARAJA MARG
SOUTH AVENUE
SOUTH AVENUE LANE
DUPLEIX RD
KRISHNA MENON MARG
SUNEHRI BAGH ROAD
KAMARAJ LANE
KEVENTER LANE
Hotel Diplomat
KUSHAK ROAD
RAJAJI MARG
KRISHNAMENON LANE
Vishwa Yuvak Kendra
PT UMA SHANKAR DIKSHIT MARG
TEEN MURTI MARG
Nehru Planetarium
AKBAR ROAD
KAUTILYA MARG
BARDOLOI MARG
Nehru Memorial Museum and Library
Gandhi Smriti
Indira Gandhi Smriti
SAFDARJUNG LANE
TEEN MURTI LANE
TUGHLAQ ROAD
JANUARY LANE
TEES
SHANTI PATH
NITI MARG
RACE COURSE ROAD
AURANGZEB ROAD
British High Commission
Gymkhana Club
Race Course
SAFDARJUNG ROAD
KAMAL ATATURK MARG
Ashok Hotel
Australian Embassy
PANCHSHEEL MARG
Delhi Riding Club
Race Course
TUGHLAQ CRESCENT
TUGHLAQ ROAD
Pakistan Embassy
Santushti Complex
PATH
RACE COURSE
Japanese Embassy
NEHRU PARK
Polo Ground
Golf Course
AUROBINDO MARG
Irish Embassy
German Embassy
Safdarjung's Tomb
VINAY MARG
SATYA SADAN
Drain
RACE COURSE
SATYA MARG
SAFDARJUNG AERODROME
Mehrauli
Jor Bagh
Yashwant Place
Delhi Flying Club
D
E
F
1
2
3
4
5

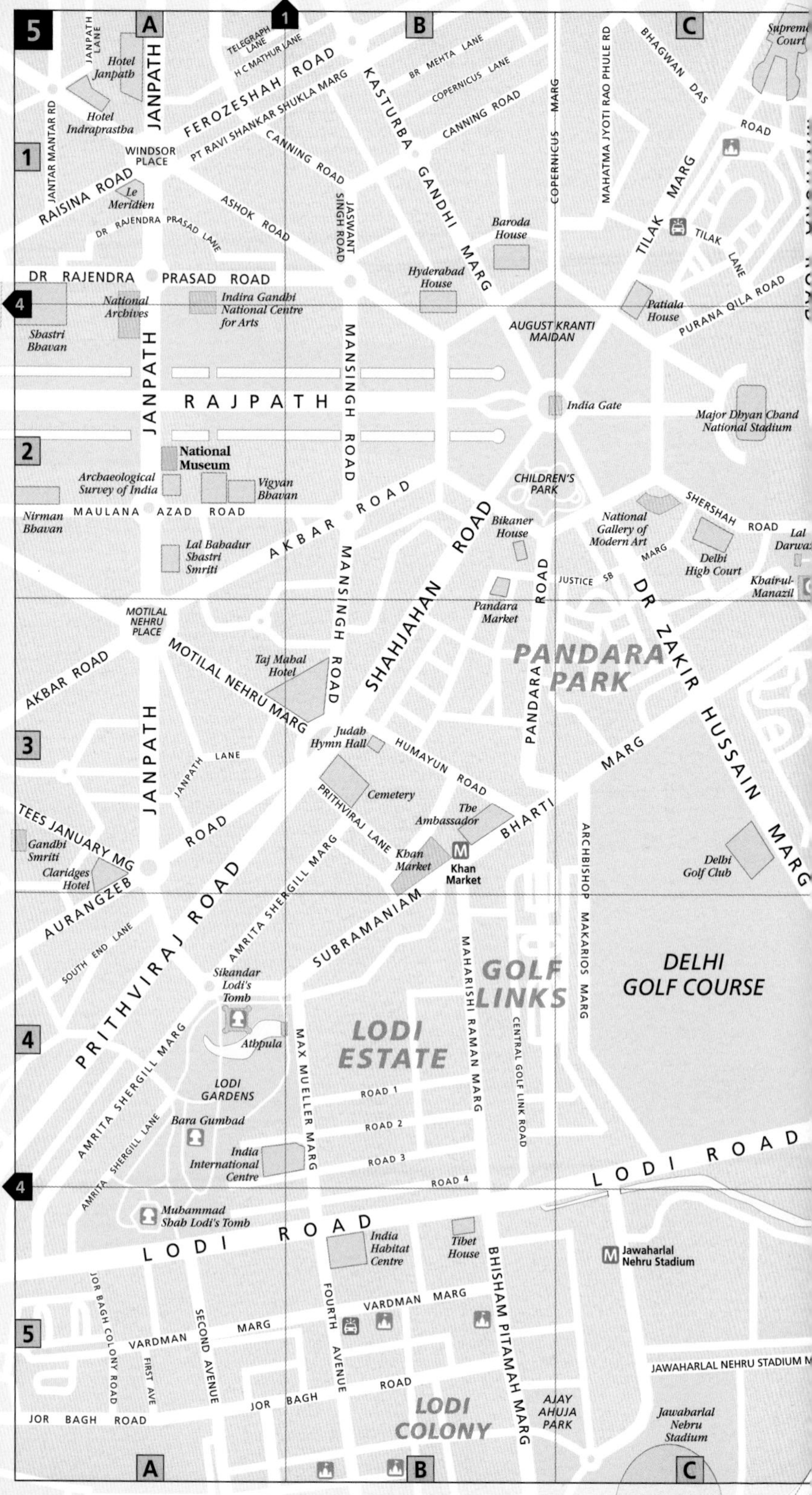

5
Hotel Janpath
Hotel Indraprastha
Janpath
Ferozeshah Road
Kasturba Gandhi Marg
Windsor Place
Raisina Road
Le Meridien
Dr Rajendra Prasad Road
National Archives
Shastri Bhavan
Indira Gandhi National Centre for Arts
Hyderabad House
Baroda House
Patiala House
August Kranti Maidan
India Gate
Major Dhyan Chand National Stadium
Rajpath
Mansingh Road
National Museum
Archaeological Survey of India
Vigyan Bhavan
Nirman Bhavan
Maulana Azad Road
Akbar Road
Lal Bahadur Shastri Smriti
Children's Park
Bikaner House
National Gallery of Modern Art
Delhi High Court
Supreme Court
Pandara Market
Pandara Park
Motilal Nehru Place
Motilal Nehru Marg
Taj Mahal Hotel
Shahjahan Road
Dr Zakir Hussain Marg
Judah Hymn Hall
Humayun Road
Cemetery
The Ambassador
Khan Market
Bharti Marg
Gandhi Smriti
Claridges Hotel
Aurangzeb Road
Prithviraj Road
Subramaniam Bharti Marg
Delhi Golf Club
Golf Links
Delhi Golf Course
Sikandar Lodi's Tomb
Athpula
Lodi Gardens
Lodi Estate
Bara Gumbad
India International Centre
Muhammad Shah Lodi's Tomb
Lodi Road
India Habitat Centre
Tibet House
Jawaharlal Nehru Stadium
Jor Bagh Road
Lodi Colony
Ajay Ahuja Park

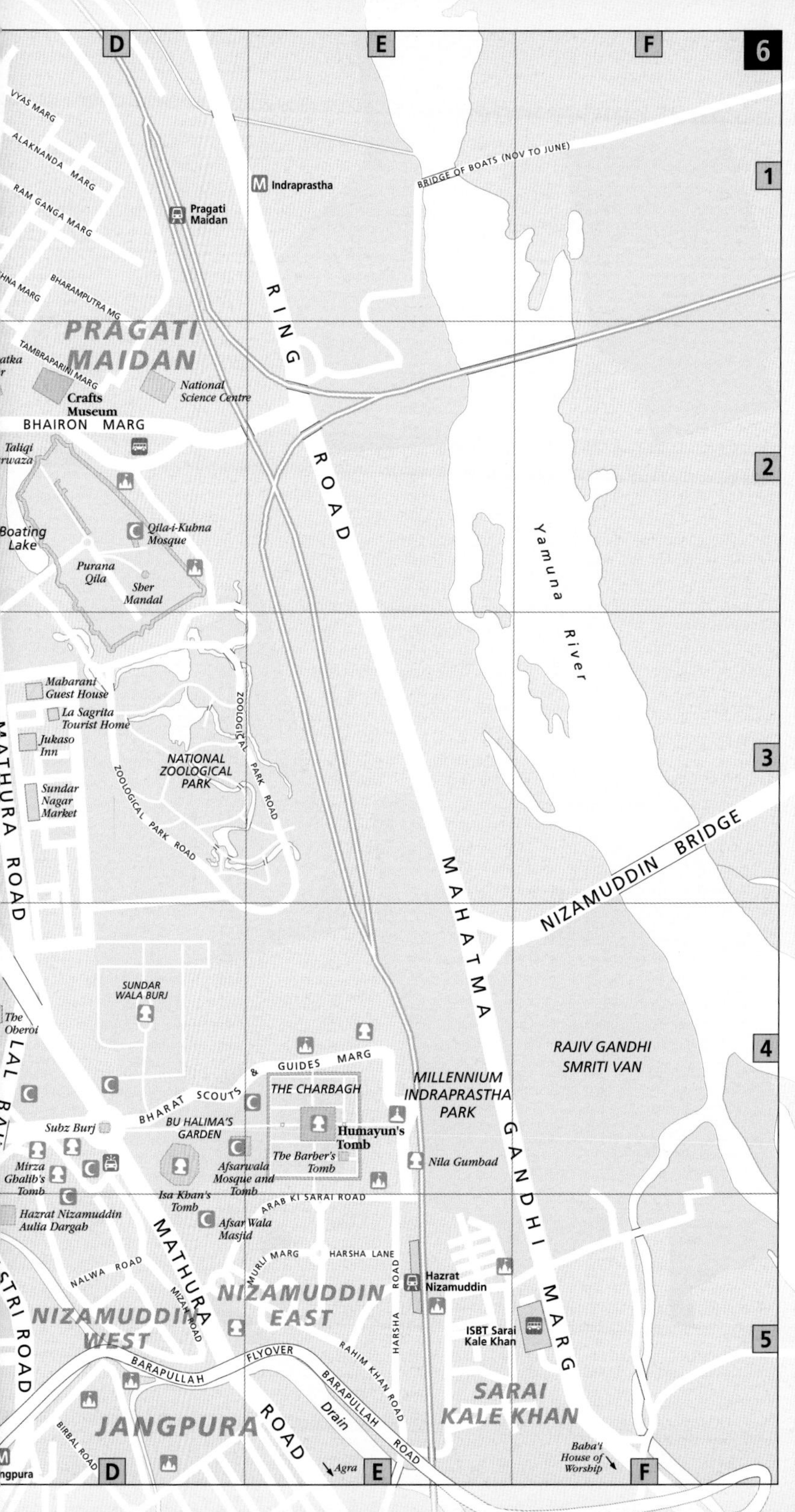

D
E
F
6
1
2
3
4
5
VYAS MARG
ALAKNANDA MARG
RAM GANGA MARG
BHARAMPUTRA MG
TAMBRAPARINI MARG
BRIDGE OF BOATS (NOV TO JUNE)
Indraprastha
Pragati Maidan
PRAGATI MAIDAN
National Science Centre
Crafts Museum
BHAIRON MARG
RING ROAD
Qila-i-Kubna Mosque
Boating Lake
Purana Qila
Sher Mandal
Yamuna River
Maharani Guest House
La Sagrita Tourist Home
Jukaso Inn
Sundar Nagar Market
MATHURA ROAD
NATIONAL ZOOLOGICAL PARK
ZOOLOGICAL PARK ROAD
NIZAMUDDIN BRIDGE
MAHATMA GANDHI MARG
SUNDAR WALA BURJ
The Oberoi
RAJIV GANDHI SMRITI VAN
BHARAT SCOUTS & GUIDES MARG
THE CHARBAGH
MILLENNIUM INDRAPRASTHA PARK
Subz Burj
BU HALIMA'S GARDEN
Humayun's Tomb
The Barber's Tomb
Nila Gumbad
Mirza Ghalib's Tomb
Afsarwala Mosque and Tomb
Isa Khan's Tomb
ARAB KI SARAI ROAD
Hazrat Nizamuddin Aulia Dargah
Afsar Wala Masjid
MURLI MARG
HARSHA LANE
HARSHA ROAD
Hazrat Nizamuddin
NALWA ROAD
MIZAH ROAD
NIZAMUDDIN EAST
NIZAMUDDIN WEST
ISBT Sarai Kale Khan
BARAPULLAH FLYOVER
RAHIM KHAN ROAD
BARAPULLAH ROAD
Drain
SARAI KALE KHAN
JANGPURA
BIRBAL ROAD
Agra
Baba'i House of Worship

Street Finder Index

BEYOND DELHI AREA BY AREA

Beyond Delhi at a Glance

The region surrounding Delhi is bounded by the snow-capped Himalayas in the north and the ravines of the River Chambal in the south. The rich alluvial plains of the Ganges and Yamuna lie at its heart, and to the west are the Aravalli Range and Thar Desert. The Rajputs and Mughals enriched the area with architectural gems of which the finest are in and around Agra and Jaipur. Mighty fortresses, luxurious palaces, mosques, tombs and temples are what draw tourists to the Delhi, Agra and Jaipur region. Away from the cities are wildlife sanctuaries, and to the north are rivers, ideal for white-water rafting and adventure sports.

Alwar *(see pp210–11)*, a former princely state, is dominated by a large hilltop fort, at the base of which lie elegant palaces, cenotaphs and gardens. Alwar is also a convenient base to explore forgotten forts and cities in and around the Sariska National Park.

Ajmer *(see pp222–3)* is best known for the shrine of the Sufi saint Khwaja Moinuddin Chishti and the ancient and stately Adhai Din ka Jhopra. The pilgrim city of Pushkar, where the annual camel fair is held, is a short distance away.

Hisar

Sikar

Alwar

Jaipur

JAIPUR AND ENVIRONS
(See pp182–229)

Ajmer

Tonk

0 kilometres 100

0 miles 50

Jaipur *(see pp186–203)*, was built by Sawai Jai Singh II in the early 1700s. In 1949 it became the capital of Rajasthan. A popular tourist destination, it is visited for its historic palaces, observatory, hilltop forts, palace-hotels and tempting markets.

◀ Panoramic view of the city from Nahargarh Fort, Jaipur

Haridwar *(see p148)*, one of North India's holiest cities, stands on the banks of the Ganges as it descends to the plains. The Kumbh Mela is held here every 12 years.

Dehra Dun

Haridwar

Roorkee

nipat

NORTH OF DELHI

(See pp140–49)

DELHI

Roorkee *(see p147)*, a small town on the way to Haridwar, lies in the heart of a rich horticultural belt. Its famous Engineering College, established in 1847, is housed in an elegant colonial building.

Mathura

Agra

Agra *(see pp154–63)*, the imperial Mughal capital during the 16th and 17th centuries, is best known for the Taj Mahal, built by Shah Jahan for his favourite wife, Mumtaz Mahal. Other Mughal monuments can be seen within and outside the city.

Gwalior

AGRA AND AROUND

(See pp150–81)

Jhansi

Orchha

Orchha *(see pp180–81)*, the early capital of the Bundela kings, is picturesquely situated on the banks of the Betwa. Its temples, palaces and cenotaphs are breathtaking.

NORTH OF DELHI

Lying between the Ganges and Yamuna rivers, this agriculturally prosperous region is held to be the cradle of Indian civilization. Its historical and mythological past extends from the ancient brick cities of the Indus Valley and the early Aryan settlements to the later Muslim and European forts and cities. Each culture has enriched the region and contributed to its remarkable diversity.

This vast plain, from about the second millennium on, has remained one of India's most densely populated areas. As time went on, ancient fortified city states developed into medieval walled towns which contained prosperous agricultural lands and flourishing markets. Many of these are today important industrial centres. Since the area has had such a diverse history, its architectural remains are an eclectic mixture of styles so that ancient brick structures, Mughal monuments and colonial churches rub shoulders with modern factories.

To the north are the pilgrim towns of Haridwar and Rishikesh, where the Ganges, India's most holy river, enters the plains. With the splendid backdrop of the Shivalik Hills, this area, rich in flora and fauna, offers exciting places for adventure sports such as white-water rafting.

To most Indians, however, this is the sacred territory of the *Mahabharata* *(see p145)*, where gods and epic heroes fought a legendary battle at Kurukshetra and where Krishna *(see pp166–7)* expounded the famous *Bhagavad Gita*. The development of ideas that led to the later compilation of the *Vedas* and *Upanishads*, the bedrock of Hindu philosophy and ethics, are believed to have taken place here as well. Panipat, the site of three decisive battles that changed the history of North India, lies close by.

To the northeast and northwest lie the now forgotten towns of Narnaul, Hansi and Sardhana, associated with the medieval Tughlaq and Sur dynasties, and European freebooters and nabobs such as Skinner, Reinhardt and his wife, Begum Samroo. Meerut, the epicentre of the Indian Mutiny, is now a busy market and trading centre.

Roadside stalls selling religious paraphernalia, a common sight outside temples

◀ Crowds gather for a ritual bath in the Ganges, Haridwar

Exploring North of Delhi

Outside of Delhi, the landscape changes dramatically. The way to Haridwar, at the foothills of the Himalayas, is lined with mango and litchi orchards. The canal network around Roorkee sustains an agriculturally prosperous rural region. On the other hand, the busy Grand Trunk Road that leads beyond Panipat and Kurukshetra all the way to the Punjab, has always been an important artery of trade and commerce. Rolling fields of paddy and wheat are dotted with electricity pylons that service this important industrial belt. Yet the odd *kos minar* (milestone pillar) and medieval fort recall another age when this was the scene of important battles and the road to the north.

St Andrew's Church at Roorkee

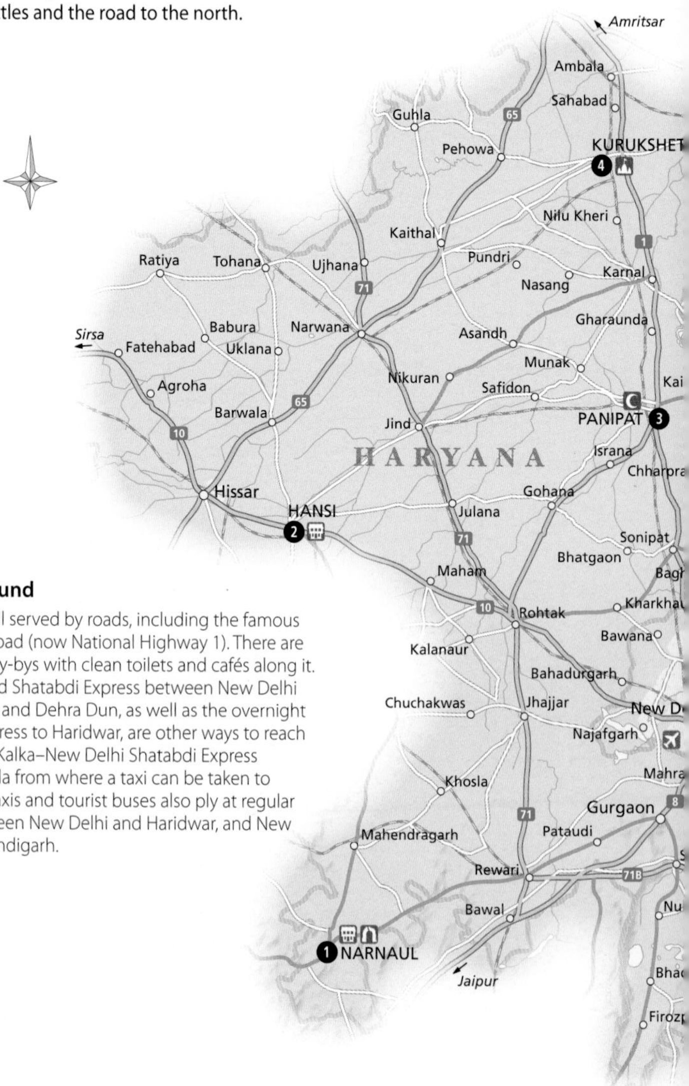

Amritsar
Ambala
Sahabad
Guhla
65
Pehowa
KURUKSHET
4
Nilu Kheri
Kaithal
1
Ratiya
Tohana
Ujhana
Pundri
Nasang
Karnal
71
Gharaunda
Sirsa
Fatehabad
Babura
Uklana
Narwana
Asandh
Munak
Agroha
Nikuran
Safidon
Kai
65
Barwala
PANIPAT 3
10
Jind
HARYANA
Israna
Chharpra
Hissar
Gohana
HANSI
2
Julana
Sonipat
71
Bhatgaon
Maham
Bagh
10
Rohtak
Kharkha
Bawana
Kalanaur
Bahadurgarh
Chuchakwas
Jhajjar
New D
Najafgarh
Khosla
Mahra
8
71
Gurgaon
Pataudi
Mahendragarh
Rewari
71B
Nu
Bawal
1 NARNAUL
Jaipur
Bha
Firozp

Getting Around

This area is well served by roads, including the famous Grand Trunk Road (now National Highway 1). There are good tourist lay-bys with clean toilets and cafés along it. The high-speed Shatabdi Express between New Delhi railway station and Dehra Dun, as well as the overnight Mussoorie Express to Haridwar, are other ways to reach Haridwar. The Kalka–New Delhi Shatabdi Express stops at Ambala from where a taxi can be taken to Kurukshetra. Taxis and tourist buses also ply at regular intervals between New Delhi and Haridwar, and New Delhi and Chandigarh.

Key

- Highway
- Major road
- Minor road
- Railroad
- State border

For keys to symbols *see back flap*

Grazing sheep tended by Gujjar tribesmen near Panipat

0 kilometres 50

0 miles 25

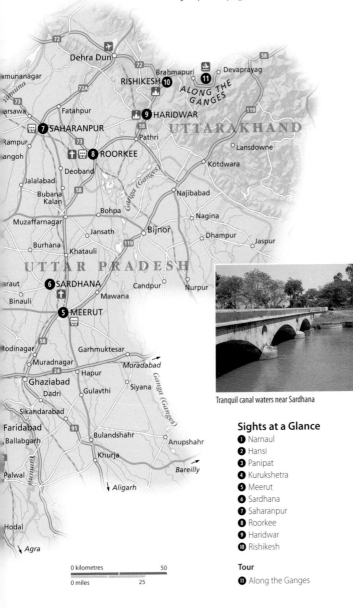

Tranquil canal waters near Sardhana

Sights at a Glance

1. Narnaul
2. Hansi
3. Panipat
4. Kurukshetra
5. Meerut
6. Sardhana
7. Saharanpur
8. Roorkee
9. Haridwar
10. Rishikesh

Tour

11. Along the Ganges

❶ Narnaul

Narnaul district. 132 km (82 miles) SW of Delhi. **Road map** C3.

Believed to have been founded by the Pandava Sahdev, the town of Narnaul is historically significant as the birthplace of the great ruler Sher Shah Sur *(see p88)* whose grandfather, Ibrahim Shah Sur, is buried here in a magnificent Afghan-style mausoleum. The Jal Mahal ("water palace"), situated in what was once an artificial lake built by Shah Quli Khan in 1591, is a Mughal-style structure; so is the Birbal ka Chatta, with its projecting balconies and pavilions. In the town's old section are some magnificent, but neglected, *havelis* with murals in the Shekhawati style *(see p216)*.

❷ Hansi

Hisar district. 137 km (85 miles) NW of Delhi. **Road map** C2.

This nondescript town is associated with two soldiers of fortune. At the end of the 18th century, the Irish adventurer, George Thomas, repaired the city's defensive wall, remodelled the ruined fort and made it his headquarters. Some 30 years later, Colonel James Skinner *(see p105)* of Skinner's Horse, built a large mansion (now derelict) here where he spent his last years. The town is scattered with monuments dating to the 12th century, including the shrine called Char Qutbs, a Sufi *dargah* of the Chishtiya order, and the 19th-century tomb of Begum Skinner, one of Skinner's 12 Indian wives.

Environs

Hissar, 26 km (16 miles) west of Hansi, was the favourite retreat of Feroze Shah Tughlaq *(see p101)*. He built palaces and forts here, now in ruins. An oddity from that time is an edifice called the Jahaz, so named as it resembles a ship.

Qalandar Shah's *dargah* at Panipat, built 700 years ago

❸ Panipat

Panipat district. 85 km (53 miles) N of Delhi on NH1. **Road map** C2. Urs of Qalander Shah (Jan–Feb).

On the flat, dusty plains of Panipat, three decisive battles were fought that changed the course of Indian history. The Mughal empire *(see pp56–7)* was established in 1526 after Babur defeated the Delhi sultan, Ibrahim Lodi, and was consolidated 30 years later when his grandson Akbar triumphed over Sher Shah's general in 1556. Finally, in 1761, the Marathas, the Mughal emperor's military arm, were routed by an Afghan invader, Ahmad Shah Abdali, paving the way for the British *(see pp58–9)*. Today, Panipat is a busy town well known for its furnishing fabrics and carpets. The 700-year-old Sufi *dargah* of Qalandar Shah is situated here. On its outskirts are *kos minars* (milestones) indicating that Panipat was part of the Grand Trunk Road *(see p164)*.

Memorial of the Third Battle of Panipat

Sacred tank on the Sannahit Sarovar in Kurukshetra

❹ Kurukshetra

Kurukshetra district.175 km (109 miles) N of Delhi on NH1. **Road map** C1. Gita Jayanti (Nov–Dec). Krishna Museum: **Tel** (017) 4429 1288. **Open** 10am–5pm daily.

Linked with 360 legendary sites of the *Mahabharata*, this strategic plain was ruled by the Kuru tribe in the later Vedic period. The 18-day epic battle between the Pandavas and Kauravas was fought on this "field of righteousness". The town of Kurukshetra is also the start of a pilgrimage circuit of 128 km (80 miles) undertaken during the solar eclipse and at Gita Jayanti in November or December, when lighted clay lamps are set afloat on the sacred waters of the tanks during a ceremony called the *deepdan*.

The main bathing tanks are the Brahmasar, with a small temple on an island, and the smaller, more sacred Sannahit Sarovar, lined with ghats and temples. Hindus believe that a dip here during the solar eclipse is very sacred for it is when the twin planets, the malefic Rahu and Ketu, try to swallow the sun to spread terror in the world. However, the sun defeats their machinations, so, after a holy dip, pilgrims donate food equal to their body weight as thanks-giving. The last solar eclipse of the 20th century occurred in August 1999, and the first of the new millennium, was on 31 May 2003. The latest took place on 21 May 2012.

The **Krishna Museum** and Gita Research Centre has a large collection that brings out the pervasiveness of the Krishna cult in Indian art.

The Mahabharata

Considered an inexhaustible fund of knowledge and ideas, the *Mahabharata* is about an eponymous battle between the Pandavas and Kauravas. Said to be first narrated by a sage, Ved Vyas, the epic was written down only between the 6th and 7th centuries BC. Eight times the length of the *Iliad* and *Odyssey* put together, the subtle moral subtext of its legends and stories codifies notions of theology and statecraft that inspired rulers down the ages.

The *Bhagavad Gita,* a later insertion of 700 stanzas, records the sermon that was given by the divine charioteer, Lord Krishna, to the Pandava prince Arjuna on the epic battlefield of Kurukshetra. It extols the virtues of performing one's moral duty without seeking reward, and condones the use of violence against injustice. Its philosophy of righteous living and the importance of one's *dharma* (duty, calling) continues to guide the lives of millions of Indians. In the 1990s, a television serial on the *Mahabharata* became so popular that life came to a virtual standstill when it was transmitted.

The battle is an allegory for the war between right and wrong. The epic's didactic tone made it an authoritative manual on moral rules and righteous conduct.

Folk art often uses the epic as a theme. This *patachitra* from Eastern India is used as a visual aid by minstrels, while *ganjifa* playing cards similarly use Arjuna as the icon for a king.

Krishna is seen as the divine charioteer who steers the mind (chariot) and five senses (the five horses that pull Arjuna's chariot) to follow the right path through life.

The Battle of the Mahabharata at Kurukshetra

The kingdom of Hastinapur and Queen Draupadi were lost by the five Pandavas when their evil cousins, the Kauravas, tricked them in a game of dice. After a long exile, the Pandavas, though outnumbered by the hundred Kauravas, were led by Krishna to victory in the Battle of the Mahabharata.

Arjuna, the skilled archer, shoots the eye of a fish reflected in water. This act won him the hand of Draupadi and the envy of the Kaurava princes.

Lord Krishna gives the sermon of the *Gita* to Arjuna on the battlefield of Kurukshetra. As the charioteer of the Pandavas in the war, this god plays a crucial role in the epic.

A cantonment house in Meerut

❺ Meerut

Meerut district. 72 km (44 miles) NE of Delhi on NH24. **Road map** D2. 1,300,000. Mon. Nauchandi Mela (Mar).

An eminent commercial and administrative town, Meerut is better known as the place where the sepoys first mutinied on 10 May 1857, igniting the Indian Mutiny *(see pp58–9)*. Today, this bustling town swirls around architectural monuments dating to the 11th and 12th centuries, such as the Jami Masjid (1019), Salar Masa-ud Ghazi's *maqbara* (1194), the tomb of Makhdum Shah Wilayat and the *maqbara* of Shah Pir (1620). Meerut's colonial heritage is, however, preserved in its manicured cantonment to the north of the old city. This is one of the country's best-planned cantonments with a broad, tree-lined mall or main road and colonial bungalows *(see p31)* with sprawling gardens along its length. The cantonment's Neo-Classical St John's Church (1822), where British residents had gathered for refuge when the revolt broke out, was the scene of a bloody massacre that fateful May day. Memorial tablets with their names and histories lie inside. The old Central Jail, associated with the worst excesses of the Mutiny and its aftermath, is now converted into a public park.

❻ Sardhana

Meerut district. 85 km (57 miles) NE of Delhi. **Road map** D2. Feast of Our Lady of Graces (2nd Sun of Nov). (to Cathedral).

Surrounded by a network of canals, Sardhana has a history inextricably linked with two flamboyant European adventurers, Walter Reinhardt and George Thomas, who had come to India to seek their fortunes in the mid-18th century *(see pp58–9)*.

Reinhardt deserted the French army in 1750 and organized a band of fierce, well-trained mercenaries who fought for various local chiefs. Called "Sombre" or "Samroo" for his swarthy complexion, he settled in Sardhana on land gifted by Najaf Khan, a nobleman of Delhi. Reinhardt was succeeded by his wife, Begum Samroo, a formidable and wily lady who converted to Catholicism in 1781. She was known throughout the region as the only Roman Catholic "queen" in India, as she led her husband's troops until her death in 1836. Her military skills, matched by her piety and philanthropy, made her popular with the locals, who still respect her memory.

Begum Samroo's palace, the grand Dilkusha Kothi, with its impressive hallway, is situated within a garden of almost 75 acres (30 ha). It now houses a charity school and orphanage. The Cathedral nearby has a white marble altar inlaid with semi-precious stones and a Carrara marble monument to the Begum sculpted by Tadolini of Rome. Now raised to the status of a basilica, this is still an important centre for Catholics. Both the palace and cathedral were built between 1822 and 1834 in a hybrid colonial style. The city is famous for its cloth industry.

The classical façade of Dilkusha Kothi at Sardhana

❼ Saharanpur

Saharanpur district.165 km (103 miles) NE of Delhi on NH24. **Road map** D1. 700,000.

Saharanpur was founded in 1340 during the reign of Muhammad-bin-Tughlaq *(see p111)*. During the Mughal period it was a popular summer resort for nobles attracted by its cool climate and plentiful game. Many of the gardens that were laid out over 200 years ago, such as the Company Bagh in the centre of town, were transformed into nurseries and botanical gardens in the 19th century, laying the foundation for the town's eventual growth into an renowned horticultural centre. Today, Saharanpur is one of North India's largest producers of luscious mangoes, while the sprawling Government Botanical Gardens, on its outskirts, is an important centre for research on the medicinal properties of plants.

Within the old city, highly skilled artisans craft items of intricately carved furniture, ornamental screens, panels and trays, brass-inlaid with traditional geometric and floral designs. Some of the finest examples of Saharanpur's woodcraft can be seen in St Thomas's Church. Also of interest are the old Jami Masjid (1530), Zabita Khan's Mosque (1779) and the old Rohilla Fort in Nawabganj.

Saharanpur's Botanical Gardens, a repository of rare plants

Stone lion at the head of the aqueduct in Roorkee

❽ Roorkee

Haridwar district. 198 km (123 miles) from Delhi on Delhi–Haridwar Rd. **Road map** D1. Roorkee Flower Show (Mar).

An illustrious university and cantonment town, this was originally a sleepy village on the banks of the River Solani. It gained significance when the Ganga Canal Workshop was set up in 1843 as part of the massive Ganga Canal Irrigation Project. This transformed the surrounding arid region into the highly productive agricultural area of today. To the north of the town is a magnificent brick aqueduct, marked with two enormous stone lions. It was considered a major engineering feat of the 19th century, and carries the water of the Ganga Canal over the River Solani. The Thomson Civil Engineering College, now the Indian Institute of Technology (IIT) Roorkee, was established in 1847 and is the country's oldest technical institution. The pleasantly sited campus, located within wooded areas, has several acclaimed research institutions. Some of the structures from the colonial period are exceptional, such as the Church of St John the Baptist (1852), with beautiful stained-glass windows. The town is also renowned for high quality replicas of 18th- and 19th-century engineering and survey equipment.

Interior of IIT Roorkee, one of India's premier engineering institutes

Mango

The mango, or *aam*, is the best-loved fruit of the country. The Mughal emperor Babur called it the "finest fruit of Hindostan." Hundreds of varieties, with exotic names and pedigrees, are available from May to July, before the monsoon arrives. While ripe mango is savoured for its sweet pulp, the raw fruit is also valued for its medicinal properties, as well as its sharp tang, and is made into pickles and chutneys eaten through the year. The popular design motif of the paisley is derived from the shape of its fruit, and mango leaves, considered auspicious, are used as buntings at festive occasions.

Langra mangoes

Pilgrims taking a dip in the holy Ganges at Haridwar

9 Haridwar

Haridwar district. 214 km (133 miles) N of Delhi. Road map: D1. 310, 500. GMVN Tourist Office, Rahi Motel (0133) 422 6430/8686. Railway Rd. Kumbh Mela (every 12 years; Feb–Mar); Ardh Kumbha Mela (every 6 years; Feb–Mar); Haridwar Festival (Oct); Dusshera (Oct–Nov).

The Ganges, India's holiest river, descends from the Himalayas to the plains at Haridwar. This gives the town such a unique status that a pilgrimage to Haridwar is every devout Hindu's dream.

Remarkably bare of ancient monuments, Haridwar's most famous "sight" and a constant point of reference is the Ganges and its numerous bathing ghats, tanks and temples. These bustling sites of ritual Hindu practices, performed by pilgrims for the salvation of their ancestors and for their own expiation, demonstrate their deep faith in the power of the river. The main ghat, Har-ki-Pauri, is named after a supposed imprint of Vishnu's feet there. Hundreds attend the daily evening *aarti* at this ghat, when leaf boats are filled with flowers, lit with lamps and set adrift on the Ganges. Further south, a ropeway connects the town to the Mansa Devi Temple across the river with a panoramic view of Haridwar. South of the town, the famous Gurukul Kangri University is renowned as a centre of Vedic knowledge, where students are taught in the traditional oral style. It also has a section displaying archaeological exhibits.

A good way to experience Haridwar's ambience, which has changed little since ancient times, is to stroll along the riverside bazaar, lined with stalls full of ritual paraphernalia – small mounds of vermilion powder, coconuts wrapped in red and gold cloth, and brass idols. The most popular items with the pilgrims, however, are the jars and canisters sold here. These are used for a vital part of Hindu worship – to carry back water from the Ganges *(Gangajal)*, which, the faithful believe, remains ever fresh.

10 Rishikesh

Haridwar district. 238 km (148 miles) N of Delhi. Road map: D1. 102,000. GMVN Tourist Office, Muni-ki-Reti (0135) 243 0799/0372. International Yoga Week (Feb).

This twin city of Haridwar, situated at the confluence of the Chandrabhaga and the Ganges, is the start of the holy Char Dham pilgrim route to the Himalayas. Muni-ki-Reti (literally "sand of the sages"), lies upstream from the Triveni Ghat and is believed to be a blessed site since ancient sages meditated here. It has several famous ashrams, such as the Sivanand, Purnanand and Shanti Kunj ashrams, which offer courses to those interested in India's ancient knowledge systems. Maharishi Mahesh Yogi, a cult figure during the 1960s, when the Beatles were his followers, also has an ashram here.

Rishikesh is a popular destination for adventure sports such as river rafting, rappelling and kayaking *(see p269)*. Eco-rafting and eco-camping are also prevalent here since the increase in environmental awareness.

Kumbh Mela

According to Hindu mythology, four drops of the immortal nectar *(amrit)* wrestled by the gods from the demons, spilled over Haridwar, Allahabad, Ujjain and Nasik. A Kumbh Mela is held once every 12 years by rotation at these venues in Magh (Feb–Mar), when the sun transits from Pisces to Aries, and when Jupiter is in the sign of Aquarius (Kumbh in Hindu astrology). Hindus believe that they can imbibe the immortal *amrit* and wash away their sins by bathing in the Ganges at this propitious time. The *mela* is regarded as the largest congregation of human beings in one place anywhere in the world, when millions come for a holy dip, and to attend the seminars, discourses and debates held in the camps of leading Hindu sages and theologians. Haridwar's last Kumbh Mela, held in 2010, attracted over ten million people. A smaller celebration, called the Ardh Kumbh (half-Kumbh), is held every six years.

Pilgrims thronging the ghats at the Kumbh Mela

⓫ River Tour Along the Ganges

From September to April, the Ganges, swollen by the monsoon rains of the upper catchment areas, becomes a torrent gushing over the rocky boulders as it hurtles out of the mountains to the plains. This is the time when a few stretches of rapids, where the flow is rough but safe, become a popular circuit for enthusiasts of white-water rafting *(see p269)*. Only organized tours, run by certified experts, are allowed. For the less adventurous, a driving tour offers a panorama of this valley of the sages whose ashrams nestle in the surrounding forests along the holy river.

The Ganges flowing serenely through a forested valley

① Kaudiyala
The starting point of the river tour, it has scenic campsites on the river bank.

② Marine Drive
This campsite is named after a Bombay promenade famous for its views.

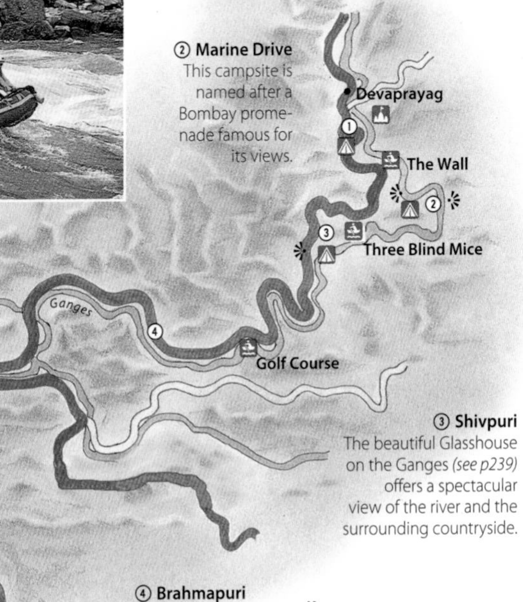

Devaprayag
The Wall
Three Blind Mice
Ganges
Golf Course

③ Shivpuri
The beautiful Glasshouse on the Ganges *(see p239)* offers a spectacular view of the river and the surrounding countryside.

④ Brahmapuri
An ashram, one of many along the Ganges, is located here.

Key
Tour route
Roads
River

⑤ Lakshman Jhula
A modern suspension bridge replaced the old rope bridge in 1929. This leads to the quieter east bank of Rishikesh where most ashrams are situated.

⑥ Rishikesh
An ancient spiritual centre, Rishikesh is serenely located on the banks of the Ganges amid lush, wooded hills.

0 kilometres 10
0 miles 5

Tips for River Rafters

Length: 36 km (22 miles).
Stopping-off points: White-water rafting can be done in leisurely stages, over two days, with a night halt at the Kaudiyala Camp. Stopover points are provided at Marine Drive, Shivpuri and Brahmapuri. However, a shorter tour of the same stretch can also be covered in one day.

AGRA AND AROUND

Agra was the imperial capital of the Mughal court during the 16th and 17th centuries, before it was shifted to Delhi. The Mughals were prolific builders and nowhere is this more evident than in the picturesque riverine region along the Yamuna which is the backdrop for its palaces, tombs, forts and gardens. Three of these, the Taj Mahal, the Agra Fort and Akbar's abandoned capital of Fatehpur Sikri, have been declared World Heritage Sites by UNESCO.

The imperial Mughal highway which still runs south along the Yamuna between Delhi and Agra is a link to the region's historical past. The rich pastoral and agricultural land around Brindavan, the supposed homeland of Krishna *(see p166)*, was the main axis of the Mughal empire. The outer fringes of this area, formed by Mathura, Bharatpur and Deeg, have wetlands that attract many rare migratory birds, such as the Siberian crane, who come each winter to the World Heritage Site of the Keoladeo Ghana National Park.

As one goes further west and south, the greens and gold of the Yamuna lands give way to the scrub and ravines along the River Chambal. This is the centre of the subcontinent: hot, dusty and vast. These awesome ravines were the preferred habitat of robbers and dacoits (armed bandits). After the decline of the Mughals, some of the more ambitious bandits declared themselves kings and built for themselves small, but powerful kingdoms with magnificent fortresses in this harsh area. Their architecture, which is a happy amalgam of traditional Hindu with Muslim building styles, can be seen in Datia, Orchha and Deeg.

Itinerant poets and musicians in this area still sing of daring kings and queens such as Laxmibai, the Rani of Jhansi. Her spirited resistance to the British forces during the Indian Mutiny of 1857 made her a popular icon during the Freedom Movement. Close by lies Gwalior. This significant princely state has a magnificent fort that goes back to the 3rd century, and splendid palaces built by its Scindia rulers.

Marble filigree screen surrounding the tombs at the Taj Mahal, Agra

◀ Red sandstone architecture of the Jahangiri Mahal, Agra Fort

Exploring Agra and Around

Agra lies in the centre of a rich and varied cultural territory. At one end of this region are the pastoral fields around the River Yamuna, and at the other, the stark and awesome ravines of the River Chambal. Between these two rivers are a number of towns, monuments and sanctuaries, making this one of the most popular travel circuits in North India. In mythology, Mathura was the sacred territory of Krishna *(see p165)* while in history, it was the centre of an influential Buddhist kingdom, and the imperial Mughal highway ran through it. Later, Jat, Rajput and Bundela kings built forts and palaces in nearby Bharatpur, Deeg, Jhansi, Datia and Orchha. Thus, this region contains some of the best examples of Indian art and architecture, while the wetlands around Bharatpur provide a natural habitat for a range of wildlife and migratory birds.

Cows near Brindavan, where they enjoy sacred status

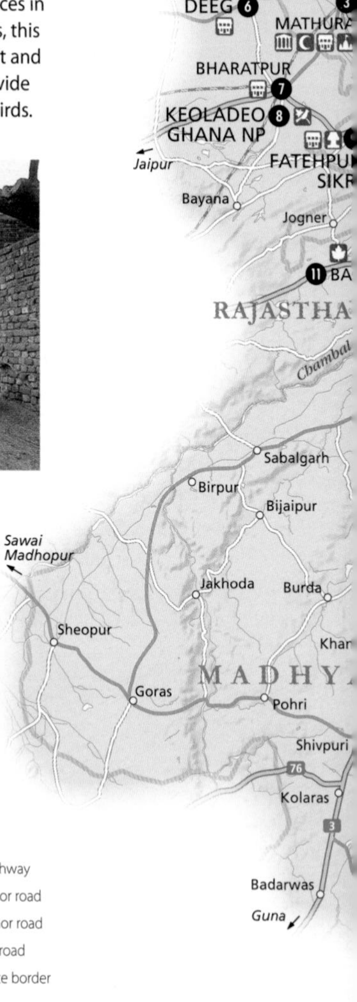

A Mughal *kos minar* on the Grand Trunk Road

Key

- Highway
- Major road
- Minor road
- Railroad
- State border

0 kilometres 50

0 miles 25

Temples and bathing ghats along the Yamuna at Mathura

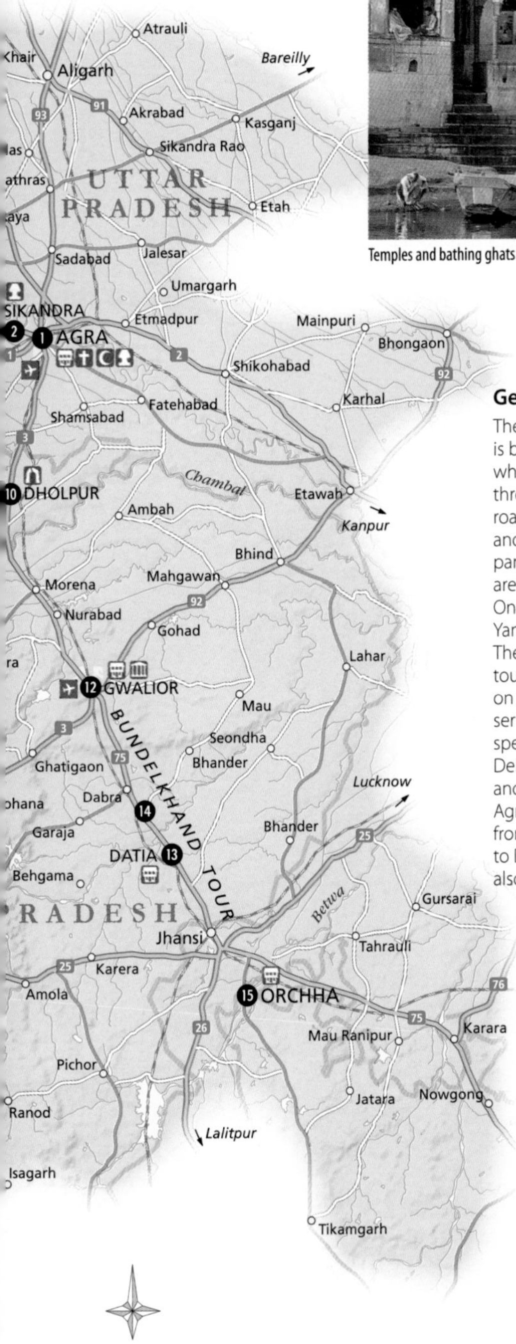

Getting Around

The best way to explore this region is by car. The National Highway (NH2) which runs from Delhi to Agra goes through Mathura. A network of smaller roads links the region beyond Mathura and Brindavan. Except in patches, particularly after the monsoon, these are generally in a good condition. Once in Mathura, a boat trip along the Yamuna is a good way to see the ghats. The Keoladeo Ghana Sanctuary provides tourists with cycle-rickshaws and guides on payment. The area is also well serviced by trains, including the high speed Shatabdi Express, which goes from Delhi to Bhopal via Gwalior and Jhansi and the Taj Express between Delhi and Agra. Several trains pass through Jhansi, from where easy car trips can be made to Datia and Orchha. Agra and Gwalior also have domestic airports.

Sights at a Glance

1 *Agra pp154–63*
2 Sikandra
3 Mathura
4 Brindavan
6 Deeg
7 Bharatpur
8 *Keoladeo Ghana National Park pp172–3*
9 *Fatehpur Sikri pp174–7*
10 Dholpur
11 Bari
12 Gwalior
13 Datia
15 *Orchha pp180–81*

Tours

5 Brajbhumi
14 Bundelkhand

For keys to symbols *see back flap*

❶ Agra

Agra was the imperial Mughal capital during the 16th and 17th centuries. It was from here that the emperors Akbar, Jahangir and Shah Jahan governed their vast empire. The city flourished under their patronage, attracting artisans from Persia and Central Asia, and also from other parts of India, who built luxurious forts, mausoleums and gardens. Agra's strategic location on the banks of the Yamuna as well as on the Grand Trunk Road linking eastern India with the west, made it a trading station, visited by merchants and travellers from all over the world. With the decline of the Mughals, Agra was captured by the Jats, the Marathas, and finally the British.

Entrance to the beautiful Jahangir Mahal, built during the reign of Akabr

Agra Fort

Open 6am–6pm daily.

Situated on the west bank of the Yamuna, Agra Fort was built by Akbar between 1565 and 1573. Its imposing red sandstone ramparts form a crescent along the riverfront, and encompass an enormous complex of courtly buildings, ranging in style from the early eclecticism of Akbar to the sublime elegance of Shah Jahan. The barracks to the north are 19th-century British additions. A deep moat, once filled with water from the Yamuna, surrounds the fort.

The impressive **Amar Singh Gate** to the south leads into the fort. To its right is the so-called **Jahangir Mahal**, the only major palace in the fort that dates from Akbar's reign. This complex arrangement of halls, courtyards and galleries with dungeons below was the *zenana* or the main harem building. In front of Jahangir Mahal is a large marble pool which, as legend says, in Nur Jahan's time used to be filled with thousands of rose petals so that the empress could bathe in its scented waters.

Along the riverfront are the **Khas Mahal**, an elegant marble hall with an exuberantly painted ceiling, characteristic of Shah Jahan's style of architecture, and two golden pavilions with typical *bangaldar* roofs *(see p311)*. These pavilions were supposedly associated with the princesses Jahanara and Roshanara, and have narrow niches where jewels could be concealed. Facing them is **Anguri Bagh** ("grape garden") with its lily-pools and candle-niches. The **Sheesh Mahal** and royal baths are to the northeast near the gloriously inlaid **Musamman Burj**, the double-storeyed octagonal tower with clear views of the Taj. This was where Shah Jahan, imprisoned by his son Aurangzeb, spent the last years of his life. **Mina Masjid** ("gem mosque"), probably the smallest in the world and the emperor's private mosque, is nearby.

Musamman Burj

To the side of Musamman Burj is the **Diwan-i-Khas**, a lavishly decorated open hall where the emperor met his court. Two thrones, in white marble and black slate, were placed on the terrace for the emperor to watch elephant fights below. Opposite is the **Machchhi Bhavan** ("fish house"), once a magnificent water palace. To its west is the **Diwan-i-Aam**, an arcaded hall within a large courtyard. Its throne-alcove of inlaid marble provided a sumptuous setting for the fabled Peacock Throne. To the northwest is the graceful **Nagina Masjid** ("jewel mosque") built by Shah Jahan for his harem, and the **Moti Masjid** ("pearl mosque").

Beyond is the **Meena Bazaar**, the fort's shopping centre, overlooked by a fine marble balcony where, according to legend, the lovely Mumtaz Mahal first met Shah Jahan. The bazaar street led directly to Delhi Gate, the original entrance, and to the Jami Masjid in the old city. Both the gate and bazaar street are now closed to the general public.

Colonnaded arches of the Diwan-i-Aam

Jami Masjid, built by Shah Jahan's favourite daughter Jahanara

VISITORS' CHECKLIST

Practical Information
Agra district. 223 km (139 miles) SE of Delhi. Road map: D3. 3,600,000. UPTDC Taj Rd, (0562) 222 6431; Government of India Tourist Office, 191 Mall Rd, (0562) 222 6368. Kailash Fair (Aug–Sep).

Transport
Kheria 16 km (10 miles). Agra Cantonment (0562) 242 1039/139; Raja ki Mandi (0562) 285 4477; Agra Fort (0562) 296 0457. Idgah (0562) 242 0324.

Jami Masjid

Open daily.

A magnificently proportioned building in the heart of the medieval town, the "Friday Mosque" was sponsored by Shah Jahan's favourite daughter, Jahanara Begum, who also commissioned a number of other buildings and gardens, including the canal that once ran down Chandni Chowk in Delhi *(see pp94–5)*. Built in 1648, the mosque's sandstone and marble domes with their distinctive zigzag chevron pattern dominate this section of the town. The eastern courtyard wing was demolished by the British in 1857 *(see pp58–9)*. Of interest are the tank with its *shahi chirag* ("royal stove") for heating water within the courtyard, and the separate prayer chamber for ladies.

A detail of the minaret

Environs

The area around Jami Masjid was a vibrant meeting place, famous for its kebab houses and lively bazaars. A stroll or rickshaw ride through the network of narrow alleys can be a rewarding experience, offering glimpses of a close-knit way of life reminiscent of Mughal Agra. This is also the city's crafts and trade centre, where a vast array of products such as jewellery, *zari* embroidery, *dhurries*, sweets, shoes and kites are available.

Some of the main bazaars are Johri Bazaar, Kinari Bazaar, Kaserat Bazaar and Kashmiri Bazaar. The quieter back lanes such as Panni Gali have fine buildings with decorative upper storeys and imposing gateways to secluded courtyards and craft workshops.

Agra City Centre

① Agra Fort
② Jami Masjid
③ Railway Station
④ St John's College
⑤ Roman Catholic Cemetery

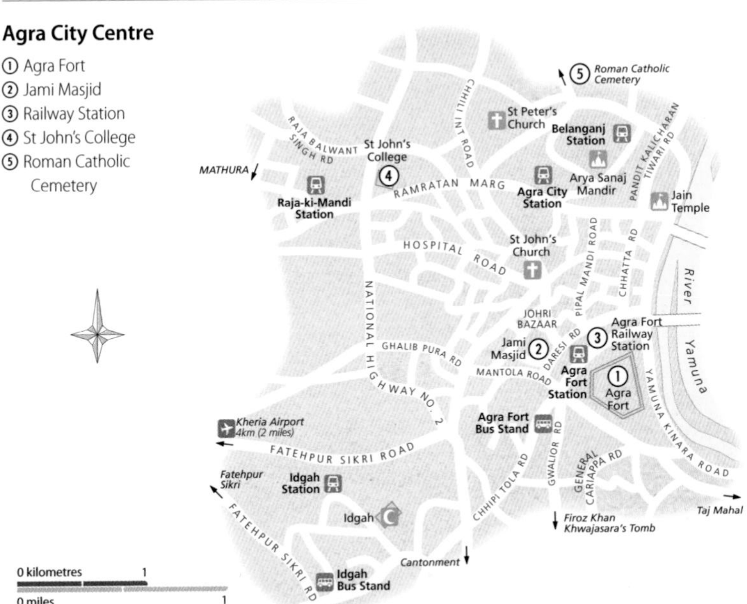

Exploring Agra: The Outer Sights

Agra's European legacy dates back to the reign of Akbar, when the first Jesuit missionaries from Portuguese-governed Goa visited his court to participate in religious debates. This marked the advent of Christianity in North India, and paved the way for future European traffic in the region. In the 18th and 19th centuries this was a great cosmopolitan centre where priests and scholars, merchants and mercenaries employed by the Scindias of Gwalior *(see p178)*, lived, traded or set up schools, colleges and impressive churches.

The red sandstone tomb built in memory of John Hessing

Auto-rickshaws parked outside the Fort Railway Station

Agra Fort Railway Station

Tel (0562) 132/135.

This memorable colonial building was constructed in 1891 as a stopover for colonial tourists visiting Agra's monuments. The octagonal bazaar *chowk* that originally connected the Delhi Gate and Agra Fort to the old city and the Jami Masjid was demolished, and the many-towered station with its French château-style slate-roofed platforms was built in its place. This is still one of Agra's most frequently-used stations; the other two are located in the cantonment and at Raja ki Mandi.

St John's College

NH2 (Drummond Rd/Mahatma Gandhi Rd). **Tel** (0562) 324 7846.

St John's College, started by the Church Missionary Society, has been described as "an astounding mixture of the antiquarian, the scholarly and the symbolic". It consists of a group of red sandstone buildings, including a hall and library, arranged around a quadrangle, all designed in a quasi-Fatehpur Sikri style by Sir Samuel Swinton Jacob *(see p198)*. The building was inaugurated in 1914 by the viceroy, Lord Hardinge, and it remains one of the region's highly lauded institutions.

Roman Catholic Cemetery

Dayal Bagh Rd, opp Civil Courts, off National Highway 2. **Open** daily.

Towards the north of the town is the Roman Catholic Cemetery, the oldest European graveyard in North India. It was established in the 17th century by an Armenian merchant, Khoja Mortenepus, on a piece of land purchased from the church as the burial ground for Agra's large Armenian trading community.

A number of Islamic-style gravestones, with inscriptions in Armenian, survive today, and include the graves of the cannon expert, Shah Nazar Khan, and Khoja Mortenepus himself. The cemetery also contains tombs of European missionaries, traders, and adventurers such as Walter Reinhardt *(see p146)*.

One of the oldest tombs belongs to the English merchant John Mildenhall (d.1614), envoy of Elizabeth I, who arrived at the Mughal court in 1603 seeking permission to trade. Other interesting graves

St John's College, designed by Sir Samuel Swinton Jacob

St George's Church in Agra Cantonment

include those of a Venetian doctor, Bernardino Maffi, and Geronimo Veroneo (once wrongly regarded by some as the architect of the Taj).

Near the chapel is the tall obelisk marking the grave of the four children of General Perron, French commander of Scindia's forces. Another Frenchman, a member of the Bourbon family and kinsman of Henry IV of France, is also buried at this site.

The largest and most impressive grave is that of John Hessing (d.1803) who first ventured out east as a soldier with the Dutch East India Company at Kandy (Sri Lanka). He came to India in 1763 and joined the service of the Nizam of Hyderabad in the south, before moving northwards to be a mercenary with Scindia's forces. His red sandstone tombstone, interestingly modelled on the lines of the Taj Mahal, was built by a local architect.

One of the tombs, in memory of Father Santos, is enclosed by a trellis frame where Hindus and Muslims tie threads, praying for the fulfillment of their wishes.

To its south, on Wazirpura Road, is the **Roman Catholic Cathedral**, constructed in the 18th century at the expense of Walter Reinhardt. An old, derelict church from Akbar's time stands next to it.

Cantonment

Bounded by Mahatma Gandhi Rd, Grand Parade Rd and the Mall Rd.

The pleasant, tree-shaded army cantonment area, with its own railway station and orderly avenues, has many interesting public buildings, churches, cemeteries and bungalows in a medley of styles dating from the British days. **St George's Church** (1826), a yellow ochre plastered building, visible even from the Taj, is a typical example of the North Indian cantonment style of architecture. JT Boileau, the architect, also built the Christ Church in Shimla.

Havelock Memorial Church (1873), constructed in a "trim Classical style", commemorates one of the British generals of the 1857 mutiny. **Queen Mary's Library** and the **Central Post Office** are other buildings in the area.

Structures such as the **Agra Club**, once the hub of British cantonment social life, and the hybrid Indo-Saracenic government Circuit House, which used to accommodate officials of the Raj, are also located in the cantonment.

Firoz Khan Khwajasara's Tomb

S of Agra, on Gwalior Rd. **Open** daily.

A signpost on the Gwalior Road indicates the turning to this unusual 17th-century octagonal tomb, standing on the edge of a lake. This is where Firoz Khan, eunuch and custodian of Shah Jahan's palace harem, is buried. The red sandstone structure stands on a high plinth and has a gateway attached to the main building. Steps lead to the upper storey where a central pavilion containing the cenotaph is located. Highly stylized stone carvings decorate the surface. Interestingly, unlike other buildings of the period, there is an absence of calligraphic inscriptions. If the tomb is closed, the *chowkidar* from the village will open the gate.

The central pavilion where Firoz Khan is buried

Gold Thread and Bead Zardozi

Agra's flourishing local craft tradition of elaborate gold thread and bead embroidery is known as *zardozi*. This technique was Central Asian in origin and came to the region with the Mughal emperors. Local craftsmen in the old city added further refinements to create garments and accessories for the Imperial court. However, with the decline of court patronage, the skill languished and almost vanished. It owes its recent revival to encouragement from contemporary fashion designers. The delicate stitches and complicated patterns in genuine gold thread and coloured beads are now widely used for both traditional and contemporary garments and accessories, including shawls and scarves, bags and shoes.

Detail of a *zari*-embroidered textile

Taj Mahal

One of the world's most famous buildings, the Taj Mahal commemorates both the Mughal emperor Shah Jahan, and Mumtaz Mahal, his favourite wife. Its perfect proportions and exquisite craftsmanship have been described as "a prayer, a vision, a dream, a poem, a wonder." This sublime garden-tomb, an image of the Islamic garden of paradise, cost nearly 41 million rupees and 500 kilos of gold. Around 20,000 workers laboured for almost 22 years to complete it in 1653.

The Dome
The 44-m (144-ft) double dome is capped with a finial.

★ Marble Screen
The filigree screen delicately carved from a single block of marble was meant to veil the area around the royal tombs.

★ Tomb Chamber
Mumtaz Mahal's cenotaph, raised on a platform, is placed next to Shah Jahan's. The actual graves, in a dark crypt below, are closed to the public.

KEY

① **Plinth**

② **Four minarets,** each 40 m (131 ft) high and crowned by a *chhatri*, frame the tomb, highlighting the perfect symmetry of the complex.

③ **The *Charbagh*** was irrigated by the waters of the River Jamuna.

VISITORS' CHECKLIST

Practical Information
Taj Mahal. **Tel** (0562) 233 0498. **Open** 6am–7pm Sun–Thu. **Closed** Fri. Taj Mahotsav (18–27 Feb). Museum: **Open** 10am–5pm Sun–Thu. **Closed** public hols.

The Lotus Pool
Named after its lotus-shaped fountain spouts, the pool reflects the tomb. Almost every visitor is photographed sitting on the marble bench here.

Pishtaq
Recessed arches provide depth while their inlaid panels reflect the changing light to give the tomb a mystical aura.

★ Pietra Dura
Inspired by the paradise garden, intricately carved floral designs inlaid with precious stones embellish the austere white marble surface to give it the look of a bejewelled casket.

Calligraphic Panels
The size of the Koranic verses increases as the arch gets higher, creating the subtle optical illusion of a uniformly flowing script.

Decorative Elements of the Taj

It is widely believed that the Taj Mahal was designed to represent an earthly replica of one of the houses of paradise. Its impeccable marble facing, embellished by a remarkable use of exquisite surface design, is a splendid showcase for the refined aesthetic that reached its height during Shah Jahan's reign. Described as "one of the most elegant and harmonious buildings in the world", the Taj indeed manifests the wealth and luxury of Mughal art as seen in architecture and garden design, painting, jewellery, calligraphy, textiles, carpet-weaving and furniture.

Detail of the marble screen with an inlaid chrysanthemum

Pietra Dura

The Mughals were great naturalists who believed that flowers were the "symbols of the divine realm". In the Taj, pietra dura *has been extensively used to translate naturalistic forms into decorative patterns that complement the majesty of its architecture.*

Flowers such as the tulip, lily, iris, poppy and narcissus were depicted as sprays or arabesque patterns. Stones of varying degrees of colour were used to create the shaded effects.

Inlaid marble above the mosque's central arch

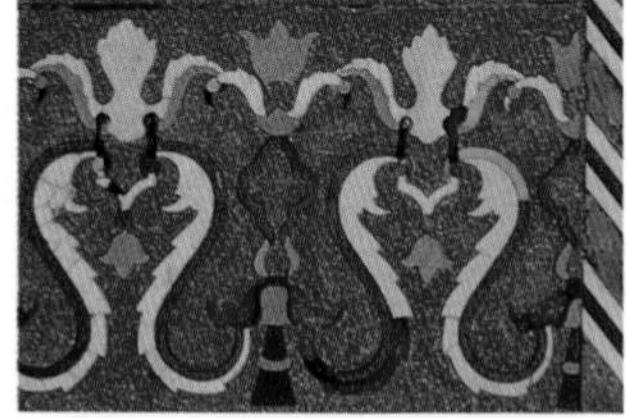

White marble, black slate and yellow, red and grey sandstone are used for decoration

Pietra Dura Craftsmanship

The Florentine technique of *pietra dura* is said to have been imported by Jahangir and developed in Agra as *pachikari*. Minute slivers of precious and semi-precious stones, such as carnelian, lapis lazuli, turquoise and malachite, were arranged in complex stylized floral designs into a marble base. Even today, artisans in the old city maintain pattern books containing the intricate motifs used on the Taj and can still re-create 17th-century designs in contemporary pieces.

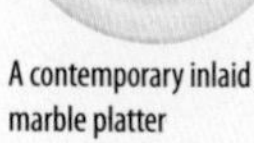

A contemporary inlaid marble platter

A single flower often had more than 35 variations of carnelian

Carved Relief Work

Decorative panels of flowering plants, foliage and vases are realistically carved on the lower portions of the walls. While the pietra dura *adds colour to the pristine white marble these highlight the texture of the polished marble and sandstone surface.*

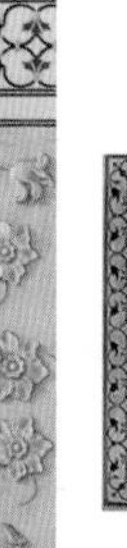

Floral sprays, carved in relief on the marble and sandstone dado levels, are framed with *pietra dura* and stone inlay borders. The profusion of floral motifs in the Taj symbolizes the central paradise theme.

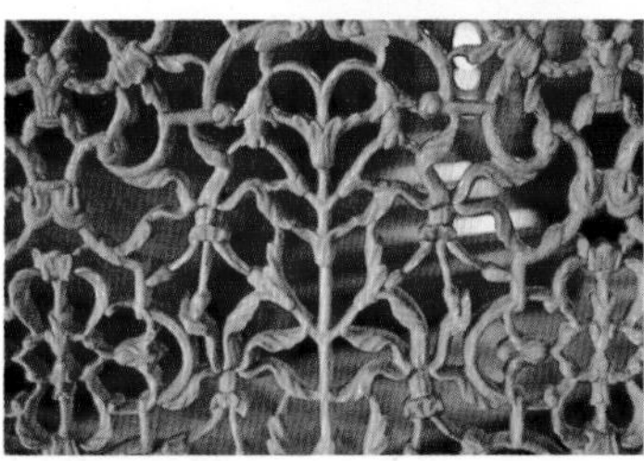

***Jaali* patterns** on the octagonal perforated screen surrounding the cenotaphs are a complex combination of the floral and geometric. The filtered light captures the intricate designs and casts mosaic-like shadows on the tombs.

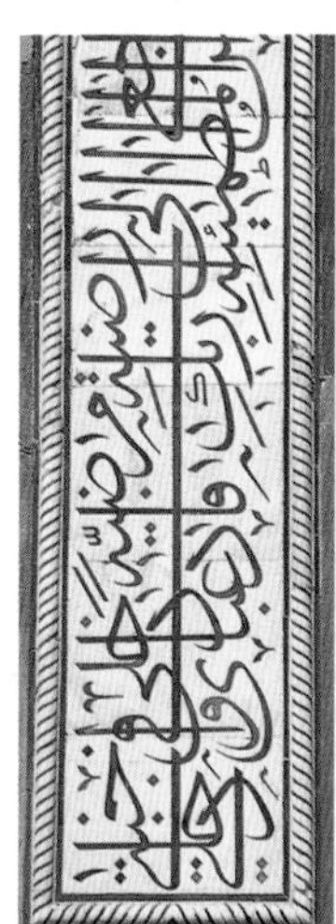

Calligraphy

Inlaid calligraphy in black marble was used as a form of ornamentation on undecorated surfaces. The exquisitely detailed panels of inscriptions of Koranic passages, which line the recessed arches like banners, were designed by the Persian calligrapher, Amanat Khan.

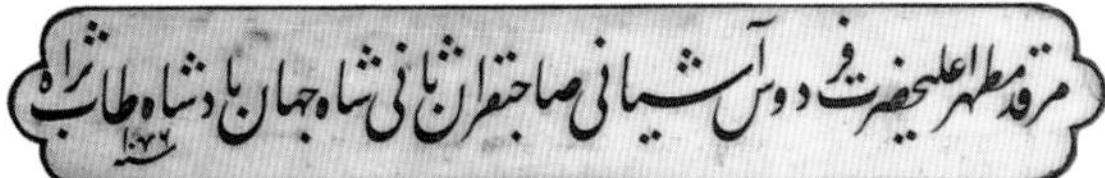

Exploring the East Bank

The picturesque east bank of the Yamuna is dotted with the remains of gardens, palaces, pavilions and the exquisite tomb of **Itimad-ud-Daulah**. North of Itimad-ud-Daulah is **Chini ka Rauza** (literally, "China tomb" after its tiled exterior), built by Afzal Khan, a poet-scholar from Shiraz who was Shah Jahan's prime minister. This large square structure is Persian in style, and at one time its surface was covered with glazed tiles from Lahore and Multan, interspersed with calligraphic panels in graceful Naskh characters. The burial chamber within has painted stucco plaster design that once must have complemented the tiled exterior.

Further upriver is the quiet, tree-shaded **Rambagh** or Aram Bagh ("garden of rest"). This is said to be the first Mughal garden laid out by Babur, the founder of the Mughal dynasty, in 1526 *(see p171)*, and his temporary burial place before his body was taken to Kabul to be interred. The spacious walled garden, divided by walkways leading to a raised terrace with open pavilions overlooking the river, was further developed by Nur Jahan.

Chini ka Rauza
1 km (less than a mile) N of Itimad-ud-Daulah. **Open** 6am–6pm daily.

Rambagh
3 km (2 miles) N of Itimad-ud-Daulah, Etmadpur. **Open** 6am–5pm daily.

Riverside pavilion at Rambagh

Itimad-ud-Daulah's Tomb

Described as a "jewel box in marble", the small, elegant garden tomb of Mirza Ghiyath Beg, entitled Itimad-ud-Daulah, the "Lord Treasurer" of the Mughal empire, was built over a period of six years from 1622 by his daughter Nur Jahan, Jahangir's favourite wife. This tomb is a combination of white marble, coloured mosaic, stone inlay and lattice work. Stylistically too, this is the most innovative 17th-century Mughal building and marks the transition from the robust, red sandstone architecture of Akbar to the sensuous refinement of Shah Jahan's Taj Mahal.

Upper Pavilion
The replica tombs of Itimad-ud-Daulah and his wife are located in the marble-screened upper pavilion.

Mosaic Patterns
Panels of geometric designs created by inlaid coloured stones decorate the dado level of the tomb.

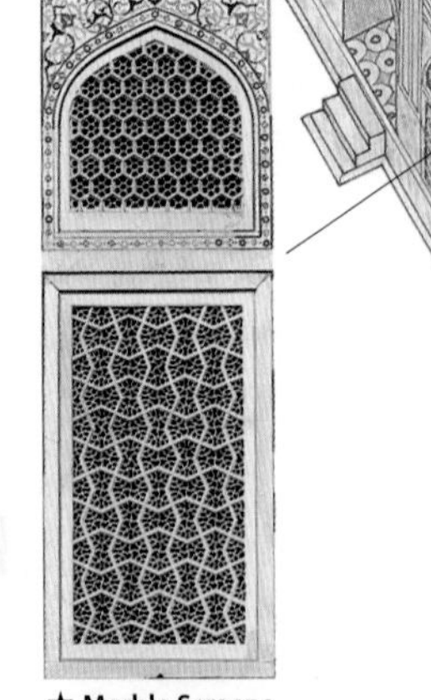

★ Marble Screens
Perforated marble screens with complex ornamental patterns are carved out of a single slab of marble.

KEY

① **Tapering pinnacles** with lotus mouldings crown the minarets.

② **The dome** with its canopy-like shape is different from the conventional domes of this period.

③ **The marble latticed balustrade**

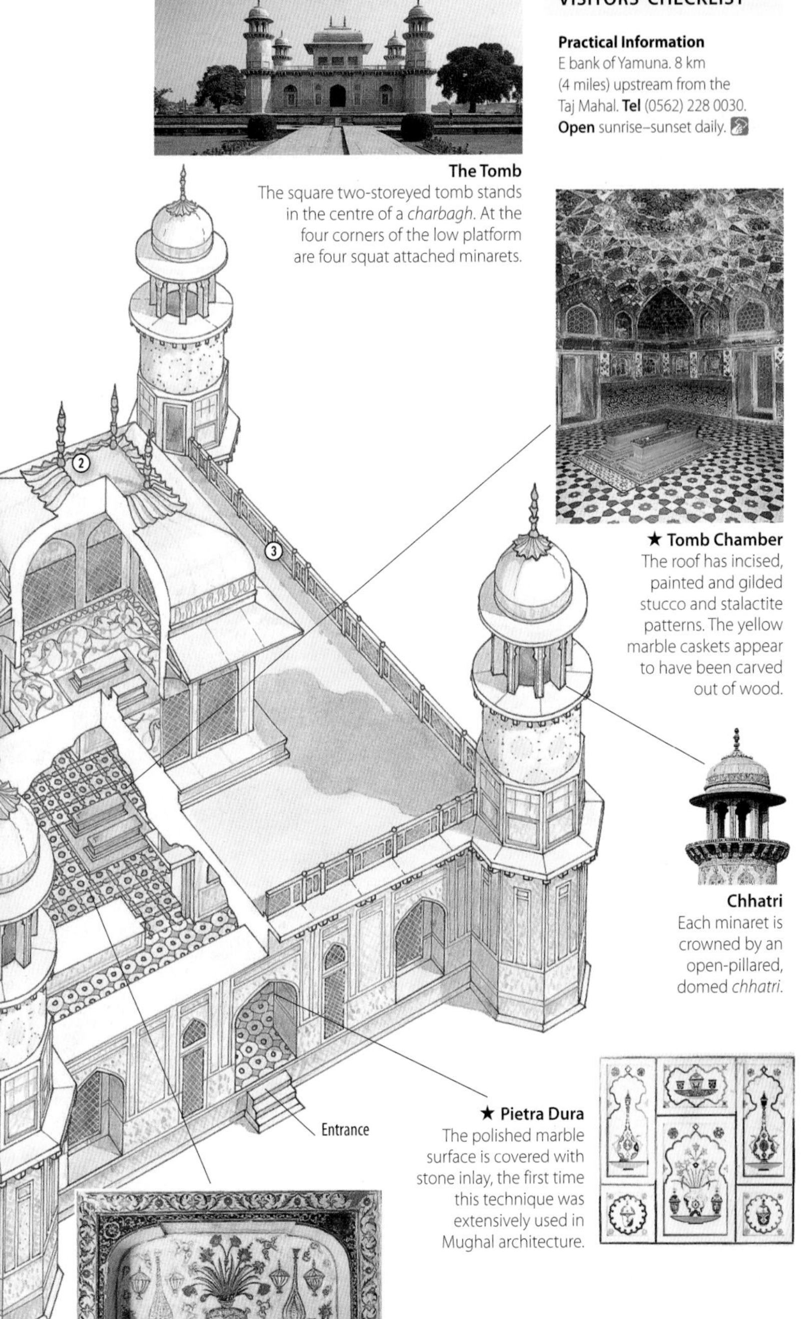

VISITORS' CHECKLIST

Practical Information
E bank of Yamuna. 8 km (4 miles) upstream from the Taj Mahal. **Tel** (0562) 228 0030. **Open** sunrise–sunset daily.

The Tomb
The square two-storeyed tomb stands in the centre of a *charbagh*. At the four corners of the low platform are four squat attached minarets.

★ Tomb Chamber
The roof has incised, painted and gilded stucco and stalactite patterns. The yellow marble caskets appear to have been carved out of wood.

Chhatri
Each minaret is crowned by an open-pillared, domed *chhatri*.

★ Pietra Dura
The polished marble surface is covered with stone inlay, the first time this technique was extensively used in Mughal architecture.

Painted Floral Patterns
Niches with painted floral bouquets, fruit, trees and wine decanters embellish the interior of the central chamber of the main tomb.

The entrance to Akbar's mausoleum at Sikandra

❷ Sikandra

Agra district. 8 km (5 miles) NW of Agra on NH2. Road map: D2. Akbar's Mausoleum: **Open** 7am–5:15pm daily. Urs at Akbar's tomb (mid-Oct).

The Mughal Emperor Akbar is buried in this small village on the outskirts of Agra. Named after Sikander Lodi, one of the last of the Delhi sultans *(see pp54–5)*, this was a pleasant garden suburb during Agra's golden age. It is widely believed that Akbar designed and started the construction of his own mausoleum which, after his death, was modified and completed by his son and successor, Jahangir. The result is this impressive, perfectly symmetrical complex with the tomb located in the centre of a vast, walled garden.

The main gateway *(see p31)* to the south is a magnificent red sandstone structure with a colossal central arch, finished with an exuberant polychrome mosaic of inlaid white marble, black slate and coloured stones. On each corner of the gateway are four graceful marble minarets, considered to be forerunners of those found later on the Taj Mahal *(see pp158–9)*.

The garden, where deer and monkeys frolic, is a typical *charbagh (see p171)*. The wide sweep of stone causeways leading to the tomb divides the area into four quadrants, each with its own fountain and sunken pond, fruit trees and bushes, now a derelict tangle.

The main tomb is a distinct departure from the conventional domed structure of the tomb of Akbar's father, the second Mughal emperor, Humayun, at Delhi *(see p87)*. The first three storeys of this majestic, four-tiered composition comprise red sandstone pavilions. Above them is an exquisite marble-screened terrace enclosing the replica tomb, which is profusely carved with floral and arabesque designs, Chinese cloud patterns, and the 99 names of Allah. The upper levels, earlier accessible through special permission, are now closed due to security reasons.

The actual tomb is within a domed sepulchre in the heart of the building, illuminated by shafts of light from an arched window. A low door at the end of the ramp ensures that every visitor bows his head with respect on entry. Just outside the complex is the **Kanch Mahal**, a double-storeyed red sandstone mansion with an ornamented façade, fretted balconies and inlaid mosaic work. Further down, on Mathura Road, is **Mariam Zamani's Tomb**, where one of Akbar's wives is buried in a square building set on a high plinth within a small garden. It was used as an orphanage by the Church Missionary Society in 1812. A church has been constructed in the compound. Further along the Agra–Delhi highway is **Guru-ka-Tal**, a unique example of the many tanks constructed by Jahangir for collecting rainwater. Broad flights of steps lead down to the water. The reservoir is now part of a *guru-dwara* complex dedicated to the ninth Sikh guru, Tegh Bahadur *(see p94)*.

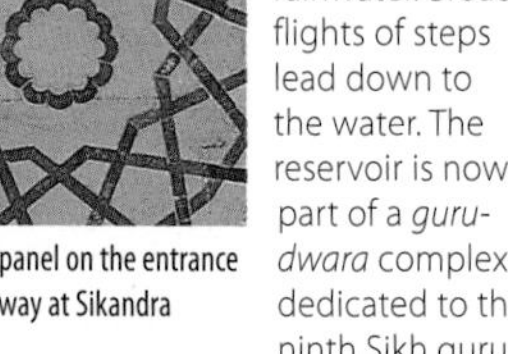
Detail of a panel on the entrance gateway at Sikandra

Environs

About 4 km (2 miles) south of Sikandra stands a lifesize red sandstone horse on the spot where Akbar's favourite steed supposedly died. Located opposite, is the gateway of **Kachi-ki-Sarai**, a historic rest house along this route.

The Grand Trunk Road

A roadside dhaba

The Grand Trunk Road, Rudyard Kipling's "stately corridor" that linked Calcutta in the east with Kabul in the northwest, was laid out by Sher Shah Sur *(see p88)* in the 16th century. In those days, it resounded with the movement of armies on campaign, and in times of peace, with the pomp and pageantry that accompanied the Mughal emperors as their court moved from Agra to Delhi.

This is still one of Asia's great roads and North India's premier highway. Some of the ancient shade-giving trees still stand, but the old caravanserais are now in ruins. Instead, at frequent intervals along the highway, there are *dhabas* for long- distance travellers, especially lorry-drivers, to stop for a cheap and filling meal of dal and *roti*, washed down with glasses of hot tea or cooling *lassi*, and to snatch a quick nap on string cots thoughtfully provided by the owner.

Vishram Ghat at Mathura where every evening at sunset oil lamps are floated on the river

❸ Mathura

Mathura district. 62 km (39 miles) NW of Agra on NH2. Road map: D3. 330,500. Old Bus Stand, Mathura. Holi (Feb–Mar), Hariyali Teej (July), Janmashtami (Aug–Sep), Annakut (Sep–Oct), Kansa Vadha (Sep).

Mathura, on the west bank of the Yamuna, is where the story of Krishna begins. A dark, cell-like room in the complex of the rather modern Sri Krishna Janmabhoomi Temple, on the periphery of the city, is revered as the birthplace of one of India's most popular gods. Further away, along the riverfront, the city's 25 ghats form a splendid network of temples, pavilions, trees and steps leading to the water. Teeming with colourful shops selling traditional items, such as its delicious *pedas* (milk sweets), this is the heart of the town.

The evening *aarti*, when small oil lamps are floated on the river, is performed at **Vishram Ghat**, where legend says Krishna rested after he killed the tyrant Kamsa. Close by is the **Sati Burj**, a red sandstone pavilion built in the 1570s, and **Kans Qila**, the site of the old fort where Sawai Jai Singh II of Jaipur constructed one of his five observatories *(see pp196–7)*.

The **Jami Masjid**, with its striking tile-work, and a number of other interesting buildings with elaborately carved façades, lie behind the riverfront. A charming oddity is the Roman Catholic Church of the Sacred Heart, built in 1860 in the army cantonment. It combines Western elements with details taken from local temple architecture.

Mathura's ancient history predates the better known legend of Krishna. From about the 5th century BC until the 4th century AD, the city prospered as a major centre of Buddhism. Under the powerful Kushana and Gupta dynasties, it was renowned throughout the ancient world as North India's cultural capital. During this period the Mathura School of Art flourished *(see pp50–51)*, and superb pieces of sculpture, made from the distinctive local white-flecked red sandstone, were carved by artisans in workshops here and exported to far off places.

A religious icon from Mathura

The **Government Museum** collection highlights the Mathura School of Art and has some exquisite pieces. These include a perfectly preserved Standing Buddha, the famous headless statue of the great Kushana king Kanishka, as well as a huge collection of carved columns, railings and fragments of narrative panels, excavated from nearby archaeological sites, depicting court scenes and religious imagery.

Also on view are artifacts from the other centres of Buddhist art, such as Gandhara (now in Pakistan), showing Graeco-Roman influences after Alexander's invasion of the northwest. There are also sections on terracotta pottery and figurines dating from the 2nd–1st centuries BC, coins and medieval stone, brass and metal objects.

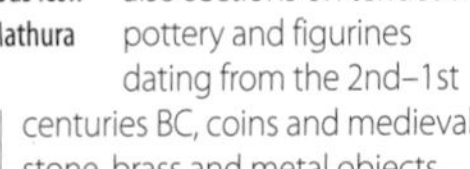

Government Museum

Dampier Nagar. **Tel** (0565) 250 0847. **Open** 10:30am–4:30pm Tue–Sun. **Closed** Mon, second Sun of month & public hols.

A boat carrying pilgrims along the Yamuna

❹ Brindavan

Mathura district. 68 km (42 miles) NW of Agra off NH2. **Road map** D3. 63,000. Old Bus Stand, Mathura. Holi (Feb–Mar), Rath ka Mela (Mar), Hariyali Teej (Jul), Janmashtami (Aug–Sep). daily.

Situated along the River Yamuna, Brindavan (literally, "forest of fragrant basil") became an important pilgrim centre after the early 16th century, when Chaitanya Mahaprabhu, a Vaishnava saint from Bengal, revived the Krishna cult. He encouraged Bengali devotees, especially widows, to settle here in ashrams endowed by wealthy Hindu merchants. However, the town's mythic origins are much older, as devout Hindus believe that the young Lord Krishna once lived here as a humble cowherd with his foster parents. So "his" cows still have the run of the streets and his name is continuously chanted in prayer halls. Stalls outside temples sell elaborate flower garlands and milk sweets called *pedas*, believed to have been loved by Krishna. All this gives the feeling that the people of Brindavan live in an enchanted time warp.

Pilgrims on the *chaurasi kos ki yatra*

This charming phenomenon is best seen in Brindavan's numerous temples and ghats, built by the Hindu kings of Amber, Bharatpur and Orchha and by rich merchants. The edge of the old town has the historic **Govindeoji Temple**, originally a seven-storeyed structure built in 1590 by Raja Man Singh I of Amber. The presiding deity is now in Jaipur *(see p186)*. Across this temple is the 19th-century **Sri Ranganathji**, an imposing Dravidian-style temple with a gold-plated ritual pillar and a fascinating museum of temple treasures. Beyond these, and within the narrow streets of the old town, are the sacred walled groves of Seva Kunj,

❺ Brajbhumi Driving Tour

Devotees believe that the area around Braj is composed of sacred *mandalas* (circuits) that map the idyllic pastoral landscape of Krishna's early life. Divided by the Yamuna, this tour partly follows the *chaurasi kos ki yatra*, a traditional pilgrimage of about 300 km (186 miles), undertaken around the Janmashtami celebrations.

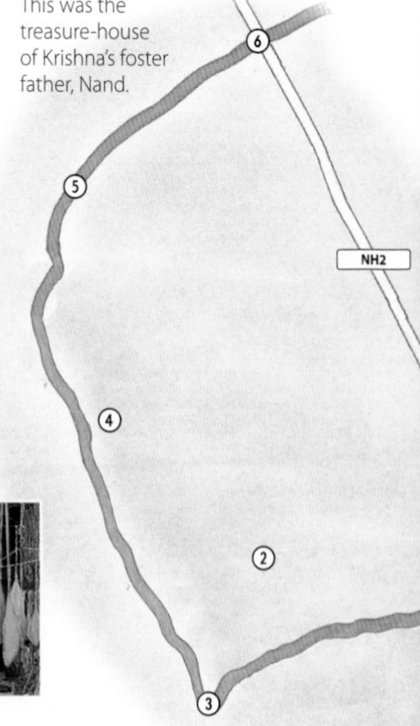

Kosi
This was the treasure-house of Krishna's foster father, Nand.

④ **Barsana**
With its 17th-century Ladliji temple, Barsana is believed to be the home of Radha.

⑤ **Nandgaon**
Krishna lived here with foster parents Nand and Yashoda after his escape from Gokul and the evil Kamsa.

③ **Govardhan**
This pilgrim town has grown around the hill that legend says Krishna lifted on his finger to shield the people of Braj from torrential rain. Nearby is Kusum Sarovar.

linked with the Raslila dance of the region *(see p34)*.

The **Shahji Temple** with its spiral columns, lies on the way to Nidhivana where Swami Haridas, the guru of Tansen *(see p178)*, developed the classic musical tradition of Dhrupad in the 16th century.

Other notable temples are the **Madan Mohan Temple**, built in 1580 with local red sandstone, on a hill next to the river. A little further are the popular **Banke Bihari Temple**, which can be approached from the main bazaar street, and the 16th-century **Jugal Kishore Temple**, adjoining the main pilgrim route to the ghats. The **Gopinath** and **Radha Raman** temples are located close to each other near Keshi Ghat. The ISKCON Temple and the Brindavan Research Institute, on the outskirts of the town, are recent additions to the town's skyline.

A Vaishanavite *sadhu*

Gopuram of the South Indian- style Ranganathji Temple

At Holi and Janmashtami *(see pp40–41)*, Brindavan is a riot of colour and dance as people celebrate the god who still enchants them and where his *lila* (divine sport) is still a living presence.

❻ Deeg

Bharatpur district. 98 km (61 miles) NW of Agra on NH2. **Road map** D3. RTDC Hotel Saras, Agra Rd, Bharatpur (05644) 22 3790. Holi (Feb–Mar), Rath ka Mela (Mar).

Once the capital of the Jat kings of Bharatpur *(see p170)*, Deeg rose to prominence after the decline of the Mughal empire in the 18th century. Its square fort, a massive edifice, has mud and rubble walls which are buttressed by 12 bastions and a shallow moat. The fortified town outside the fort once had grand mansions, lush gardens and pools, but these now lie unkempt and forlorn. Deeg's Raja Suraj Mal and his son, Jawahir Singh, were also builders of lavish pleasure palaces. Of these, the most remarkable is the **Water Palace** *(see pp168–9)*, built in celebration of the monsoon. This was a favourite summer retreat of the Bharatpur kings.

② Radhakund
Said to be Radha's personal bathing pool, it has a special sanctity for her devotees.

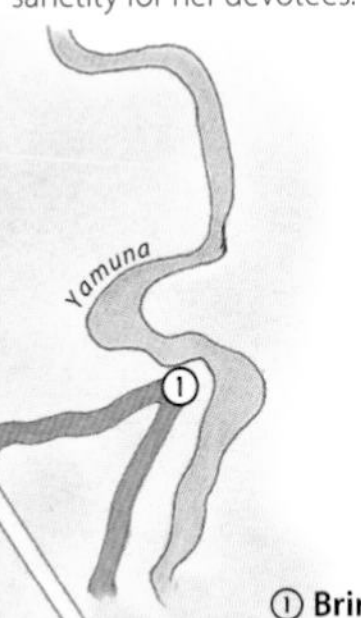

① Brindavan
An important pilgrim centre, it is separated from Mathura by the River Yamuna.

Key

Tour route

Roads

Rivers

0 kilometres 5

0 miles 2

Tips for Drivers

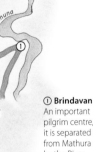

Length: 105 km (65 miles).
Stopping-off points: Brindavan has good hotels and restaurants and is the ideal base for the tour. Both Radhakund and Barsana have UPSTDC tourist bungalows, and Govardhan and Kosi have petrol stations. However, private transport will be a more convenient way to explore this region.

The Krishna Cult

Sanjhi, Brindavan's paper stencil craft

A peacock feather, a flute and the colour blue announce the presence of Krishna. Named after his dark skin, this most human of gods still haunts the glades and forests along the Yamuna. A naughty child who was passionately fond of milk and butter, Krishna is also the charming flute-player whose flirtatious dalliance with Radha is a metaphor for the complex metaphysics of temporal and spiritual love, widely celebrated in art and literature.

Deeg Water Palace

The magic of the monsoon and the traditions of music and dance associated with it inspired the Bharatpur kings to build a romantic "water palace" at their summer capital, Deeg. A lyrical composition of sandstone and marble pavilions, gardens and pools, this late 18th-century marvel, built by Raja Suraj Mal, used a number of innovative special effects that simulated monsoon showers, even producing rainbows. The skilful cooling system drew water from a huge reservoir that originally took two days to fill. The coloured fountain-jets are now played only during the Jawahar Mela.

Nand Bhavan
Huge terracotta water pitchers placed inside its innovative double roof insulated its interior against the heat of summer.

★ Sawan Pavilion
Shaped like an upturned boat, its ingenious water system created a semi-circle of falling water.

Mughal Marble Swing
This was a part of Suraj Mal's war booty, now placed in front of Gopal Bhavan.

KEY

① **Bhadon Pavilion**

② **Gopal Sagar Tank**

③ **Rup Sagar Tank**

④ **Kishan Bhavan**

⑤ **The roof-level reservoir** had water drawn to it from four wells. Pipes led from holes in its sides to supply the chutes and fountains with a continuous stream of water.

⑥ **Charbagh**

★ Gopal Bhavan
This elegant complex is flanked by the boat-shaped Sawan-Bhadon pavilions. Its numerous overhanging kiosks and balconies are reflected in Gopal Sagar from which it seems to rise. The interior still retains the original furnishings and objets d'art of this palace.

★ Keshav Bhavan
Heavy lithic balls were placed on the roof here. When water gushed up the hollow pillars and pipes inside the arches, the balls rolled on the roof to produce "thunder".

VISITORS' CHECKLIST

Practical Information
Bharatpur district. 95 km (59 miles) NW of Agra. **Road map** D3.
Open 9:30am–5:30pm daily.
Closed Fri, the day after Holi (Mar).
Jawahar Mela (Sep). Mon.

Transport

Lotus Quoins
Placed at each corner of the plinth, these urns were inspired by Mughal designs.

Suraj Bhavan
A pillared, secluded pavilion with a splendid view of the *charbagh*, it was part of the *zenana* enclosure.

Monsoon Architecture

Coloured water fountains at Deeg

In the dry areas of North India, light and wind direction guided architecture. Underground rooms, water channels, fountains, latticed screens, terrazzo floors and open courtyards were devices to keep homes cool before the advent of electricity. The Sawan-Bhadon pavilions at Deeg, named after the months of the monsoon (July–August), are an architectural style inspired by the rainy season. Built to savour the thunder and rain of the monsoon, such pavilions adorned forts and palaces.

❼ Bharatpur

Bharatpur district. 55 km (34 miles) W of Agra. **Road map** D3. 2,552,600. opp RTDC Hotel Saras Circle, Agra Rd (05644) 22 2542. Jaswant Mela (Oct).

Most famous for its bird sanctuary, the kingdom of Bharatpur, on the eastern edge of Rajasthan, came into prominence during the declining years of the Mughal Empire. It was founded by the fearless Jats, a community of landowners. Their most remarkable leader was Raja Suraj Mal (r.1724–63), who in 1733 captured and fortified the city of Bharatpur, thereby laying the foundations of his capital. This powerful ruler defied the reigning Mughal emperor, stormed Delhi and Agra and brought home the massive gates of Agra Fort and installed them at his own fort at Deeg's Water Palace *(see pp168–9)*, near Bharatpur. A prolific builder as well, he used the loot from Mughal buildings, including a swing (now in Deeg), to embellish the forts and palaces he built throughout his kingdom.

In the centre of the town is **Lohagarh** ("iron fort"), which withstood repeated attacks by the Marathas and the British until it was finally captured by Lord Lake in 1805. When built, it was a masterpiece of construction with massive double ramparts made of solid packed mud and rubble that were surrounded by impressive moats. Most of the outermost ramparts have disintegrated, but the inner ones are intact and are distinguished by two towers, the Jawahar Burj and Fateh Burj, built to mark successive Jat victories over the Mughals and the British. The Victory Column at Jawahar Burj carries an inscription with the genealogy of the Jat kings. Both its north and south gates were part of the loot from the imperial Mughal capital at Delhi.

The State museum at Lohagarh fort, Bharatpur

Three palaces were built in the fort by the rustic Jats in a surprisingly fine mix of Mughal and Rajput stylistic detail. The royal apartments, in Mahal Khas, had unusual octagonal chambers in the corners with colourful painted walls, but these are now the site of a pharmaceutical college. The other two palaces were located around the Katcheri (court) Bagh, and now house the **State Museum**, where a rare collection of 1st- and 2nd-century stone carvings and terracotta toys from nearby excavations can be seen.

An interesting sunken *hamam* is close by.

Figure of Krishna, State Museum

In 1818, Bharatpur became the first Rajput state to sign a treaty of alliance with the British East India Company. A later maharaja was a keen collector of Rolls Royce cars, which he converted for use on tiger and duck.

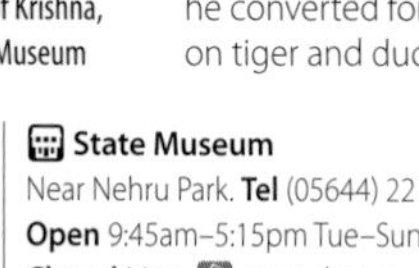

State Museum
Near Nehru Park. **Tel** (05644) 22 8185. **Open** 9:45am–5:15pm Tue–Sun. **Closed** Mon. extra charges.

The moat and ramparts of Lohagarh

❽ Keoladeo Ghana National Park

See pp172–3.

❾ Fatehpur Sikri

See pp174–7.

❿ Dholpur

Dholpur district. 54 km (34 miles) S of Agra. **Road map** D3. 130,200. Bharatpur, (05644) 22 2542.

Situated on the banks of the River Chambal, the small town of Dholpur was strategically located on the route from Delhi

The lakeside temples of Machkund near Dholpur

to the Deccan, making it the target of invading armies. In 1504, Sikandar Lodi set up camp here for a month on his march against Gwalior. Some 20 years later, Babur made this a royal domain of his new empire. The ruined Shergarh Fort, said to be 1,000 years old, is in Dholpur and so is a modest 19th-century palace (closed to the public) which can only be seen through an ironwork railing. The palace has a number of art deco rooms covered with European tiles. Dholpur is today associated with the beige-coloured sandstone quarried nearby, used in buildings all over Rajasthan and made famous by Lutyens, who used it for the building of New Delhi *(see pp72–3)*.

Environs

Dholpur town is a convenient base to explore a number of fascinating neighbouring sites. **Machkund** (3 km/2 miles west), has over 100 temples along its lake. Its waters are said to heal all skin diseases. **Damoh**, a popular picnic spot, has 76 waterfalls. **Talab Shahi** (40 km/25 miles) has the remains of hunting lodges developed by the Jat rulers of Dholpur for their numerous European guests.

Off the beaten track is **Jhor** (16km/10 miles), where in 1978, Babur's 400-year-old Lotus Garden was discovered.

⓫ Bari

Dholpur district. 84 km (68 miles) SW of Agra. **Road map** D4. ℹ Bharatpur, (05644) 22 2542.

The site of an old 100-acre (40 ha) garden once so dense that sunlight could not reach the ground, Bari was where Emperor Shah Jahan built a number of pleasure pavilions. Located nearby is the Vana Vihar Ram Sagar Wildlife Reserve, home to crocodiles, sambhar, wild boar and several species of migratory bird. Remains of an old fort built by Feroze Shah Tughlaq can also be seen here.

Shah Jahan's palace gate, Bari

Babur and the Paradise Garden

The Garden of Fidelity in the *Babur Nama*

The concept of the Paradise Garden, the hallmark of Mughal landscape design, was introduced by the first Great Mughal, Babur. Yearning for the natural beauty of Ferghana, his homeland in Central Asia, he recreated the Persian paradise garden based on Islamic geometric and metaphysical concepts of design.

The *charbagh* was an enclosed garden divided into four quarters, representing the four quarters of life, by a system of raised walkways, sunken groves and water channels. Water was the central element, for it was regarded by the rulers of Central Asian desert kingdoms as the source of life. The intersecting water channels met at a focal point which contained a pavilion for the emperor, seen as a representative of God on earth.

The Mughals used their gardens as living spaces, and also as settings for their garden tombs *(see p33)*. The Jhor garden of paradise, sometimes referred to as the Lotus Garden, was laid out in 1527, barely a year after Babur invaded India. Three water channels, Babur's hot bath, a tank and a pavilion are all that remain of the original garden, which once covered several acres (2 ha).

8 Keoladeo Ghana National Park

A World Heritage Site regarded as one of the world's most important bird sanctuaries, Keoladeo Ghana derives its name from a Shiva temple (Keoladeo) within a dense *(ghana)* forest. This once-arid scrubland was first developed by the Bharatpur rulers in the mid-18th century by diverting the waters of a nearby irrigation canal to create a private duck reserve. Extravagant shooting parties for viceroys and other royal guests were held here, and horrifying numbers of birds were shot in a single day. Today, the park spreads over 29 sq km (11 sq miles) of wetlands, and attracts a wide variety of migrant and water birds who fly in each winter from places as distant as Siberia. Keoladeo's dry area has a mixed deciduous and scrub vegetation and is home to many mammals such as the nilgai antelope.

Bharatpur's wetlands, which hold one of the world's finest heronries

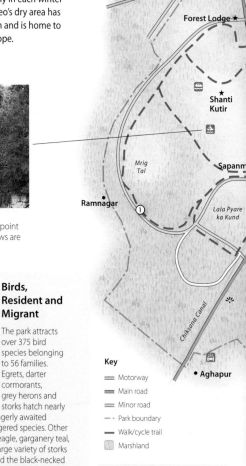

Around the Park
Expert boatmen navigate the wetlands and point out bird colonies. Bicycles and cycle-rickshaws are also available for touring the forest paths.

Jaipur
NH11
Forest Lodge
Shanti Kutir
Mrig Tal
Sapanm
Ramnagar
Lala Pyare ka Kund
Chiksana Canal
Aghapur

Key

- Motorway
- Main road
- Minor road
- Park boundary
- Walk/cycle trail
- Marshland

Birds, Resident and Migrant

The male Sarus crane dances to attract his mate

The park attracts over 375 bird species belonging to 56 families. Egrets, darter cormorants, grey herons and storks hatch nearly 30,000 chicks every year. The park's most eagerly awaited visitor, the Siberian crane, is now an endangered species. Other birds include the peregrine falcon, steppe eagle, garganery teal, snake bird and the white ibis. Among the large variety of storks are the open-bill stork, the painted stork and the black-necked stork, considered to be the world's tallest stork. When standing on its coral-coloured legs, the bird rises to a height of 2 m (6 ft), with a wing spread of 2.5 m (8 ft). The Sarus crane, a symbol of fidelity in Indian mythology, woos its partner for life with an elaborate mating dance.

Baby cormorants

KEY

① **Dry scrubland** provides good grazing for many species of deer and cattle.

② **A stone plaque** near the temple records the number of past bird shoots.

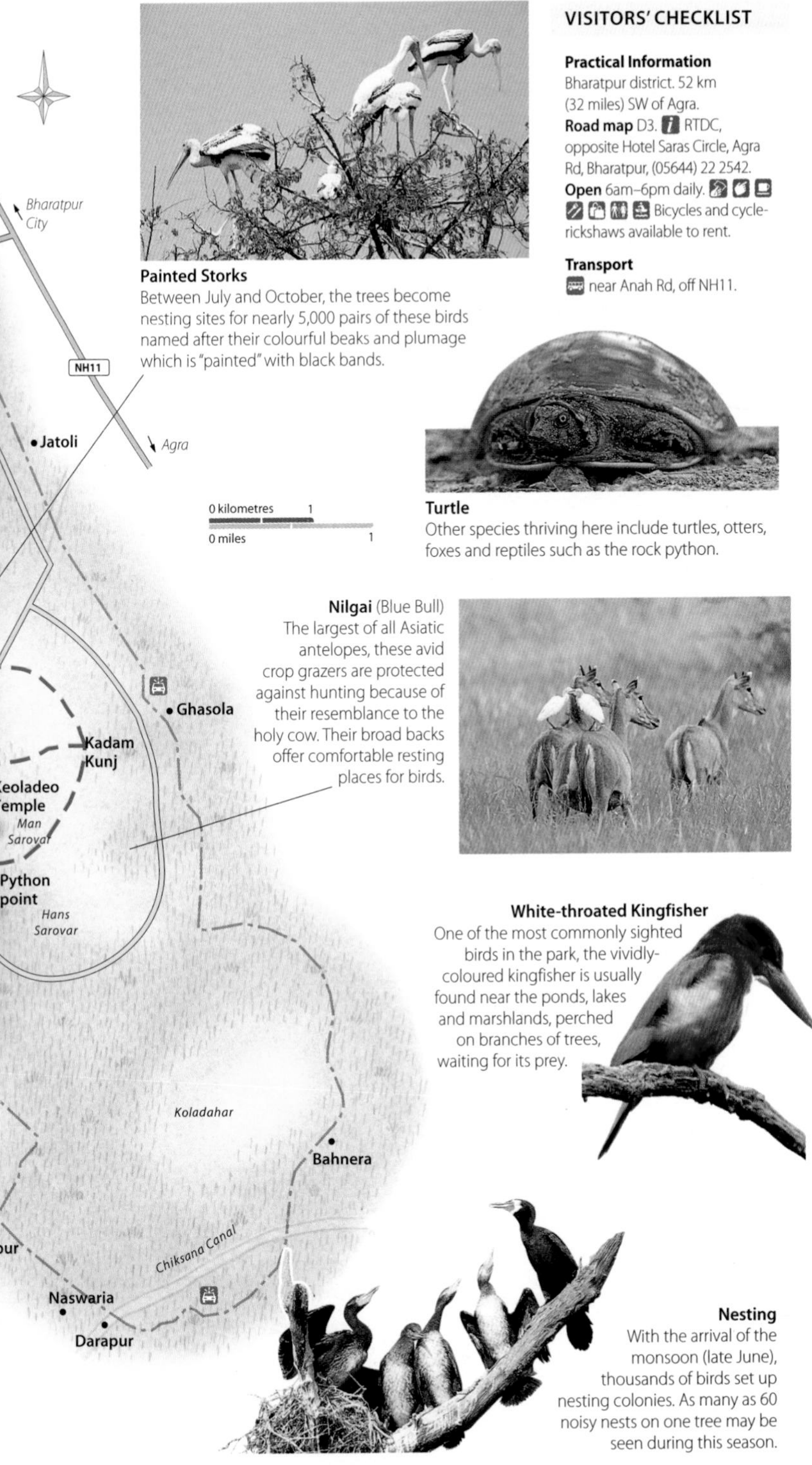

Painted Storks
Between July and October, the trees become nesting sites for nearly 5,000 pairs of these birds named after their colourful beaks and plumage which is "painted" with black bands.

Turtle
Other species thriving here include turtles, otters, foxes and reptiles such as the rock python.

Nilgai (Blue Bull)
The largest of all Asiatic antelopes, these avid crop grazers are protected against hunting because of their resemblance to the holy cow. Their broad backs offer comfortable resting places for birds.

White-throated Kingfisher
One of the most commonly sighted birds in the park, the vividly-coloured kingfisher is usually found near the ponds, lakes and marshlands, perched on branches of trees, waiting for its prey.

Nesting
With the arrival of the monsoon (late June), thousands of birds set up nesting colonies. As many as 60 noisy nests on one tree may be seen during this season.

VISITORS' CHECKLIST

Practical Information
Bharatpur district. 52 km (32 miles) SW of Agra.
Road map D3. RTDC, opposite Hotel Saras Circle, Agra Rd, Bharatpur, (05644) 22 2542.
Open 6am–6pm daily. Bicycles and cycle-rickshaws available to rent.

Transport
near Anah Rd, off NH11.

For keys to symbols *see back flap*

9 Fatehpur Sikri

Built by Mughal Emperor Akbar in 1571 in honour of the famous Sufi saint, Salim Chishti, Fatehpur Sikri was the Mughal capital for 14 years. An example of a Mughal walled city with defined private and public areas and imposing gateways, its architecture, a blend of Hindu and Islamic styles, reflects Akbar's secular vision as well as his style of governance. After the city was abandoned, some say for lack of water, many of its treasures were plundered. It owes its present state of preservation to the initial efforts of Lord Curzon *(see p61)*, a legendary conservationist.

Pillar in the Diwan-i-Khas
The central axis of Akbar's court, supported by carved brackets, was inspired by Gujarat buildings.

Jami Masjid

Khwabgah
The emperor's private sleeping quarters, this "chamber of dreams" with murals and Persian calligraphy has an ingenious ventilating shaft near his bed.

Entrance

★ Turkish Sultana's House
The elaborate dado panels and delicately sculpted walls of this ornate sandstone pavilion make the stone seem like wood. It is topped with an unusual stone roof with imitation clay tiles.

Diwan-i-Aam
This large courtyard with an elaborate pavilion was originally draped with rich tapestries and used for public hearings, receptions and celebrations.

★ Panch Mahal
A five-storeyed open sandstone pavilion, it overlooks the Pachisi Court, where Akbar's queens savoured the cool evening breezes. Its decorative screens were probably stolen after the city was abandoned.

VISITORS' CHECKLIST

Practical Information
Agra district. 37 km (23 miles) W of Agra. **Road map** D3. UPTDC, 64 Taj Rd, Agra, (0562) 222 6431. **Open** 7am–7pm daily.

★ Diwan-i-Khas
Perhaps a debating chamber, the real function of this unique structure is still unknown.

Jodha Bai's Palace

Birbal's House

④

⑤

Ankh Michauli
Sometimes identified as the treasury, this building has mythical guardian beasts carved on its stone struts. Its name means "blind man's buff".

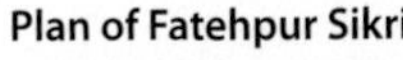

Plan of Fatehpur Sikri

Fatehpur Sikri's royal complex contains the private and public spaces of Akbar's court, which included the harem and the treasury. The adjoining sacred complex containing the Jami Masjid, Salim Chishti's tomb and the Buland Darwaza, are separated from the royal quarters by the Badshahi Darwaza, an exclusive royal gateway.

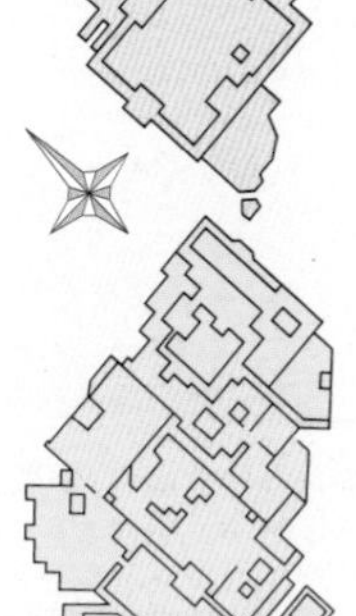

Key

- Area illustrated above
- Other buildings
- Sacred complex (Jami Masjid)

KEY

① **Abdar Khana**

② **Anoop Talao** or pool is associated with Akbar's legendary court musician Tansen who, it is said, could light oil lamps with the magic of his voice.

③ **Haram Sara complex**

④ **Maryam's House**

⑤ **Pachisi Court** is named after a ludo-like game played here by the ladies of the harem.

Exploring Fatehpur Sikri

The principal buildings of the imperial palace complex, clustered on a series of terraces along the sandstone ridge, formed the core of Akbar's city. Stylistically, they marked the absorption of Gujarat into the Mughal Empire and reveal a successful synthesis of pre-Islamic, Hindu and Jain architecture (as in the carved brackets) with the elegant domes and arches of Islamic buildings. The concentric terraces clearly divide the public spaces from the private royal quarters. The buildings, mostly in Akbar's favourite red sandstone, were quarried from the ridge on which they stand.

Stone "tusks" at the Hiran Minar, a memorial to Akbar's favourite elephant

Aerial view of Fatehpur Sikri

Even today, the access to the city that was Akbar's capital is provided by a straight road he built, then lined with exotic bazaars. It leads visitors through the Agra Gate to the triple-arched **Naubat Khana**, where the emperor's entry used to be announced by a roll of drums. The imperial palace complex is entered from the west through the Naubat Khana and opens into the spacious cloistered courtyard of the **Diwan-i-Aam**, where Akbar gave public audiences. A passage behind it leads into the so-called "inner citadel" which contains the **Diwan-i-Khas**, **Khwabgah** and **Anoop Talao**, along with the the treasuries and the **Abdar Khana** where water and fruit for the royal household were stored. It also contains the curiously named **Turkish Sultana's House**. Though probably built for one of Akbar's wives, the identity of the "Turkish Sultana" is unclear. The great courtyard in front of the Diwan-i-Khas is the **Pachisi Court**, named after the central open space that resembles the board game of *pachisi*, similar to ludo.

The **Haram Sara**, or harem complex, was a maze of interconnected buildings beyond Maryam's House or **Sunehra Makan** ("golden house"), named after its rich frescoes and gilding. The massive and austere exterior of the harem leads to **Jodha Bai's Palace**, a large inner courtyard, surrounded by pavilions decorated with azure glazed tiles on the roof. A screened viaduct, presumably for privacy, connected the palace to the **Hawa Maha**l facing a small formal garden. The **Nagina Masjid**, adjoining the garden, was the royal ladies' private mosque. The two-storeyed pavilion popularly said to be **Birbal's House**, situated to the east of Jodha Bai's palace, has spectacular carving on the exterior and interior of its unusual layout. Beyond this lies a large colonnaded enclosure surrounded by cells, meant probably for the servants of the harem, and the royal stables.

The **Hathi Pol** and **Sangin Burj**, the original gateways to the harem, lead to the outermost periphery of the palace complex. This was laid out in concentric circles around the inner citadel and is made up of ancillary structures, such as the caravanserais, the domed *hamams* and waterworks. The **Hiran Minar** ("deer tower"), believed to be a memorial to Akbar's favourite elephant, was probably an *akash deep* ("heavenly light") with lamps suspended from stone "tusks" to guide visitors.

Entrance to Birbal's House

Jami Masjid

This grand open mosque towers over the city of Fatehpur Sikri and was the model for several Mughal mosques. Flanked by arched cloisters, its vast *namazgah* has monumental gates to the east and south. However, the spiritual focus of the complex is the tomb and hermitage of the Sufi mystic, Salim Chishti, as popular today as it was in the days of its Mughal patrons.

Tomb of Sheikh Salim Chishti
Exquisite marble serpentine brackets and almost transparent screens surround the inner tomb which has a mother-of-pearl canopy inlaid with sandalwood.

Hujra
Symmetrically flanking the main mosque, this pair of identical cloistered prayer rooms has flat-roofed pillared galleries that run round the complex.

Badshahi Darwaza
Akbar used the steep steps of this royal gateway to enter the complex. The view of the sacred mosque, directly across, greeted his entry.

Corridors

Buland Darwaza
Erected by Akbar, the huge 54 m (177 ft) gateway later inspired other lofty gates. Young boys dive from its ramparts into the pool below to fish for coins.

Making a Wish in Chishti's Tomb

Ever since Akbar's childlessness was ended by the remarkable prediction of Salim Chishti in 1568, the saint's tomb has become the haunt of those in search of a miracle. The *dargah*, lavishly endowed by both Akbar and his son Jahangir, attracts crowds of supplicants who make a wish, tie a small cotton thread on the screen around the tomb, and go back confident that the saint will make it come true.

A thread tied to a screen in Chishti's tomb

The strikingly ornamental façade of Gwalior Fort

⓬ Gwalior

Gwalior district. 118km (73 miles) S of Agra on NH3. **Road map** D4. 1,100,000. Tansen Residency, 6-A, MG Rd, (0751) 223 4557. Tansen Music Festival (Oct–Nov).

This royal seat of the Scindias is dominated by the massive **Gwalior Fort**. The interior owes some of its finest features to the Tomar musician-king, Man Singh (r. 1486–1517). Near the ornate Hindola Gate, one of three gateways located near the old city, is the romantic Gujari Mahal (1510) built by Man Singh for his tribal wife, the beautiful Mrignayani. It now houses the outstanding **Archaeological Museum**. His main palace, the Man Mandir, with an amazing variety of ornamental glazed tile patterns, is considered the most remarkable example of an early Hindu palace. In the city below the fort, the 19th-century Italian palazzo-style **Jai Vilas Palace** houses the Scindia Museum. Famous for a magnificent crystal staircase and furniture, its vast Durbar Hall has Venetian chandeliers that weigh three tons. A silver model train, laden with brandy and cigars, once used to serve guests at the spectacular royal feasts held here.

Frieze in Gwalior fort

Other notable sights are the tombs of Tansen and Muhammad Ghaus, as well as early temples such as Teli ka Mandir *(see p30)* and the Sas-Bahu ka Mandir.

Gwalior Fort
Open 8am–6pm daily. Son et Lumière: 8:30pm daily.

Archaeological Museum
Open 10am–5pm Sat–Thu. **Closed** Fri & public hols.

Jai Vilas Palace
S of Fort. **Open** 10am–5pm Tue–Sun. **Closed** Wed & public hols.

Gwalior Gharana of Music

Akbar, Tansen and Guru Ramdas

The Gwalior Gharana is one of the oldest schools of North Indian classical music. Its greatest achievement was the adaptation of folk music into the orthodox Dhrupad mode, a contribution of Raja Man Singh and Mrignayani, whose tribal music wove a spell on the king. This form was given lively expression by Gwalior-born Tansen, Akbar's court musician, who developed a range of lyrical new *ragas (see p34)*.

The Datia Palace, built in 1620, displays fine architectural complexity

⓭ Datia

Datia district. 187 km (116 miles) S of Agra. **Road map** D4. 90,600. UPTDC, Hotel Veerangana, Shivpuri Rd, Jhansi, (0517) 244 2402.

The main focus of this ghostly town is the five-storeyed Datia Palace, an outstanding building of great structural complexity. Built by the Bundela king Bir Singh Deo in 1620, its sinister underground chambers still exude an eerie ambience. The finely painted royal apartments within the main courtyard are connected to the galleries around them by double-storeyed bridges.

Another important historic building is the later Rajgarh Palace, which offers a pan- oramic view of the entire walled town.

⓮ A Tour of Bundelkhand

Gwalior and the adjoining region of Bundelkhand, named after the Bundela Rajputs, make up a culturally distinctive area in Central India. Innumerable forts and monuments, situated in a boulder-strewn landscape of great beauty, still echo with stories of the valour and pageantry of the Bundela Rajput courts, and warriors such as the Rani of Jhansi. The area's glorious history and refined cultural traditions are reflected in the architectural treasures of Gwalior, the magical, medieval town of Orchha, and the hilltop temples of Sonagiri.

① **Gwalior** The capital city of many great dynasties since its origins in the 1st century AD, Gwalior is the most splendid of the "gateways" to the Bundelkhand region.

② **Pawaya**
The remains of an ancient fort can be seen in this capital of the Nag kings (3rd century AD) from the highway at Dabra.

③ **Sonagiri**
This impeccably maintained complex of 77 Jain temples is approached through a thriving pilgrim settlement.

④ **Datia**
This erstwhile Bundela capital surrounded by numerous small lakes, has scenically located palaces on hillocks.

Agra
Dabra
Sind
Bundelkhand
Betwa
Lalitpur

Key

Tour route

Other roads

Rivers

0 kilometres 20

0 miles 10

⑤ **Jhansi**
The town is best known for its impressive fort and the heroic Rani Laxmi Bai, who died leading her troops in the 1857 Indian Mutiny.

⑥ **Orchha**
The temples, cenotaphs and tiered palaces here are perfect examples of Bundelkhand architecture *(see pp180–81)*.

⑦ **Taragram**
Its fascinating handmade paper factory is an interesting experimental centre aimed at upgrading local craftsmanship.

Tips for Drivers

Length: 120 km (75 miles).
Stopping-off points: Gwalior, Sonagiri, Datia, Jhansi, Taragram, Orchha. After Gwalior, there is a petrol pump at Dabra on NH3. Accommodation in the form of state tourism hotel and guesthouses is available at Gwalior, Jhansi and Orchha. Local buses run between the major stops.

The 16th-century Chaturbhuj Temple at Orchha

⓮ Orchha

Tikamgarh district. 238 km (148 miles) S of Agra. **Road map** E5. **i** MPTDC, Sheesh Mahal; (07680) 252 624. Ramnavami (Mar–Apr), Dussehra (Sep–Oct).

Orchha is dramatically positioned on a rocky island, enclosed by a loop of the River Betwa. Founded in 1531, it was the capital of the Bundela kings until 1783, when it was abandoned in favour of Tikamgarh.

Crumbling palaces, pavilions, *hamams*, walls and gates, connected to the town with an impressive 14-arched causeway, are all that remain today. Three main palaces, **Raj Mahal** (1591), **Jahangiri Mahal** (1598) and **Rai Praveen Mahal** are massed symmetrically together. Rai Praveen Mahal was named after a royal paramour and Jahangiri Mahal after the Mughal prince who spent a mere night here.

There are three beautiful temples in the old town, the Ram Raja, the Chaturbhuj and the Laxminarayan. A unique blend of fort and temple styles, the **Chaturbhuj Temple**, dedicated to Vishnu, has huge arcaded halls for massed singing and a soaring spire towering over the area.

Lying along the Kanchana Ghat of the Betwa are 14 hauntingly beautiful *chhatris* of the Orchha rulers. Along with the many *sati* pillars in Jahangiri Mahal's museum, these are reminders of Orchha's feudal past when *sati* queens jumped into their husband's funeral pyres.

Jahangiri Mahal

Named after the Mughal emperor Jahangir, who spent one night here with his Bundela ally Bir Singh Deo, this is an excellent example of Rajput Bundela architecture. The many-layered palace has 132 chambers off and above the central courtyard and an almost equal number of subterranean rooms. The square sandstone palace is extravagantly embellished with lapis lazuli tiles, graceful *chhatris* and ornate *jaali* screens. The palace also has a modest museum.

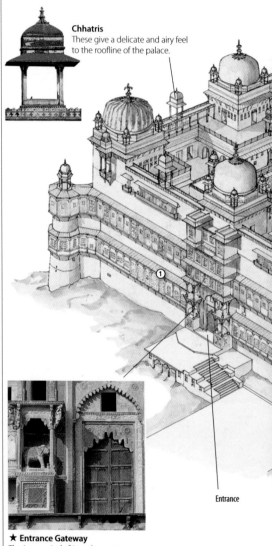

Chhatris
These give a delicate and airy feel to the roofline of the palace.

①

★ Entrance Gateway
The impressively fringed entry gate, flanked by stone elephants, offers a good view of River Betwa.

Entrance

★ Screened Corridor
A screened corridor runs round the fourth level which has eight pavilions with lavishly painted interiors, separated by courts.

VISITORS' CHECKLIST

Practical Information
Palace Complex.
Open 8am–6pm daily.
Closed public hols. MPTDC, Sheesh Mahal.
Museum: **Open** 10am–5pm.

Glazed Tilework
Geometric lapis motifs decorate the outer façade at the upper levels.

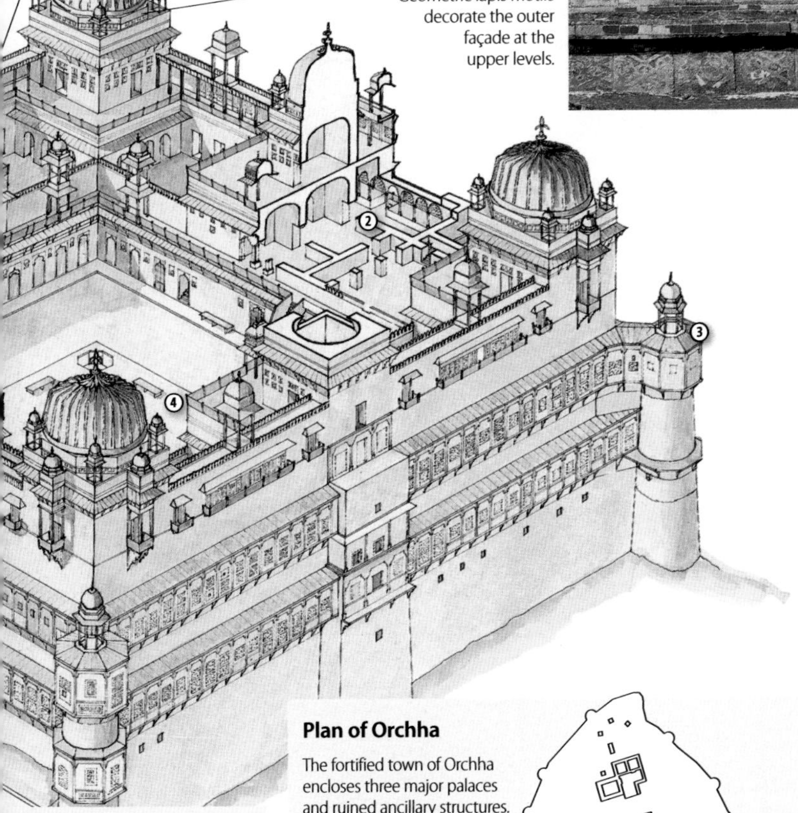

KEY

① **Carved niches** line the outer walls.

② **Jahangir's bedroom**

③ **Fortified bastions** protect the palace.

④ **The central courtyard** can be viewed from each part of the palace and has a small museum in a set of rooms that run along it.

Plan of Orchha

The fortified town of Orchha encloses three major palaces and ruined ancillary structures.

1 Jahangiri Mahal
2 Sheesh Mahal
3 Raj Mahal
4 Rai Praveen Mahal
5 *Hamam*
6 Stable

Key

Area illustrated above

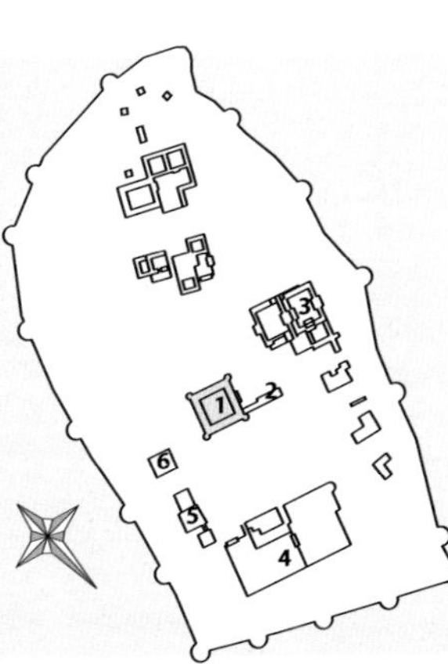

JAIPUR AND ENVIRONS

The Jaipur region of Rajasthan lies on the eastern fringes of the Thar Desert, a semi-arid land cut southwest to northeast by the craggy Aravalli Hills. Studded with hilltop and jungle forts, the region offers valleys and plains that glitter with palaces and pavilions, pleasure gardens and temples. Once ruled by proud Rajput princes, this territory is still sustained by memories of a feudal past that is kept alive by its splendid architectural remains and deep-rooted traditional culture.

At the end of the 11th century, the Kachhawahas of Jaipur established their kingdom at Amber. In the region around it lay other Rajput kingdoms – the Chauhan stronghold of Ajmer that would soon fall to Muslim forces, and the massive Rathore jungle fort of Ranthambhore, which would later become a Mughal preserve. By the 18th century the fierce feudal lords of Shekhawati would become vassals of Amber-Jaipur, while Jat kings would rule over Bharatpur, the only non-Rajput kingdom in the area.

The early Rajput states engaged in bitter internecine clan wars, but with the rise of the Delhi sultans *(see pp54–5)*, their energies were directed at keeping their lands safe from the marauding Muslim troops. Finally, under the Mughal emperor Akbar, military and matrimonial alliances paved the way for peace in the region. The result was a cultural and social synthesis which produced some outstanding art and architecture. The British also followed this policy of appeasement and offered the princes military protection in return for their loyalty. The rule of the princely states ended when, after Independence, they were incorporated into the modern Indian state of Rajasthan, with Jaipur as the administrative capital.

But despite democracy, the Rajput feudal tradition, with its code of loyalty to the local chieftain, and immense pride in their past, remains alive. This is perhaps what has preserved the extraordinary culture of the region, so that for many it still remains the romantic land of forts, palaces and kings it was in medieval times.

Devotees at the sacred ghats of Pushkar

◀ Women in bright saris by the Hawa Mahal, or "Palace of the Winds", Jaipur

Exploring Jaipur and Environs

This historically rich territory is centred around the old capital of Amber and the "newer" city of Jaipur with its palace, observatory, temples and bazaars and impressive modern buildings. To Jaipur's north are the attractive Samode palace and Shekhawati areas, while to its northeast is the wooded area of the Aravallis, where Alwar, a former princely state, and the Sariska National Park are situated. To the southwest, past the textile towns of Sanganer and Bagru, are the religious sites of Ajmer and Pushkar. Southeast of Jaipur lies Chaksu, a pilgrim centre, and Tonk, once the site of a powerful medieval kingdom, beyond which is the spectacular tiger sanctuary of Ranthambhore, nestling beneath the grand ramparts of a historic medieval fort.

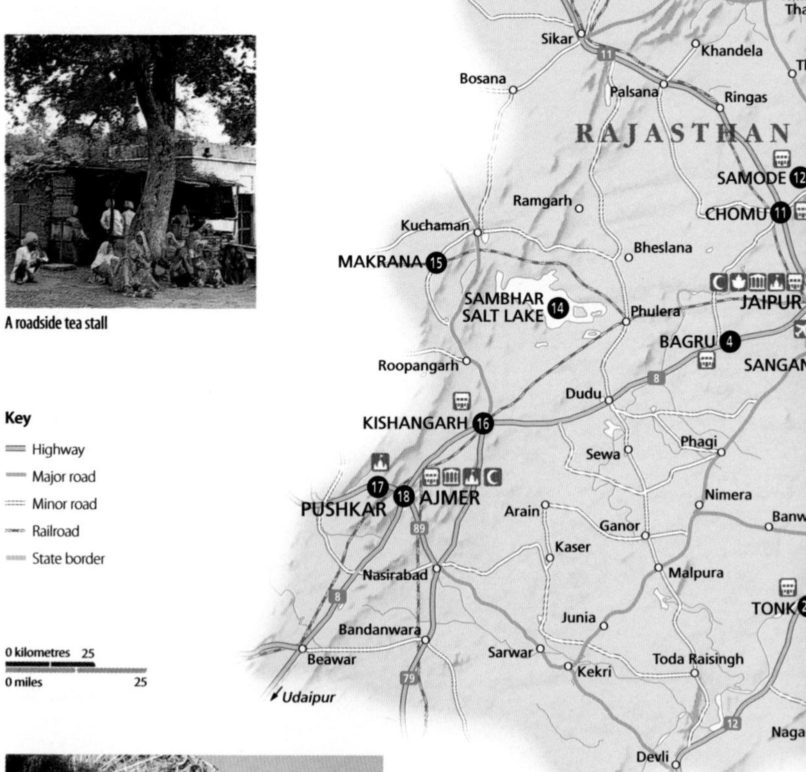

A roadside tea stall

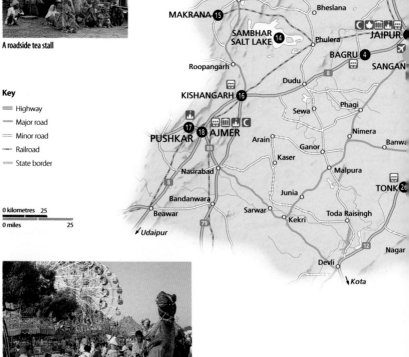

Pushkar's spectacular cattle fair in progress

Getting Around

Jaipur's airport is at Sanganer *(see p286)*, and two superfast trains (the Pink City Express and Shatabdi Express) connect the city to Delhi. Air-conditioned luxury coaches from Delhi to Jaipur are run by Rajasthan Tourism *(see p291)*. The rest of the region is best explored by road. The Palace on Wheels and Royal Rajasthan on Wheels *(see p289)* offer luxury rail tours for well-heeled tourists who wish to savour the trip through the desert in royal comfort.

A sacred tank at Galta

Maota Lake in front of Amber Palace

Printed textiles drying in the sun at Sanganer

Sights at a Glance

1. *Jaipur (see pp186–203)*
2. *Amber (see pp204–7)*
3. Sanganer
4. Bagru
5. *Alwar (see pp210–11)*
6. Siliserh
7. Rajgarh
8. *Sariska National Park (see pp214–15)*
9. Bairat
10. Bhangarh
11. Chomu
12. Samode
14. Sambhar Salt Lake
15. Makrana
16. Kishangarh
17. *Pushkar (see pp220–21)*
18. *Ajmer (see pp222–5)*
19. Chaksu
20. Tonk
21. Sawai Madhopur
22. *Ranthambhore National Park (see pp228–9)*
23. Indergarh

Tours

13. Shekhawati

For keys to symbols *see back flap*

❶ Jaipur

A labyrinth of fascinating bazaars, opulent palaces and historic sights, Jaipur offers a chance to see the medieval alongside the modern. On its colourful streets, camels jostle for space with motorbikes, and turbaned village elders rub shoulders with youngsters in jeans. Often called the Pink City because its prominent buildings are washed with this colour, Jaipur's old walled area has the City Palace Museum, a medieval astronomical observatory, and bazaars that sell everything from precious jewellery to camel skin shoes. Recent additions include a multi-arts centre, yet the city's focal point is still the myriad-windowed pink Hawa Mahal, the Palace of Winds.

Govind Dev Temple, dedicated to Krishna

City Palace Museum

See pp192–5.

Govind Dev Temple

Jaleb Chowk, behind City Palace.
Open 5–11am, 6–8pm daily.
Holi (Mar), Janmashtami (Jul–Aug), Annakut (Oct–Nov).

The presiding deity of this unusual temple is the flute-playing Krishna (also known as Govind Dev). This image, originally from the Govindeoji Temple in Brindavan *(see p166)*, was brought to Amber in the late 17th century to save it from the iconoclastic zeal of Aurangzeb. It is believed that this temple was once a garden pavilion called Suraj Mahal, where Sawai Jai Singh II lived while his dream-city Jaipur was being built. Legend has it that one night, the king awoke from his sleep to find himself in the presence of Krishna who demanded that his *devasthan* ("divine residence") be returned to him. Jai Singh then moved to the Chandra Mahal, at the opposite end of the garden, and installed the image as the guardian deity of Jaipur's rulers. Devotees are allowed only a brief glimpse of their god seven times a day, and on special festivals such as Janmashtami *(see p43)*.

Jai Niwas Bagh

Open 6am–10pm daily.

Just behind the temple is the 18th-century Jai Niwas Bagh, planned as a private leisure ground for the ladies of the royal household. Inspired by the classic Mughal *charbagh*, it has features such as water channels and fountains. Towards the north of the sight is **Badal Mahal**, a five-arched hunting pavilion on the banks of the Talkatora. Its ceilings still bear faint traces of the cloud *(badal)* patterns.

A view of the walled city of Jaipur

Sights at a Glance

1. City Palace Museum
2. Govind Dev Temple
3. Jai Niwas Bagh
4. Talkatora
5. Chaugan Stadium
6. Tripolia Bazaar
7. Jantar Mantar
8. Hawa Mahal
9. Govt Central Museum

Talkatora

N of Jai Niwas Bagh. **Open** daily.

The Talkatora is an artificial tank that existed before Jaipur was built. This may have been one of the reasons why this site was chosen for the new city. When excavated, it was surrounded on three sides by a lake known as Rajamal ka Talab, making it look like a *talkatora*, literally a "bowl in a lake". Sawai Jai Singh II was particularly fond of this rather secluded spot and used to breed crocodiles here. The original lake was later filled in and developed as a residential area.

Chaugan Stadium

Brahmpuri: **Open** 5am–8pm daily.

This large open area near the City Palace derives its name from *chaugan*, an ancient Persian form of polo played with a curved stick. In the past, this area was used for festival processions, wrestling matches, as well as elephant and lion fights. The maharajas and nobility watched from the pavilions of Chini ki Burj (which still retains some of the old blue and white tilework), Moti Burj, Chatar ki Burj and Shyam ki Burj, all located here. *Chaugan* is not played any more, but the stadium is the venue for the famous Elephant Festival held at the time of Holi *(see p42)*.

VISITORS' CHECKLIST

Practical Information

261 km (162 miles) from Delhi on NH8. 3,073,500. RTDC, Swagatam Complex (0141) 220 0595. Rajasthan Tourism, MI Rd, (0141) 511 0598. Mon–Sat. Kite Flying (mid-Jan), Elephant Festival (Feb–Mar), Gangaur (Mar–Apr), Teej (Jul–Aug).

Transport

Sanganer. Sindhi Camp.

A mahout and his caparisoned elephant at a festival

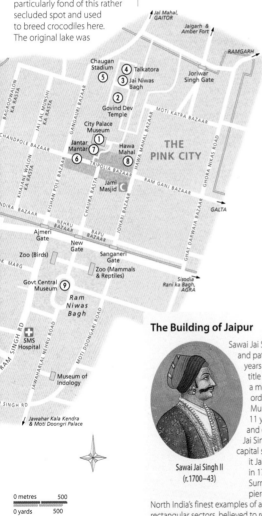

Jal Mahal, GAITOR
Jaigarh & Amber Fort
RAMGARH
Chaugan Stadium ⑤
④ Talkatora
③ Jai Niwas Bagh
② Govind Dev Temple
City Palace Museum ①
Jantar Mantar ⑦
⑥
Hawa Mahal ⑧
Jami Masjid
Joriwar Singh Gate
THE PINK CITY
BAGROOWALON KA RASTA
JAI LAL MUNSHI KA RASTA
GANGAURI BAZAAR
MOTI KATRA BAZAAR
CHANDPOLE BAZAAR
HAWA MAHAL BAZAAR
GHORA NIKAS ROAD
TRIPOLIA BAZAAR
RAM GANJ BAZAAR
KHAJANE WALON KA RASTA
KISHAN POLE BAZAAR
CHAURA RASTA
JOHARI BAZAAR
INDIRA BAZAAR
GALTA
NEHRU BAZAAR
BAPU BAZAAR
GHAT DARWAJA BAZAAR
Ajmeri Gate
New Gate
Sanganeri Gate
Zoo (Birds)
Zoo (Mammals & Reptiles)
Govt Central Museum ⑨
Sisodia Rani ka Bagh, AGRA
Ram Niwas Bagh
SMS Hospital
JAWAHARLAL NEHRU ROAD
MOTI DOONGARI ROAD
Museum of Indology
Jawahar Kala Kendra & Moti Doongri Palace

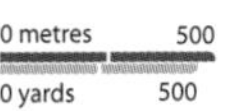

Key

Street-by-Street area

The Building of Jaipur

Sawai Jai Singh II (r.1700–43)

Sawai Jai Singh II, a brilliant statesman, scholar and patron of the arts, ruled for over 40 years and was awarded the title of "Sawai" ("one-and-a-quarter"), a metaphor for one who is extra-ordinary, by Mughal emperor Muhammad Shah when he was just 11 years old. Along with Bengali scholar and engineer, Vidyadhar Chakravarty, Jai Singh supervised the building of a new capital south of Amber and named it Jaipur ("city of victory"). Work started in 1727 and took six years to complete. Surrounded by a crenellated wall pierced by seven gates, Jaipur is one of North India's finest examples of a planned urban city. Its grid of nine rectangular sectors, believed to represent the nine cosmic divisions of the universe, is actually based on a geometric and pragmatic plan with a system of main streets, intersected by spacious market squares. Jai Singh encouraged traders and artists to settle here, giving tax incentives to merchants to ensure economic prosperity.

Street-by-Street: Around Badi Chaupar

The Badi Chaupar ("large square") is at one end of the colourful Tripolia Bazaar. There have been few changes to the original 18th-century plan of streets and squares. Narrow pedestrian lanes branch out of the main streets where artisans fashion puppets, silver jewellery, and other local crafts in tiny workshops. Behind are the *havelis* of eminent citizens, some now used as schools, shops and offices. The area is a hub of activity, rich with pungent smells and vibrant colours, with temple bells adding to the cacophony of street sounds.

Gangaur Festival
A colourful procession of bullock carts marks Gangaur festivities in spring.

Ishwar Lat
Ishwari Singh built this tower in 1749 to commemorate his victory over his stepbrother, Madho Singh I.

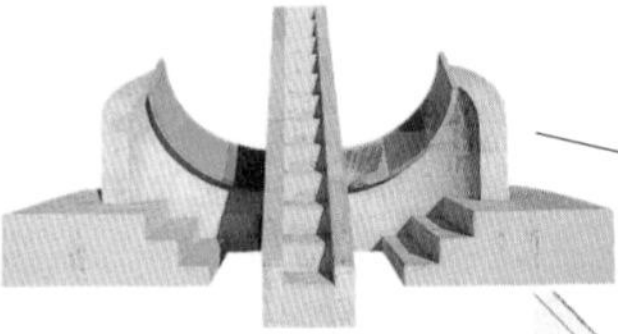

★ Jantar Mantar
Jai Singh II's observatory of astronomical instruments looks like a set of futuristic sculptures (*see pp196–7*).

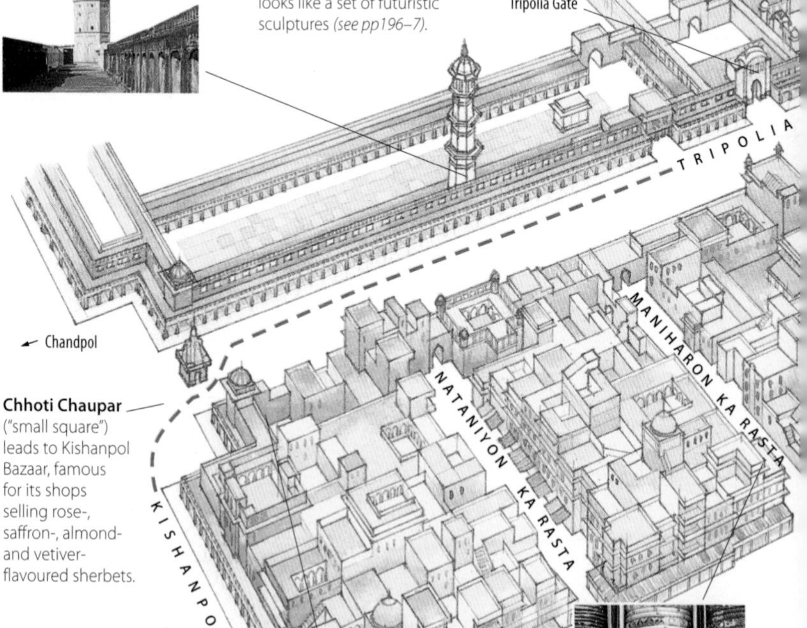

City Palace

Tripolia Gate

TRIPOLIA

Chandpol

MANIHARON KA RASTA

NATANIYON KA RASTA

KISHANPOL BAZAAR

Chhoti Chaupar
("small square") leads to Kishanpol Bazaar, famous for its shops selling rose-, saffron-, almond- and vetiver-flavoured sherbets.

Maharaja Arts College

Flower Sellers
Marigolds and other flowers made into garlands sell briskly as offerings to beloved deities in temples and roadside shrines.

Lac Bangles
Maniharon ka Rasta is full of tiny workshops of lac bangle-makers.

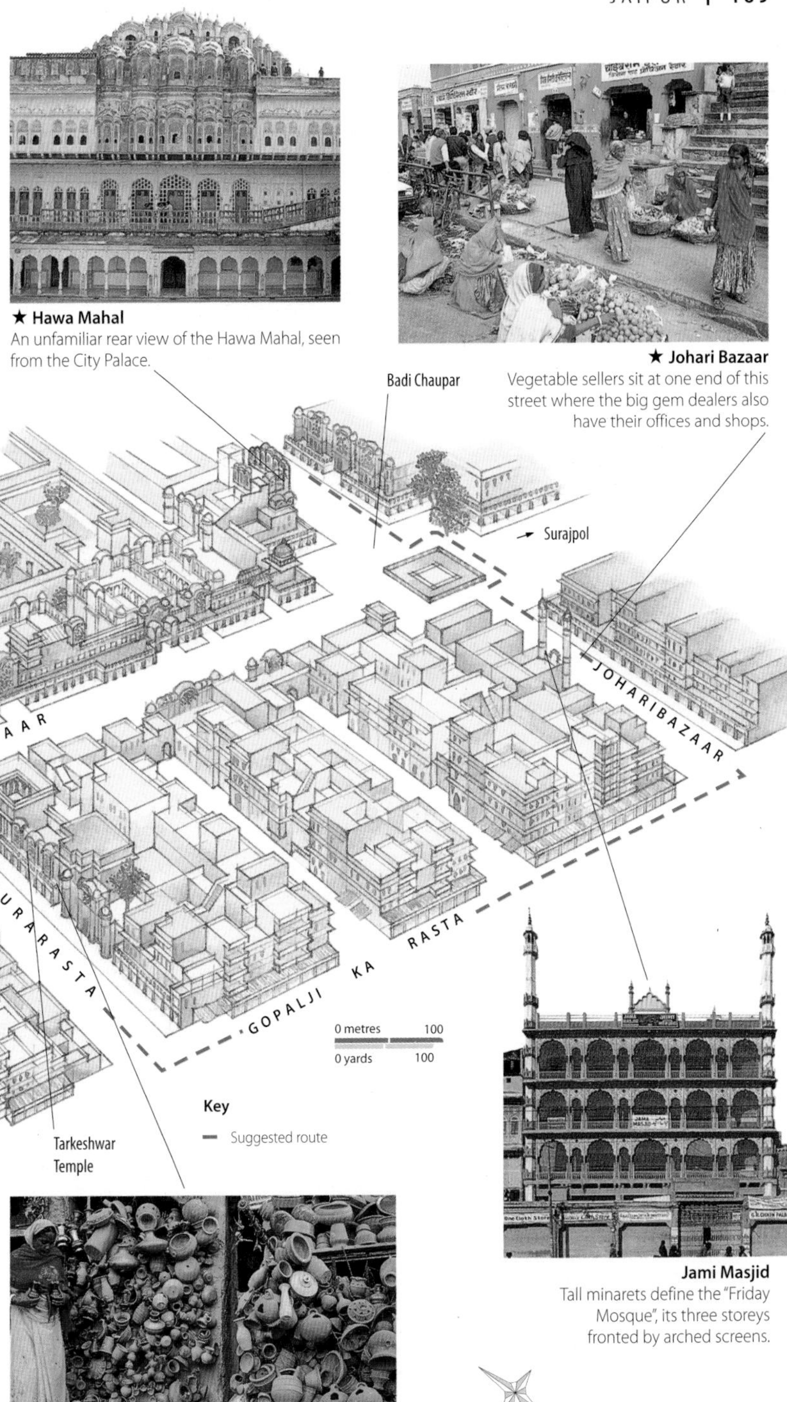

★ Hawa Mahal
An unfamiliar rear view of the Hawa Mahal, seen from the City Palace.

★ Johari Bazaar
Vegetable sellers sit at one end of this street where the big gem dealers also have their offices and shops.

Jami Masjid
Tall minarets define the "Friday Mosque", its three storeys fronted by arched screens.

Pottery Shop
Large terracotta urns, pots of all sizes, bells, statues, foot-scrapers and oil lamps made by traditional craftsmen are sold here.

Hawa Mahal

Sireh Deori Bazaar. **Tel** (0141) 261 8862. **Open** 9am–5pm daily. **Closed** Holi & public hols. extra charges.

A whimsical addition to Rajasthan's rich architectural vocabulary, the fanciful Hawa Mahal or "Palace of Winds" was erected in 1799 by the aesthete Sawai Pratap Singh (r.1778–1803). Its ornate façade has become an icon for the city, a tiered baroque-like composition of projecting windows and balconies with perforated screens. Though five storeys high it is just one room deep, with walls no thicker than 20 cm (8 inches). Built of lime and mortar and painted pink, this structure was so designed to enable the purdahed ladies of the harem to watch unnoticed the colourful street scenes and state processions on Sireh Deori Bazaar below. Visitors are permitted to climb up the winding ramp to the top.

Pratap Singh was a poet, composer and patron of the arts. A devotee of Krishna, he dedicated the Hawa Mahal to him, and many believe that when seen from afar, the building looks like the *mukut* (crown) that often adorns Lord Krishna's head.

A gateway towards the west leads into the complex and to the administrative offices and the **Archaeological Museum**.

Archaeological Museum

Tripolia Bazaar. **Open** 9am–5:30pm. **Closed** Fri & public hols.

Façade of Hawa Mahal

Tripolia Bazaar

To the south of the City Palace is one of the walled city's busiest streets and bazaars. The shops here mainly sell an enormous range of metal goods and kitchenware. The pavements outside the shops attractively display utensils in brass, copper, aluminium and steel as well as crowbars, chisels and other assorted hardware. Sometimes, handicrafts, plastic and paper products, such as the traditional red cloth-bound *bahi khathas* (account books) still used by merchants and moneylenders, are also laid out. At Badi Chaupar, towards the end of the street, are flower-sellers with baskets full of fragrant roses, marigolds, tuberoses and jasmine, and shops selling silver jewellery, hand-embroidered *jootis* (slippers) and feather-light cotton quilts. In the centre of this lively commercial artery stands the majestic Tripolia ("triple-arched") Gate. Constructed in 1734, this was once the main entrance to the palace and on festive occasions, crowds watched the royal entourage of the maharaja and his nobles *(thakurs)*, clad in ceremonial robes, seated on elephants and horses, pass through this impressive gate. Today, its use is confined to members of the royal family and their special guests, and a guard on duty reminds visitors that this is not a public thoroughfare.

Detail of a painted gate

A short distance from Tripolia Gate, towards the east, is the well-maintained **Nawab Saheb ki Haveli**, named after Nawab Faiz Ali Khan, Ram Singh II's *(see p198)* prime minister. This 18th-century mansion was once the residence of Vidyadhar Chakravarty *(see p187)*, who is believed to have chosen this site to supervise the building of the new city of Jaipur. Its enclosed terrace offers some marvellous views of the city. Other *havelis* of eminent citizens can be seen in the narrow alleys off the main street. Some of these gracious old buildings are still occupied by descendants of the original owners, others have been rented out to schools, shops and offices.

Nawab Saheb ki Haveli

Open 10am–6pm daily.

A view of Tripolia Gate with Ishwari Singh's victory tower seen in the distance

Jewellery

Be it the fabulous emeralds and rubies sported by former maharajas and their queens or the splendid silver and bone ornaments worn by peasants, jewellery is an integral part of Rajasthani culture. Even camels, horses and elephants are adorned with specially designed anklets and necklaces. Jaipur is one of the largest ornament-making centres in India, and *meenakari* (enamelling) and *kundankari* (inlaying) are two traditional techniques for which it is most famous. In the 16th century, Man Singh I *(see p53)*, influenced by the prevailing fashions of the Mughal court, brought the first five Sikh enamel workers from Lahore to his state. Since then, generations of highly skilled jewellers have lived and worked here. Jaipur caters to every taste, from chunky silver ornaments to elegant designs intricately set in gold with precious stones.

A jewelled trinket box with a *kundankari* lid has the lower portion worked in fine meenakari with traditional floral patterns in red, blue, green and white.

Sarpech, the cypress-shaped turban ornament, was a fashion statement introduced by the Mughal emperors in the early 17th century to display their finest gems. Rajput rulers, impressed by Mughal flamboyance, sported dazzling ornaments like this piece of enamelled gold set with emeralds, rubies, diamonds and sapphires with a pearl drop.

The skill of setting stones can be seen in the crowded alleys of Haldiyon ka Raasta, Jadiyon ka Raasta and Gopalji ka Raasta. An inherited art, the trade of jewellery is in the hands of artisans' guilds.

Meenakari embellishes the obverse side of *kundan* jewellery, for the Rajasthani love of adornment decrees that even the non-visible back of a piece of jewellery, which touches the wearer's skin, must be as beautiful as the front.

Kundankari uses a highly refined gold as the base, which is then inlaid with lac and set with precious and semi-precious stones to provide the colour and design. Purified gold wire outlines the design and also conceals the lac background.

Jaipur is now a centre of lapidary, specializing in the cutting of emeralds and diamonds that come from Africa, South America, and parts of India. Gem-cutters learn their skill by cutting garnets.

City Palace Museum

Occupying the heart of Jai Singh II's city, the City Palace has been home to the rulers of Jaipur since the first half of the 18th century. The sprawling complex is a superb blend of Rajput and Mughal architecture, with open, airy Mughal-style public buildings leading to private apartments. The opulence and exquisite craftsmanship is a tribute both to the wealth of the former maharajas and their lavish patronage of the arts. Today, the complex is open to the public as the Maharaja Sawai Man Singh II Museum, popularly known as the City Palace Museum. The beautiful Chandra Mahal, once the residence of the maharaja, is also open to visitors.

★ Pritam Chowk
The "Court of the Beloved" has four delicately painted doorways representing the seasons.

Sileh Khana
The erstwhile armoury houses the museum's collection of weapons, some lavishly decorated, and is considered among the finest in India.

★ Mubarak Mahal
This sandstone "Welcome Palace" was built in 1900 by Madho Singh II to receive guests, hence the name. It is now the costume and textile gallery.

KEY

① Crafts demonstration area
② Riddhi-Siddhi Pol
③ Shops
④ Transport gallery
⑤ Ticket counter

★ Rajendra Pol
Flanking the gateway are two large elephants, each carved from a single block of marble.

Chandra Mahal
Each floor of this seven-storeyed palace is extravagantly decorated and has a specific name according to its function. The top floor affords great city views.

VISITORS' CHECKLIST

Practical Information
City Palace Complex. **Tel** (0141) 408 8888. **Open** 9am–5pm daily. **Closed** public hols. (including use of audio guide). Director's permission needed to see Ram Singh II's Reserve Collection of photos.

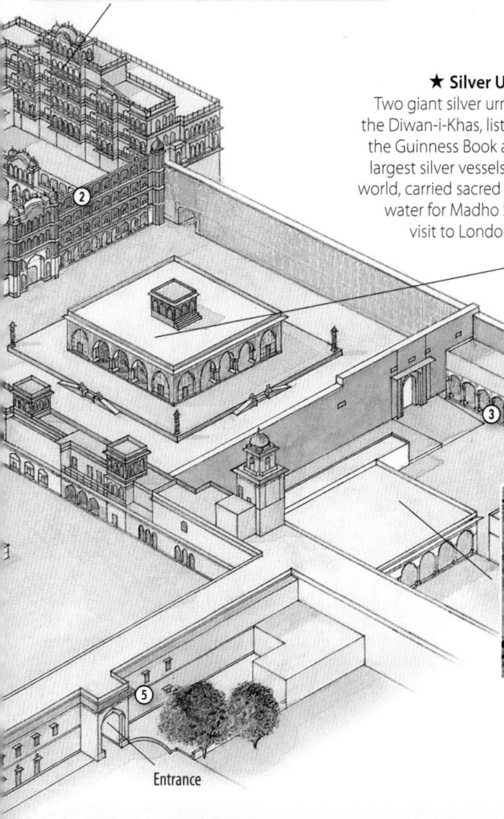

★ Silver Urns
Two giant silver urns in the Diwan-i-Khas, listed in the Guinness Book as the largest silver vessels in the world, carried sacred Ganges water for Madho Singh II's visit to London in 1901.

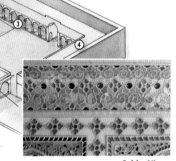

Sabha Niwas
Sparkling glass mirrors embellished with intricate designs are among the many stunning features in the Durbar Hall (audience hall).

The City Palace

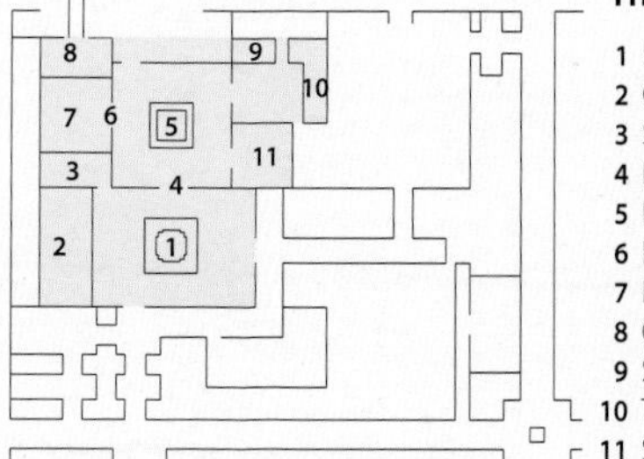

1 Mubarak Mahal
2 Crafts Demonstration Area
3 Sileh Khana
4 Rajendra Pol
5 Diwan-i-Khas
6 Riddhi-Siddhi Pol
7 Pritam Chowk
8 Chandra Mahal
9 Shops
10 Transport Gallery
11 Sabha Niwas (Durbar Hall)

Key

Building area

0 metres 200
0 yards 200

Exploring the City Palace Museum

The Maharaja Sawai Man Singh II Museum provides a splendid introduction to the arts and crafts and the courtly pomp and ceremony of Jaipur in the old days. In their long reign, which spanned almost a thousand years, the Kachhawaha rulers amassed a fabulous collection of treasures – rare manuscripts, miniature paintings, carpets, textiles, costumes and weaponry, palanquins and chariots. These are some of the royal and historical memorabilia displayed here. Initially a private collection open only to select visitors and dignitaries, in 1959 it was formally declared a state museum that is open to the public.

The palatial interior of the Chandra Mahal

Chandra Mahal

The beautiful Chandra Mahal (Moon Palace) or Satkhana Mahal (Seven Storied Palace) is located in the north-west of the vast City Palace. It was planned and built by Jaipur's chief architect Vidhyadhar Chakravorty for Maharaja Sawai Jai Singh II *(see p187)*, and was completed in 1734.

Each of the seven floors is luxuriously decorated with paintings, floral decorations, tiling and mirrors. The ground and first floors of the palace house the extensive art collection of the Maharaja Sawai Man Singh II Museum. Artworks include life-sized portraits of Jaipur rulers by the German artist AH Muller (1878–1952) and miniatures of the Rajasthani, Persian and Mughal schools. Enamelware, weaponry, carpets, and dresses and costumes worn by former royals of Jaipur complete the collection.

The second floor, Suhk Niwas (Hall of Pleasure), has an open terrace. Possibly built in honour of Sawai Jai Singh's beloved queen, Sukh Kanwar, it is decorated with colourful floral designs and Mughal miniatures. Rang Mandir (Temple of Colour), the third floor, is embellished with mirrors in the walls, pillars and ceilings, as is the fourth floor, Shobha Niwas (House of Beauty), which also has exquisite blue tiles and gold leaf. The fifth floor, Chhavi Niwas (Hall of Images), is decorated with blue-and-white painted floral designs and was the maharaja's retreat during the rainy season. Sri Niwas (Shining Hall), the sixth floor, offers mirrored ceilings and rows of double columns through which there are magnificent views of the hills and city. Finally, the top-floor, Mukut Niwas (House of the Crown), is an open marble pavilion affording panoramic views of the walled city.

One of the rare Mughal miniatures in the Chandra Mahal

Textiles and Costumes Gallery

A glittering collection of textiles and costumes from the royal *toshakhana* (treasure house) is displayed on the ground floor of **Mubarak Mahal**. Also known as the Welcome Palace, this was a reception centre for visiting dignitaries. On view here are rich brocades, known as *kimkhabs*, from Surat, Aurangabad and Varanasi, exquisitely embroidered and handloom-woven shawls from Kashmir, embroidered silks, embossed velvets and light, gossamer muslins typical of Dhaka (today in Bangladesh), which collectively represent India's great textile tradition.

The expert and refined craftsmanship that existed in Jaipur almost three centuries ago is visible in the wide variety of hand-blockprinted textiles from nearby Sanganer and tie-and-dye *(bandhini)* pieces specially produced by the printers and dyers from the palace workshops. Equally breathtaking is the incredible range of well-preserved royal garments. Dazzling gathered skirts and long, flowing veils *(odhnis)*, decorated with delicate *zari* (gold thread embroidery) and *gota* (gold or silver frill), worn by the ladies of the court, vie for attention with the brocaded robes, waistbands *(patkas)*, pyjamas and turbans that comprised the male attire. The most striking of these royal robes is the enormous pale pink *atamsukh* ("comfort of the soul") of Sawai Madho Singh I (r.1750–68), who was 2 m (7 ft) tall and 1.23 m (4 ft) in girth, and weighed 230 kg (500 lbs)! This long, quilted cloak-like robe, worn usually by men in winter, is embossed with gold work. There is also a rare gold-brocaded velvet throne cover, bearing seal marks that date to 1605, and an intricately woven gold and silk circular *thal-posh* (dish-cover).

The lattice screens that run round the balcony here once enabled royal ladies and their retinues to watch the proceedings of the durbar hall without being seen.

A tissue *ghaghara*, early 20th century

Sabha Niwas (Durbar Hall)

Leading from the Mubarak Mahal is a magnificent gateway with a brass door that opens into a stately courtyard and the fascinating Sabha Niwas (Hall of Public Audience). Also sometimes referred to as Diwan-e-Aam, it was built during the reign of Maharaja Sawai Pratap Singh (1778–1803), a period that saw great development in local architectural and building skills.

The spacious, richly decorated assembly hall is built on a raised platform supported by artistically dressed marble columns. It was used by the maharajas for formal durbars (royal courts), ceremonies and receptions. The hall housed an art gallery for many years, but a conservation programme has restored its former status and sparkling decor. Visitors now have the sense of a real durbar as it used to be when Sawai Man Singh II, Jaipur's last maharajah, would hold his public audiences here. The last durbar took place in March 1949.

Arms Gallery

This gallery, known as the Sileh Khana, is located near the Mubarak Mahal. Some of the exhibits, displayed under exuberantly painted ceilings, are reputed to be the finest examples of weapons used in medieval India and are a tribute to the Rajput warrior's worship of arms. Whether specially commissioned, or acquired by the maharajas, the weapons in the royal armoury were both lethal and exquisitely crafted. On view are a range of swords, daggers and *katars*, a dual-edged blade with a grip handle, which would have been worn hitched to the waistband. Some are of green or white jade and are carved, while others are studded with jewels. Hilts are engraved with hunting scenes, images of gods and goddesses, or topped with the heads of exotic birds and animals.

Diamond-studded dagger with pistols

Among the swords on display is one belonging to Raja Man Singh I (r.1590–1619) weighing about 5 kg (11 lbs). Another, made by Abdullah Isfahani, bears the emblem of the Shah of Persia. There are two swords of Jahangir and Shah Jahan and also Akbar's gold-encrusted helmet, shaped like a turban. A fascinating section displays gunpowder containers, some made of ivory, others decorated with mother-of-pearl inlay on shell.

The gallery's collection also contains such gut-wrenching exhibits as a lotus-shaped steel mace belonging to Jai Singh I. When rammed into the enemy's stomach, it would spring into a deadly fan of sharp spikes and disembowel the victim.

Entrance to the Sileh Khana arms gallery, flanked by field guns

Transport Gallery

A comparatively recent addition is the Transport Gallery situated near the Art Gallery. It exhibits palanquins, chariots, *ikkas*, buggies and carriages from the old Buggi Khana which fell into disuse after the motor car became popular with the maharajas.

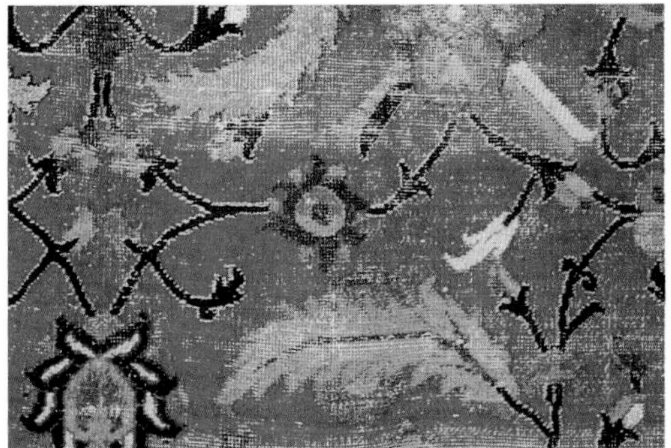
Fragment of a 16th-century Persian carpet

Jantar Mantar

Of the five observatories built by Sawai Jai Singh II, the one in Jaipur is the largest and best preserved; the others are in Delhi *(see p81)*, Ujjain, Mathura and Varanasi. A keen astronomer himself, Jai Singh was aware of the latest astronomical studies in the world, and was most inspired by the work of Mirza Ulugh Beg, the astronomer-king of Samarkand. Built between 1728 and 1734, this observatory resembles a giant sculptural composition of 16 instruments and has been described as "the most realistic and logical landscape in stone". Some of the instruments are still used to forecast how hot the summer months will be, the expected date of arrival, duration and intensity of the monsoon, and the possibility of floods and famine.

Narivalaya Yantra
Inclined at 27°, these represent the two hemispheres and are sundials that calculate time by following the solar cycle.

Unnatansha Yantra
was used to determine the positions of stars and planets at any time of day or night.

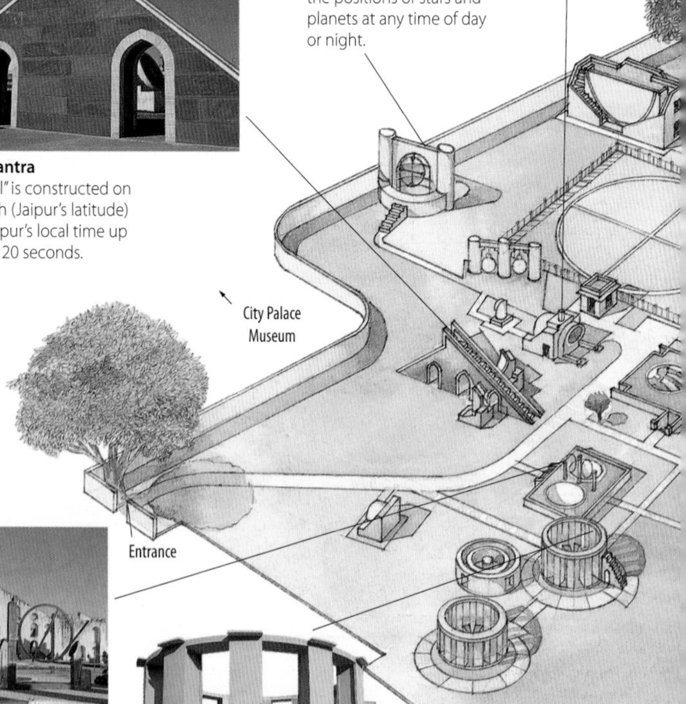

Laghu Samrat Yantra
This "small sundial" is constructed on Latitude 27° North (Jaipur's latitude) and calculates Jaipur's local time up to an accuracy of 20 seconds.

City Palace Museum

Entrance

Chakra Yantra
A brass tube passes through the centre of two circular metal instruments through which the angle of stars and planets from the equator can be observed.

★ Ram Yantra
Vertical columns support an equal number of horizontal slabs in two identical stone structures that comprise this instrument. The readings from these determine the celestial arc from horizon to zenith, as well as the altitude of the sun.

Jantar Mantar
The complex of stone and metal instruments was repaired with the addition of marble inlay by Madho Singh II in 1901.

VISITORS' CHECKLIST

Practical Information
Chandni Chowk, outside City Palace. **Tel** (0141) 261 0494. **Open** 9am–5pm daily. **Closed** Holi & public hols. extra charges. Son et Lumière: 6:30pm daily.

★ Samrat Yantra
Jai Singh believed that gigantic instruments would give more accurate results. This 27-m (90-ft) high sundial forecasts the crop prospects for the year.

Hawa Mahal

Rashivalaya Yantra
This is composed of 12 pieces, each of which represents a sign of the zodiac and so faces a different angle and constellation. This unique *yantra* is still used by astrologers to make accurate horoscopes.

★ Jai Prakash Yantra
Two sunken hemispheres map out the heavens. This instrument is believed by some historians to have been invented by Jai Singh himself to verify the accuracy of all the others in the observatory.

South of the Walled City

By the end of the 19th century, Jaipur had spread far beyond the boundaries established by Sawai Jai Singh II. Much of the area outside the walled city was developed by the enlightened ruler, Sawai Ram Singh II (r.1835–80). This able administrator also modernized the city by adding many civic amenities such as good roads, street lighting and running water. As Jaipur expanded, it incorporated the pleasure palaces and hunting lodges existing on its outskirts. The still-gracious city we see today is a harmonious blend of the old and the new.

The Indo-Saracenic-style Government Central Museum (Albert Hall)

Government Central Museum

Ram Niwas Bagh. **Tel** (0141) 257 0099. **Open** 9:45am–5:15pm Sun–Tue. extra charges.

Designed by Sir Samuel Swinton Jacob, Albert Hall or the Government Central Museum was commissioned by Sawai Ram Singh II to honour the visit of Albert, the Prince of Wales, in 1886. Swinton Jacob had perfected the Indo-Saracenic style of architecture, a hybrid form that combined modern European with traditional Indian elements to create a highly ornamental style used for many public buildings during the Raj.

This grand multi-layered building, with its domes, parapets and balustrades, is located in the centre of the Ram Niwas Gardens. Its ground floor displays decorative shields and embossed salvers in Jaipur's famed metalware, life-sized models of rural scenes, good examples of Jaipur's glazed pottery, and even an Egyptian mummy. The first floor has a fine collection of Mughal and Rajput miniature paintings. Other items on display include wood carvings, lacquer work, ivory pieces, jewellery, textiles and pottery objects. The museum's greatest treasure, one of the world's largest Persian garden carpets (1632), is housed in the Durbar Hall.

Museum of Indology

Nilambara, Prachaya Vidya Path, 24 Gangwal Park, Malviya Nagar. **Tel** (0141) 260 7455. **Open** 10am–5pm daily.

The large mansion of the reputed scholar, Acharya RC Sharma "Vyakul", is now home to a privately owned museum that displays his unusual personal collection. Among the exhibits are impressive displays of maps, coins, manuscripts, textiles and jewellery, fossils, gems and clocks. The museum's charm, however, lies in its idiosyncrasies, such as a map of India painted on a grain of rice, a copy of Rajasthan's oldest newspaper (1856), and letters written, incredibly, on a single strand of hair.

Moti Doongri

Jawaharlal Nehru Marg. **Open** 5am–1:30pm & 4:30–9:30pm daily.

Moti Doongri owes its florid exterior to Sawai Man Singh II, who converted the old fort of Shankargarh into a palace and added turrets in the style of a Scottish castle. In 1940 he married the beautiful Princess Gayatri Devi of Cooch Behar, and this palace with its modernized interior became the venue for glittering parties hosted by the glamorous couple for their wide circle of friends. After his death in 1970, the maharani, by then a Member of Parliament, lived here for some years to keep in touch with her constituency. The palace, a private property, is perched on a low hillock, with only its ramparts and the tall spire of an ancient Shiva temple visible from the road.

At the foot of Moti Doongri is the white marble **Lakshmi Narayan Temple**. This generously endowed building was erected in 1988 on a piece of land sold by the Jaipur royal family for a token sum to the Birlas, a powerful industrial family. Though the sale was disputed and created a huge uproar in the local press, the temple is now a popular place of worship, admired for its carvings.

Lakshmi Narayan Temple, a white marble addition to the Pink City

The luxurious interior of Rambagh Palace

Statue Circle

Bhagwan Das Rd.

This popular landmark is a traffic roundabout, circling an imposing white marble statue of Sawai Jai Singh II, commissioned by the Sawai Jai Singh Benevolent Trust. It was installed in 1968 and is now a lunch-hour recreation spot for office workers and for evening joggers.

Facing the statue to the left is the **Birla Planetarium**. The complex comprises two modern buildings: the science museum with an auditorium, and the planetarium. The main entrance of the building is a replica of Amber Fort's Ganesh Pol *(see p205)*. Exhibitions and sales of Rajasthani handicrafts are held here periodically.

Statue of Sawai Jai Singh II

Birla Planetarium

Statue Circle, Prithviraj Rd. **Open** 11am–8pm daily. **Tel** (0141) 238 5094.

Rambagh Palace

Bhawani Singh Rd. **Tel** (0141) 221 1919. open to non-residents.

The Rambagh Palace, now a splendid hotel *(see p241)*, has had a colourful past. From its modest origins in 1835 as a small, four-roomed garden pavilion for Ram Singh II's wet nurse, it was used as a hunting lodge after she died in 1856. Later, when Ram Singh II's son, Madho Singh II, returned from England, he transformed it with the help of Swinton Jacob into a royal playground with squash and tennis courts, a polo field and indoor swimming pool. In 1933 it was selected as the official residence of Madho Singh's adopted son and heir, Man Singh II, who invited Hammonds of London to re-do the interiors, adding a red and gold Chinese room, black marble bathrooms and fabulous Lalique crystal chandeliers, fountains and an illuminated dining table.

Surrounded by fairy-tale gardens, this was the perfect setting for Man Singh and his wife. Rambagh became the official residence of the Head of State of the new Rajasthan Union in 1949, and a hotel in 1957.

Raj Mahal Palace

Sardar Patel Marg. **Tel** (0141) 414 3000. open to non-residents.

Now a grand heritage hotel, this 18th-century palace, less opulent than the Rambagh Palace, occupies a special place in the history of Jaipur. Built in 1739 for Sawai Jai Singh II's favourite queen, Chandra Kumari Ranawatji, it was used as a summer resort by the ladies of the court. In 1821, it was then declared the official home of the British Resident in Jaipur. However, the most glamorous and memorable phase of its colourful history dates to the time when Man Singh II and Gayatri Devi moved here from Rambagh Palace in 1956. Among the celebrities they entertained were Prince Philip, a polo player like Man Singh, and Jackie Kennedy.

Jawahar Kala Kendra, a centre that promotes art and culture

Jawahar Kala Kendra

Jawaharlal Nehru Marg. **Tel** (0141) 270 6560. **Open** 7am–10pm daily.

Designed by Indian architect Charles Correa in 1993, this remarkable building offers tribute to contemporary Indian design. Imaginatively patterned after the famous grid system of the city, each of the nine squares or courts houses a *mahal* named after a planet. Each *mahal* displays selected exhibits of textiles, handicrafts and weaponry, while in the centre there is a grand open-air plaza where performances of traditional Rajasthani music and dance are also held.

Polo – A Royal Game

Polo, said to be Central Asian in origin, was brought to India by the Muslim conquerors. Its requirement of superior cavalry skills made it a popular sport among Rajput royalty and the army. Man Singh II was a dashing polo player and formed the Jaipur polo team and club in the 1930s. Ironically, he died in England in 1970, playing the game he loved so well. Jaipur is still a well-known venue, and distinguished visitors such as Prince Philip and Prince Charles have played polo here.

A Jaipur polo player in action

Beyond Jaipur: East

Enclosing a narrow valley, a parallel range of hills runs along Jaipur's eastern periphery from Sanganer in the south up to Amber and beyond. This combination of rocky terrain and thickly wooded slopes provided an attractive environment for the rulers and nobility who built temples, garden pavilions and palaces here for themselves. The area is also known for its wildlife, particularly monkeys, after whom the valley is fittingly named the Valley of Monkeys.

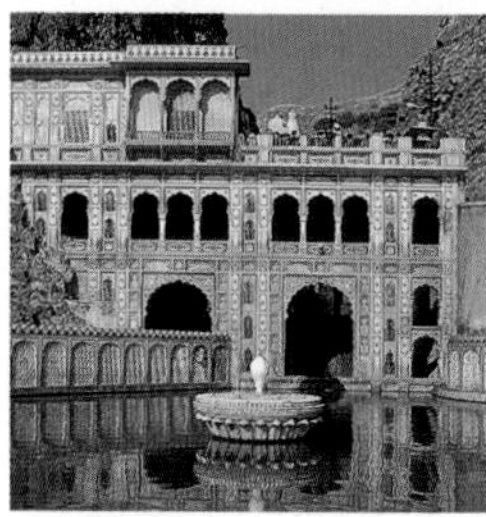

A sacred tank at Galta, whose waters are said to have healing powers

Galta

10 km (6 miles) E of Jaipur on Agra Rd.

The picturesque Galta gorge plunges down the hillside to join the Jaipur–Agra road. A great sage, called Galav, is supposed to have lived and performed penance here. Deep within the gorge is Galta Kund, an 18th-century religious site with two main temples dedicated to Ram and Vishnu; the Achariyon ki Haveli; and a number of smaller shrines and now derelict buildings. High on the ridge is the Surya Temple.

At different levels are sacred tanks, fed throughout the year by natural spring water flowing from a rock resembling a cow's mouth. The water is said to have curative powers. The two *baradaris* on either side of the complex have fairly well-preserved frescoes depicting legends from Krishna's life, including a ceiling profusely painted with gorgeous lotus blooms; others depict the maharaja playing polo.

From the summit there are spectacular views of Jaipur, but do beware of monkeys in search of food. More than 5,000 monkeys live here, attracting tourists who watch them splash about in the water tanks. Visitors can purchase peanuts to feed to the monkeys at the temple gate, but should be prepared to be mobbed. The macaques are bold and aggressive, but the langurs are not so persistent.

Sisodia Rani ka Bagh

Purana Ghat. 6 km (4 miles) E of Jaipur on Agra Rd. **Tel** (0141) 232 1534. **Open** 8am–5pm daily. Son et Lumière: 5–8pm (additional charge).

This terraced garden was laid out in the 18th century for Sawai Jai Singh II's second wife, a Sisodia princess from Udaipur. The marriage was one of convenience, to foster better relations between the two powerful princely states, and one of the conditions was that the new queen's son would succeed to the Jaipur throne. To escape the ensuing and inevitable palace intrigues, the queen decided to shift to a more private home outside the walled city.

Her little double-storeyed palace is surrounded by beautiful gardens artfully planted with fragrant bushes of jasmine, where peacocks dance amid the spray of fountains and gurgling water channels. The interiors are decorated with lively murals depicting episodes from Krishna's life, hunting scenes and polo matches, mythical beasts and heroic events. Behind the gardens, temples coated in the yellow wash that is used throughout the compound are open for worship at midday and in the early evening. Not surprisingly, this enchanting place has become a popular set location for Indian films.

Environs

Opposite Sisodia Rani ka Bagh is **Vidyadhar ka Bagh**, a small and beautiful 18th-century garden laid out in the valley between two hills. Designed along the lines of a Mughal garden with fountains, shady trees and flowerbeds, it is dedicated to the courtier traditionally credited with designing Jaipur *(see p187)*. An evening visit to the renovated garden is particularly magical because the bases of the surrounding hills are lit up, illuminating the garden against the night sky.

Ghat ke Balaji

6 km (4 miles) N of Sisodia Rani ka Bagh towards Galta. **Tel** (0141) 268 0964.

Behind Sisodia gardens, a double flight of steps ends in a pair of tall gateways leading to a small temple dedicated to the popular monkey-god Hanuman (also

Sisodia Rani ka Bagh, laid out as a formal Mughal *charbagh*

Elegant *chhatris* of deserted buildings lining the Ghat ki Guni road

known as Balaji). This endearing deity is cherished by the local people who treat him with tender care, and in winter wrap his image in a muffler and quilt to keep him warm. The monkeys that inhabit the area are equally well looked after. Every evening at 4pm, a charming ritual takes place when, to the call of the priests, hordes of silver grey langurs with black faces and long tails descend on the temple for a meal specially cooked for them. Then, swishing their tails, they head back to the valley that bears their name.

Ghat ki Guni

6 km (4 miles) E of Jaipur on Agra Rd.

In the 18th and 19th centuries the ministers and dignitaries of the Jaipur court created a tranquil summer retreat in this valley, when the area would bustle with the constant coming and going of aristocracy. Now, the deserted *havelis*, temples and bathing ghats are all that remain of this once exclusive resort. On either side of the road are dense rows of niched façades perforated by tiny windows and arched *chhatris*, elegant eaves and domes, while among the ruins and winding alleys, a number of tea-stalls and little shops selling trinkets and souvenirs have sprung up.

Ramgarh

40 km (25 miles) E of Jaipur.

Ramgarh is the site of one of the earliest fortresses of the Kachhawahas. It was built by the dynasty's founder, Duleh Rai (r.1093–1135), after he defeated the local Meenas by attacking them on a Diwali night when they were forbidden to carry weapons.

A lake created here in the 19th century was once Jaipur's main source of drinking water but has been dry for several years due to insufficient rainfall. On its northern bank is Ramgarh Lodge, an elegant hunting lodge built in 1931 for the Jaipur royal family. It is now a pleasing heritage hotel and makes a relaxing retreat from Jaipur.

Hanuman – The Monkey God

Hanuman statue

A much loved figure in the pantheon of Hindu gods *(see pp28–9)*, Hanuman appears wherever Rama is worshipped. In the *Ramayana* *(see p41)*, this loyal trooper and his monkey army play a crucial role in the defeat of Ravana and the rescue of Sita. To this day, warriors, acrobats and wrestlers regard him as their patron deity. The cult of Hanuman as a martial god and protector is so widespread that even a simple stone daubed with orange vermilion paste *(sindur)* signals his presence.

Yet, he has another more loveable side which widens the circle of his devotees. They believe this fearless warrior, who set Lanka afire and decimated Ravana's army, is ignorant of his own miraculous powers. Not only can he cure disease and exorcise evil spirits; he can cure infertility because his celibacy gives him that power. Others believe he also knows the secrets of yoga and the finer points of music and Sanskrit grammar. By combining the might of a martial god with the endearing qualities of the monkey he resembles, Hanuman becomes a link between warrior princes and simple peasants.

Beyond Jaipur: North

Towering above Jaipur are the two dramatic fortresses of Nahargarh and Jaigarh that guard the approach from the north to both Amber and the new capital of Jaipur. Today, they recall a bygone age when warrior clans fought for supremacy. The surrounding rocky terrain also has the remains of fortified walls, temples and shrines, *havelis* and the ornate marble cenotaphs of the Kachhawaha kings.

Nahargarh

9 km (5 miles) NW of Jaipur on Amber Rd. **Tel** (0141) 513 4038. **Open** 10am–5:30pm daily. **Closed** public hols.

The forbidding hill-top fort of Nahargarh ("tiger fort") stands in what was once a densely forested area. The fierce Meena tribe ruled this region until they were defeated by the Kachhawahas. Legend says that this was the site of the cenotaph of Nahar Singh, a martyred Rathore warrior, and when Sawai Jai Singh II ordered that its fortifications be strengthened to defend the newly-built Jaipur, the warrior's spirit resisted all construction until a priest performed tantric rites. Successive rulers further expanded the fort. Madho Singh II added a lavish palace called Madhavendra Bhavan for his nine queens. Laid out in a maze of terraces and courtyards, it has a cool, airy upper chamber from which the ladies of the court could view the city. Its walls and pillars are an outstanding example of *arayish*, a plaster-work technique that is hand-polished with a piece of agate to produce a marble finish.

Pundarik ki Haveli

Shastri Chowk, Brahmpuri. **Tel** (0141) 513 4038. **Open** 8am–5pm daily.

Lying to the east of Nahargarh, on the way to Gaitor, is the Brahmpuri area where the grand *havelis* of the pundits and scholars of the Jaipur court once stood. One mansion was the residence of Pandit Ratnakar Pundarik, a Brahmin courtier during the reign of Sawai Jai Singh II who, it is said, conducted the *puja* that appeased the spirit of Nahar Singh. Fortunately, this *haveli* has survived the ravages of time and is partly occupied. A portion is now a protected monument to preserve the superb frescoes decorating the walls and ceilings of the living rooms. These lively paintings depict gods and goddesses, courtly scenes and festival processions. One also portrays life on the different floors of the seven-storeyed Chandra Mahal *(see pp192–3)*.

Gaitor

Brahmpuri. **Open** 10am–5:30pm Mon–Sat. **Closed** Sun & public hols.

The marble cenotaphs of the Kachhawaha kings are enclosed in a walled garden just below Nahargarh Fort. Sawai Jai Singh II chose this to be the new cremation site after Amber was abandoned *(see p207)*. Ornate, carved pillars support the marble *chhatris* erected over the platforms where the maharajas were cremated. One of the most impressive cenotaphs is that of Jai Singh II himself. It has 20 marble pillars, carved with mythological scenes and

Maharani ki Chhatri

One of the exquisite, well preserved murals at Pundarik ki Haveli

The picturesque Jal Mahal during the monsoon

topped by a white marble dome. Another is that of Sawai Ram Singh II, with stone pillars and dome panels carved with images of Hindu deities and scenes from Krishna's life. There is another sandstone and marble *chhatri* in memory of Madho Singh II. The most recent cenotaph was erected in 1997 in memory of Jagat Singh, the only son of Sawai Man Singh II and Gayatri Devi.

Environs

The *chhatris* of the official wives of the Jaipur kings are located in a separate enclosure called **Maharani ki Chhatri**, outside the Jorawar Singh Gate of the walled city, on the road to Amber. Set in a pleasant garden, the complex with its cupolas and carved pillars was restored in 1995.

Maharani ki Chhatri
Amber Rd. **Open** 9am–4:30pm daily. **Closed** public hols.

Jal Mahal

Amber Rd, opp Trident Hotel.
Open restricted entry.

During the monsoon when water fills the Man Sagar lake, the Jal Mahal or "water palace" seems to float serenely on the calm waters of the lake. Built in the mid-18th century by Madho Singh I, it was based on the Lake Palace at Udaipur where the king spent his childhood. Later it was used as a lodge for duck shooting parties, and even today, a large number of waterbirds can be sighted here. A terrace garden is enclosed by arched passages, and at each corner is a semi-octagonal tower capped by an elegant cupola.

Environs

Sawai Jai Singh II performed a number of Vedic *yagnas* on the western banks of Man Sagar. Dating to that period are traces of a **Yagna Stambha** ("pillar") where he performed a horse sacrifice, and the **Kala Hanumanji**, a temple dedicated to the popular monkey god.

To the north of Jal Mahal is the splendidly restored **Kanak Vrindavan Temple,** dedicated to Krishna, where the image of Govind Dev *(see p186)* was lodged before it was taken to the City Palace. This picturesque complex, with its well-landscaped gardens, fountains and pavilions, makes a popular picnic spot.

Jaigarh

Amber Rd. **Tel** (0141) 267 1848.
Open 9am–4:30pm.
Closed public hols.

Legendary Jaigarh, the "victory fort", watches over the old capital of Amber, its great, crenellated outer walls delineating the edge of a sharp ridge for 3 km (2 miles) from north to south. Located within the fort is one of the world's few surviving cannon foundries. Its most prized possession is the monumental Jai Van, cast in 1720 and believed to be the world's largest cannon on wheels. Its 6-m (20-ft) long barrel has fine carvings of elephants, birds and flowers. Ironically, despite its impressive size, the cannon remained a work of art and was never fired.

An interesting sight is the massive Diva Burj, a tower on whose uppermost seventh storey a huge oil lamp would be lit on the king's birthday and during Diwali, until the top two storeys were struck down by lightning. The fort has two temples and a large palace complex built over 200 years by different rulers. Located here are the Subhat Niwas (audience hall), the profusely painted Aram Mandir (an airy pleasure pavilion), the residential Laxmi Niwas with baths, and a small theatre for music, dance and puppet shows. The fort's intricate system of collecting and storing rainwater in huge tanks located in the courtyard is unique. Legend has it that Man Singh I's vast treasure, amassed during his military campaigns, was hidden within these tanks. In 1976, the government carried out a massive but unsuccessful hunt, to the extent of draining the water tanks in hope of locating this legendary trove.

The famous Jai Van

The ramparts of Jaigarh Fort, a feat of military engineering

❷ Amber Fort

The fort palace of Amber was the Kachhawaha citadel until 1727, when their capital moved to Jaipur. However, successive rulers continued to come here on all important occasions to seek the blessings of the family deity, Shila Devi. The citadel was established in 1592 by Man Singh I on the remains of an earlier 11th-century fort, but various buildings added by Jai Singh I (r.1621–67) constitute its magnificent centrepiece.

Elephant ride on the cobbled pathway to the fort

★ Sheesh Mahal
The flame of a single candle, reflected in the tiny mirrors embedded in this chamber, transforms it into a starlit sky.

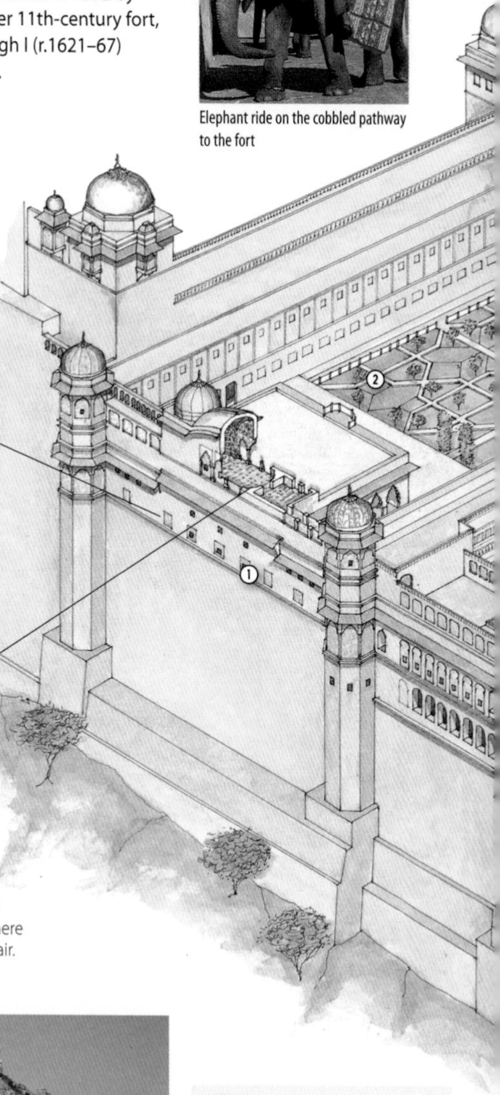

Jas Mandir
This hall of private audience has latticed windows, a floral ceiling of elegant alabaster relief work and glass inlay. A marble screen here overlooks the Maota Lake and wafts in cool air.

Location of Amber Fort
Protected by Jaigarh Fort, the massive ramparts of Amber Fort follow the contours of a natural ridge.

KEY

① **Jai Mandir**

② **Aram Bagh**, the pleasure garden.

③ **Sukh Niwas**

④ **Diwan-i-Aam**

⑤ **Sattais Katcheri**

VISITORS' CHECKLIST

Practical Information
Jaipur district. 11 km (6 miles) N of Jaipur. **Road map** C3.
Tel (0141) 253 0293.
Open 9:30am–4:30pm daily.
Closed public hols.
Son et Lumiere: 7:30pm daily.

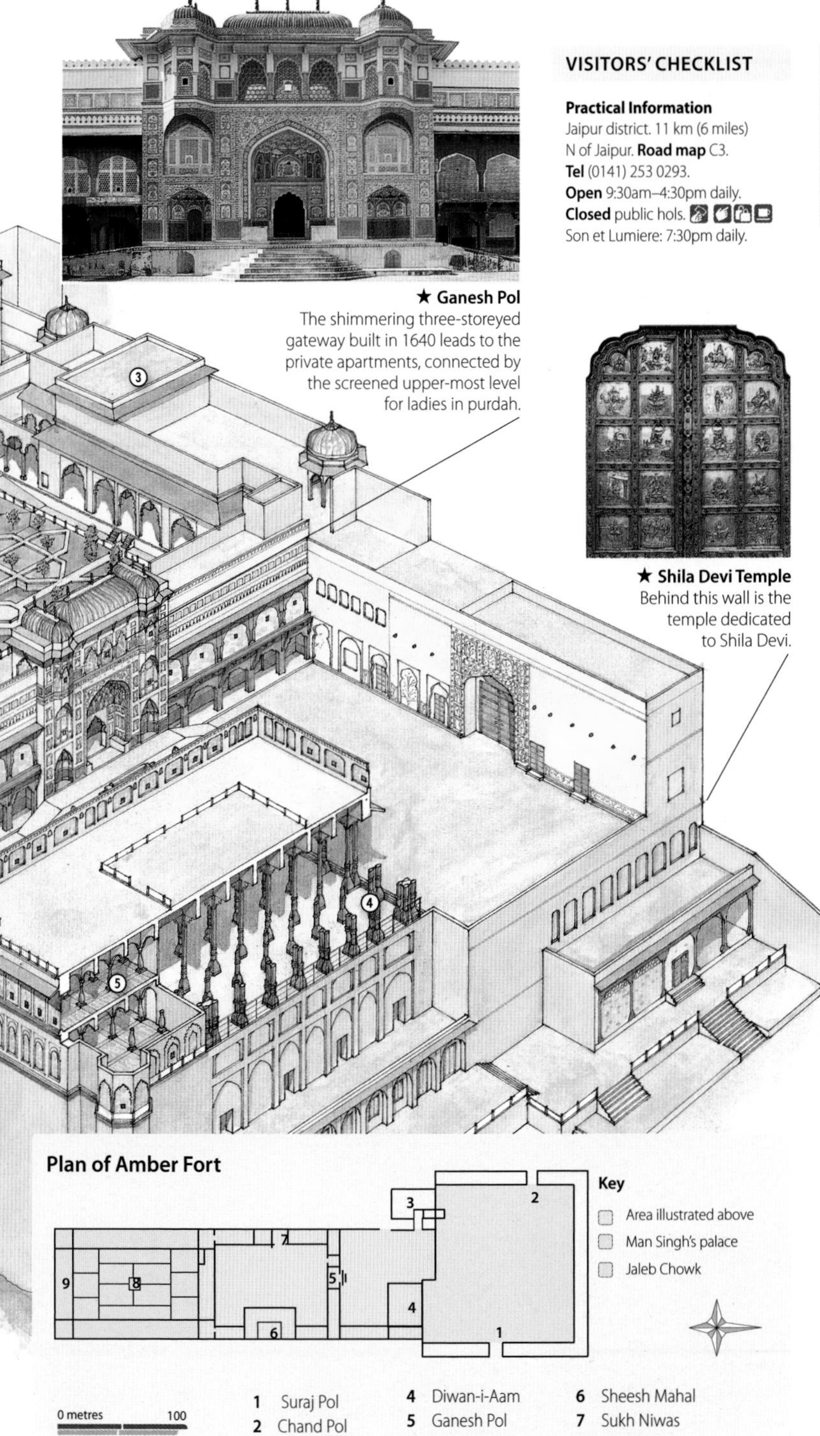

★ Ganesh Pol
The shimmering three-storeyed gateway built in 1640 leads to the private apartments, connected by the screened upper-most level for ladies in purdah.

★ Shila Devi Temple
Behind this wall is the temple dedicated to Shila Devi.

Plan of Amber Fort

Key

- Area illustrated above
- Man Singh's palace
- Jaleb Chowk

1 Suraj Pol
2 Chand Pol
3 Shila Devi Temple
4 Diwan-i-Aam
5 Ganesh Pol
6 Jai Mandir
6 Jas Mandir
6 Sheesh Mahal
7 Sukh Niwas
8 *Baradari*
9 Zenana

Exploring Amber (the Old Capital)

Crowning the crest of a hill, Amber Fort offers a view of Maota Lake, two formal gardens, and the historic old town at the base of the hill, dotted with the remains of an older capital before it shifted to the precincts of the fort. Some of the old *havelis* and numerous temples here are well-preserved, while stepwells and lakes point to the existence of a self sufficient township where the Mughal emperor Akbar stopped by on his annual pilgrimage.

Sattais Katcheri, where the revenue records were written

The Fort Complex
The main entrance to the historic Amber Fort is through the imposing **Suraj Pol** ("sun gate"), so called because it faces the direction of the rising sun, the Kachhawaha family emblem. This gate leads into a huge flagged courtyard, **Jaleb Chowk**, literally, "the square where elephants and horses are tethered". Originally the fort's parade ground, its central area is surrounded on three sides by guard rooms. A flight of steps leads to the **Shila Devi Temple**, which contains the image of the Kachhawaha family deity, a stone *(shila)* goddess Kali, brought here by Man Singh I from Bengal in 1604. The temple has ornately carved silver doors presented by the second wife of the last maharaja in 1939, silver oil lamps and grand pillars of green marble carved to look like banana trees.

The next courtyard has the **Diwan-i-Aam**, the space for public audience. Near it are 27 *(sattais)* airy colonnades, called the **Sattais Katcheri**, where scribes once sat to record revenue petitions.

The magnificent **Ganesh Pol** is a beautifully painted gateway to three private palaces built around an enclosed Mughal-style garden *(see p171)*, **Aram Bagh**. Each of these pleasure-palaces has some special feature. **Sukh Niwas** has doors carved from fragrant sandalwood, and water cascades over marble chutes to cool the interior. The marble **Jai Mandir**, at the other end of the garden, contains the superb **Sheesh Mahal** studded with mirrors. The adjoining **Jas Mandir** has a marble screen across its eastern façade that overlooks the Maota Lake.

The lake, which provided water to the fort, is surrounded by two exquisite gardens. The **Kesar Kyari Bagh** has star-shaped flower beds once planted with saffron *(kesar)* flowers, while **Dilaram Bagh**, built in 1568 as a resting place for Emperor Akbar on his way to Ajmer, is a clever pun on the name of its architect, Dilaram ("heart's ease"). A small archaeological museum is located near Dilaram Bagh.

The furthermost end of the fort, which was also its oldest section, was converted into the **Zenana** ("women's quarters") by Man Singh I to house his 12 wives and concubines. The apartments bear the distinct stamp of Mughal *zenana* architecture, with screens and covered balconies for the protection and purdah of the royal ladies. Faint traces of frescoes are still visible on the walls. In the centre of the courtyard is a colonnaded pavilion called the **Baradari**.

Kesar Kyari Bagh, named after rare saffron flowers once planted in its star-shaped flower beds

Bharmal ki Chhatri, the old cenotaphs of the Kachhawaha rulers

The Township

The **Chand Pol** ("moon gate"), directly opposite Suraj Pol, leads to the old town outside the fort. The **Narsimha Temple**, built in the early 15th century by the Kachhawaha king Narsingh Dev, is the first of many on this route. The temple itself is only a small part of a derelict palace complex which was the site of past coronations before the Amber rulers abandoned it for the fort.

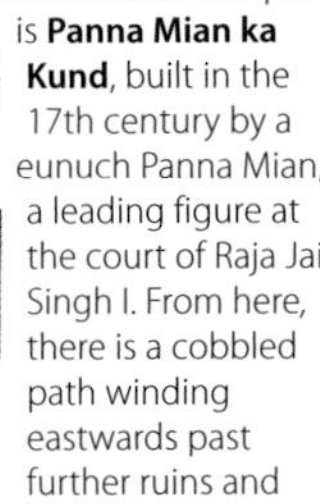

Marble carving in Narsimha Temple

East of this lies the beautiful **Jagat Shiromani Temple**, erected in the early 17th century by Man Singh I in memory of his eldest son, Jagat Singh. A remarkable *toran* (carved lintel) adorns the doorway of the temple which has images of Vishnu, Radha and Krishna. Legend says that the Krishna image was brought here in the 16th century by the saint-poetess Mira Bai, famous for her devotion to Lord Krishna, from Chittorgarh, her home in southern Rajasthan.

Situated further east is the **Sanghi Jutharam Temple** which at one time had a beautiful 12-sided well, a small garden and several chambers. It is now protected by the Archaeological Survey of India (ASI). To its north-east lies the **Ambikeshwar Mahadev Temple**, dedicated to a manifestation of Shiva. One of the oldest temples here, it now stands 3 m (10 ft) below ground level and is said to be slowly sinking.

North of the Ambikeshwar Temple is **Panna Mian ka Kund**, built in the 17th century by a eunuch Panna Mian, a leading figure at the court of Raja Jai Singh I. From here, there is a cobbled path winding eastwards past further ruins and out through **Kheri Gate**, one of the old gates of Amber, leading to a popular picnic spot called **Sagar**, with its two terraced lakes. These were once important sources of water supply during times of siege. Located in a depression formed by the surrounding hills, just behind Jaigarh Fort, the site still bears traces of an elaborate water transport system in which elephants were used to carry water up to the fort.

These monuments lie to the west of the main Jaipur–Delhi highway that cuts across the town. The main market and the Amber bus stand are also located along this road, which is now almost entirely occupied by tiny wayside eateries and souvenir shops. Further along this road, to the north, stands the **Akbari Mosque**, built by Emperor Akbar in 1569 on one of the spots where he stopped to pray on his way to Ajmer *(see pp222–3)*. The basic structure of the mosque remains intact even though it has been often repaired.

Further westwards down this road is **Bharmal ki Chhatri**, a walled enclosure containing a group of memorials. This was the old cremation site for the rulers of Amber until a new spot was established at Gaitor *(see pp202–3)* after the capital moved from Amber to Jaipur.

Steps criss-crossing down to the water in the partly restored Panna Mian ka Kund

Marble statue of a Jain *tirthankara* at Sanganer's Sanghiji Temple

3 Sanganer

Jaipur district. 16 km (10 miles) SW of Jaipur. **Road map** C3. ✈ 🚗 daily.

Two ornate triple-arched gateways lead into Sanganer, a colourful town renowned for its blockprinted cotton textiles. According to local lore this tradition of blockprinting goes back to the 16th century when Sanga, one of the 18 sons of Prithviraj, the Kachhawaha ruler of Amber, re-established the town. Printers from nearby villages were asked to migrate to this new settlement to develop a range of textiles for the Jaipur court. It was Sanganer's river, with its mineral powers of fixing the colours of the dyes, that gave this printing village its fame and wealth. Today, the town resounds with the thud of printing, as craftsmen work in their sheds amidst bolts of cloth, dye-soaked pads and wooden blocks. Most of the printers and dyers in the town belong to a guild with retail outlets that sell reasonably priced fabric, tailored linen and accessories.

Sanganer is also a centre of handmade paper, a spin-off from textile printing, and Jaipur's famous Blue Pottery *(see p260)*. Raja Man Singh I of Amber *(see p53)* set up the first workshops here to produce this special type of hand-painted pottery, inspired by Persian and Chinese blue and white tiles, so popular at the Mughal court.

Tucked away in the old walled town is an impressive 11th-century Jain temple. The **Sanghiji Temple** was probably built by a Jain trader with additional donations from the town's other wealthy merchants. Like other Jain temples found elsewhere in Rajasthan, this too is lavishly decorated with ornate stone carvings that include images of all the 24 Jain *tirthankaras* (saints) and a beautiful statue of Mahavira, the founder of Jainism, in the innermost sanctuary.

Frieze at Sanghiji Temple

Sanganer is now a busy suburb of Jaipur city and the location of its airport.

4 Bagru

Jaipur district. 32 km (20 miles) SW of Jaipur past Sanganer on Ajmer Rd. **Road map** C3. 🚌 🚗 daily.

The small village of Bagru is yet another traditional textile printing centre. Unlike the refined prints of Sanganer, Bagru's are bolder and more earthy, and originally had a limited colour palette of red and black. The indigo, yellow and green that we see today are later additions. The origins of blockprinting in Bagru date back some 300 years, when the first few printing families were brought to this village by the then *thakur* of Bagru, an important fiefdom of the Jaipur kings. Over time, more printers settled here, lured by state patronage as well as the abundant supply of water, so essential for printing.

Bagru's printers *(chhipas)* supplied the fabric that was used by the local farming communities as both stitched and unstitched garments. As the demand for blockprinted textiles increased, their clientele became more varied and their range of products more diversified. Yet, in many ways, little has changed and this is one of the few places to see the printing process at work. Craftsmen still follow the traditional methods of resist-printing, blockprinting and bleaching, and though the use of synthetic dyes has crept in, some colours, such as black and yellow, are still extracted from vegetable and mineral matter.

Faded wall paintings outside the palace at Bagru

Blockprinted Textiles

Delicate flowers and foliage, paisleys, birds and animals on a white background are Sanganer's typical motifs. Handed down from father to son, these designs were inspired by the flower studies of miniature paintings *(see pp36–7)* and Mughal *pietra dura* motifs *(see pp160–61)*. Blockprinting can be seen in the workshops of the city's Chhipa Mohalla, where each stage of this ancient technique, from chiselling intricate patterns on wooden blocks, to dyeing the fabric in huge copper vats on wood-fed fires, and printing, is all done by hand. In the more complex designs, a single motif may use up to ten different colours with as many blocks, each with a different design. In the final stage, swathes of printed cloth are spread on riverbanks or hung on huge frames to dry under the sky.

Textile printing is done with wooden blocks. These are dipped in dye to print the cloth stretched across a low stool. Earlier, colours were extracted from vegetable and mineral matter. Pomegranate rinds, saffron, madder root, turmeric and the indigo plant were some natural sources. Chemicals have now replaced some natural dyes.

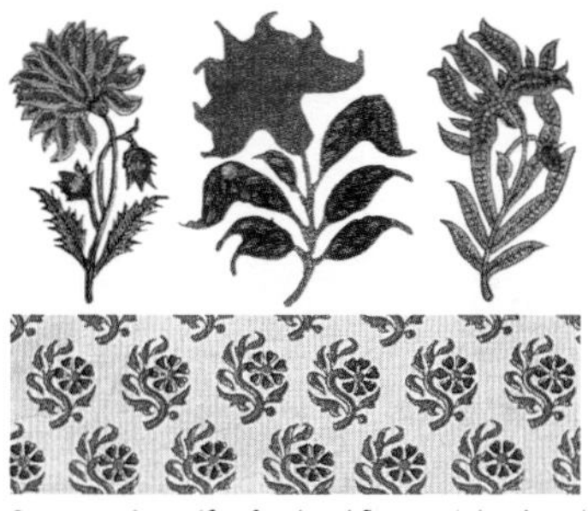

Sanganeri motifs of stylized flowers (*phool*) and leaves (*buti*) in soft colours recreate a field of dainty flowers.

Wooden printing blocks are carved by hand with popular design motifs. Traditional designs have today been enlivened by inputs from modern Indian fashion designers.

Bagru's floral, figurative and geometric motifs are printed on a coarse cotton cloth that is made into blouses and gathered skirts worn by local women. However, in recent years, these earthy prints have become popular in urban centres too.

Handmade Paper

The Kagazi Mohalla, the colony of papermakers, recycles scraps of cloth and silk thread to produce an impressive range of decorative and functional paper products. Fabric is first converted into pulp and then flattened on a wire mesh. The thin sheets of paper are finally peeled off and hung up to dry. These craftsmen jealously preserve their trade secrets and seldom marry outsiders.

Sheets of handmade paper hung to dry

❺ Alwar

Situated between Mughal and Rajput territories, Alwar's place in history was manipulated by its rulers who made shrewd alliances to gain political leverage. Alwar's growth from a vassal state of the Kachhawaha kings to a significant Rajput state came about after Pratap Singh captured the fort of Bala Qila in 1775. Later, as the British cultivated it as a friendly base in Rajputana, there followed a burst of architectural extravagance that went along with a lavish round of tiger shoots, as its rulers tried to rival the glittering lifestyle of their cousins in Jaipur. Today, Alwar is a dusty provincial town with some remarkable monuments, mostly visited by tourists on their way to the Sariska National Park.

City Palace

Near Collectorate.
Open 10am–4:30pm.

A stunning profusion of architectural features marks this palace, with Rajput *bangaldar* eaves and elegant *chhatris* alongside Mughal floral tracery and *jaalis*. Built in 1793, the palace is now largely occupied by the District Collectorate and Police Headquarters, so it is best viewed from the large central courtyard. A stairway flanked by two marble kiosks leads from here to the Durbar Hall and Sheesh Mahal, where special entry permission is required.

A door on the right of the courtyard leads to the **City Palace Museum**, spread over three halls of the upper storey. These contain some treasures of the erstwhile rulers, such as their famed collection of miniature paintings of the Alwar, Jaipur and Mughal schools. The 7,000 rare manuscripts in Persian, Arabic, Urdu and Sanskrit include an illuminated Koran, a version of the rare and precious *Gulistan* of the great Persian poet Sa'adi, as well as the *Babur Nama* or "Memoirs of Babur" (1530). The awesome armoury display includes the swords of Mohammed Ghori, Akbar and Aurangzeb, and a macabre coil called *nagphas*, used for strangling enemies. The first room contains a silver dining table with dividers, through which moving metal shoals of swimming fish can be seen. Behind the palace, across a magnificent *kund,* is the cenotaph of Maharaja Bakhtawar Singh (r.1791–1815). It is locally known as **Moosi Maharani ki Chhatri** after his mistress who performed *sati* here when he died. One of Rajasthan's most elegant monuments, blending brown sandstone and white marble, its carved pavilion has domed arches with exquisite floral tracery, and ceilings adorned with fading gold leaf paintings of mythological characters and courtly scenes.

Dagger, City Palace Museum

The elegant marble pavilion at Moosi Maharani ki Chhatri

From the *Gulistan*, an 18th-century Mughal manuscript, City Palace Museum

City Palace Museum

Open 10am–4:30pm. **Closed** Fri & public hols.

Moosi Maharani ki Chhatri

Open 10am–4:30pm. **Closed** Fri & public hols. Shoes not allowed.

Bala Qila

Open daily. Written permission is needed from the office of the Superintendent of Police, City Palace.

Perched on a steep hill above the city, easily accessible by car, the Bala Qila was originally a 10th-century mud fort. Several additions were made to it by the Jats and Mughals (Babur is said to have spent a night here) until it was finally captured in 1775 by Pratap Singh of Alwar. Now a police wireless station, this sprawling fort was defended by 66 large and small towers. The frescoed palace within, the Nikumbh Mahal, was named after its first occupants, the Nikumbh Rajputs. The entire city can be seen from the fort's extensive ramparts, which give an idea of its scale and of the engineering skills that went into its building. Also visible are the ruins of Salim Mahal, named after Jahangir (Salim), who was exiled here after he plotted to kill Abu'l Fazl, Akbar's official biographer and one of the "nine gems" of his court.

Company Bagh

Vivekanand Marg. **Open** 6am–6pm.

A lovely garden when it was laid out in 1868, the Company Bagh is now a shadow of its former

The aqueduct which brought water from Siliserh to the Company Bagh

VISITORS' CHECKLIST

Practical Information
Alwar district. 150 km (93 miles) NE of Jaipur. **Road map** C3. 315,300. TRC, near Railway Station, Alwar, (0144) 234 7348; Paryatan Bhavan, MI Road, Jaipur, (0141) 511 0595. daily. Jagannathji Fair (Mar–Apr), Laldas Mela (May), Sawan Teej (Jul–Aug), Diwali (Oct–Nov).

Transport
Nehru Marg. Manu Marg.

self. It was originally named after Alwar's British ally and protector, the East India Company. Later, it was christened Purjan Vihar by Maharaja Jai Singh. An enchanting greenhouse here is named "Simla", because it reminded the maharaja of the British summer capital in North India. A 3-km (2-mile) long aqueduct, made of solid stone masonry, brought water from a reservoir at Siliserh to this garden.

Fateh Jang's Tomb

Near Alwar Railway Station.
Open 9:30am–4:30pm.

The tomb of Fateh Jang, one of Shah Jahan's ministers, is a five-storeyed monument, constructed in 1647. Dominated by an enormous dome, its walls and ceiling have raised plaster reliefs, and fine calligraphic inscriptions can be seen on the first floor. A school now occupies the tomb's compound.

Environs

To the north of Alwar, located at the edge of Vijay Sagar Lake, is the 105-roomed **Vijay Mandir Palace**, built to look like an anchored ship by Jai Singh (r.1892–1937). A great builder of palaces, the eccentric Jai Singh had the famous 100-roomed Moti Doongri palace-fortress to the south of the Company Bagh blown up because it offended his sensibilities. Vijay Mandir was his last official residence and he lived here for many years. The former ruling family still occupies it and reserves the right of admission to it.

Alwar is full of apocryphal stories of Jai Singh's strange tastes. His Bugatti cars were "buried" after he tired of them, and he once famously ordered a custom-made gold Lancaster car that resembled the King of England's coronation coach, minus the horses!

Alwar Town Map

1. Bala Qila
2. City Palace Complex
3. Company Bagh
4. Fateh Jang's Tomb

For keys to symbols *see back flap*

❻ Siliserh

Alwar district. 13 km (8 miles) SW of Alwar. **Road map** C3. Tourist Office, opposite Railway Station, Alwar, (0144) 234 7348.

This enchanting spot is midway between Alwar and Sariska National Park *(see pp214–15)*. The 10.5 sq km (4 sq miles) Siliserh Lake, in a valley bounded by low forested hills, is still the main reservoir supplying water to Alwar and the surrounding area. Perched on a hillock overlooking the lake is the water palace built in 1845 by the king of Alwar, Vinay Singh, for his beautiful wife, a local village girl, so that she could be near her family home. This once-grand palace is now a hotel and an ideal place for a quiet getaway, as the only sounds one hears are those made by cormorants, ducks and other waterbirds. Pathways lead up the foothills and around the lake where the remains of old cenotaphs still stand. From the palace's open terrace there are wonderful views of the sun setting over the lake.

Rajgarh Fort, once the capital of the Alwar kings

❼ Rajgarh

Alwar district. 35 km (22 miles) S of Alwar. **Road map** C3. Tourist Office, opposite Railway Station, Alwar, (0144) 234 7348. Miter Vihar Colony, (0144) 2334984. Sadulpur.

Overlooking a picturesque valley, with green fields and citrus groves, is the grand hilltop fort of Rajgarh, the old capital of the Alwar rulers. Built by the founder of the dynasty, Pratap Singh, in the mid-18th century, its status as the capital was brief, and in 1775, when Pratap Singh captured Bala Qila *(see p210)*, the court moved to Alwar. The fort, however, with its once beautiful Sheesh Mahal, frescoed walls and secret passages, was maintained as a summer residence, but over time it fell into disuse until finally it was abandoned. The town, too, at the foot of the hill, wears a desolate look.

❽ Sariska National Park

See pp214–15.

❾ Bairat

Alwar district. 64 km (40 miles) SW of Alwar. **Road map** C3. Tourist Office, opposite Railway Station, Alwar, (0144) 234 7348.

Nowhere is the age and majesty of the Aravalli Hills as apparent in the region as it is at Bairat. The striking topography of giant rocks, variously textured and shaped, provides a dramatic backdrop for an excavated, ancient archaeological site that dates back to the 3rd century BC. One of the cities along the main north-south trade route, this was a major Buddhist centre. A rock edict of Emperor Ashoka (273–232 BC) was found here, and at one end of the village, off a dirt track, high on a hillock locally known as Bijak ki Pahadi, are the remnants of a Buddhist monastery and circular temple. It is believed to be India's oldest free-standing structure. Historians have identified it as a *chaitya* hall or chapel which was once supported by 26 octagonal wooden columns.

Siliserh Palace, built on a hillock overlooking the lake

Bairat's history, however, goes back to the time of the *Mahabharata* (around the 9th century BC), when this land formed part of a kingdom comprising much of eastern Rajasthan, and was ruled by King Virat from his capital of Viratnagar (present Bairat). It was here that the Pandavas *(see p145)* spent the 13th year of their exile. Locals believe that one of the Pandava brothers, the mighty Bhim, lived at **Bhim ki Doongri** ("Bhim's hillock"), and that Arjuna created the River Banganga when he struck an arrow into the earth. King Virat joined the Pandavas in the battle at Kurukshetra, and his daughter married Arjuna's son, Abhimanyu.

On the other side of town, near the rock edict, is an early 17th-century garden mansion dating to Jahangir's reign. Within the compound is a Jain temple, and just outside is the charming 16th-century hunting lodge where Akbar camped } on his way to Ajmer. Locally known as the Chhatri, it was built on a raised platform, with five well-sculpted pavilions.

Remains of the circular temple dating to the Buddhist period, Bairat

⑩ Bhangarh

Alwar district. 56 km (35 miles) S of Sariska via Thana Gazi. **Road map** C3. Tourist Office, opposite Railway Station, Alwar, (0144) 234 7348.

A bumpy ride from Sariska will take you to the abandoned city of Bhangarh, a fascinating site said to be a Kachhawaha clan citadel before Amber. Local legend says that the place was deserted when cursed by an evil magician, and many of its structures were transported to the new capital, Ajabgarh. Built in the early 17th century by Madho Singh, the younger brother of Amber's Raja Man Singh I *(see p53)*, Bhangarh, also known as the "City of Ten Thousand Homes", exemplifies the hierarchy of traditional town planning.

A colonnaded stone pathway lined with market kiosks, stables or residences leads to the inner sanctum at the foot of the hills, where a ruined palace, derisively called Randiyon ka Mahal ("palace of the prostitutes") remains, overlooking the Someshwar Temple, still in use. Three other temples dot the sprawling site, of which the Mangala Devi Temple, with a corbelled dome and finely carved exterior, is by far the most imposing.

Carved bracket from the Mangala Devi Temple, Bhangarh

Environs

On the road to Bhangarh is Ajabgarh, built by Madho Singh's grandson as a new settlement for the people of Bhangarh. Part of the old town is under water, but a fort and some ruins may still be seen.

The Pandavas in Exile

The great epic, the *Mahabharata (see p145)*, describes how, after losing the Pandava kingdom and wife Draupadi to the wicked Kauravas at a game of dice, Prince Yudhishthira, along with his brothers, Bhim, Arjuna, Nakul and Sahdev, were banished to 13 years of exile. The last year was the most crucial and had to be spent in complete anonymity for, if recognized, it meant another 12 years of exile. Forced to accept these rigid terms, the Pandavas roamed the country, spending their 13th year in disguise at the court of King Virat. The story of the Pandavas, their exile and the final battle are important components of the land's folklore, while sites such as Kurukshetra *(see p144)*, associated with their adventures, are venerated pilgrim spots.

The five Pandava brothers, from a popular TV serial

8 Sariska National Park

Designated a tiger reserve under Project Tiger *(see p227)* in 1979, the park sprawls over 800 sq km (308 sq miles) with a core area of 480 sq km (185 sq miles). The Aravallis branch out at Sariska, forming low plateaux and valleys that harbour a wide spectrum of wildlife in the dry jungles. Formerly the private hunting ground of Alwar State, Sariska owes a debt to the strict game and protection laws laid down by its conservation-conscious rulers, which preserved its natural habitat and wildlife. A 17th-century fortress and several ancient temple ruins, such as the Pandupol Temple, also lie within the park.

Langur Monkeys
These black-faced primates with long tails are known as Hanuman langurs.

Sariska Palace
An elegant 19th-century hunting lodge of the Alwar rulers, this palace, now a luxury hotel, has a collection of vintage photographs of past hunts, and period furnishings.

Endangered Species
Rampant poaching in the past years has depleted the park's tiger population. Approximately five remain.

Water Holes
To combat the chronic shortage of water in the region, the Forest Department has laid out a series of water holes at Pandupol, Bandipol, Slopka, Kalighati and Talvriksha. These make good vantage points to view wildlife, especially at sunset, when herds of animals flock to them to quench their thirst.

Flora

The dry deciduous forests of Sariska come to life during the brief spring and early summer when the flowering *dhak* (Butea monosperma) and laburnum bloom. The date palm begins to bear fruit, while berries, locally known as *kair* (Capparis decidua) appear on the bushes.

VISITORS' CHECKLIST

Practical Information

Alwar district. 103 km (22 miles) NE of Jaipur. **Road map** C3. Field Director, Project Tiger Sanctuary, Sariska (0144) 284 1333. **Open** 6–10am, 3–6pm. **Closed** Jul–Sep. extra for personal vehicles or jeeps.

Transport

Alwar.

Jackal

Jackals and hyenas often lead trackers to a tiger kill. Along with panthers and jungle cats, these carnivores feed on the many species of deer, nilgai or blue bull, wild boar and porcupine in the forest.

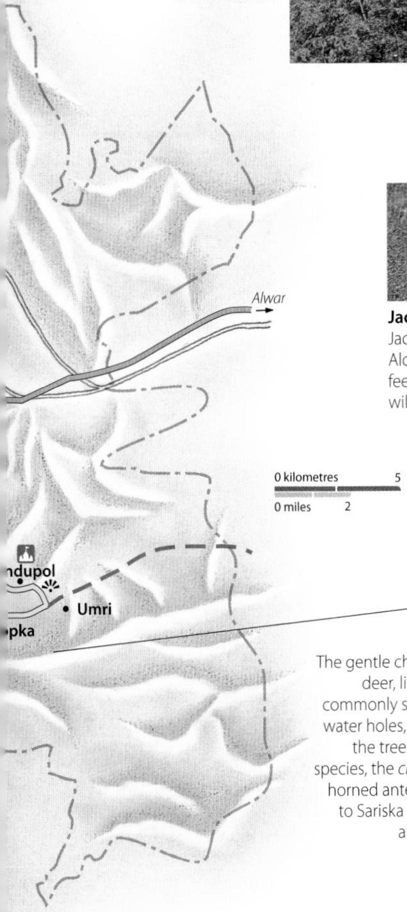

Alwar

ndupol

Umri

pka

Cheetal

The gentle cheetal or spotted deer, like the sambar, is commonly seen at the park's water holes, or resting under the trees. The other deer species, the *chowsingha* (four-horned antelope), is specific to Sariska and can be seen around Pandupol.

Grey Partridge

The hides at Kalighati and Slopka are ideal for observing the park's birdlife, such as the crested serpent eagle, the great Indian horned owl, wood-peckers, kingfishers and partridge.

Key

- Major road
- Minor road
- Park border
- Trails

For keys to symbols *see back flap*

⓫ Chomu

Jaipur district. 32 km (20 miles) NW of Jaipur. **Road map** C3. Paryatan Bhawan, Khasa Kothi Hotel Campus, MI Rd, Jaipur, (0141) 511 0598. daily.

The small town of Chomu links Jaipur with the Shekhawati region. Traces of a grander past are visible in its once impressive fort, handsome *havelis* and stepwells. But Chomu's charm lies in its rural ambience, where bullocks and camels plough the fields, and the unique four-pillared well is the main source of water. In the market, tractor spare parts and tubewell pump-sets vie for attention with hand-carts spilling over with mounds of cucumbers and *ber (Zizyphus mauritiana)*, a berry for which the region is famous.

⓬ Samode

Jaipur district. 42 km (26 miles) NW of Jaipur. **Road map** C3. Paryatan Bhawan, Khasa Kothi Hotel Campus, MI Rd, Jaipur, (0141) 511 0598. daily. Gangaur festival (Mar–Apr).

Samode's romantic palace, immortalized in films such as *The Far Pavilions*, is the main reason why this minor Rajput hamlet is now a luxurious tourist destination. Erected in the late 19th century by a powerful noble of the Jaipur state, this jewel-like palace nestles among the hills below an older hill fort.

The fairy tale Samode Palace, a luxurious retreat set amidst rugged hills

A flight of stairs leads up to a massive gateway and into the palace. Its simple exterior is highly deceptive for, surrounding the vast central courtyard, are spacious rooms on three levels. Of these, the chambers on the uppermost level are the most opulent. The Durbar Hall, Sheesh Mahal and Sultan Mahal are embellished with dazzling mirrorwork and elaborate murals that depict courtly life, hunting scenes and religious themes, along with floral and geometric motifs. The murals represent the best of the Jaipur style and are said to rival those at Jaipur's Chandra Mahal *(see pp192–3)* and Tonk's Sunehri Kothi *(see p226)*. The palace is now a luxury hotel *(see p241)*, but non-guests can pay an entrance fee to see it.

A short distance away is Samode Bagh where the more adventurous can stay in one of the 50 deluxe tents pitched in the formal garden. Other points of interest are the abandoned old fort at the end of a strenuous walk up 376 steps, and the quaint little village where a wide variety of local handicrafts such as lac bangles and *jootis* (slippers) are available.

The Painted Havelis of Shekhawati

In the many little towns of Shekhawati are the ancestral homes of some of India's leading industrialist families, such as the Birlas, Dalmias and Goenkas. These sprawling old *havelis* with their exuberantly frescoed walls *(see p33)* were built between the late 18th and early 20th centuries by the local Marwari merchants who had migrated to the port-cities of Bombay and Calcutta to seek their fortunes. Their interaction with the British and exposure to modern urban and industrial trends influenced their lifestyles, and their homes reflected the new ideas they brought back with them, as well as their newfound wealth and social status.

A "pop art" view of Rajput chieftains

The entrance to Biyani Haveli, Sikar

The style and content of the Shekhawati frescoes are a telling comment on the urbanization of a traditional genre. The local artists still followed the one-dimensional realism of traditional Indian painting *(see pp36–7)*, but juxtaposed among the gods, goddesses and martial heroes are images from a changing world. In their celebration of contemporary "pop" themes, the frescoes of British ladies, top-hatted gentlemen, brass bands and soldiers, trains, motor cars, aeroplanes, gramophones and telephones, symbolize the emerging industrial society of the late 19th century.

⓭ A Tour of Shekhawati

Northeast of Jaipur, situated along the old camel caravan trade route, lies Shekhawati, or the "garden of Shekha", named after Rao Shekha, a fiercely independent ruler who consolidated the region in the 15th century. Today, the region resembles a vast open-air museum full of frescoed mansions. A network of excellent roads through semi-arid scrubland connects most towns and villages where the painted *havelis* of India's leading merchant families stand today in ghostly splendour.

Gods and goddesses frolic on the wall of Biyani Haveli, Sikar

④ Mandawa
The fort-palace is now a charming hotel and a convenient base from which to visit the neighbouring towns.

③ Fatehpur
This picturesque mid-15th century town is best known for the Singhania, Goenka and Jalan *havelis*.

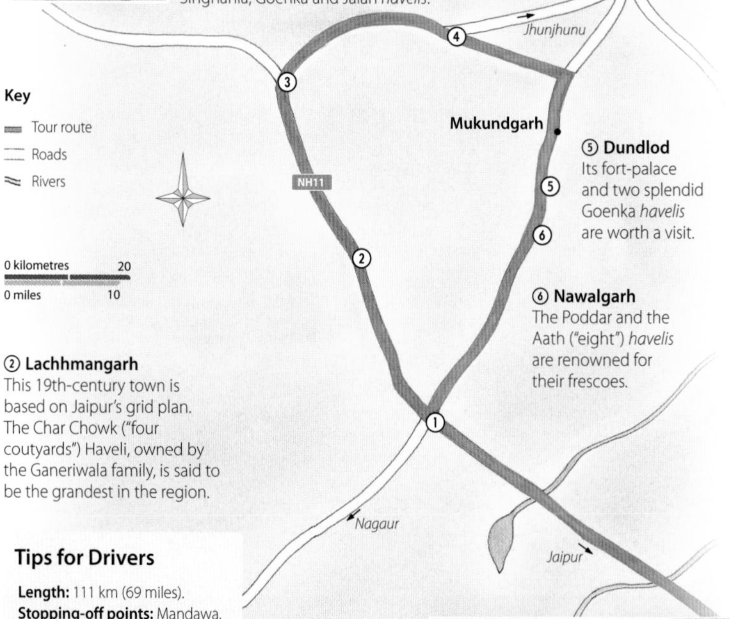

Jhunjhunu

Mukundgarh

NH11

Key

Tour route

Roads

Rivers

0 kilometres 20

0 miles 10

⑤ Dundlod
Its fort-palace and two splendid Goenka *havelis* are worth a visit.

⑥ Nawalgarh
The Poddar and the Aath ("eight") *havelis* are renowned for their frescoes.

② Lachhmangarh
This 19th-century town is based on Jaipur's grid plan. The Char Chowk ("four coutyards") Haveli, owned by the Ganeriwala family, is said to be the grandest in the region.

Nagaur

Jaipur

Tips for Drivers

Length: 111 km (69 miles).
Stopping-off points: Mandawa, Dundlod, Mukundgarh, Fatehpur and Nawalgarh have good hotels. Petrol pumps are at regular intervals on the main road. Apart from NH11, the lesser roads towards Jhunjhunu are poor, but there are roadside eateries at intervals selling mineral water, hot and cold drinks and snacks.

① Sikar
Sikar's charm lies in its *havelis*, bazaars and rural ambience.

⓮ Sambhar Salt Lake

Jaipur district. 70 km (44 miles) NE of Ajmer. **Road map** B3. Shakambri Mata Mela (Oct).

Sambhar Lake is among the six crucial sites in India designated by the World Wide Fund for Nature (WWF) as a wetland of international importance. This vast inland saline lake spreads over an area of roughly 230 sq km (89 sq miles) and is fed by four river streams. During November and December, several species of migratory bird, especially flamingoes, can be seen here.

A number of local legends are connected with the lake's origin, and a Shiva temple and two sacred tanks dedicated to mythological princesses are an indication of the lake's antiquity. The place, however, came into prominence after it was noticed by Babur in the 16th century. Since then, it has been a major source of salt for the country. One of the reasons for this is that after a good monsoon, the water level can rise by up to 1 m (3 ft), but over winter, the lake turns brackish due to capillary action caused by evaporation, drawing up salt from underground deposits.

The little township that has grown around the lake survives on the extraction and packaging of salt. Men, women and even children can be seen working away at the countless trenches and mounds that are spread across the ghostly-white terrain. This has now become a highly commercial business, and though only one state-owned company has the monopoly, there has been an unprecedented growth in the numbers of private manufacturers. Many *bunds* (small dams) have been illegally constructed in the catchment area to retain rainwater for small-scale operations. This has affected not only the flow of water into the lake but has also put a considerable strain on its ecosystem.

Flamingoes in flight over Sambhar Lake

⓯ Makrana

Nagaur district. 80 km (50 miles) N of Ajmer. **Road map** B3. 95,000. Khadim Hotel, Ajmer. daily.

Great slabs of hewn marble indicate that Makrana is a highly commercial stone-quarrying centre. The quarries stretch over a distance of 20 km (12 miles) and produce the highly-prized, luminous white marble that was used to build the Taj Mahal *(see pp158–9)*. Quarrying began several centuries ago, and traditional open-pit methods are still used to excavate the stone. The demand for good quality marble has not lessened, and nearly 50,000 tons are mined annually and transported throughout the country.

Marble quarrying at Makrana, a stone-quarrying centre in the region

The town is also a good place to pick up gifts and souvenirs. Many small workshops have sprung up where artisans carve statues, pillars, vases, lamps and other objects for local sale and export. Objects are also sent to Agra where marble inlayers recreate the same delicate floral patterns as seen in the Taj Mahal *(see pp160–61)*.

Salt packaging at Sambhar Salt Lake

Phool Mahal Palace in a picturesque setting

⓰ Kishangarh

Ajmer district. 30 km (19 miles) NE of Ajmer on NH 8. **Road map** B4. 155,000. Khadim Hotel, Ajmer.

Of all Rajputana's princely states, this was the smallest. It was established in the early 17th century by Kishan Singh, a Rathore prince from Jodhpur, on lands near Ajmer. The king's sister was one of Jahangir's wives, a privilege that gave him a special status at the Mughal court. An obvious outcome of this proximity was that the Kishangarh kings tried to emulate the cultured lifestyle of the Mughal emperors, and when the arts lost imperial patronage under the leadership of the austere Aurangzeb, this tiny state became a haven for several migrant miniature painters.

The old city is certainly worth exploring as it remains much as it was in the past. The narrow streets are lined with *havelis*, some of which have been converted into shops, and on the pavements are vendors selling all kinds of merchandise, including red chillies for which the region is famous. The **Phool Mahal**, a privately-owned palace which is now a heritage hotel *(see p241)*, has an idyllic setting on the banks of a lake that attracts a variety of waterbirds. Shady balconies, courtyard gardens and brass doors flanked by paintings hint at its past glory.

Roopangarh Fort, built in the 17th century, now a charming heritage hotel

Phool Mahal
Tel (01463) 24 7405/7505.

Environs

The 17th-century Roopangarh Fort, 25 km (15 miles) from Kishangarh, was once the capital of the state. Among the riches of this splendid heritage hotel is a rare collection of the famous Kishangarh miniatures.

The Kishangarh School (1735–70)

In the mid-17th century, many miniature painters left the imperial atelier and moved to the Rajput, Central Indian and Punjab hill states, where each court evolved its own distinct regional style. Kishangarh's School of Painting flourished under the reign of Raja Sawant Singh (r.1748–64) who was a mystic, poet and Krishna devotee. His talented court painter, Nihal Chand, immortalized the love story of the king and his court singer in lyrical, romantic paintings where they are portrayed as Radha and Krishna. They are often surrounded by animals and birds, also in pairs, celebrating the union of the gods. The most famous painting is the portrait of Bani Thani, as the court singer was known. She is depicted in profile with a sharp nose and very elongated eyes and tapering wrist and fingers. This highly stylized form of portraiture became the hallmark of the Kishangarh School.

Portrait of Bani Thani

⑰ Street-by-Street: Pushkar

A peaceful pilgrim town of lakes and 400 temples, Pushkar derives its name from *pushpa* (flower) and *kar* (hand) after a legend that says that its lakes were created from the petals that fell from the divine hands of Brahma, the Creator *(see pp28–9)*. Today, life revolves around its lakeside ghats, temples and vibrant, colourful bazaars, and it is this harmonious mix of the spiritual and commercial that draws people to Pushkar.

Villagers at the Fair
Hundreds of thousands of people, camels and cattle attend the annual fair, said to be one of Asia's largest.

Residential area

Dhanna Bhagat Temple

0 metres 100
0 yards 100

SADAR BAZAAR

To Savitri Temple

PARIKRAMA MARG

Badi Ganeshji Temple

Parshuram Temple

★ Brahma Temple
This is one of the few temples in India dedicated to Brahma who, as myth says, was cursed by his wife Savitri when, in her absence, he invited Gayatri, a tribal girl, to take her place in an important ritual.

Pushkar Lake
On top of a hill, by the sacred lake at Puskhar, is the temple of Savitri. Across the lake, on another hill, is the Gayatri Temple.

Key

— Suggested route

Rangaji Temple

This temple is conspicuous for its South Indian style of architecture. Its *gopuram* (pagoda) towers over the area. The temple is not open to foreign visitors.

VISITORS' CHECKLIST

Practical Information

Ajmer district. 144 km (89 miles) SW of Jaipur. **Road map** B4. 15,000. 9am–8pm daily. Pushkar fair (Nov). No eggs, meat or alcohol available/allowed. RTDC, Hotel Sarovar, Pushkar Lake, (0145) 277 2040.

Transport

RTDC, Hotel Sarovar, Pushkar Lake, (0145) 277 2040.

Women at Sadar Bazaar

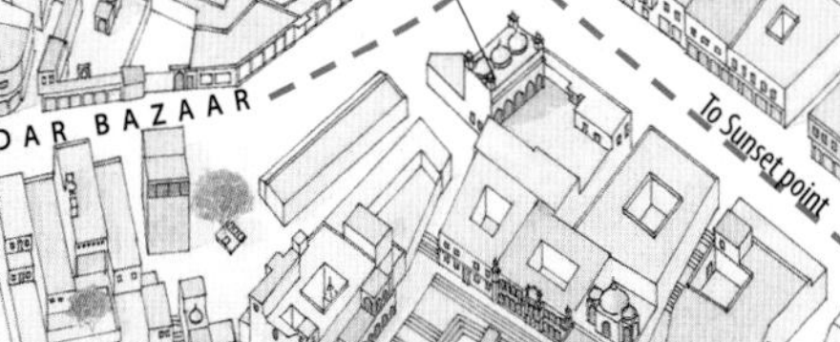

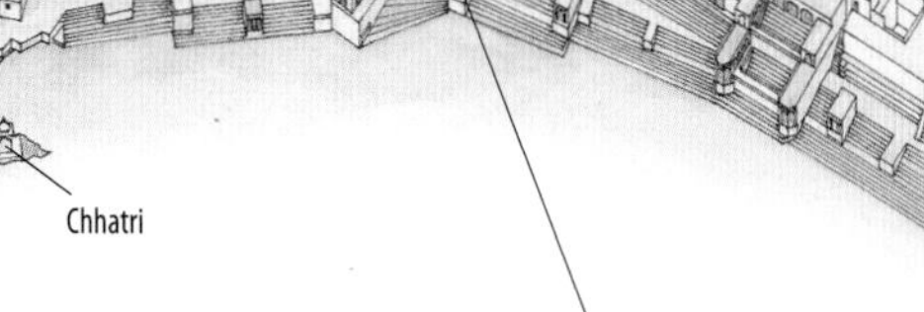

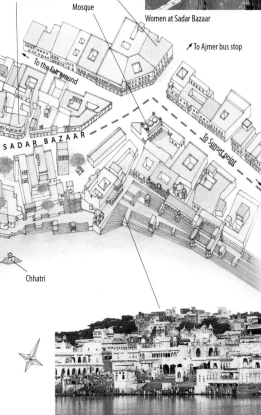

★ Ghats

Pushkar has 52 ghats. Devout Hindus make at least one pilgrimage to Pushkar and bathe at the holy ghats to wash away their sins and thereby earn themselves salvation.

Camel race at the Pushkar fair

Pushkar Mela

In the Hindu month of Kartik (Nov), ten days after Diwali, this quiet town and its environs come alive as the much-anticipated annual cattle fair gets going. Several campsites and temporary tents suddenly appear to accommodate the thousands of pilgrims, tourists and villagers who come here with herds of cattle, horses and camels to participate in this spectacular event.

Pushkar has always been the region's main cattle market for local herdsmen and farmers buying and selling camels and indigenous breeds of cattle. Over the years, this trade in livestock has increased in volume and has become one of Asia's largest cattle fairs.

In the vast, specially-built amphitheatre that lies on the outskirts of the town, camel, horse and donkey races and contests take place amid lusty cheers from a huge audience.

A festive funfair atmosphere prevails over Pushkar during the Mela's two-week duration. Giant ferris wheels and open-air theatres offer amusement, while food and souvenir stalls do brisk business. In the evenings, people huddle round campfires, listening to the haunting strains of Rajasthani folk ballads.

The fair reaches a crescendo on the night of the full moon *(purnima)*, when pilgrims take a dip in the holy lake. At dusk, during the mesmerizing *deepdan* ceremony, hundreds of clay lamps on leaf boats are lit and set afloat in a magical tableau.

18 Ajmer

Famous throughout the subcontinent as the holiest Muslim pilgrim centre after Mecca, Ajmer's prominence in history is connected to the *dargah* of a Sufi saint, Khwaja Moinuddin Chishti. The Mughals made Ajmer the provincial capital of their territories in Rajputana, and it was here that Sir Thomas Roe, the first British ambassador, presented his credentials to Jahangir in 1615. Although the *dargah* is still its most important landmark, Ajmer is also known for its proximity to another famous pilgrimage centre, Pushkar. The town is framed by undulating hillocks dotted with evocative ruins. The picturesque environs of Anasagar Lake with charming pavilions, are popular with picnickers.

Taragarh Fort

Taragarh Rd. **Tel** (0145) 262 7426.
Open sunrise–sunset daily.

The rugged, sprawling 7th-century "Star Fort" occupies the summit of Beetli Hill. A series of five gateways lead into this once-impregnable citadel, said to be the earliest hill fort in the country. Many ruined buildings lie within it, among which are a mosque, still in use, and the shrine of Miran Sayyid Hussain, a 12th-century governor of the fort. The later structures were added by the British whose troops occupied the fort in the 19th century.

Dargah Sharif

See pp224–5.

Adhai Din ka Jhonpra

N of Dargah Sharif, Nalla Bazaar.
Open 10am–4:30pm. **Closed** Mon & public hols.

This impressive complex of pillared cloisters is all that remains of a mosque built around AD 1198 by the ruler of the Slave dynasty, Qutbuddin Aibak. Some say that the mosque's name, which means "a hut of two-and-a-half days", indicates the time taken to build it. However, it is more likely that it refers to the duration of a religious fair held during the Urs in the 18th century. Like the Quwwat-ul-Islam mosque at Delhi's Qutb complex *(see p117)*, also built at the same time, pillars and fragments from nearby Hindu and Jain temples were used for its construction. The mosque itself, said to have been built over a demolished Jain college, stands on a platform cut out of the hillside, with ten shallow domes supported by 124 columns. The glory of the structure is an exquisite seven-arched screen in front of the many-pillared hall. Each arch is different from the next, and every column is ornamented with delicate engravings and calligraphic inscriptions in both Kufic and Tughra (early Arabic scripts). The sheer exuberance of the decoration and ingenious use of materials led Cunningham, the first Director-General of the Archaeological Survey of India, to describe it as "one of the noblest buildings the world has produced".

The Dargah Sharif dome rising above the surrounding houses

Government Museum Ajmer

Near bus stand. **Tel** (0145) 262 0637.
Open 10am–4:30pm daily.
Closed public hols.

Akbar's fort and palace was the first seat of Mughal power in Rajasthan and was later used by the British as an arsenal. On the orders of Viceroy Lord Curzon, it was converted into a museum in 1908. Formerly known as the Rajputana Museum, its varied collection highlights sculpture and other antiquities gathered from sites all over Rajasthan. The most impressive exhibits are the sculptures dating from the 4th to 12th centuries, of which the most remarkable are the four-armed Vishnu seated on Garuda, and a door-frame from the ancient site of Baghera, depicting the ten *avataras* of Vishnu. Other important displays include antique coins, inscriptions, copper plates, paintings and weapons.

Nasiyan Temple

Anok Chowk, Prithviraj Marg.
Open summer: 8am–5pm; winter: 8:30am–5pm daily.

Built in the 19th century, the "Red Temple" in the heart of Ajmer is a

The exquisitely carved seven-arched façade of the Adhai Din ka Jhonpra

The Aravalli Range, picturesquely framing the Anasagar Lake

VISITORS' CHECKLIST

Practical Information
Ajmer district. 135 kilometres (112 miles SW of Jaipur).
Road map B4. 543,000.
RTDC Hotel Khadim, (0145) 262 7426. Urs (July).

Transport
Near Hotel Khadim.
Station Rd.
Sanganer.

fine example of a Jain religious building. Just behind the main temple (closed to non-Jains) is the double-storeyed Svarna Nagari Hall. It is elaborately decorated with coloured glass mosaics, and large gilded wooden figures re-create scenes from Jain mythology, such as the birth and life of Rishabhdeva, the first Jain *tirthankar* (saint).

Anasagar Lake

Circular Rd. **Open** 7am–10pm.

This tranquil lake to the north of the city is named after Anaji (r.1135–50), the grandfather of Prithviraj Chauhan. Charmed by its scenic beauty, Jahangir laid out a garden, Daulat Bagh, and Shah Jahan built the marble pleasure pavilions.

Overlooking this popular picnic spot is a grand colonial building, now the Circuit House, where the British Resident once lived.

Mayo College

Shrinagar Rd. **Tel** (0145) 266 1286. Can visit with Principal's permission.

Set up in 1875 by Lord Mayo as an "Eton of the East" for Rajput princes, the school's main building, designed by Charles Mant, is a jewel of Indo-Saracenic architecture *(see p31)*. Its early students were allowed to live in their individual "houses" with English private tutors and family retainers. Some, such as the prince of Alwar, would ride to school after vacations on an elephant. After 1947, commoners were allowed entry, and today, along with its girls' section, Mayo is rated as one of India's best public schools.

Lord Mayo

Ajmer Town Map

① Dargah Sharif
② Adhai Din ka Jhonpra
③ Goverment Museum Ajmer
④ Nasiyan Temple
⑤ Anasagar Lake
⑥ Mayo College

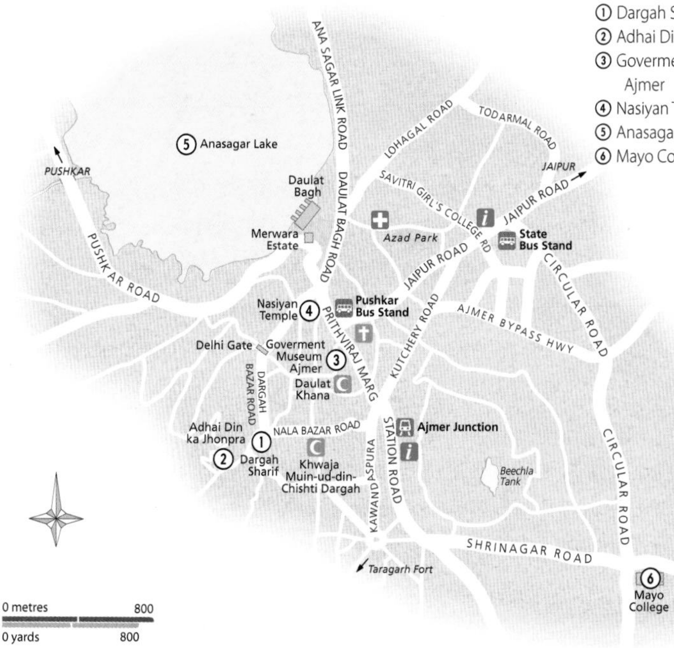

0 metres 800
0 yards 800

Dargah Sharif

A revered Muslim pilgrim centre since the 12th century, the Dargah Sharif contains the tomb of the famous Sufi saint Khwaja Moinuddin Chishti (1143–1236), popularly called Garib Nawaz, or "protector of the poor". Reputed to possess miraculous powers, the saint draws people of every faith to his *dargah* to seek favours and blessings. It is said that the saint entered his cell to pray in seclusion until his death on the sixth day. Each year, six days in the seventh lunar month (October) are marked as his Urs (death anniversary celebrations). Over the years, the saint's royal devotees built grand extensions to the tomb, so that today the *dargah* complex, teeming with pilgrims and tourists, is virtually a township in itself.

★ Mehfil Khana
Built in 1888 by the fabulously wealthy Nizam of Hyderabad, this is the venue for all-night *qawwalis*.

★ Shahjahani Masjid
Emperor Shah Jahan built this marble mosque. The Mughals made many such generous endowments.

***Qawwali* Singers**
Qawwalis (see p34), always sung by a group, are specially composed to sing the saint's praises in front of his tomb.

★ Mazar Sharif
Chishti's tomb, begun during the saint's lifetime by Iltutmish, was completed in the 16th century by Emperor Humayun. Later Mughal princes added to it. A marble dome surmounts the simple brick tomb, enclosed by a silver railing and a marble lattice screen.

KEY

① **Ibadat Khana** (prayer hall)
② **Nizam Gate**
③ **Shahjahani Gate**

Akbar's Mosque
Akbar, Chishti's most illustrious devotee, walked from Agra to Ajmer twice: once for enabling his conquest of Chittor, and again after the birth of his heir, Prince Salim, the future Jahangir.

VISITORS' CHECKLIST

Practical Information
Ajmer district. 141 km (87 miles) SW of Jaipur. **Road map** B4. RTDC TO Hotel Khadim (0145) 262 7426. **Open** daily. Urs (July).

Pilgrims
People of every faith come to seek favours and bring flowers and *chadors* as thanksgiving offerings.

Dargah Bazaar

Buland Darwaza
This imposing entrance doorway was erected by one of the Khilji rulers. A flag is hoisted over its ramparts to mark the start of the Urs ceremony held each October.

Degs
Two enormous *degs* (iron cauldrons), one nearly 10 ft (3 m) in diameter, are used during the Urs for cooking a special rice pudding, *tabarrukh*. After they have been emptied, professional divers "loot" the *degs* by jumping in and scooping out the dregs.

Dargah Bazaar
The long road that lies outside the Nizam Gate, the main entrance to the complex, is the location of a bustling market. Colourful stalls and kiosks sell baskets of rose petals as well as *chadors* for devotees to offer at the *dargah*.

A 15th-century manuscript, Arabic and Persian Research Institute, Tonk

⓳ Chaksu

Jaipur district. 43 km (27 miles) S of Jaipur on NH12. **Road map** C4. 35,000. Shitala Ashtami (Mar–Apr).

This sleepy little village on the road from Jaipur towards Sawai Madhopur is known for its small white temple dedicated to Shitala Mata, the goddess who wards off disease, especially smallpox. A hundred steps lead to the shrine, around which devotees gather for a gossip session after propitiating the deity. Shitala Mata is much venerated in parts of rural Rajasthan where many diseases are still fatal. Every year in March or April a fair is held here, which attracts a large number of pilgrims. Food is cooked a day before Ashtami, the eighth and most auspicious day after the new moon, and offered cold to the goddess to ensure her protection.

⓴ Tonk

Tonk district. 96 km (60 miles) S of Jaipur on NH12. **Road map** C4. 1,422,000. daily. Id (Feb–Mar).

The small principality of Tonk, the only Muslim kingdom in Rajasthan, was created by the British in the early 19th century to appease the powerful Pathan warlord, Amir Khan. The legacy of its *nawabs* is evident throughout the old city. They constructed the imposing Jami Masjid, as well as a number of fine painted mansions, of which the **Sunehri Kothi** ("golden mansion"), built in 1824 by Amir Khan in the old palace complex, is the most spectacular. Magnificent enamelled mirror-work and gilded stucco cover the walls and ceilings of its jewel-like interior, the windows are fitted with stained-glass and the floors beautifully painted. The old city also has many Raj-style bungalows that were once the homes of the British Resident and his entourage.

The *nawabs* were dedicated patrons of art and literature. In the late 19th century, the third ruler established a grand centre of Islamic art, now known as the **Maulana Abul Kalam Azad Arabic and Persian Research Institute**. Its collection of rare Arabic and Persian manuscripts includes several illuminated Korans, such as Aurangzeb's *Alamgiri Koran Sharif* and the *Koran-e-Kamal,* prepared on the orders of Shah Jahan. There are also translations of the epics, the *Ramayana* and the *Mahabharata,* inscribed in exquisite Persian as well as Arabic calligraphy.

Sunehri Kothi
Partially operational. Enquire at MAKA Arabic & Persian Research Institute.

MAKA Arabic and Persian Research Institute
Near new bus stand.
Open 10am–5pm Mon–Sat.
Closed Sun. **Tel** (01432) 24 7389.

㉑ Sawai Madhopur

Sawai Madhopur district. 172 km (107 miles) SE of Jaipur. **Road map** C4. 121,000. Mon–Sat. Shivaratri (Feb), Ganesha Chaturthi (Aug–Sep).

An important railway junction and entry point to the Ranthambhore National Park, Sawai Madhopur is named after its founder Sawai Madho Singh I (r.1750–68). The historic 10th-century Ranthambhore

A cart stands outside a village hut on the outskirts of Sawai Madhopur

A rooftop view of the distant Indergarh Fort

Fort (now in the park), a strategic point on the main route to Central India, was the scene of many terrible battles between its Rajput chieftains and the invading armies from Delhi and Agra. The fort was attacked by Alauddin Khilji *(see pp54–5)* and later by Akbar in 1569. This later battle has been glorified in Mughal miniatures and bards have sung about the heroic deeds of its Rajput defenders.

The fort was eventually handed over to the Amber kings *(see pp204–5)*. This jungle fort, despite its ruined state, looks daunting. Its massive gateways, ramparts and bastions make entry a tricky affair. Within it is an 8th-century temple dedicated to Ganesha, whose priest receives sacks of letters, sometimes addressed simply to "Shri Ganesha, Ranthambhore", especially during the marriage season, in order to invoke the deity's blessings. Clumps of grass, tied together by newlyweds for luck, are also seen along the way to the fort temple.

Environs

About 37 km (24 miles) west of Sawai Madhopur is the sprawling **Uniara Palace**. Further towards Tonk, past **Hathi Bhata**, a life-sized elephant carved out of a single rock, is the picturesque **Kakod Fort**. East of Sawai Madhopur, is the vast **Mansarovar Lake**.

22 Ranthambhore National Park

See pp228–9.

23 Indergarh

Kota district. 52 km (33 miles) S of Sawai Madhopur. **Road map** C4. Indergarh Fort: **Open** 8am–5pm daily, on request to the caretaker who lives below the fort. Donation optional.

This small town, founded by Raja Indrasal in 1605, lies huddled beneath the ramparts of a picturesque hill fort which is clearly visible from the flat rooftops of houses where, in summer, people sleep at night. Though dilapidated, some fort areas still bear traces of exquisite murals depicting colourful court scenes and legends. Indergarh's two main temples, one dedicated to Bijasan Mata (a form of Durga) and the other to Kuanwalji (Lord Shiva), are popular places of worship for pilgrims.

Tale of the Tiger

The tiger plays a major role in Indian myth, as a symbol of supreme power, kingship and manhood. In Puranic legend it is Durga, the fearsome goddess with ten arms, who rides a tiger and defeats the invincible buffalo-headed demon, Mahishasura. Yet, for all its aura of strength and power, the tiger is a vulnerable creature today.

Durga riding a tiger, detail of a miniature painting

Statistics claim that at the turn of the 20th century, India's tiger population was about 40,000, but by 1972, the figure had dropped to roughly 1,800. This was when a special Task Force of the Indian Board for Wildlife constituted Project Tiger to address the alarming issue of dwindling tiger populations across the country. In the first year of Project Tiger, nine wildlife sanctuaries were declared tiger reserves, one of them being Ranthambhore.

There are now 27 Project Tiger Reserves, and the number of tigers has grown substantially, though persistent habitat destruction, illegal poaching and trading of tiger parts for medicinal and other derivatives in many Far Eastern countries continue to threaten the life of this supreme predator.

㉒ Ranthambhore National Park

This park lies in the shadow of the Aravalli and Vindhya mountain ranges and covers a core area of 400 sq km (155 sq miles). Its razor-sharp ridges, deep boulder-filled gorges, lakes and jungle are the habitat of carnivores such as the caracal, panther, jackal and hyena, as well as species of deer, and a rich variety of resident and migratory birds. The most famous resident, however, is the endangered tiger, and it is a unique experience to catch glimpses of this majestic and fascinating animal. Like other parks in the region, this was originally the Jaipur state's hunting grounds and became a Project Tiger Reserve in 1973.

Rajbagh
Ruined pavilions stand on the banks of Rajbagh Talao, one of the three lakes in the park.

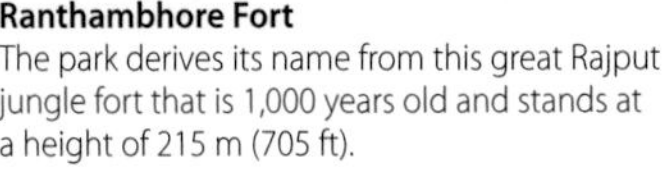

Ranthambhore Fort
The park derives its name from this great Rajput jungle fort that is 1,000 years old and stands at a height of 215 m (705 ft).

Sambar Stag
Large herds of sambar are seen around the lakes, wallowing in the water, swimming and feeding on aquatic plants, unperturbed by jeeps and visitors.

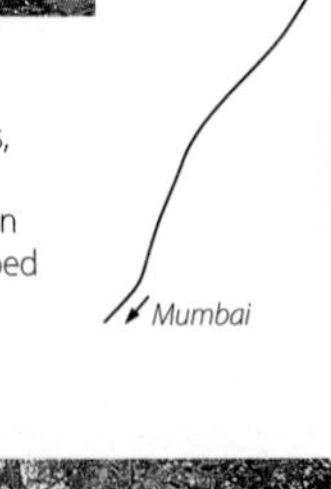

Banyan Tree
India's second-largest banyan tree *(Ficus bengalensis)* lies in the grounds of Jogi Mahal. Its several spreading branches are all supported by roots.

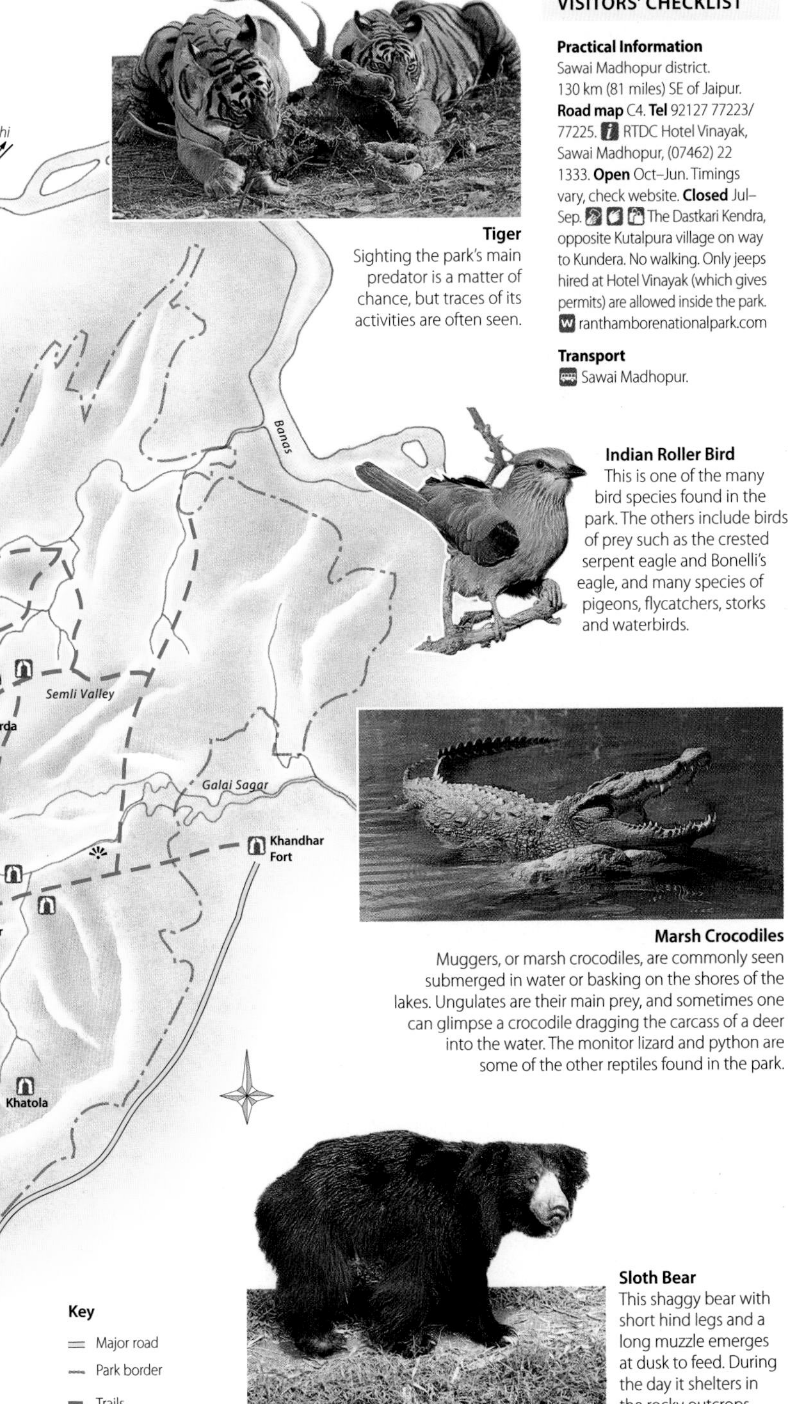

Tiger
Sighting the park's main predator is a matter of chance, but traces of its activities are often seen.

Indian Roller Bird
This is one of the many bird species found in the park. The others include birds of prey such as the crested serpent eagle and Bonelli's eagle, and many species of pigeons, flycatchers, storks and waterbirds.

Marsh Crocodiles
Muggers, or marsh crocodiles, are commonly seen submerged in water or basking on the shores of the lakes. Ungulates are their main prey, and sometimes one can glimpse a crocodile dragging the carcass of a deer into the water. The monitor lizard and python are some of the other reptiles found in the park.

Sloth Bear
This shaggy bear with short hind legs and a long muzzle emerges at dusk to feed. During the day it shelters in the rocky outcrops and is difficult to sight.

VISITORS' CHECKLIST

Practical Information
Sawai Madhopur district. 130 km (81 miles) SE of Jaipur. **Road map** C4. **Tel** 92127 77223/ 77225. RTDC Hotel Vinayak, Sawai Madhopur, (07462) 22 1333. **Open** Oct–Jun. Timings vary, check website. **Closed** Jul–Sep. The Dastkari Kendra, opposite Kutalpura village on way to Kundera. No walking. Only jeeps hired at Hotel Vinayak (which gives permits) are allowed inside the park.
ranthamborenationalpark.com

Transport
Sawai Madhopur.

For keys to symbols *see back flap*

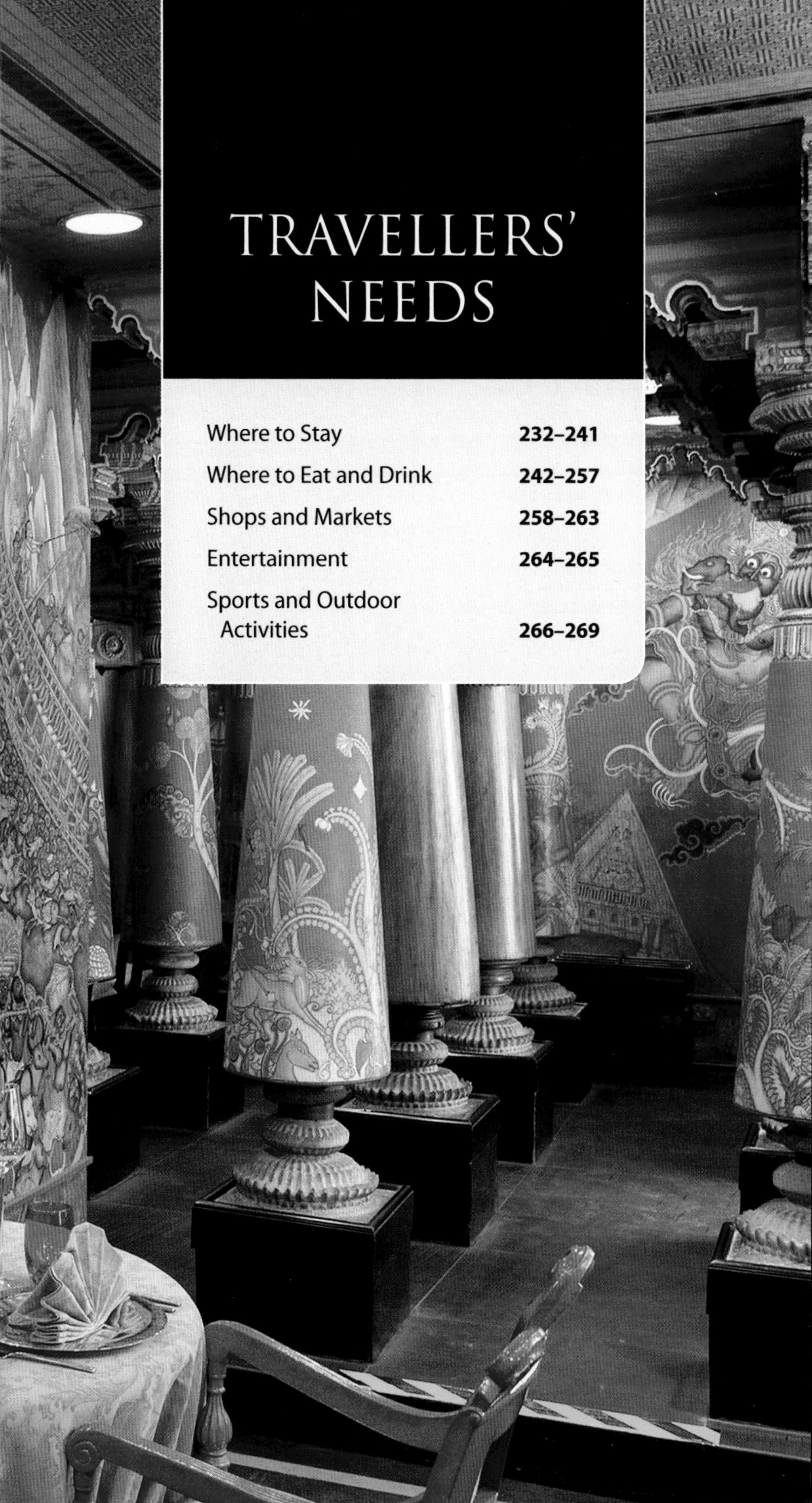

TRAVELLERS' NEEDS

WHERE TO STAY

Popularly known as the Golden triangle, the Delhi, Agra and Jaipur region receives the largest number of tourists in India. Naturally, this area has a wide range of places to stay, though prices, particularly in Delhi and Agra, can be higher than the rest of the country. Jaipur and the rest of Rajasthan offers a huge variety of accommodation with a lot of competitively priced heritage and boutique options. The choice of accommodation available throughout the region ranges from upmarket luxury hotels run by international or leading Indian chains, to guesthouses and youth hostels. In addition, there are state-run tourist hotels, with comfortable board and lodging at reasonable rates. On the more exotic side are the grand old palaces and lovingly restored *havelis* of the region which re-create the lavish lifestyles of former rulers and aristocracy. For the budget traveller, there is a choice of ashrams and small guest-houses, sometimes with extremely basic facilities. For more information on places to stay in this region, refer to the detailed listings on pages 238–41.

Hotel Chains, Grading and Facilities

At the top end of the range are the five-star deluxe hotels which provide luxurious accommodation for the international visitor. Many of these are part of national chains, such as **Oberoi**, **ITC Hotels** and **Taj Group**, or of international groups such as the **Sheraton** and **Radisson**.

Below them are the four- and three-star hotels, guesthouses and tourist lodges, some of which may offer additional facilities, such as a pool or tennis court. International television channels are generally available though some heritage properties may not have televisions at all. In Agra and Jaipur, palaces, bungalows and *havelis* have been converted into heritage hotels, which have been tastefully decorated and furnished in traditional style.

The hotels run by the large international and national chains are fully air-conditioned and offer a wide range of services such as a resident doctor, shopping arcades and patisseries, banqueting halls, a 24-hour coffee shop, bars and gourmet restaurants. For the business traveller, there are business and conference centres equipped with computers for personal use and access to the Internet. Desk jacks and modems are provided for personal computers and laptops. Wi-Fi is widely available, although not always free (strangely Wi-Fi is more likely to be free in cheaper accommodation).

High tea service at Jaipur's Rambagh Palace *(see p241)*

Additional facilities include beauty parlours and fitness centres, swimming pools and tennis courts. The front desk can often make bookings for golf and other activities. Some hotels even have a regular palmist, tarot card reader or astrologer. Even in the lower-priced hotels and in older properties, bathrooms are usually in Western style. Room service, safe deposits and daily laundry are standard in more expensive places. The reception desk can advise on tours, and large hotels have travel agencies on the premises.

Agra's ITC Mughal, renowned for its innovative architecture *(see p240)*

Luxury Hotels

India has many award-winning luxury hotels which match the best in the world in their elegance, professional services, and wide range of facilities. Architecturally, many of them have cleverly combined traditional Indian and modern design, while their interiors are sumptuously decorated with the best of Indian crafts and textiles. A number of these hotels are renowned for their gourmet restaurants, stunning spas and expansive grounds, such as the Imperial in Delhi or Amarvilas in Agra.

◀ Lavish interiors of award-winning restaurant, Spice Route, at The Imperial *(see p238)*

Heritage Hotels

Several palaces and stately homes, particularly in Rajasthan, have been restored and converted into hotels. These come under the banner of **Heritage Hotels Association of India**. There is an amazing variety of these lovingly restored palaces and *haveli* mansions in this region. These are classified as grand, classic and ordinary, and are priced accordingly.

Middle-range Hotels

These are three- and four-star establishments that may lack the stylish decor, slickness and range of facilities of five-star hotels. Though smaller in size they are always comfortable, clean and well-serviced. The rooms are generally air-conditioned with attached baths that have hot and cold running water. Some are surrounded by extensive gardens and may even have cafés and business centres.

Boutique hotels have also become fashionable and are quite welcoming. They offer excellent accommodation; some are small chains, while many are independently operated. The middle-range category also includes establishments that can be classified as great value and offer modern and comfortable rooms. They are a reliable option and come equipped with most modern conveniences. Certain hotels can be classified as rural retreats and offer guests a chance to immerse themselves in the local life of the region. Many of these hotels have unique settings and have received local certifications for environmentally sensitive practices.

Budget Hotels and Tourist Lodges

Budget hotels are usually found in the older sections of cities, near the railway and bus stations. You can also stay with families under the Paying Guest Scheme. You can find short-term paying guest accommodation in Delhi through the Delhi Tourism Office *(see p275)* or your travel agent. In Agra, the tourist information counter at the railway station can supply addresses, and in Jaipur, **Rajasthan Tourism (RTDC)** has an official and comprehensive list of families under a good Paying Guest Scheme administered by them. There are many home-stays in this region and while some offer only basic facilities, there are other more opulent versions. They also offer great food and often cookery classes. **Munjeeta Travel**, based in the United Kingdom, can organize Homestay Tours across India.

Dharamshalas and *ashrams* are rest houses for pilgrims run by religious trusts, but anyone can stay, as in the **International Rest House** in Brindavan, or **Ramakrishna Mission** and **Sri Aurobindo Ashram** in Delhi *(see p235)*, provided the rules of the place are strictly followed. They charge absurdly low rates. In cities, *dharamshalas* in the older sections may have dubious standards of hygiene, and the facilities can amount to a bare room with no bedding, shared with others, along with the bathroom. The rates in Delhi are higher than in the rest of the region. The wide network of tourist "bungalows" or lodges established by state tourism departments, and the national India Tourism Development Corporation's (ITDC) **Ashok Group**, make travelling to lesser-known places easier. The rates are reasonable, and there is a choice of dormitories as well as double rooms with attached bathrooms.

Basic and typical *dharamshala* in Haridwar

Luxurious and spacious club room at Claridges, New Delhi *(see p238)*

Guesthouses

The term "guesthouse" can be a misnomer. Both mid-range and budget hotels can have "guesthouse" appended to their name, and so the prices and the services can vary enormously. If you opt for a lower priced one, do make it a point to inspect the room before checking in, especially the bathroom, which may contain an Indian-style toilet. The better guesthouses all have air-conditioning and attached baths with Western toilets. Many even offer service apartments with modern amenities. In Jaipur, some families have converted all or part of their large *havelis* into guesthouses, providing meals on order.

Youth Hostels

There is a network of youth hostels across India, including the YWCA and YMCA *(see p275)*. They offer very low rates, although the YMCA's are pricier with better facilities and are found only in selected cities. Though it is not necessary to be a member of Youth Hostel International to gain entry, during the busy season its members do get priority and always get lower rates. Rooms and dormitories are both usually available, and the rules of the hostel must be respected.

National Parks and Camping Sites

The national parks have several places to stay in, but no dedicated camping sites. At the Pushkar fair grounds, Rajasthan Tourism sets up a **Tourist Village** on a large campsite and offers cottages and tents during the Pushkar season. A few hotels in Rajasthan have fixed Rajasthani tents which are extremely luxurious. In Uttar Pradesh, apart from private operators like award-winning **Aquaterra**, there are river rafting campsites on the River Ganges run by **GMVN** Rishikesh.

A view of the main swimming pool at the Rajvilas Hotel in Jaipur *(see p241)*

Prices and Discounts

Rates vary between cities, with Delhi and Agra being the most expensive, and the small town hotels being very cheap at times. The five-star luxury and the palace or heritage hotels are at the top end of the scale (although with the plethora of palaces in Rajasthan you can find one to suit most budgets). Those run by the state tourism development corporations can vary from state to state, with Delhi being the most expensive. Prices at the guest-houses swing from high to low.

Most hotels offer discounts during the low season from April to September. This can bring the original rates down by almost 50 per cent at times. Every October, hotels raise their rates by a nominal percentage. Various taxes are charged, over and above the listed rates, as notified by the government from time to time. Sometimes, foreigners have to pay the dollar room rate, plus any additional taxes on the listed price. This is payable in foreign currency or in rupees.

Taxes

Although the government has abolished the 10 per cent hotel expenditure tax on rooms, it does levy a luxury tax which varies from state to state, from 5 to 20 per cent. Expect to pay luxury tax on the published tariff for fare on discounted rooms. VAT, about 12.5 per cent in most states, has replaced the sales tax on food and beverages.

Hidden Extras

Services for which you may be charged extra could include bottles of mineral water, breakfast (although this is often included), laundry, extra bedding, telephone calls, emails and faxes, the mini bar in your room, and special pay channels on television (you should read the screen or your room service folder before pressing the remote). Hotels usually charge extra for transport to and from the hotel. When telephoning, it is cheaper to use the pay phones in the lobby or at outside STD booths *(see p284)*.

Picturesque surroundings of the Glasshouse on the Ganges in Rishikesh *(see p239)*

Booking, Checking In and Out

It is a good idea to make hotel bookings well in advance, especially for the peak October to March tourist season when many conferences and cultural festivals take place. You can email or telephone your requirements, but do insist that you are sent a written confirmation. Check-out time is usually noon, though at smaller establishments they are not so particular and calculate by the day. Before checking out, do study your bills carefully and retain all the receipts. Most hotels will take a copy of your passport on arrival so it is a good idea to have photocopies on you if you do not want to part company with your passport for any period of time. There are often extensive forms to be filled in on check-in too.

Touts

At the airport or railway station you may be besieged by touts *(see p259)*, many of whom also operate as taxi and three-wheeler drivers, who insist on taking you to hotels where they get a commission. The best solution is to have prior bookings. Failing this, the tourism counter at the airport or station will help you find a place suitable to your needs. If touts continue to pester you, speak to the nearest policeman. You may be told that your hotel is full, burned down or that there is a riot in that area – be prepared to be persistent with taxi or rickshaw drivers.

Aesthetic living room of the grand presidential suite at Taj Palace, Delhi *(see p238)*

Facilities for Children

The staff at hotels are usually very good with children. Many hotels will willingly add an extra bed for a child in your room at a small extra charge. Very few provide baby-sitting services; you should check at the front desk, but usually parents are expected to look after their children. Most hotels do not have any special facilities for children.

Travellers with Disabilities

Only the newer and fancier hotels make an effort to provide ramps, special lifts and wheelchairs for disabled travellers. However, you can always seek the help of the staff. Many of the older hotels, especially in Rajasthan, which are converted from palaces and private mansions, have several levels within them, with no ramp or lifts for easy movement. Do check out these facilities before making your bookings.

Tipping

Tips are expected even though there may be a service charge on bills. The amounts are at the discretion of the guest, starting with ₹10 for car parking attendants, slightly more for a porter, and 10 per cent of the total bill for waiters. Some hotels have a tip box in the lobby.

Recommended Hotels

The many hotels featured in this guide have been selected keeping in mind a broad spectrum of travellers, from backpackers to business travellers, and across as wide a price range as possible for their excellent facilities, good location and usually great value. They have been listed according to region for your convenience and will provide excellent accommodation and facilities based on your budget.

The hotels have broadly been divided into seven categories: Luxury, Heritage, Great Value, Boutique, Rural Retreat, Tourist Lodge and Guesthouse. Throughout our listings, we have marked recommended hotels as DK Choice. These establishments have been highlighted in recognition of an exceptional feature – a stunning location, notable history, great ambience or outstanding value.

DIRECTORY

Hotel Chains

Ashok Group
Scope Complex, Core-8, 7 Lodhi Rd, Delhi.
Tel (011) 2436 0303.
W theashokgroup.com

ITC Hotels
ITC Maurya, Sardar Patel Marg, New Delhi.
Tel (011) 2611 2233.
W itchotels.in

Sheraton
District Centre, Saket, New Delhi.
Tel (011) 4266 1122.
W starwoodhotels.com/sheraton

Radisson
National Highway 8, Mahipalpur Rd, Delhi.
Tel (011) 2677 9191.
W radissonblu.com

Taj Group
Taj Mahal, Mansingh Rd, Delhi. **Map** 5 B3.
Tel (011) 2302 6162.
W tajhotels.com

Oberoi Group
The Oberoi, Dr Zakir Hussain Marg, Delhi. **Map** 6 D4.
Tel (011) 2389 0606.
W oberoihotels.com

Heritage Hotels

Heritage Hotels Association of India
Mandawa Haveli, Sansar Chandra Rd, Jaipur.
Tel (0141) 237 1194.
W indianheritagehotels.com

Paying Guest Accommodation

Munjeeta Travel
12 Cavendish Rd, Woking, Surrey GU22 OEP, UK.
Tel (01483) 77 3331.
W munjeetatravel.com

RTDC
Govt Hostel, MI Rd, Jaipur. **Tel** (0141) 237 1641.
Swagatam Tourist Campus.
Tel (0141) 511 0598.

Dharamshalas and Ashrams

International Rest House
Shri Krishna-Balaram Temple, Brindavan.
Tel (0565) 254 0021.

Ramakrishna Mission
Ramakrishna Ashram Marg, Delhi.
Tel (011) 2358 7110.
W rkmdelhi.org

Sri Aurobindo Ashram
Aurobindo Marg, Delhi.
Tel (011) 2656 7863.
W sriaurobindoashram.net

National Parks and Camping Sites

Aquaterra Adventures
S–507, Greater Kailash II, Delhi. **Tel** (011) 2921 2641. **W aquaterra.in**

GMVN Tourist Office
Muni-ki-Reti, Rishikesh.
Tel (0135) 243 0799.
W gmvni.com

Tourist Village
Pushkar.
Tel (0145) 277 3074.

Heritage Hotels

The title "heritage hotel" is given to some palaces and *havelis* that have been discreetly modernized to meet the needs of international travellers and run as high-class hotels. Fitted with modern plumbing and air-conditioning and with facilities such as swimming pools and tennis courts, such hotels take care that their history, architecture and innate elegance are suitably highlighted. The interiors display old sepia photographs, memorabilia and exquisite furniture tended by a caring staff, often old family retainers. The high tariffs of such hotels are compensated for by their special ambience.

Neemrana Fort Palace, Neemrana
Built in 1464, this fort was one of India's first heritage hotels. Meticulously restored to recreate the original plan and architecture, its interior is an eclectic blend of traditional design and its modern interpretations *(see p241)*.

Castle Mandawa, Mandawa
This mid-18th century fortress is now a charming heritage hotel and an ideal base to explore the painted *havelis* of Shekhawati. Live entertainment by Rajasthani folk dancers and musicians, and camel rides are some of its attractions *(see p241)*.

Samode Palace, Samode
All the grandeur of royal Rajasthan is visible in this opulent painted palace. Its magnificent Durbar Hall and Sheesh Mahal are now reception areas where guests can dine *(see p241)*.

Hotel Pushkar Palace, Pushkar
The lake-side palace, once the property of the Maharaja of Kishangarh, is now a popular hotel in this temple town. Its location is ideal for views of the bathing ghats, the rugged Aravalli Hills and the town's 400 temples.

Narain Niwas Palace, Jaipur
Surrounded by sprawling gardens and mango orchards, this traditional palace was built in 1928.

The Hill Fort, Kesroli
This seven-turreted fort is believed to be 600 years old. Built on top of a small hillock, it commands a splendid view from its high ramparts and is a perfect base from which to visit neighbouring sites and sanctuaries.

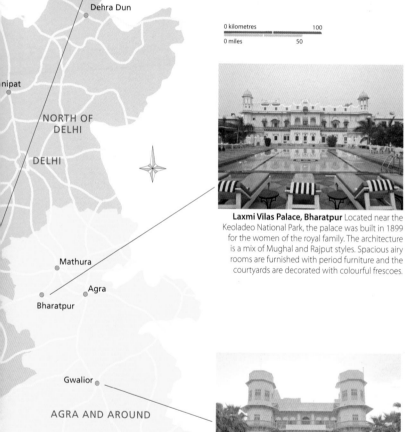

Dehra Dun

0 kilometres 100

0 miles 50

nipat

NORTH OF DELHI

DELHI

Mathura

Agra

Bharatpur

Gwalior

AGRA AND AROUND

Jhansi

Laxmi Vilas Palace, Bharatpur Located near the Keoladeo National Park, the palace was built in 1899 for the women of the royal family. The architecture is a mix of Mughal and Rajput styles. Spacious airy rooms are furnished with period furniture and the courtyards are decorated with colourful frescoes.

Usha Kiran Palace, Gwalior
The Maharaja of Gwalior's official guesthouse is now a pleasant hotel with an old-world charm *(see p240)*.

Where to Stay

Delhi

New Delhi

Prince Polonia ₹
Great Value **Map** 1 B3
2325–26 Tilak Gali, off Main Bazaar Paharganj
Tel *(011) 4762 6600*
W hotelprincepolonia.com
Situated in a busy backpacker area conveniently close to Connaught Place. Modern facilities, free Wi-Fi, and a rooftop swimming pool.

YWCA Blue Triangle ₹
Great Value **Map** 1 B5
Ashoka Rd, Connaught Place
Tel *(011) 2336 0133*
W ywcaofdelhi.org
Clean, basic rooms and a friendly, safe atmosphere. Recommended by young, female travellers.

YWCA International ₹
Great Value **Map** 1 B5
10 Parliament Street
Tel *(011) 2334 5235*
W ywcaindia.org
Comfortable, basic rooms at this centrally located hostel. Good for solo women travellers.

Jyoti Mahal ₹₹
Boutique **Map** 1 B3
2488–90 Nalwa Street, Chuna Mandi, off Main Bazaar, Paharganj
Tel *(011) 2358 0523*
W jyotimahal.net
Excellent heritage-style property in a central location. Stylish decor and a lovely rooftop restaurant.

Master Bed & Breakfast ₹₹
Boutique
R–500 New Rajender Nagar
Tel *(011) 2874 1089*
W master-guesthouse.com
A delightful option with just three stylish rooms and lovely communal areas. Delicious breakfast.

Palace Heights ₹₹
Great Value **Map** 1 C5
D26–28 Connaught Place
Tel *(011)4546 0000*
W palaceheights.com
This plush property, at an enviable location in the heart of Connaught Place, offers stylish rooms and a good restaurant, *Zaffran*.

Ahuja Residency ₹₹₹
Guesthouse **Map** 5 B4
193 Golf Links
Tel *(011) 2461 1027*
W ahujaresidency.com
Stylish, spacious rooms with modern amenities. Also offers service apartments across Delhi.

Claridges ₹₹₹
Luxury **Map** 5 A3
12 Aurangzeb Rd
Tel *(011) 3955 5000*
W claridges.com
Stylish rooms at this slightly old-world hotel. Outdoor pool and an array of dining options.

ITC Maurya ₹₹₹
Luxury **Map** 3 B4
Diplomatic Enclave, Sardar Patel Marg
Tel *(011) 2611 2233*
W itchotels.in
Premier hotel that has an exquisite art collection and smart rooms. Favoured choice for state guests and foreign dignitaries. Enjoy fine dining at the popular *Dum Pukht*.

Maiden's ₹₹₹
Heritage
7 Sham Nath Marg, Old Delhi
Tel *(011) 2397 5464*
W maidenshotels.com
Established in 1903, this is one of Delhi's oldest hotels with classic style and great views of the Delhi Ridge.

Taj Palace ₹₹₹
Luxury **Map** 3 A4
Diplomatic Enclave, Sardar Patel Marg
Tel *(011)2 611 0202*
W tajhotels.com
A beautiful location and elegant rooms complemented with modern facilities. A lovely place for high tea.

DK Choice

The Imperial 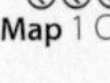
Luxury **Map** 1 C5
1 Janpath (close to Connaught Place)
Tel *(011)2334 1234*
W theimperialindia.com
Experience a graceful confluence of the colonial heritage and the magnificence of modern Delhi at this hotel. Designed as a part of Lutyen's vision of Delhi, this elegant hotel has hosted Gandhi and Nehru while they discussed issues related to India's independence. Today it offers evocative charm, nostalgic decor, award-winning restaurants, world-class spa and every modern amenity.

The Oberoi ₹₹₹
Luxury **Map** 6 D4
Dr Zakir Hussain Marg
Tel *(011) 2389 0606*
W oberoihotels.com
Impressive hotel with views of the Delhi Golf Course and Humayun's Tomb. Fantastic Sunday brunch.

Price Guide
Prices are based on one night's stay in high season for a standard double room, inclusive of service charges and taxes.

₹	up to ₹4000
₹₹	₹4000 to 10000
₹₹₹	over ₹ 10000

The Park ₹₹₹
Boutique **Map** 1 C5
15 Parliament Street
Tel *(011) 2374 3000*
W theparkhotels.com
Close to the historic Jantar Mantar, the hotel has an array of stylish rooms and good restaurants. Rejuvenate at the spa or the pool.

Vivanta by Taj ₹₹₹
Luxury **Map** 5 B3
Sujan Singh Park, Subramania Bharti Marg
Tel *(011)6626 1000*
W vivantabytaj.com
At a stone's throw away from Lodi Gardens and Khan Market, this hotel has smart decor, great restaurants and a lovely pool.

Nizamuddin

B Nineteen ₹₹
Boutique **Map** 6 E5
B–19 Nizamuddin East
Tel *(011) 4182 5500*
W bnineteen.com
Set against Humayun Tomb, this lovely B&B has comfortable rooms and facilitates access to kitchen.

The Lodhi 
Luxury
Lodhi Road **Map** 5 C4
Tel *(0124) 465 3333*
W thelodhi.com
Formerly the Aman, this opulent property has rooms with private plunge pools and balconies.

Elegant decor of the bar, InSomnia, at Vivanta by Taj, Delhi

Old Delhi

Hotel Broadway ₹₹
Heritage **Map** 2 E3
4/15A Asaf Ali Rd (Near Delhi Gate)
Tel *(011) 4366 3600*
W hotelbroadwaydelhi.com
Stylish, with old-world charm and themed restaurants. Organizes heritage walks of Old Delhi.

South Delhi

Tree of Life B&B ₹
Guesthouse
D–193, Saket
Tel *981 027 7699*
W tree-of-life.in
Close to the Saket metro station and the Qutb Minar, this B&B offers comfort and modern amenities.

Amarya Villa ₹₹₹
Boutique
A–2/20, Safdarjung Enclave
Tel *(011) 4103 6184*
W amaryagroup.com
Stylish three-storey villa offers nine spacious rooms, each themed on one of nine auspicious gemstones or *navratna*. Pretty terrace garden.

The Manor ₹₹₹
Luxury
77 Friends Colony West
Tel *(011) 4323 5151*
W themanordelhi.com
Charming hotel with lovely grounds. Acclaimed fine-dining restaurant, *Indian Accent*. Modern amenities.

The Rose ₹₹₹
Boutique
T–40 Hauz Khas Village
Tel *(011) 6450 0001*
W therosenewdelhi.com
Homely yet modern hotel with contemporary decor, lovely café and an art gallery. Lively ambience.

Further Afield

The Leela Ambience Gurgaon ₹₹₹
Luxury
Ambience Island, Gurgaon
Tel *(0124) 477 1234*
W theleela.com
Elegant property featuring fully serviced rooms and residences, award-winning restaurants, pool and spa. Next to Ambience Mall.

Tikli Bottom ₹₹₹
Rural Retreat
Tikli Bottom, Gairatpur Bas, Gurgaon
Tel *931 337 0853*
W tiklibottom.com
Lutyens-style four-bedroom *haveli*, surrounded by farmland. Food is sourced from the organic farm; pool facilities.

A spacious and exquisite room at The Imperial, Delhi

North of Delhi

HARIDWAR: Teerth ₹
Great Value
Subhash Ghat, Har-ki-Pauri
Tel *(0133) 422 5211*
W hotelteerth.com
Basic accommodation close to the Ganges, with rooms offering views of the main ghat, Har-ki-Pauri.

HARIDWAR: Haveli Hari Ganga ₹₹
Luxury
Pilibhit House, 21 Ramghat
Tel *(0133) 426 5207*
W havelihariganga.com
Right on the river, a lovely hotel with option for yoga on the ghats.

RISHIKESH: Bhandari Swiss Cottage ₹
Great Value
High Bank, Tapovan Bypass Rd
Tel *(0135) 243 2939*
W bhandariswisscottage.com
Picturesque views across the river and valley. Basic rooms with a verandah and a good restaurant.

RISHIKESH: Divine Ganga Cottages ₹
Rural Retreat
Tapovan, Laxman Jhula
Tel *(0135) 244 2175*
W divinegangacottage.com
Renovated rooms with great views and a charming garden restaurant.

DK Choice

RISHIKESH: Camp Silver Sands ₹₹
Rural Retreat
Beach no. 12, Badrinath Rd
Tel *(011) 2921 2760*
W aquaterra.in
A perfect place to relax, rejuvenate and be one with nature. Tented camps on the river bank with campfire and delicious food. Enjoy white-water rafting and adventure sports with one of the most acclaimed adventure companies in India.

RISHIKESH: Rainforest House ₹₹
Rural Retreat
Badrinath Rd, Brahmpuri
Tel *800 677 9298*
W rainforest-house.com
Beautiful, quiet oasis with stylish rooms and a lovely café serving classic Italian and local cuisine.

RISHIKESH: Ananda ₹₹₹
Luxury
Narendra Nagar, Tehri Garhwal
Tel *(0124) 451 6650*
W anandaspa.com
Try this award-winning spa-resort with great views, for ayurvedic and holistic treatments.

RISHIKESH: Glasshouse on the Ganges ₹₹₹
Heritage
23rd Milestone Badrinath Rd, Gular-Dogi
Tel *941 207 6420*
W neemranahotels.com
Exclusive resort with classic rooms and a private beach. Garden with tropical plants and rare birds.

Agra and Around

AGRA: Amar Yatri Niwas ₹
Tourist Lodge
181/1, Tourist Complex Area, Fatehabad Rd,
Tel *(0562) 223 3030*
W amaryatriniwas.com
This hotel offers spacious rooms and an on-site café and restaurant.

AGRA: Mayur Tourist Complex ₹
Tourist Lodge
Fatehabad Rd
Tel *(0562) 403 2310*
W mayurcomplex.com
Little cottages with lawns and a swimming pool. Basic amenities.

AGRA: Hotel Taj Plaza ₹₹
Great Value
Taj East Gate Rd
Tel *(0562) 694 1550*
W tajplaza.in
Comfortable rooms with great rooftop views of the Taj Mahal.

For more information on types of hotels *see page 235*

Lush interiors of a room at Usha Kiran Palace, Gwalior

AGRA: Howard Plaza ₹₹
Great Value
Fatehabad Rd
Tel *(0562) 404 8600*
W howardplazaagra.com
A range of rooms with modern amenities including gym, pool, spa and good on-site restaurant.

DK Choice

AGRA: Amarvilas ₹₹₹
Luxury
Taj East Gate Rd
Tel *(0562) 223 1515*
W oberoihotels.com
Elegant rooms with private balconies and glorious views of the iconic Taj Mahal. Rich decor inspired by the Taj. Unwind at the spa, relax by the pool, and dine at two acclaimed restaurants.

AGRA: Grand Imperial ₹₹₹
Heritage
MG Rd
Tel *(0562) 225 1190*
W hotelgrandimperial.com
Well-appointed rooms with four-poster beds. Vintage decor inspired by the Mughal era.

AGRA: ITC Mughal ₹₹₹
Luxury
Fatehabad Rd
Tel *(0562) 402 1700*
W itchotels.in
Award-winning hotel set in verdant gardens. Opulent property with charming rooms and excellent service.

BHARATPUR: Bharatpur Ashoka - Forest ₹₹
Tourist Lodge
Inside Keoladeo National Park
Tel *(0564) 422 2722*
W forestlodgebharatpur.com
Experience nature from this sylvan retreat in the bird sanctuary. Rooms with balconies. Row boats to get you closer to nature and birds.

BHARATPUR: Birder's Inn ₹₹
Boutique
Bird Sanctuary Rd
Tel *(0564) 422 7346*
W birdersinn.com
Nestled close to the Keoladeo National Park, this renovated lodge has stylish rooms and lush gardens.

BHARATPUR: Chandra Mahal Palace ₹₹₹
Heritage
Peharsar, Jaipur–Agra Rd
Tel *(011) 2506 6241*
W heritagehotelsofindia.com
Well-appointed rooms with antique furniture and interiors inspired by Mughal architecture.

BHARATPUR: Royal Farm ₹
Rural Retreat
Village Barso, Fatehpur Sikri Rd
Tel *941 431 5457*
W royalguesthousebharatpur.com
Comfortable homestay owned by naturalists working at Keoladeo Park. Food with ingredients from organic garden. Guesthouse also.

BRINDAVAN: Bhaktivedanta Ashrama & MVT Guest House ₹
Guesthouse
Bhaktivedanta Swami Marg Raman-Reti
Tel *999 772 5666*
W mvtindia.com
Ideally located behind the famous ISKCON temple, simple and comfortable rooms at this retreat with manicured lawns.

DHOLPUR: Raj Niwas Palace ₹₹₹
Heritage
Dholpur
Tel *766 5002 151*
W dholpurpalace.com
Grand red sandstone palace with lavish interiors, luxurious rooms and manicured gardens.

FATEHPUR SIKRI: Goverdhan Tourist Complex ₹
Tourist Lodge
Shahcoolie, Fatehpur Sikri
Tel *(05613) 282 643*
W fatehpursikriviews.com
Well-equipped rooms set around a beautiful, central garden. Enjoy scenic views and food at the multi-cuisine restaurant.

GWALIOR: Deo Bagh Hotel ₹₹₹
Heritage
Opposite Janaktal, Agra–Mumbai Highway
Tel *(0751) 282 0357*
W neemranahotels.com
Luxurious property with opulent rooms and exquisite interiors. Serene ambience and magnificent views of Char Bagh and Nau Bagh.

GWALIOR: Usha Kiran Palace ₹₹₹
Heritage
Jayendraganj Lashkar
Tel *(0751) 244 4000*
W tajhotels.com
Housed in a century-old palace, this regal property has an array of stylish rooms and a lovely spa.

MATHURA: Abhinanden ₹
Great Value
Goverdhan Chauraha NH 2
Tel *976 086 6595*
W hotelabhinandan.com
Comfortable hotel with spacious rooms and contemporary decor. Modern amenities.

ORCHHA: Orchha Homestay ₹
Rural Retreat
Lakshmi Mandir Rd, Ganj Mohalla
Tel *999 338 5405*
W orchha.org
Five simple and comfortable rooms, offering an opportunity to live with locals and gain a unique cultural experience. Homely meals. Cycle tours and walks on request.

ORCHHA: Sheesh Mahal MPTDC ₹₹
Heritage
Jahangir Mahal,
Tel *(0768) 025 2624*
W heritagehotelsofindia.com
Government-run property, offers lovely rooms with a combination of old-world charm and modern facilities. On-site restaurant.

Jaipur and Environs

AJMER: Heritage Haveli Inn ₹
Guesthouse
Kutchery Rd
Tel *(0145) 262 1607*
W haveliheritageinn.com
Housed in a 150-year-old building, this friendly B&B has a range of rooms; home-cooked food.

ALWAR: Dadhikar Fort ₹₹
Heritage
Dadhikar Village
Tel *995 044 9900*
W dadhikarhotels.com
Perched on a hilltop, this stunning fort with elegant rooms provides the perfect getaway from hectic city life. Traditional local cuisine.

CHURU: Malji Ka Kamra ₹₹
Heritage
Behind Jain Market, Churu, Shekhawati
Tel *(01562) 25 4514*
W maljikakamra.com
Renovated 20th-century *haveli*, with magnificent rooms and stunning frescoes. Traditional cuisine and grand sunset views.

JAIPUR: Hotel Pearl Palace ₹
Great Value
51 Hathroi Fort, Hari Kishan Somani Marg
Tel *(0141) 237 3700*
W hotelpearlpalace.com
A range of rooms with intricate artwork, and modern amenities. Friendly service; rooftop restaurant.

JAIPUR: Diggi Palace ₹₹
Heritage
Diggi House, Shivaji Marg, C-Scheme
Tel (0141) 237 3091
W hoteldiggipalace.com
Spacious rooms with a blend of old-world charm and modern luxury. Hosts the famous Jaipur Literary Festival. Cookery courses.

JAIPUR: Mosaic Guest House ₹₹
Rural Retreat
Siyaram Ki Doongri, Amber
Tel *(0141) 253 0031*
W mosaicsguesthouse.com
Beautiful guesthouse adorned with mosaic artwork by the French owner. Rooftop lounge with grand views of the Amber Fort.

JAIPUR: Pratap Bhavan B&B ₹₹
Guesthouse
A–4 Pratap Bhawan, Jamnalal Bajaj Marg, C-scheme
Tel *982 907 4354*
W pratapbhawan.com
Lovely homestay with traditional decor and modern facilities. Wildlife photography tours and walks can be organised by the owners.

JAIPUR: Umaid Bhawan ₹₹
Boutique
D1–2A, behind Collectorate, (Via) Bank Rd, Bani Park
Tel *(0141) 231 6184*
W umaidbhawan.com
Elegant hotel with exquisitely painted interiors and traditional handicrafts. Rooftop restaurant and courtyard swimming pool.

JAIPUR: Rajvilas ₹₹₹
Luxury
Oberoi Rajvilas
Tel *(0141) 268 0101*
W oberoihotels.com
Sprawling, large, royal resort in a beautiful fort setting. Magnificent suites, luxury tents and landscaped gardens.

JAIPUR: Rambagh Palace ₹₹₹
Heritage
Bhawani Singh Rd
Tel *(0141) 238 5700*
W tajhotels.com
Relax and unwind at this palatial hotel, embodying opulence and a sense of history. A range of beautifully appointed rooms with unique themes. Rejuvenate at the regal Jiva Spa.

JAIPUR: Samode Haveli ₹₹₹
Luxury
Gangapole
Tel *(0141) 263 2407*
W samode.com
Aesthetic rooms and heritage suites with lavish decor. Charming garden views. State-of-the-art spa.

JAIPUR: The Farm ₹₹₹
Boutique
Pritvisinghpura, Dhankiya Rd, Bad ke balaji, Ajmer highway
Tel *982 802 3030*
W thefarmjaipur.com
Charming rooms with eclectic art decor and quirky design features such as tables made from Enfield motorbikes. Large grounds.

KISHANGARH: Phool Mahal Palace ₹₹
Heritage
Phool Mahal Palace
Tel *(01463) 24 7405*
W royalkishangarh.com
With the majestic Kishangarh Fort as the backdrop, comfortable rooms; striking frescoes.

DK Choice

MANDAWA: Mandawa Haveli ₹₹
Heritage
Near Sonthaliya Gate, Mandawa
Tel *(0141) 237 4112*
W mandawahotels.com
Beautifully restored *haveli* with incredible frescoes, combining old-world charm and modern facilities. Rooms are lavishly designed. Central courtyard and a good option for rooftop dining. Enjoy splendid views of the Nahargarh Fort from the terrace.

NAWALGARH: Apani Dhani ₹
Rural Retreat
Old Jhunjhunu Rd, Nawalgarh, Shekhawati
Tel (01594) 22 2239
W apanidhani.com
Relax at this ecolodge with comfortable rooms. Winner of 2013 Responsible Tourism Award.

NEEMRANA: Neemrana Fort Palace ₹₹₹
Luxury
Neemrana Village, 122nd Milestone, Delhi–Jaipur Highway
Tel *(01494) 24 6007*
W neemranahotels.com
Relax at the luxurious rooms with unique themes or be adventurous with camel rides and zip-lining.

PUSHKAR: Inn Seventh Heaven ₹
Boutique
Next to Mali ka Mandir, Chotti Basti
Tel *(0145) 510 5455*
W inn-seventh-heaven.com
Restored ancient *haveli* with beautiful themed rooms and fantastic rooftop restaurant.

SAMODE: Samode Palace ₹₹₹
Heritage
Samode Village, Tehsil Chomu
Tel *(01423) 240 014*
W samode.com
Upscale property that blends traditional decor and modern luxury. Beautiful rooms and suites.

SARISKA: Sariska Tiger Camp ₹₹
Rural Retreat
Village Dhawala, Jaipur Rd
Tel *(0144) 288 5311*
W sariskatigercamp.com
A good option for the family, this hotel offers comfortable rooms, grounds and swimming pool.

SAWAI MADHOPUR: Ranthambhore Bagh ₹₹
Rural Retreat
Ranthambhore Rd
Tel *823 9166 777*
W ranthambhorebagh.com
Run by a wildlife photographer; offers both rooms and luxury tents. Fantastic campfire dinners.

SAWAI MADHOPUR: Sher Bagh ₹₹₹
Luxury
Sherpur–Khiljipur Village
Tel *746 225 2120*
W sujanluxury.com
Unwind in wilderness at this tented safari camp. Pool, campfire and jungle spa.

The magnificent Rambagh Palace, Jaipur

For more information on types of hotels *see page 235*

WHERE TO EAT AND DRINK

The unique flavours of Indian food depend heavily on the imaginative blend of spices and the use of fresh ingredients. Once, availability of local fruits and vegetables dictated menus in restaurants, which meant that a standard restaurant would offer a seasonally-changing choice of Mughlai preparations and a smattering of colonial fare, such as roast lamb with mint sauce, fried fish, and vegetables *au gratin*. Today, eating habits, especially in Delhi, have become much more sophisticated, and most Indians, when they dine out, prefer food that is quite different from what is cooked at home. The search for new culinary experiences has led to the proliferation of excellent speciality restaurants, as well as fast food and pizza parlours. These newer, fancier, and more cosmopolitan establishments have added to the eating-out scene, but traditional Indian food, such as succulent kebabs, rich aromatic curries, or even the simple dal and *roti* served at *dhabas,* still remain popular. The listings of restaurants on pages 250–57 are organized by area to help visitors choose where and what kind of food they wish to eat.

Coffee bars and fast food outlets in Connaught Place, New Delhi

Restaurants

There is an array of eateries in Delhi, ranging from snack bars in markets to speciality restaurants in luxury hotels. Every commercial area has mobile vans which offer low-priced sandwiches, burgers and Indian-style Chinese chowmein and soups. South Indian eating places are widespread and good value for money with a wide choice of dishes. Other places specialize in North Indian tandoori meats and fish. Many of the American fast food giants, such as Pizza Hut, McDonald's and Dominos are firm favourites in the capital. Agra and Jaipur also have a wide range of restaurants where good quality international cuisine is served. The five-star hotels here house some exceptional fine-dining restaurants. Most places are open from 11am to midnight. It is a good idea to book in advance for the popular gourmet restaurants. Late hour or early meals are best had at the 24-hour coffee shops found inside the hotels.

Speciality Restaurants

Upmarket restaurants that specialize in international cuisines such as Japanese, Italian and Spanish are immensely popular, particularly in Delhi. Most of these restaurants are in luxury hotels, though a few independent ones are located in places such as the Hauz Khas Village and Greater Kailash in Delhi. Diva, run by gastronome Ritu Dalmia, is one such restaurant. It serves excellent Italian fare. The prices may be a bit steep, but the food and stylish ambience are worth it. Visitors can also find authentic Tibetan and Mediterranean food in select places. Most restaurants in Jaipur serve traditional Rajasthani dishes such as the *kej sangari* (desert beans) or *gutta* curry (curry made with yoghurt). Delhi and Agra have many restaurants that serve delicious Mughlai or Punjabi meals, prepared using traditional age-old recipes.

Coffee Shops

All big hotels have 24-hour coffee shops where guests can get snacks and light meals. Western coffee shop chains such as Costa Coffee and Starbucks can be found around Delhi. At busy market places, there are also coffee shop-like cafés that are open from 10am to midnight, offering a variety of refreshments and simple multi-cuisine dishes that may range from Indian to Indianized Western and Chinese. It is safer to order the more common dishes, and to avoid the fish and prawns specials.

A light prosciutto starter at Diva in Greater Kailash, New Delhi

Breakfast on the ramparts of Kesroli Fort

Roadside and Market Food Stalls

The roadside food stalls or *dhabas* offer a typical Indian meal, which includes a couple of basic curries, usually vegetarian, and hot *rotis*. However, it should be kept in mind that the dishes are made to suit an Indian palate, which prefers spicy food; when ordering, insist that the meal be made without the spices. It is advisable to eat at stalls that appear to have a rapid turnover, as the food will be freshly cooked. For health precautions, see page 281. Visitors could also try the local savoury and sweet shops that serve an assortment of fried snacks such as potato and flour fingerlings, spiced nuts and delicious, syrupy sweets. *Kulfi* (Indian ice cream) and the regional specialities of Rajasthan such as *pyaaz kachori* (fried pastry filled with spiced onions) are also recommended. Most Indian cities have become quite tourist friendly, with food stalls offering a variety of Western-style soups and salads, as well as baked delicacies. The majority of the menus are written in English.

Vegetarian Food

Most roadside food stalls in India are strictly vegetarian. Delhi, Agra and Jaipur have excellent vegetarian restaurants, which include the ubiquitous South Indian eateries that offer vegetarian *thalis*. Some of them display signs that read: "Cooked in pure *ghee*" or "Cooked in *ghee* made from cow's milk" which is meant to advise pure vegetarians. Cake shops also advertise eggless cakes. In the holy cities of Haridwar, Rishikesh and Pushkar, restaurants will not serve eggs, meat and alcohol.

Alcohol

There are strict restrictions on serving alcohol in the Delhi, Agra, and Jaipur region, and only restaurants and hotels with a liquor permit are allowed to serve alcoholic drinks, though there are liquor shops in all cities. A few places are licensed to serve only beer. Larger hotels have their own bars and sell both "Indian-Made Foreign Liquor" (whisky, rum, gin, vodka and beer), as well as many foreign brands. Drinking one's own liquor in a restaurant is not permitted. Selling and buying alcohol on the 1st and 7th of each month, national holidays and notified election days is also prohibited and these are hence, "dry days".

Prices and Tipping

Prices are fixed everywhere, even at roadside stalls. At luxury hotels, the rates are high and there are added taxes, but eating at most restaurants and coffee shops is generally affordable, and at the roadside stalls, it is quite cheap. The prices are always listed on the menu and diners should cross-check the figures on the bill. Waiters do expect to be tipped, and ten per cent of the bill is an appropriate amount.

Recommended Restaurants

Delhi, Agra and Jaipur offer an impressive range of cuisines, from Italian and Mediterranean to Japanese and Korean. Traditional Indian fare includes North Indian as well as South Indian dishes that have rich, flavourful curries and soft, fluffy whole-grain breads. Modern or contemporary Indian cooking experiments with the old, classic recipes to create innovative, delectable food. The following listings place restaurants in six geographical areas: New Delhi, Old Delhi, South Delhi, North of Delhi, Agra and Around, and Jaipur and Environs, and they have been carefully selected to cater to all tastes and preferences. The specially recommended restaurants, marked as DK Choice, stand out for the unique experience they offer– either the superb cuisine, a delightful ambience, excellent value, or a combination of these.

A roadside stall selling popular street food in Agra

The Flavours of Delhi, Agra and Jaipur

This region's traditional food is renowned for its range. Delhi's finest flavours are preserved in Mughlai cuisine and a long heritage of vegetarian fare. Jaipur and Agra are famous for spicy snack foods, made fragrant with cloves, cardamom and pepper, with spice levels toned down for the faint-hearted. Tandoori food *(see pp246–7)*, still considered a culinary upstart by traditionalists, is increasingly popular today. The wide variety of delicately flavoured milk sweets must also be tasted to experience the full talents of the region's cooks.

Bayleaves, cinnamon, cardamom, cumin, cloves and turmeric

Fresh local produce on a stall in a Delhi vegetable market

Delhi

Delhi, with its wide variety of Indian and foreign residents, offers food from virtually every part of India, as well as abroad. However, its unique culinary heritage is preserved in ancient recipes, handed down through generations of chefs and served in the Old City's eateries. Even prime ministers are known to have made their way here to savour the authentic Mughlai dishes, still cooked in huge brass pots over wood fires. Often tucked away in smoky warrens, these modest places are an essential part of the authentic Delhi culinary experience. Spices are ground fresh each day and their heady smells float out as they are lovingly cooked. Stuffed bread *(paratha)* is another Old Delhi speciality – it even has a lane named after it. No visitor to Delhi should miss the colours and smells of its fruit and vegetable markets. Vendors sing out bargain prices to tempt buyers, while keeping a sharp eye out for competitors. For centuries, the Indian street stalls have provided the raw materials for gifted cooks. Spices are an integral part of the culinary tradition and each region has its own secret combinations and recipes.

A small selection from the vast range of Indian breads

Regional Dishes and Specialities

Most of the food in this region is classified as vegetarian or non-vegetarian and, broadly, it reflects the traditional Hindu and Muslim culinary styles. Curried or dry vegetables are served with a range of breads.

Found throughout the region, the *aloo poori*, along with the *paratha*, appears at breakfast or a main meal. Mutton (which can mean goat meat too in India) and chicken form the core of Mughlai food, often served in curried stews such as *korma* and *rogan josh*.

Mint and chillies

Stewed lentils, called dal, are the staple comfort food throughout North India and are eaten with rice or bread. Milk is the main ingredient of desserts, often dressed temptingly with delicate silver sheets and slivers of nuts.

Poori are puffy, deep-fried breads, served with spicy potato *(aloo)* or other vegetable, curried or dry.

Fiery red chillies being dried before being ground into powder

Agra

In Agra, almost every neighbourhood or market has a *halwai* shop. This is the Indian version of a deli, except that you will only find vegetarian food and sweets here. It is possible to get a full meal, served on a *thali*, or just a savoury snack.

A typical *thali* meal will include dal, curried potatoes, pumpkin and other seasonal vegetables. *Pooris* and rice are eaten with the curried or dry vegetables, along with *raita*, chutneys and pickles, served in small bowls. *Thalis* are modestly priced.

Halwai shops are rather sophisticated now: levels of hygiene have improved, and bottled water is available. Service is prompt and orders are yelled across to the kitchen, usually situated at the back.

Jaipur

Be prepared to have your palate tickled with robust flavours when you eat in Jaipur. Rajasthani food, vegetarian or not, is robust and highly spiced. Fresh batches of the round onion *masala kachauri* are fried in huge woks from morning to night and served on leaf plates. *Lal maas*, a rich, red mutton dish, is the region's signature offering, along with the vegetarian *gatta* curry. Millet breads *(bajra rotis)*, served with chutneys, local vegetables and berries, are another speciality. Curds, set overnight in clay vessels, are churned with sugar and cardamom to make a frothy drink called *lassi*. This is often served in delicate terracotta cups which, like leaf plates, reflect ancient practices that helped to conserve precious water in a desert region.

Bazaar vendor cooking samosas in a *tawa* (wok)

BAZAAR FOOD

The sizzle of *ghee* on hot griddles, the splutter of spices as they are added and the aromas of food cooked lovingly in huge vats and pans are traditional bazaar wiles to tempt customers. As for curries, there is a bewildering variety to choose from: from the rich red of the mutton korma, served with a range of breads, to the turmeric based *karhi* with yellow dumplings, served with rice. Food courts with a range of regional and traditional cuisines have sprung up close to these bazaars and attract customers all day. Food may be washed down with hot, sweet, milky *masala chai* (tea flavoured with cinnamon, cardamom and ginger).

Korma is fragrant with cardamom and cloves. This rich, creamy curry is eaten with either Indian bread or rice.

Dal combines lentils with a heady mix of onions, garlic and spices. It is considered India's "soul food".

Gulab Jamun may be served hot or cold. These syrupy little dough balls are often topped with ice cream.

The Flavours of the Tandoor

A wood-fired clay oven, the tandoor, is used all over Western Asia. Its entry into the mainstream of Indian cooking began with the arrival of Punjabi refugees at the time of Partition *(see pp62–3)*. Meats or vegetables are marinated in a spiced yoghurt mixture, then speared onto long skewers and slowly cooked in the tandoor until the outer skin is crisp and smoky. Tandoori breads are rolled by hand, flung up in the air to stretch, deftly caught and then fired in the tandoor. Tandoori cuisine is undoubtedly the most popular "finger food" of this region.

Raita, a cooling yoghurt salad dip

Barra Kebab features robustly flavoured lamb chops

Murg Tikka is a spicy cube *(tikka)* of chargrilled boneless chicken

Mughlai Kebab is minced lamb spiced in the Mughlai style

Tandoori Murgh, a whole spring chicken *(murgh)*, is the original tandoori delicacy

Reshmi Kebab, made with minced chicken, gets its name from being as smooth as silk *(resham)*

Seekh Kebab, uses spicy minced lamb, and is named after the skewer *(seekh)*

ON THE TANDOORI MENU

Achari Murg: chicken kebabs in a strong pickle *(achar)* marinade.

Achari Paneer Tikka: cottage cheese *(paneer)* chunks in a sharp pickle *(achar)* marinade go well with a chilled beer.

Afghani Murg: grilled chicken basted with butter and spices.

Bharwan Tamatar: tomatoes *(tamatar)* stuffed with a spicy potato filling. This squishy dish must be eaten in one bite.

Boti Kebab: chunks of mutton, grilled medium-rare.

Dahi ka Kebab: the base of this delectable melt-in-the-mouth kebab is strained curds *(dahi)*.

Galouti Kebab: richly spiced, finely minced mutton patties that melt in the mouth. However, the pepper in them has a slow fuse so take care.

Hariyali Murg: grilled spring chicken in a green marinade, often featuring coriander.

Kakori Kebab: cardamom-flavoured soft kebabs originally devised for a toothless *nawab* by the royal chef of Kakori.

Kalmi Kebab: chicken twists with soft buttery marinade.

Kathal Kebab: often called a vegetarian lamb substitute, this jackfruit kebab tastes like a mutton *shami* kebab.

Lehsuni Murg Tikka: garlicky *(lehsun)* chicken kebabs.

Machli Tikka Ajwani: fish *(machi)* kebab flavoured with the oregano-like herb *ajwain*.

Malai Makai Seekh: creamy sweetcorn *(makai)* kebabs, served chargrilled on skewers.

Mutton Chop Adrakhi: ginger *(adrak)* features in this dish.

Paneer Pudina Tikka: cottage cheese kebab flavoured with mint *(pudina)*.

Pasanda: boneless, flattened lamb in a cardamom-based marinade. Garnished with roasted almonds and sultanas.

Pickles and Chutneys

No Indian meal is complete without accompanying relishes, set in small bowls alongside the main meal. Raw mango pickle is a favourite, the tender fruit mixed with spices and mustard oil. Raw mango is also a base for spicy chutneys with fresh coriander, mint and chillies. Among other popular chutney bases are red tomatoes and garlic. Pickled shallots are often served with tandoori platters. Shredded ginger, pickled in lime juice, turns pink with time and aids digestion. Sweet pickles are flavoured with cloves.

Mango, mint and tomato chutneys, among the many varieties that accompany a meal

Tandoori Gobhi is spiced florets of cauliflower *(gobhi)* lightly grilled in the tandoor

Paneer Tikka, delicately grilled chunks of cottage cheese *(paneer)*

Tandoori Sabzi feature assorted skewered, grilled vegetables *(sabzi)*

Bharwan Simla Mirch are barbecued green and red peppers *(simla mirch)* with a spicy potato stuffing

Bharwan Aloo are potatoes *(aloo)* that are scooped out and stuffed with a spicy filling, then grilled

Hariyali Kebabs are green *(hara)* kebabs made of lentils and spinach

Tandoori chef with a whole leg of lamb *(raan)* for the oven

Sabzi Seekh Kebab: served on skewers, this is a vegetarian *(sabzi)* variation of the popular *seekh* kebab.

Seekh Kebab Roll: A soft *rumali* (handkerchief) bread is rolled round a *seekh* kebab, spiced with mint chutney and onion rings.

Shami Kebab: finely minced meat, stuffed with chopped onions, ginger and fresh coriander. Raisins may be added.

Tandoori Bater: marinated quails *(bater)* skewered and chargrilled.

Tandoori Bhindi: tender whole okra *(bhindi)*, smeared in tandoori marinade and grilled to a crunchy finish.

Tandoori Jhinga: marinated jumbo prawns *(jhinga)* garnished with pomegranate seeds.

Tangri Kebab: chicken drumstick kebabs.

Tandoori Khumb: Kashmiri mushrooms *(khumb)* are spiced and grilled to a creamy bite.

Tandoori Pomfret: a whole marinated fish, served with onion rings, lemon and mint chutney.

Tandoori Raan: grilled leg of lamb, marinated in spiced yoghurt dressing.

Tandoori Salad: features seasonal vegetables such as peppers, tomatoes and lotus root.

A Glossary of Typical Indian Food

The essence of traditional Indian food lies in the infinite variations in the blending and combination of a variety of spices. Chillies need not be used and, in fact, are often regarded as the inputs of a poor cook who uses them to camouflage the lack of subtlety in his seasonings. A typical menu in the region includes meat, lentils, vegetables and *tandoori* dishes, accompanied by rice and *rotis*. Street food is extremely popular with locals, and consists of savoury snacks, eaten through the day.

Snacks

Sweet and savoury snacks are an important part of the Indian diet.

Aloo Tikki
Stuffed potato cutlet cooked on a griddle.

Chaat
The most popular items are *papri*, made of fritters, chickpeas, potatoes, yoghurt and spicy sauces; and *golguppas*, puffed flour crisps filled with cumin-spiced water and chickpeas.

Idli and Dosa
Popular South Indian steamed rice cakes and crisp pancakes, served with coconut curry and a spicy lentil curry, are a national breakfast favourite.

Jalebi
Crisp, golden coils of flour batter dipped in a rose-flavoured syrup.

The *chaat-wallah's* variety of savouries served in mouth-watering combinations

Pakora
Vegetables or cottage cheese fried in gramflour batter.

Skewered tikkas

Samosa
Deep-fried pastry triangles filled with spiced potato and peas.

Tikkas
Marinated and char-grilled small chunks of chicken, mutton, fish and cottage cheese. The *burra* kebab is meat with bone from the rib, prepared in the same way.

Main Non-Vegetarian Dishes

Often spicy and rich, these are among the most delicious examples of Indian cuisine.

Bhuna Gosht
A dry meat curry, stir-fried slowly till tender.

Butter Chicken
Tandoori chicken with a rich tomato and butter sauce.

Dal Gosht
Meat with lentils.

Dil Bahar Dopiaza
A spicy mutton stew in a thick sauce made with onions.

Kadhai Murg
Chicken curry stir-fried in a wok.

Kofta
Meatballs in broth.

Lal maas
A Rajasthani mutton dish cooked with red chillies. A variation is *safed maas*, a "white" curry with almonds and cashew nuts.

Nargisi Kofta
The Mughlai version of Scotch Eggs – hard-boiled eggs covered in minced meat and served in a spicy sauce.

Murg Mussallan
A masala roast chicken, sometimes stuffed with hard-boiled eggs.

Rogan josh, a meat dish

Korma
Braised meat or chicken cooked on a slow fire with yoghurt and spices.

Nihari
Stewed lamb shanks, usually cooked all night over embers. It is eaten for breakfast during the month of Ramadan.

Rogan Josh
Cubes of mutton cooked with red chillies and spices.

Saag Gosht
Meat cooked with spinach.

Red chilli

Curry leaves and *masur* dal

Vegetarian Dishes

Traditionally, only seasonal vegetables *(sabzi)* were used, limiting the choice of dishes.

Aloo Gobhi
Potatoes *(aloo)* cooked with cauliflower *(gobhi)* and ginger.

Aloo Methi
Browned potatoes and fenugreek *(methi)* leaves.

Baingan ka Bharta
Smoked aubergine puréed with onions and tomatoes.

Bhindi Piaz
Okra and onions (seasonal).

Dum Aloo
Potatoes with yoghurt and spices cooked over low heat.

Gatta Curry
Gramflour dumplings in a delicate, aromatic sauce.

Kadhi
Fried gramflour dumplings cooked in a yoghurt and gramflour-thickened sauce.

A streetside restaurant specializing in *parathas*

Kair Sangri
Small local berries cooked with spinach-like leaves.
Khumb-matar Curry
A mushroom and pea curry.
Malai Kofta
Cottage cheese dumplings in a thick tomato gravy.
Masala Baingan
Stuffed aubergines (eggplants) braised in oil.
Paneer
Paneer (cottage cheese), an all time favourite, is cooked in a variety of combinations. *Palak paneer* is with spinach, and *matar paneer* with peas.
Paneer Makhani
Cottage cheese in a tomato and butter sauce.
Sarson ka Saag
Mustard leaves cooked in milk and served in a puréed form with butter.

Lentils

Dal, a lentil curry, is the staple meal. *Masur* and *moong* are two varieties.
Chhola Bhatura
Chickpeas thickly coated with a spicy sauce eaten with a puffed, deep-fried bread *(poori)*.

Chhola Bhatura

Dal Makhani
Unhulled dal cooked in cream and butter.
Rajma Curry
A red kidney-bean curry.
Sambhar
A South Indian speciality made with *arhar* dal and a special curry powder.

Breads

Common breads cooked on a griddle are the *chapati*, paper-thin *roomali roti* and *paratha*. *Pooris* are deep fried, while tandoori breads include the tandoori and *khastha roti* and *naan*.

Rice

Biryanis and *pulaos* are eaten with *raitas* (whipped yoghurt mixed with onions, tomatoes, coriander and green chillies), and a wide range of pickles and chutneys.
Biryani
Mutton or chicken korma is layered with rice, cooked on a slow charcoal fire, and flavoured with saffron.
Navratan Pulao
Rice cooked with nine types of vegetables.
Yakhni Pulao
Rice and mutton cooked in stock flavoured with aniseed and whole spices.

Sweets

Sweets are mainly milk-based.
Gajar ka Halwa
Grated carrots cooked in milk and sugar and browned with pistachios and almonds.
Gulab Jamun
Deep-fried milk and flour dumplings in a thick syrup.
Kulfi
Hand-churned ice-cream flavoured with pistachios.
Phirni A Mughlai riceflour pudding, flavoured with saffron *(kesar)*.
Rabri
Thickened milk and sugar garnished with nuts.
Rasmalai
A flatter version of the *rasgulla (paneer* balls in a thin syrup) in a mildly flavoured creamy sauce.

Gajar ka Halwa

Drinks

Elaichi Chai
Cardamom-flavoured tea.
Lassi
Whipped yoghurt shake.
Nimbu Pani
Fresh, sweetened or salted lime juice with water or soda.
Panna
Peeled raw mango boiled, puréed, and mixed in water with salt, sugar and cumin.
Sherbet
A flavoured sweet drink.

Paan

Betel leaf packed with areca nut, lime *(catechu)* paste, and other ingredients such as cardamoms and cloves.

Paan, a good digestive, can be made to suit individual tastes

Where to Eat and Drink

Delhi

New Delhi

The Shim Tur ₹
Korean **Map** 1 B3
3 F, Navrang Guest House, Tooti Galli, Main Bazaar, Paharganj
Tel *981 038 6717*
The rustic restaurant serves simple home-made style food. Try their *kimbap* (sushi) or the DIY fried pork. Their alcoholic beverage, *Soju*, is quite popular.

Kwality ₹
North Indian **Map** 1 C5
7 Regal Building, Connaught Place
Tel *(011) 2374 3352*
Serves North Indian fare such as tandoori *rotis* and kebabs. Their *chhola bhatura* (spicy chickpeas) is a crowd favourite.

Saravana Bhavan ₹
South Indian Vegetarian **Map** 1 C5
46 Janpath
Tel *(011) 2331 6060*
Very popular South Indian diner that serves great *thalis* and *dosas*. The mini tiffin, with a little bit of everything, is fantastic.

Triveni Tea Terrace ₹
Snacks **Map** 2 D5
205, Opposite FICCI, Mandi House
Tel *981 011 8115* **Closed** *Sunday*
Part of a cultural and arts complex, serves delicious dishes such as *palak paneer* and kebabs in a peaceful, arty setting.

Big Chill ₹₹
Multi-cuisine **Map** 5 B3
68A Khan Market
Tel *(011) 4175 7588*
Famous for their range of cakes and milkshakes such as Mississippi Mud Pie and Malted Oreo Shake. The vast menu also includes pizzas and lasagne.

Khan Chacha ₹₹
North Indian **Map** 5 B3
50, First floor, Khan Market
Tel *(011) 2463 3242*
Savour scrumptious tandoori food – kebabs, *tikkas* and *roomali* rolls. Try the chicken *tikka* roll and the mutton *seekh*. Expect long queues.

Pind Balluchi ₹₹
North Indian **Map** 1 C5
13 Regal Building, Connaught Place
Tel *(011) 4372 0507*
Colourful, rustic interiors and a wide selection of hearty Punjabi dishes. The kebabs are succulent and fresh.

Daniell's Tavern ₹₹₹
North Indian **Map** 1 C5
The Imperial, 1, Janpath
Tel *(011) 4111 6634*
The menu here charts the culinary expedition of a British explorer duo in 18th-century India. Try their East India Fish Curry and the Railway Chicken.

Dhaba ₹₹₹
North Indian **Map** 5 A3
The Claridge's, 12, Aurangzeb Rd
Tel *(011) 3955 5082*
In kitschy interiors that recreate popular roadside eateries, the restaurant serves outstanding traditional Punjabi and tandoori dishes. The chef's special *thali* and *balti* meat are must-haves.

Elan ₹₹₹
Multi-cuisine **Map** 5 B4
The Lodhi, Lodi Rd
Tel *(011) 4363 3333*
Serves an eclectic mix of flavours from around the world. The Mediterranean and Southeast Asian dishes are excellent and the contemporary courtyard setting makes a great place to enjoy a glass of good wine.

Latitude 28 ₹₹₹
Multi-cuisine **Map** 5 B3
9, 2nd Floor, Khan Market
Tel *(011) 2462 1013*
Fresh salads and great fish dishes; a great place to break for a leisurely lunch while shopping.

Lodi Garden Restaurant ₹₹₹
Mediterranean **Map** 5 A5
Opposite Mausam Bhawan, Near Gate 1, Lodi Rd
Tel *(011) 3310 5163*
The garden restaurant, lit with colourful lanterns, is enchanting. Their rosemary and thyme quinoa and home-made fig ice cream are highly recommended.

Price Guide
The price ranges are for a meal for one, including tax and service charges but not alcohol.

₹	under ₹300
₹₹	₹300 to 900
₹₹₹	over ₹900

Sevilla ₹₹₹
Spanish **Map** 5 A3
The Claridges, 12, near Lodi Rd, Aurangzeb Rd
Tel *(011) 3955 5082*
Authentic Spanish food in a beautiful outdoor setting with individual gazebos. Try the *paella valencia* (a rice dish with meat and vegetables).

Spice Route ₹₹₹
Asian **Map** 1 C5
The Imperial, Janpath
Tel *(011) 4111 6605*
The ornate interiors resemble those of a South Indian temple. The varied dishes on the menu represent the original course of spices from Kerela through Sri Lanka, Thailand and Vietnam.

Varq ₹₹₹
Contemporary Indian **Map** 5 B3
The Taj Mahal Hotel, 1, Mansingh Rd
Tel *(011) 6656 6162*
Traditional Indian recipes but with a contemporary twist. Try their signature dishes such as Varqui Crab, apricot kebabs, and Baileys *rabdi*.

Veda ₹₹₹
North Indian **Map** 1 C4
H27, Outer Circle, Connaught Place
Tel *(011) 4151 3535*
With plush red velvet decor and sparkling crystal chandeliers, the ambience dominates the dining experience here, but the food is good too. Their signature dal Veda, chicken *makhani* and *dahi ke* kebabs are recommended.

The elegant interiors of Varq

Wasabi ₹₹₹
Japanese **Map** 5 B3
Taj Mahal Hotel, 1 Man Singh Rd
Tel *(011) 6651 3585*
Watch the chefs perform the elaborate knifework of the Teppanyaki style of cooking. All ingredients are fresh and are flown in from Tokyo daily. The food is excellent and there is a wonderful sake bar that offers an impressive collection of Japanese sakes.

Nizamuddin

Three Sixty Degree ₹₹₹
Multi-cuisine **Map** 6 D4
The Oberoi, Dr Zakir Hussain Marg
Tel *(011) 2436 3030*
In addition to their renowned Sunday brunch, Three Sixty Degree is popular for its delicious Japanese food and wood-fired pizzas. The service is excellent.

Old Delhi

Karim's ₹
North Indian **Map** 6 D5
16, Gali Kababian, Jama Masjid
Tel *(011) 2326 4981*
An institution in Old Delhi, Karim's has been serving tasty Mughlai kebabs and juicy tandoori *raan* (leg of lamb) for over 100 years. The Chicken *Jahangiri* is also recommended.

Chor Bizarre ₹₹
North Indian **Map** 2 E3
Hotel Broadway, 4/15A Asaf Ali Rd
Tel *(011) 4366 3600*
Eclectically designed restaurant that serves authentic, flavoursome Kashmiri food. Try the delicious *gushtaba* (spiced meat balls cooked in yoghurt).

South Delhi

Naivedyam ₹
South Indian
1, Hauz Khas Village
Tel *(011) 2696 0426*
Offers delicious, reasonably-priced South Indian dishes. The *thali* and the *rasam vadai* are recommended, as is a close look at the exquisite wall paintings.

Elma's ₹₹
Multi-cuisine
31, 2nd floor, Hauz Khas Village
Tel *(011) 2652 1020*
Furnished with big, comfortable armchairs, Elma's is perfect for those in need of a laid-back repast. The extensive menu includes mezze platters and lamb roulade, but the highlight is their indulgent array of cakes such as red velvet and apple crumble.

Kitschy decor of the Japanese restaurant, Wasabi

Oh! Calcutta ₹₹
Bengali **Map** 2 D5
Ground Floor, International Trade Towers, E Block, Nehru Place
Tel *(011) 3040 2415*
Acclaimed Bengali restaurant that serves authentic *kosha mangsho* (a traditional spicy mutton dish) – a must-try. Their fish fry is also quite popular.

DK Choice

Park Balluchi ₹₹
North Indian **Map** 1 B3
Inside Deer Park, near Hauz Khas Village
Tel *(011) 2685 9369*
Located amid the lush greenery of the Deer Park, Park Balluchi serves classic North Indian food such as *tikkas* and kebabs. Their signature dishes include the popular dal Balluchi and tandoori *gulnar* (marinated cauliflower florets slowly cooked in the tandoor). The staff is friendly and efficient.

Sagar Ratna ₹₹
South Indian
18, Defence Colony Market
Tel *(011) 2433 3658*
Famed for enormous 1 m- (4 ft-) long family *dosas*, Sagar Ratna is an excellent place to get the true taste of South India. The restaurant serves great vegetarian *thalis* and authentic South Indian filter coffee.

Tamura ₹₹
Japanese
S16 Uphar Commercial Complex, Green Park Extension Market
Tel *(011) 2653 5769*
Apart from the regular sushi dishes, Tamura serves lesser-known Japanese fare such as salmon rice in Japanese tea and sweet pork in vegetable stew. It also has a well-stocked bar. There is another branch in New Friends Colony.

TLR – The Living Room ₹₹
Multi-cuisine
31, Hauz Khas Village
Tel *(011) 4608 0544*
Spread over three floors, this is an excellent place for a relaxed lunch. In the evenings, the restaurant comes alive as a bar with live music and other events.

Yeti ₹₹
Tibetan/Nepalese
2nd Floor, 50A Hauz Khas Village
Tel *(011) 4067 8649*
This simple, comfortable restaurant serves well-prepared specialties from the high Himalayas – momos, *thukpa* and *sukuti sadeko* (buffalo jerky).

Bukhara ₹₹₹
North Indian **Map** 3 B4
ITC Maurya, Diplomatic Enclave, Sardar Patel Marg
Tel *(011) 4621 5125*
Rated amongst the best tandoori restaurants, with a lively open kitchen that serves rich, bold flavours. The dal Bukhara is very popular.

Diva ₹₹₹
Italian
M-8A, M Block Market, Greater Kailash II
Tel *(011) 3310 6265*
Award-winning restaurant that serves scrumptious Italian fare along with an excellent collection of wines. The menu changes seasonally.

Dum Pukht ₹₹₹
North Indian **Map** 3 B4
ITC Maurya, Diplomatic Enclave, Sardar Patel Marg
Tel *(011) 3310 5108*
Pristine marble interiors in a magnificent gold and blue decor, complement the traditional slow-cooked courtly cuisine. Try the *Shahi Nehari* (stewed lamb shanks with spices), Dum Phukt *biryani* and the *kheer* (rice pudding). Reservation recommended.

For more information on types of restaurants *see page 243*

Guppy by ai ₹₹₹
Japanese **Map** 5 B5
28, Main Market, Lodi Colony
Tel *(011) 3310 7928*
Run by the renowned Olive Bar & Kitchen group, the restaurant serves outstanding Japanese food in an Animé-style setting. Their Mushroom Suimono soup, California rolls, garlic fried rice and flambéd blueberry crêpes are highly recommended.

DK Choice

Indian Accent ₹₹₹
Contemporary Indian
The Manor, 77 Friends Colony West
Tel *(011) 4323 5151*
Try the award-winning chef Manish Mehrotra's inventive dishes such as tandoori bacon prawns with wasabi cream, chicken *tikka quesadillas* and butter chicken *kulcha*. Or opt for the chef's tasting menu for a broader experience of modern Indian cuisine – old classics with an experimental twist. Tables are only available at 7pm and 9:45pm. There is live music on Saturdays.

Beautiful *diya* trees at Indian Accent

Kainoosh ₹₹₹
Contemporary Indian
122–124 DLF Promenade Mall, Vasant Kunj
Tel *(011) 3310 6161*
Feast on enormous *thalis* that include nutmeg-infused lamb *kofta* and cardamom-saffron chicken. It also has a great bar, Keya, right next door.

La Piazza ₹₹₹
Italian
Hyatt Regency Delhi, Ring Rd, Bhikaji Cama Place
Tel *(011) 6677 1338*
Sunday brunch is very popular. The wide-ranging, tempting choices on the à la carte menu include signature dishes such as the pan-seared sea bass or wood-fired pizzas.

The ornatly designed dining room at Kainoosh

Nanking ₹₹₹
Asian
6C, Local Shopping Complex, Vasant Kunj
Tel *(011) 2613 8939*
Friendly restaurant, well-known for its dim sums, fried corn curd and sticky spare ribs. The *kung pao* chicken is absolutely delicious.

Olive at the Qutub ₹₹₹
Mediterranean
One Style Mile, Haveli 6, Mehrauli
Tel *981 023 5472*
Situated in the shadow of the Qutub Minar, the rustic restaurant serves perfectly grilled bass, seafood risotto and blue cheese gnocchi.

Orient Express ₹₹₹
Continental **Map** 3 A4
Taj Palace Hotel, Diplomatic Enclave
Tel *(011) 2611 0202*
A 5-star dining experience themed on the legendary train that transverses Europe. The restaurant is ornately styled as a railway carriage to create just the right ambience. The menu reflects the cuisine of the various regions the train journeys through. Dinner only.

Smokehouse Bar & Grill ₹₹₹
Multi-cuisine **Map** 5 B3
17, First Floor, Khan Market
Tel *(011) 3310 5615*
Offers a wide array of meat and seafood dishes. Guests can gorge on juicy tenderloin and lamb patties or crunchy prawn skewers. Also has a branch in Hauz Khas.

Swagath ₹₹₹
Multi-cuisine
14, Defence Colony Market
Tel *(011) 2433 0930*
Serves some of the most delicious regional dishes from Tamil Nadu and Mangalore in the capital and is best known for its seafood. Other cuisines such as Chinese and Continental also feature on the menu.

Thai High ₹₹₹
Asian
1091/1, Ambawatta Complex, Kalkadass Marg, Mehrauli
Tel *(011) 2664 4289*
Offers a wide range of tempting Thai dishes. Try the signature Thai High chicken and *yam phak krob* (crispy vegetables in a tangy sauce). Diners can sit outside and admire a beautiful view of the Qutub Minar.

The Great Kabab Factory ₹₹₹
North Indian
1st Floor, MGF Metropolitan Mall, Saket
Tel *(011) 3310 6148*
Serves an extraordinary 160 varieties of succulent kebabs, including quite a few vegetarian options as well. They have branches in Connaught Place, Noida and Mahipalpur.

The Kylin Experience 
Asian
24 Basant Lok, Vasant Vihar
Tel *958 200 1010*
Try the generous sushi platter, Indonesian *gado-gado* (mixed vegetable salad with peanut sauce dressing) and asparagus tempura rolls with the finest Japanese sake. The earthy interiors have a number of nice, cosy nooks.

Key to Price Guide *see page 250*

North of Delhi

Haridwar: Ahaar ₹
Indian
Kulri Bazaar Mal Rd, Survey Colony
Tel *983 757 2655*
Offers delicious northern favourites such as *Sarson ka Saag* and dal *Makhani*, as well as good South Indian food.

Haridwar: Mid-Way Resort ₹
Multi-cuisine
Raiwala, Haridwar–Rishikesh Rd
Tel *976 000 0929*
A perfect stop-off between Haridwar and Rishikesh, Mid-Way Resort offers a wide range of dishes. The bar here has an excellent collection of wines.

Haridwar: Shivalik ₹
Multi-cuisine
Hotel Shivalik, Lalita Rao Bridge, Railway Rd
Tel *(0133) 422 6868*
This hotel diner specializes in authentic Gujarati food. Also serves North Indian, Chinese and Continental fare.

Haridwar: Haveli Hari Ganga ₹₹
Multi-cuisine
21, Pilibhit House, Ramghat
Tel *(0133) 426 5207*
Inspired by the flavours of India, Southeast Asia and Europe, the food here is fresh and delicious. The Haveli also has a rooftop café that offers a beautiful view of the Ganges river.

Rishikesh: Chotiwala ₹
Indian
Swarg Ashram, across Shivanand Jhula
Tel *(0135) 243 4070*
Established in 1958, Chotiwala is an institution in Rishikesh. Their special *thali* and *aloo poori* are highly recommended.

Rishikesh: Devraj Coffee Corner ₹
Multi-cuisine
Opposite Laxman Jhula
Tel *(0135) 244 2089*
This restaurant serves healthy vegetarian fare. Try their signature dishes such as brown bread with yak cheese and aubergine lasagne. They have a quaint little bookshop next door.

Rishikesh: Green ₹
Italian
Swarg Ashram
Tel *(0135) 243 1242*
Serves a wide variety of wholesome lasagne and pizzas. A fairly reliable free Wi-Fi connection is also available.

Rishikesh: Ishan ₹
Multi-cuisine
Lakshman Jhula
Tel *(0135) 249 192*
Ishan is a popular travellers' hangout with extensive menu options. The spinach lasagna, in particular, is scrumptious.

Rishikesh: New Bhandari Swiss Cottage ₹
Multi-cuisine
High Bank Area, Bypass Rd, Shivanand Nagar, Tapovan
Tel *(0135) 243 5322*
The cottage serves great food – from signature dishes such as tofu steaks with mushroom sauce to the usual travellers' favourites of hummus and lasagne.

Rishikesh: Pyramid Café ₹
Multi-cuisine
Kirmola/Laxman Jhula, Opposite the Post Office
Tel *805 782 5597*
Popular café that serves a range of home-made jams, tofu, hummus, as well as freshly-brewed Kerala coffee and organic cocoa beans. They have live music and DJ evenings.

DK Choice

Rishikesh: Ramana's Organic Restaurant ₹
Multi-cuisine
Close to Divine Ganga Cottages, Tapovan
Tel *901 275 4681*
Closed *Monsoon*
Popular dishes include different kinds of pasta and *momos*. A lovely organic garden provides the ingredients for fresh, delicious salads. Proceeds from the café go to the Ramana's Garden Children's Home, a shelter for children at risk. You can attend cookery classes at the café or volunteer at the shelter.

Rishikesh: Royal Café ₹
Multi-cuisine
Laxman Jhula, Near Laxman Moorti,
Tel *(0135) 244 2778*
A popular rooftop restaurant that serves a variety of vegetarian burgers, Tibetan *momos* and pancakes.

Rishikesh: Sanskriti Vedic ₹
Indian
Near Shivanand Hospital, Ramjhulla, opposite Shivanand Ashram
Tel *(0135) 244 2444*
The organic vegatarian menu here has been designed according to the principles of Ayurveda and offers healthy, nourishing dishes. Guests can also choose vegan, gluten-free and dairy-free meals.

Rishikesh: Tattva ₹
Multi-cuisine
Pundir's Organic Store, Tapovan
Tel *(0135) 243 4798*
A rooftop restaurant that serves healthy, organic produce. They have a great shop for travellers which sells miso, tofu, granola, herbal teas and yoga mats.

Rishikesh: Holywater ₹₹
Multi-cuisine
Hotel Ganga Kinare, 237 Virbhadra Rd
Tel *901 554 4000*
Holywater has lovely outdoor seating that takes advantage of the river-side location. The indoor dining space has an elegant decor. Excellent vegetarian food.

Rishikesh: Glasshouse on the Ganges ₹₹
Multi-cuisine
Glasshouse on the Ganges, 23rd Milestone, Badrinath Rd
Tel *941 207 6420*
Sit on the scenic banks and enjoy a picturesque view of the river. North Indian cuisine with a smattering of Italian, Chinese and Continental dishes.

View of Chotiwala, a popular eatery in Rishikesh

For more information on types of restaurants *see page 243*

The exquisitely furnished Bellevue at Oberoi Amarvilas

Agra and Around

Agra: Dasaprakash ₹₹
South Indian
18/163A/6, Minto Rd, Vibhav Nagar
Tel *(0562) 401 6123*
Excellent vegetarian restaurant that offers delicious *dosas*, *thalis* and a wide range of chutneys.

Agra: Pinch of Spice ₹₹
Multi-cuisine
1076/2, Fatehabad Rd, Tajganj
Tel *(0562) 404 5353*
Try the *rogan josh* (lamb cooked in aromatic spices and butter) or any dish from the tandoor. The buffet is quite popular.

Agra: Pizza Hut ₹₹
Italian
8, Handicraft Nagar, Fatehabad Rd
Tel *(0562) 406 4051*
The fast-food chain offers Indian-style pizzas with flavoursome tandoori *paneer* or chicken topppings, in addition to the usual offerings.

Agra: Zorba the Buddha ₹₹
Vegetarian
E-19, Shopping Arcade, Sadar Bazaar
Tel *(0562) 222 6091*
A popular restaurant – try their delicious *paneer* dishes and the *malai kofta*.

Agra: Al Fresco ₹₹₹
Italian
Trident Hotel, Fatehabad Rd
Tel *(0562) 223 5000*
Savour succulent grilled meats and super thin-crust pizzas that are seasoned with fresh herbs from their own kitchen garden.

Agra: Bano ₹₹₹
Multi-cuisine
ITC Mughal, Fatehabad Rd
Tel *(0562) 402 1700*
The breakfast and the lunch buffet here is immensely popular as it allows a diverse sampling of beautifully prepared food from around the world. It has an inviting ambience is inviting and the service is excellent.

Agra: Bellevue ₹₹₹
Multi-cuisine
The Oberoi Amarvilas, Taj East Gate
Tel *(0562) 223 1515*
With an extensive à la carte menu and a huge buffet, diners are completely spoilt for choice. Luxurious interiors in vibrant blue provide the perfect backdrop.

Agra: Dawat-e-Nawab ₹₹₹
North Indian
Radisson Blu, Taj East Gate
Tel *(0562) 405 5555*
Definitive fine dining – an extravagant six-course meal in a resplendent setting. Try the special mutton *biryani* with one of their delicious gravies.

DK Choice

Agra: Esphahan ₹₹₹
North Indian
The Oberoi Amarvilas, Taj East Gate
Tel *(0562) 223 1515*
Enjoy the delicately flavoured cuisine of Mughal India while listening to live instrumental traditional music. The restaurant is softly lit and has an elegant, earthy decor. As it is extremely popular, Esphahan has two seperate seating timings in the evening – 6:30pm and 9:30pm.

Agra: Jhankar ₹₹₹
North Indian
The Gateway Hotel, Fatehabad Rd
Tel *(0562) 660 2000*
Serves excellent kebabs and a wide range of vegetarian dishes. The atmosphere is lively with regular music and dance events.

Agra: Peshawri ₹₹₹
North Indian
ITC Mughal, Fatehabad Rd
Tel *(0562) 402 1700*
The award-winning restaurant features a variety of delectable dishes cooked in the tandoor. The dal Bukhara, their signature dish, is simply divine. Chicken *khurchan* with *roomali rotis* is also recommended.

Bharatpur: Hotel Pelican ₹
Multi-cuisine
Hotel Pelican, Near Keoladeo National Park, Bird Sanctuary Rd
Tel *941 424 7066*
A perfect choice for bird-watchers; Pelican has a rooftop restaurant that offers a panoramic view of the beautiful bird sanctuary. The portions are large and the food, delicious.

Bharatpur: Bharatpur Ashoka ₹₹
Multi-cuisine
Hotel Bharatpur Ashoka, Forest Lodge, Inside Keoladeo National Park
Tel *(0564) 422 2722*
Surrounded by lush green trees inside the national park, this is an idyllic spot to have a leisurely lunch or dinner. The restaurant serves Continental, Chinese and regional delicacies.

Bharatpur: The Spoonbill ₹₹
North Indian
Near Tourist Reception Centre
Tel *(0564) 422 3 571*
Popular restaurant at a convenient location; a stone's throw from the Keoladeo National Park. Serves good, hearty meals and hosts traditional dance performances in the evenings.

The regal setting of Daawat-e-Nawab, Radisson Blu Agra

Bharatpur: The Sunbird ₹₹
Multi-cuisine
Near Bird Sanctuary Entrance Gate
Tel *(0564) 422 5701*
A mix of good North Indian fare along with other cuisines. Their lunchtime buffet is fairly popular. There is an outdoor seating area as well.

Fatehpur Sikri: Gulistan Tourist Complex ₹₹
Multi-cuisine
UPSTDC, Gulistan Tourist Complex
Tel *(05613) 282 490*
North Indian is the primary cuisine here, though some Continental classics also feature on the menu. The dining room is pleasant and spacious.

Gwalior: Kwality ₹₹
Multi-cuisine
Captain Upmanyu Singh Marg, Behind SP Office, City Centre
Tel *(0751) 241 0456*
Even though it serves a variety of cuisines, Kwality is renowned for its Mughlai dishes and rich North Indian food.

Gwalior: Volga ₹₹
North Indian
Jayendraganj, Shinde Ki Chhawani
Tel *(0751) 408 7100*
Their dal *makhani* and butter chicken is very popular. The restaurant is well-liked by locals and tourists alike.

Gwalior: Yellow Chilli ₹₹
Multi-cuisine
Ground Floor, Alaknanda Towers 2, Plot No C-8, City Centre
Tel *(0751) 406 5000*
The perfect place to relish delectable dishes from different parts of India – try the crispy *Amritsari machchli* (fish) from Punjab, Chowringhee chili chicken from Calcutta and rich *dum aloo* curry from Kashmir.

Gwalior: Silver Saloon ₹₹₹
North Indian
Usha Kiran Palace Hotel, Jayendraganj Lashkar
Tel *(0751) 244 4000*
Traditional recipes from the royal kitchens to tempt your palate and live perfomances of classical music to create the perfect ambience at this courtyard restaurant.

Meerut: Alfa ₹₹
Multi-cuisine
Bombay Bazaar, near Hanuman Chowk
Tel *(0121) 266 0532*
Try the North Indian dishes, such as the tikkas prepared with mustard or *paneer butter masala*.

Orchha: Betwa Resort ₹₹
Multi-cuisine
The Orchha Resort, Kanchanghat, District Tikamgarh
Tel *(0768) 025 2222*
Serves a variety of Indian, Chinese and Continental cuisine. Diners can opt to sit outdoors and enjoy a beautiful view.

Orchha: Kaleva ₹₹
Multi-cuisine
The Orchha Resort, Kanchanghat, District Tikamgarh
Tel *(0768) 025 2222*
Choose from a wide selection of regional specialities as well as international favourites. There is also an excellent vegetarian buffet. Cultural performances enliven the evenings.

Orchha: Sheesh Mahal ₹₹
North Indian
MPTDC Sheesh Mahal, Jahangir Palace
Tel *(0768) 025 2624*
The majestic dining room in this heritage fort serves an excellent buffet and also presents an extensive à la carte menu.

Jaipur and Environs

Ajmer: Bhola Hotel ₹
Vegetarian
Agra Gate, Station Rd
Tel *(0145) 243 2844*
Serves reasonably priced, flavourful vegetarian fare from the tandoor. Their vegetarian *thali* is one of the best in the city

Ajmer: Honeydew ₹₹
Multi-cuisine
Near KEM Resthouse, Station Rd
Tel *(0145) 262 2498*
One of the most popular restaurants in the city, it is renowned for its tandoor dishes and Chinese sizzlers. The staff is courteous and attentive.

Scenic view of the Orchha Cenotaphs from Kaleva

Alwar: Peppers ₹₹
Multi-cuisine
Near Delhi Public School, Alwar City
Tel *988 749 0946*
Enjoy Chinese and Continental dishes in a beautiful outdoor setting that is surrounded by lush green trees and hills. Serves only vegetarian food.

Alwar: Hill Fort Kesroli ₹₹₹
Multi-cuisine
Village Kesroli, Near MIA Post-Office
Tel *982 949 9901*
Live puppet shows entertain guests dining in this lovely courtyard restaurant. The buffet and an à la carte menu offer plenty delectable of choices.

Jaipur: Copper Chimney ₹
Multi-cuisine
Maya Mansion, Opposite GPO, MI Road
Tel *(0141) 237 2275*
Generous servings of tasty North Indian fare and some regional dishes such as the Rajasthani mutton and the delicately spiced *gutta* curries.

The airy courtyard of Silver Saloon

For more information on types of restaurants *see page 243*

A delectable spread of North Indian dishes at Peacock restaurant

Jaipur: Indian Coffee House ₹
South Indian
Near Ajmeri Gate, MI Rd
Tel *(0141) 236 2024*
This coffee house has been a popular meeting place in the city for decades and is famous for its filter coffee and delicious South Indian fare.

Jaipur: Special Lassiwala ₹
Snacks
315, MI Rd
Tel *966 718 8811*
There are several establishments in the city with the same name, but the original Lassiwala is situtated right next to an alley and serves sweet and salty *lassi* (yoghurt shake). It is worth getting there early in the day, before they run out.

Jaipur: Peacock ₹
Multi-cuisine
Hotel Pearl Palace, 51, Hathroi Fort
Tel *(0141) 237 3700*
The restaurant serves excellent North Indian dishes. The rooftop dining area, covered with a peacock canopy, has a beautiful view of the Hathroi Fort.

Jaipur: Anokhi ₹₹
Café
C11, 2nd Floor, Prithviraj Rd, C-Scheme
Tel *(0141) 400 7245*
Closed *Public Holidays*
An extension of Anokhi's flagship showroom, the café serves a variety of fresh, healthy salads, pizzas and sandwiches. Their French press organic coffee is a favourite among tourists.

Jaipur: Barbeque Nation ₹₹
North Indian
City Plex 1, Ashram Marg, Tonk Rd
Tel *(0141) 313 8001*
This popular restaurant serves incredible chicken and mutton kebabs. The menu also offers equally good vegetarian kebab options, as well as North Indian classics such as dal *makhani* and the sweet *gulab jamuns*.

DK Choice

Jaipur: Chokhi Dhani ₹₹
Vegetarian
Chokhi Dhani Village Resort, 12 Mile, Tonk Rd
Tel *(0141) 516 5000*
Serves a mouthwatering range of traditional Rajasthani dishes such as desert beans and *yoghurt pakoda curry*. The resort has eight beautiful dining areas that showcase different styles of dining in Rajasthan. The meals are usually accompanied by puppet shows and live music. Dine at the Chokhi Dhani to really experience the culture of Rajasthan.

Jaipur: Dasaprakash ₹₹
South Indian
5, Kamal Mansion, MI Rd
Tel *(0141) 237 1313*
Centrally located, this popular restaurant chain serves paper thin *dosas*, flavourful *sambhar* and amazing *thalis*. The fried rice *idlis* served with mint chutney and crispy *vadas* with *sambhar* are also recommended.

Jaipur: Diggi Palace ₹₹
Multi-cuisine
Diggi House, Shivaji Marg, C-Scheme
Tel *(0141) 237 3091*
The beautiful restaurant at this quaint palace hotel is surrrounded by lovely gardens. The flavours reflect the quality of ingredients – most grown organically at the owner's farm. Offers cookery courses as well.

Jaipur: Four Seasons ₹₹
North Indian
D-43, A2, Subhash Marg, C-Scheme
Tel *(0141) 331 9277*
The traditional Indian dishes such as *dum aloo* and dal *makhani* are absolutely delicious. The restaurant only serves vegetarian fare. Prior booking is advisable.

Jaipur: Jaipur Baking Company ₹₹
Multi-cuisine
Jaipur Marriott, Ashram Marg, Near Jawahar Circle
Tel *(0141) 456 7777*
A delicatessen and bakery that offers great cakes and muffins. They serve gourmet sandwiches, burgers and savoury pastries too.

Jaipur: LMB ₹₹
Vegetarian
100, Johari Bazaar, Pink City
Tel *(0141) 400 1616*
The highlight of the restaurant is its wide array of sweets. It also serve scrumptious *chat*. The *Raj Kachori, aloo tikki* and *badam* (almond) milk are recommended. LMB is very popular and, hence, quite busy.

Jaipur: Nahargarh Fort Restaurant ₹₹
North Indian
Nahargarh Fort
Tel *(0141) 514 8044*
Enjoy magnificent view of the Jaipur countryside while dining at the fort's rooftop restaurant. The food here is delicious and the menu offers good mocktails.

Jaipur: Natraj ₹₹
North Indian
Panch Batti, MI Road
Tel *(0141) 237 5804*
One of the oldest restaurants in the city. The Rajasthani *thali* here truly showcases the cuisine of the state – hearty, rich and spicy. They also have a good in-house sweet shop.

Jaipur: Niro's ₹₹
Multi-cuisine
Panch Batti, MI Road
Tel *(0141) 331 9372*
A local favourite, the restaurant is considered a landmark on the bustling MI Road. Serves outstanding North Indian and Chinese cuisine.

The lovely garden restaurant at Diggi Palace

Key to Price Guide *see page 250*

Jaipur: Baluchi ₹₹₹
Pan Indian
The Lalit, Jagatpura Rd, Malviya Nagar
Tel *(0141) 331 9237*
Specialises in marinaded meats and artisanal breads, baked in an iron tandoor rather than the usual clay one.

Jaipur: Marble Arch ₹₹₹
Multi-cuisine
Jai Mahal Palace, Civil Lines
Tel *(0141) 660 1023*
The breakfast buffet has a wide selection of English, French and Indian dishes. The staff is friendly and attentive.

Jaipur: Samode Haveli ₹₹₹
Rajasthani
Gangapole
Tel *(0141) 263 2407*
The authentic flavours of regional Rajasthani cuisine vie with the ambience to define the dining experience here. The exquisite hand-painted murals and beautiful frescoes in the dining hall are breathtaking.

Mandawa: Castle Mandawa ₹₹₹
Multi-cuisine
Mandawa Village, Jhunjhunu
Tel *(01592) 223 124*
Live music and dance shows complement the excellent buffet of Indian and Continental dishes. There are three beautiful dining areas – the terrace, an indoor dining hall and a verandah bar.

Nawalgarh: Apani Dhani ₹₹
Vegetarian
Old Jhunjhunu Rd
Tel *(01594) 222 239*
The restaurant offers healthy, home-made vegetarian dishes. Most of the ingredients are sourced from Apani Dhani's organic gardens. They also conduct cookery classes.

Nawalgarh: Jharoka ₹₹
North Indian
Grand Haveli, Bawri Gate, Jhunjhunu
Tel *(01594) 225 301*
Choose to sit in an elegant dining room or a lovely outdoor seating area in the courtyard. Jharoka serves tasty regional dishes and North Indian fare.

Nawalgarh: Thikana ₹₹
Rajasthani
Hotel Heritage Thikana, Near Bawri Gate
Tel *(01594) 222 152*
Feast on traditional home-cooked Rajasthani delicacies. The fresh produce comes from their own farm.

The spacious and earthy interiors of Baluchi

Pushkar: Derby's Café ₹
Vegetarian
Hotel U-Turn, Vahara Ghat, Chotti Basti
Tel *992 873 7798*
The rooftop café has an amazing view of the Pushkar lake and the Vahara ghat. Serves tasty Indian and Italian cuisine.

Pushkar: Funky Monkey Cafe ₹
Café/ Bakery
Mahadev Chowk, Chotti Basti
Tel *982 987 3439*
This cosy little café is immensely popular with tourists. It serves delicious pancakes, sandwiches and shakes. Their decadent home-made chocolate banana bread is simply divine.

Pushkar: Honey & Spice ₹
Vegetarian
Laxmi Market, Old Rangji Templer
Tel *941 324 7156*
This popular restaurant serves delicious, healthy dishes such as a variety of vegetable stews and brown rice. Their banana-honey bread is excellent.

The serene ambience at Marble Arch, Jai Mahal Palace

Pushkar: Om Shiva ₹
Multi-cuisine
Town Centre
Tel *(0145) 277 2647*
In addition to its great-value buffet, the Italian food at this garden restaurant is very popular.

Pushkar: Sixth Sense ₹
Multi-cuisine
Inn Seventh Heaven, Next to Mali Ka Mandir, Chotti Basti
Tel *(0145) 510 5455*
Serves a delectable range of pizzas, waffles and *thalis*, as well as large selection of fresh garden salads. The dishes are served via an ingenious pulley system at this rooftop restaurant.

Pushkar: Tibetan Kitchen ₹
Tibetan
Near Dadudura Temple, Chotti Basti
Tel *(0145) 510 51745*
Known for its mix vegetable *thentuk* (noodles) and *momos*, this restaurant is an excellent place to try authentic Tibetan cuisine. The yak cheese special with the mint *nana* (mocktail) is outstanding.

Pushkar: Pink Floyd Cafe ₹₹
Multi-cuisine
Chotti Basti, near Marwar Bus Stand
Tel *982 807 2591*
The lovely rooftop restaurant is run by ardent Pink Floyd fans and is a great place for music lovers to relax. The ambience is friendly and relaxed with classic Pink Floyd music plaing in the background. The menu offers a variety of dishes – the cheese omlette is recommended.

SHOPS AND MARKETS

The colourful markets of the region carry a vast and exciting range of handicrafts. The government-run state emporia are well stocked with merchandise at fixed and reasonable rates. Shopping arcades of larger hotels cater to travellers who are hard-pressed for time, though their more sophisticated boutiques are usually pricier. For the more adventurous, there are the street stalls and bazaars that offer glimpses of local colour, and where bargaining is a way of life. Delhi has some of the region's most elegant shops *(see pp122–3)*, but the charming bazars of Jaipur and Agra offer visitors a chance to actually observe skilful craftsmen at work. In the smaller towns beyond the main cities, local crafts are often sold in quaint village stores or on the roadside.

Pavement hawkers selling fruits and vegetables in Jaipur

Opening Hours

Most shops usually open at 10am and shut by 7:30pm, though the smaller markets keep longer hours and many 24-hour shops are opening up. The government-run emporia close an hour earlier. Food markets open at dawn and stay open until late evening, while the temporary bazaars that spring up at different localities on festivals or particular week days stay open until late at night. In Jaipur and Agra, the closing day is Sunday, but in Delhi, each locality has its own weekly holiday. Shopping centres in the New Delhi area are closed on Sundays, but in South Delhi and Karol Bagh, the closing days are Monday or Tuesday. By law all shops are required to remain closed on the main national holidays, that is Republic Day (26 Jan), Independence Day (15 Aug) and Mahatma Gandhi's birthday (Martyr's Day, 2 Oct).

How to Pay

The rupee (₹) is accepted everywhere. The bigger stores accept international credit cards such as VISA, MasterCard, American Express and Diners, and usually display signs prominently inside the shops. But they are still not very common in the smaller shops and towns, and it is always sensible to keep some cash handy when travelling. Traveller's cheques can be encashed at local branches of the State Bank of India *(see p282)*, but again, this facility may not be available in the smaller towns.

Connaught Place shopping complex, Delhi

Bright glass and plastic bangles can be found at any bazaar in Delhi

Bargaining

Bargaining is an essential part of the shopping experience in India, and at the smaller markets, prices are quoted with the expectation that customers will haggle. Some of the most familiar scenes at all bazaars are those of local shoppers indulging in long and often acrimonious discussions with shopkeepers about price and quality. Most shopkeepers are tourist savvy today and will usually quote a higher price to foreigners. The best way to check out prices is to browse through a fixed-price shop like a government emporium. This will also give you an idea of quality. However, the price you offer to pay should be realistic and not so low that you miss out on a good purchase altogether. If this price is still not accepted by the shopkeeper, an old and usually very effective bargaining tactic is to walk away feigning indifference.

All the bigger and fancier shops and boutiques, retail outlets of manufacturers and the government emporia have fixed prices with no scope for bargaining. Increasingly, in fact, more shops are tagging their goods with labels that clearly indicate item prices.

A stall selling multicoloured paper kites in Jaipur

Rights and Refunds

By law all shops are obliged to give you a receipt or cash memo for all purchases. When buying, insist on getting one to which sales tax, generally seven or ten per cent of the total cost, has been added. Often the shopkeeper will say that you can save on the tax if you do not take a receipt, but do insist on one nevertheless. Refunds or the exchange of damaged goods are impossible without one and it is absolutely essential for the more expensive purchases. Bigger shops can be fussy about taking back goods but you can talk to the manager if absolutely necessary.

If the shop is going to ship your purchases, make sure that you know all the costs involved, including taxes. Also, insist that all the paperwork is done correctly and you have copies of it all. If you wish you can also ship the larger purchases yourself through the international courier services *(see p284)*.

Antiques

Antiques and art objects that are more than 100 years old cannot be taken out of the country. If in doubt about your purchases, consult the office of the Archaeological Survey of India *(see p272)*. You should also get a certificate from the shop stating the age of the artifact.

Touts

In the larger markets that are frequented by tourists, persistent touts can be a problem. Ignore the offers of fantastic bargains because the prices you pay are often suspect. Also beware of polite young men inviting you home for a cup of tea because "home" will be a shop down the lane. Tourist buses will of course stop at their selected shops but you don't have to buy anything from them. Try to shop for expensive things at big shops with price tags on their goods and beware of of shops with "government-approved" boards as these are usually private enterprises.

Bazaars

A visit to a traditional Indian bazaar is worth it for the experience rather than the actual shopping. These lively places offer fantastic bargains and a colourful atmosphere. Most bazaars are located in the heart of the old cities, where narrow lanes are lined with rows of shops selling a variety of merchandise, from car spare-parts, machinery, cooking utensils and provisions to textiles and jewellery. Vegetables and other fresh produce are sold on the roadside. Most cities also have weekly bazaars, and rural India has seasonal *haats* that travel from village to village for the local people to shop for everything from agricultural equipment and clothes to pots and pans. The bazaars in Agra and Jaipur were originally craft guilds and some still specialize in specific local crafts such as textiles, jewellery, marble inlay and leatherwork, where you can watch the craftsmen at work, admire their skills and buy directly from them.

Delicately inlaid marble

A streetside stall where bargaining skills are essential

Government Emporia

The central government and the state governments all run shops selling handicrafts and handloom textiles that are special to their region or state. The prices are fixed and the products genuine. Rajasthali, the Rajasthan emporium, concentrates on handicrafts from Jaipur. While Delhi is a centre for emporia from all the states, neither Agra nor Jaipur offer the same range of regional products. October is a good time for bargains and discounts.

Roadsides flooded with colourful, seasonal fruit

Anokhi, Jaipur, combining traditional designs with modern-day use

Shopping in Agra

The exquisite *pietra dura* work at the Taj Mahal is still practised in Agra by descendants of craftsmen who worked on the historic monument. Replicas of the delicate semi-precious stone inlay designs are found on marble and alabaster boxes and bowls, tabletops, chessboards and trays readily available in Agra's bazaars. Large wall panels and ornate sofa backs can be made to order and shipped directly abroad. Plain marble, red sandstone and soapstone items are also popular. Another beautiful craft is *zardozi* embroidery done on silk or velvet with gold and silver thread and sequins to create dress material, bags, jackets and shoes.

Agra is renowned for its shoe industry. The designs are somewhat basic, but the shoes are sturdy and certainly worth their price.

You can also shop for cotton *dhurries* woven in modern or traditional designs.

North of Delhi

Smaller towns near Delhi have their own craft specialities. There are several weaving centres producing pile carpets which are sent to Delhi and other cities to be sold. **Panipat** is famous for its attractive cotton floor coverings and woven home furnishings. In **Saharanpur**, you will find all kinds of woodcarved items in intricate designs and brass inlay work ranging from tables and screens to boxes and ashtrays.

Shopping in Jaipur

Jaipur is truly a shopper's paradise. The range of textiles and handicrafts available here includes an irresistible selection of fabrics (embroidered, block-printed, tie-and-dyed), as well as ready-made garments. Rolls of colourful quilts in light layered cotton, but surprisingly warm, are piled high on streetside shops, and government emporia and larger shops stock the beautiful Mughal designed woollen carpets that are made in Jaipur. The city is known for its jewellery which ranges from folk designs in silver to the elegant and more pricey gold jewellery in *meenakari* and *kundan* work *(see p191)*. There is also a wide variety of handmade leather goods, from *jootis* and bags to saddles and wallets, while in furniture, there is a dazzling choice of carved and painted tables, chairs, screens, wall brackets, candle-holders and lamp stands.

Jaipur blue pottery

Jaipur was a centre of miniature painting, and artists now sell perfect reproductions at a fraction of the price of originals. Both the religious *pichhwai* and the narrative *phad* cloth paintings make wonderful wall hangings. Blue pottery is another of Jaipur's traditional crafts, using delicate Persian, Turkish and Indian designs on vases, door-knobs and tiles.

Around Jaipur

Both Sanganer and Bagru *(see p208)* are famous for their blockprinted textiles dyed in vegetable colours. In Rajasthan every village has its own artisans. The cobblers produce brightly decorated sandals and bags, potters mould clay into delightful terracotta bowls and plates, and the woodcarver will have wide-eyed puppets hanging on the walls of his workshop. The village markets teem with brightly dressed men and women responding to the cajoling and loud calls of hawkers. Among the traditional metal cooking pots and modern clothes made of synthetic fabric, there are toys and trinkets, lacquer bangles and silver jewellery.

Weaving a carpet on a traditional pit-loom

DIRECTORY

Government Emporia

Handloom House
21, MI Rd, Jaipur.
Tel (0141) 236 5331.

Khadi Ghar
MI Rd, Jaipur.
Tel (0141) 237 3745.

Oswal Emporium
30, Munoro Rd, Sadar Bazaar, Agra.
Tel (0562) 222 5711.

Rajasthali
MI Rd, opposite Ajmeri Gate, Jaipur.
Tel (0141) 510 3329.

Rajasthan State Handloom Dev. Corp. Ltd.
Gulab Path, Chomu House, Jaipur.
Tel (0141) 237 1109.

Jewellery

Amrapali
Tholia Building, Panch Batti, MI Rd, Jaipur.
Tel (0141) 237 7940.

Bhuramal Rajmal Surana
Johari Bazaar, Jaipur.
Tel (0141) 257 0429.

Dwarka's
61 B, Sardar Patel Marg, C Scheme, Jaipur.
Tel (0141) 236 9798.

Gem Palace
MI Rd, Jaipur.
Tel (0141) 237 4175.

Koh-i-Noor
41, MG Rd, Agra.
Tel (0562) 246 0855.

Munshi Ganeshi Lal & Son
9, MG Rd, Agra.
Tel (0562) 233 0168.

Silver Mountain
Shop No. 141, Mirza Islam Rd, Jaipur. **Tel** (0141) 400 1603.

Surana Jewellers
B 7E, Surana Enclave, Sawai Ramsingh Rd, Jaipur.
Tel (0141) 237 2544.

Textiles

Anokhi
C 11, 2nd Floor, KK Square, Prithviraj Rd, Jaipur.
Tel (0141) 400 7244.

Cottons
Hari Bhawan, Jacob Rd, Civil Lines, Jaipur.
Tel (0141) 222 3870.

Naika
Tholia Building, MI Rd, Jaipur.
Tel (0141) 236 2664.

Ratan Textiles
Shop No. 5, Shalimar Bagh, Chitrakoot Ajmer Rd, Tagore Nagar, Jaipur.
Tel (0141) 222 2526

Shilpi Handicrafts
Near Siliberi, Sanganer.
Tel (0141) 273 1106.

Soma Shop
5, Jacob Rd, Civil Lines, Jaipur.
Tel (0141) 222 2778.

Embroidered Textiles

Indian Crafts Gallery
Fatehabad Rd, Agra.
Tel (0562) 223 0336.

Thar Inc.
65, Mathur Vaishya Nagar, Tonk Rd, Sanganer, Jaipur.
Tel (0141) 272 1913.

Carpets and Dhurries

Ambika Exports
Naila House, Moti Doongri Rd, Jaipur.
Tel (0141) 261 5059.

Jaipur Rugs
G 250, Mansarovar Industrial Area, Jaipur. **Tel** (0141) 239 8948.

Kanu Carpet Factory
8/166/E, Purani Mandi, Fatehabad Rd, Taj Ganj, Agra.
Tel (0562) 233 1307.

Paintings and Objets D'art

Juneja Art Gallery
6–7, Ground Floor, Lakshmi Complex, MI Rd, Jaipur.
Tel (0141) 403 4964.

Saurashtra Oriental Arts
3–4, Opposite Ayurveda College, Inside Zoravar Singh Gate, Amer Rd.
Tel (0141) 263 0242.

Shree Ganpati Arts
S-17, Golimar Garden, Amer Rd, Jaipur.
Tel (0141) 267 2212.

Ved Pal Sharma Banno
Shop No. 1401, Chanakya Marg, Subhas Chowk, Jaipur.
Tel (0141) 260 3450.

Blue Pottery

Neerja International
Anand Bhawan, Jacob Rd, Civil Lines, Jaipur.
Tel (0141) 411 2609

Handmade Paper

Salim's Paper
Gramodyog Rd, Sanganer.
Tel (0141) 273 0222.

Books, Tea and Spices

Books Corner
Shop No. 82, MI Road, Jaipur.
Tel (0141) 236 6323.

Bookwise
Mall 21, MI Rd, Jaipur.
Tel (0141) 236 4755.

Grah Sangrah Dept Store
Khasa Kothi Circle, Villa Station Rd, Jaipur.
Tel (0141) 220 3600.

Maharaja Exports
Fatehabad Rd, Near MG Tower, Agra.
Tel (05612) 400 5622.

Saroj Handicrafts and Arts
A-2, Tilak Marg, C-Scheme, Nandanam Apts, Jaipur.
Tel (0141) 511 0927.

Shoes

Bharat Boot House
87, Johari Bazaar, near LMB Hotel, Jaipur.
Tel (0141) 257 7914.

Mojari
Bhawani Villa, Gulab Path, Chomu House, Jaipur.
Tel (0141) 237 7037.

Marble Inlay

Akbar International
289, Fatehabad Rd, Agra.
Tel (0562) 233 0076.

Ganesi Lal International
Clarks Shiraz, Agra.
Tel (0562) 222 6114.

UP Handicrafts Complex
Handicrafts Nagar, Fatehabad Road, Taj Ganj, Agra.
Tel (0562) 233 3167.

Bazaars

Agra
Johari Bazaar
Cotton dhurries.
Kinari Bazaar
Jewellery and *zari* work.
Taj Ganj
Marble inlay.

Jaipur
Johari Bazaar, Gopalji ka Rasta, Haldiyon ka Rasta
Jewellery and tie-and-dye textiles.
Khajanewalon ka Rasta
Marble carving.
Kishanpol Bazaar
Tie-and-dye textiles.
Maniharon ka Rasta
Lac bangles.
Nehru Bazaar
Embroidered *jootis*.
Ramganj Bazaar
Shoes.

What to Buy

The bazaars, markets and boutiques of Delhi, Agra and Jaipur showcase the wide range of the region's arts and crafts. In many places shoppers have the joy of watching artisans at work and buying directly from them. The quality can vary, but the range is unbelievable, from exotic, aromatic spices to ceramics and handicrafts, carpets, textiles and jewellery. There are also elegant contemporary interpretations of traditional design.

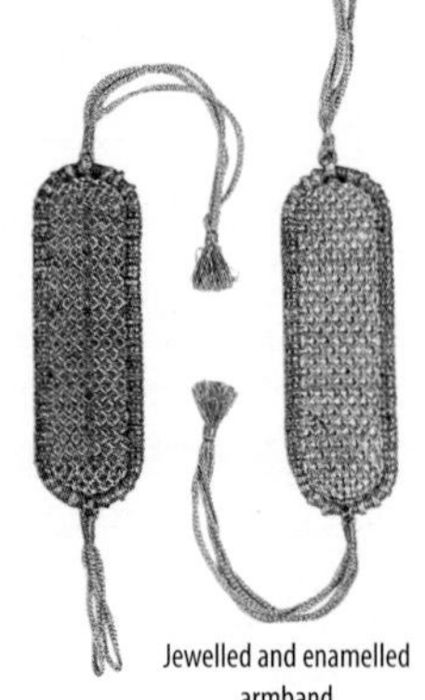

Jewelled and enamelled armband

Jewellery

Antique and jewellery shops stock exquisite pieces of gem-encrusted *kundan* and enamelled *meenakari* jewellery. Also available are the silver ornaments worn by local men and women.

Silver anklets, bracelet and armband

Hand-crafted cutlery

A pencil holder

A goblet in mixed metal

Metal

Bronze and brass objects of everyday use, such as pots, lamps or boxes, are widely available along with an exciting range of artifacts in silver and other metals created by contemporary designers.

Brass pots *(lotas)*

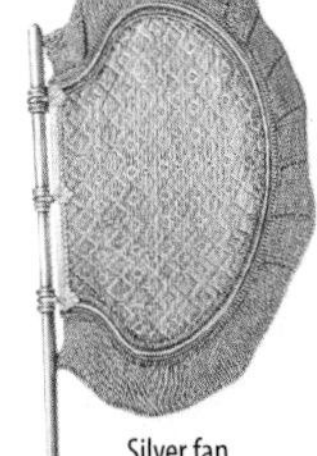

Silver fan *(pankha)*

Pottery

Abundant earthenware vessels and toys made by local potters can be seen stacked along the roadside. Commonly found are a sophisticated range of patterned tableware from Khurja, and Jaipur's famous blue pottery.

Door-knobs

Terracotta votive figure

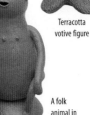

A folk animal in terracotta

Tiles with floral motifs

Jaipur blue pottery jar with lid

Textiles

Blockprints and silk and cotton woven textiles in a dazzling choice of colours and designs can be bought by the yard or ready-made garments, scarves and saris. Floor coverings are either the thick pile carpets or the colourful cotton dhurries used in Indian homes.

Pile carpet with floral design

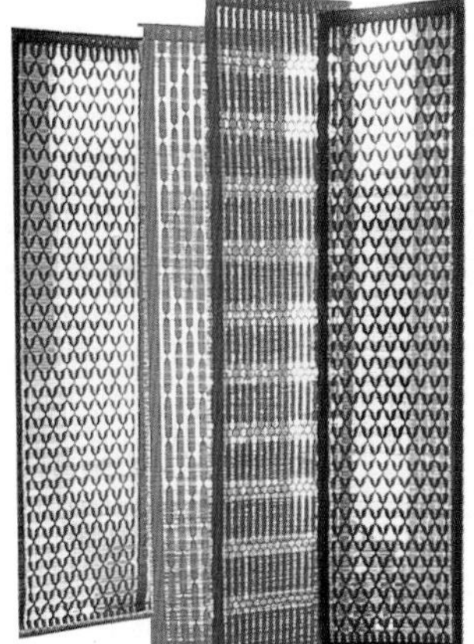

Window blinds

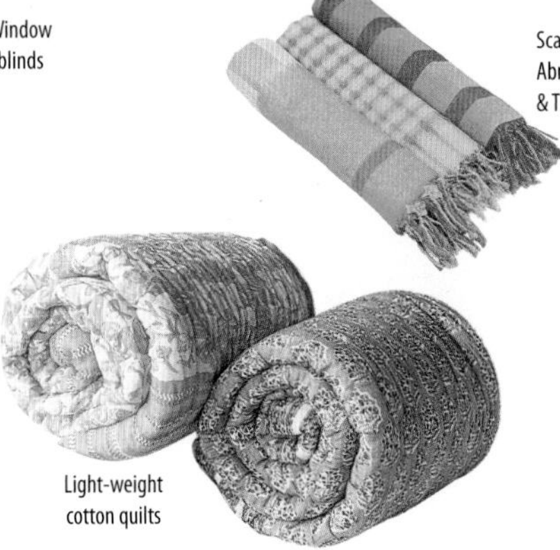

Scarves by Abraham & Thakore

Light-weight cotton quilts

Herbal Products

Traditional natural remedies have been re-invented to suit the contemporary need for eco-friendly cosmetics, soothing oils and lotions, tea and joss sticks (incense).

Joss sticks *(agarbatti)*

Traditional perfumes (attar)

Herbal tea

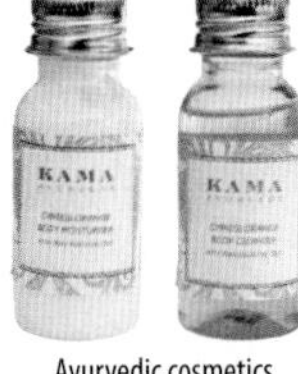

Ayurvedic cosmetics

Natural Rosewater

Soap

Handicrafts

Materials such as handmade paper, leather, stone and wood are used to make decorative and functional objects such as shoes, plates, boxes and puppets.

Handmade paper box

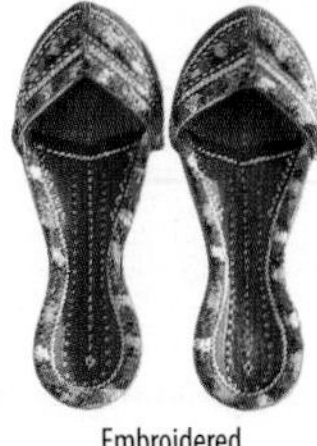

Embroidered slippers

ENTERTAINMENT

Except for Delhi, which offers a wide range of cultural entertainment round the year *(see pp124–5)*, options in most other cities are often restricted to the cultural fare offered by the hotels. Although both Agra and Jaipur have a strong tradition of folk and classical performing arts, these can only be seen during the peak season. One reason for this is that most Indians prefer to spend their evenings or holidays with the family. As outings invariably include children, the cinema is a favourite, while religious festivals, which offer free entertainment, are also popular. However, dining out is a rising fad among the urban elite.

Information Sources

Your travel agent is the best source of information on what is happening, where and when. Otherwise, calendars of cultural events are available from the tourist offices and also at hotels. Local newspapers also list daily events and advertise major cultural festivals, such as the Taj Mahotsav *(see p45)*. Small tourist-oriented local publications, such as *Jaipur Vision*, available at book shops and hotel receptions, also carry listings of cinemas, restaurants and bars, swimming pools and shops.

Booking Tickets

All the larger hotels in the region have regular evening performances of classical music and dance in their main restaurants. The dinner cover charge usually includes the performance. But if a show at a theatre or hall is announced, the tickets are available at the venue and your hotel or travel agent will be able to book them for you.

Classical Music and Dance

Kathak and Hindustani music *(see pp34–5)* flourished in this region, patronized first by the Mughals, and later by the regional courts. In an attempt to revive these traditional art forms, classical dance and music festivals are now held regularly in the cities during the peak tourist season sponsored by various cultural organizations. Among auditoria, the **Sur Sadan** in Agra, and the **Ravindra Manch** in Jaipur, are the most popular venues, while on special occasions, well-known dancers also perform before the main deity of the Govind Dev Temple in Jaipur. In Mathura and Brindavan the religious festivals of Holi and Janmashtami also attract classical dancers and singers. The devotional Sufi *qawwali*, originally based on the classical *raga* idiom *(see p34)*, is now a popular concert form. However, the best places to hear authentic *qawwalis* are at the Sufi shrines at Ajmer and Fatehpur Sikri where they are a daily ritual, while during the Urs festivities, special all-night soirées are held.

A Rajasthani folk dancer, dressed in a traditional costume

The *bhopa* musicians performing round a campfire

Folk Theatre, Music and Dance

Few areas in this region can match the colour and vibrancy of Rajasthan's indigenous folk forms. Sadly, folk theatre and itinerant storytellers like the *phad* bards are fast losing their audiences and can often only be seen in smaller places. Yet, since Jaipur is the capital state, some of the best bards and dancers come here to perform at urban centres such as the **Jawahar Kala Kendra**. The *ghumar* dance, performed by women during religious festivals and weddings, and the *kalbelia* or snake dance of a nomadic tribe can be seen at hotel shows.

Folk singers, such as the *bhopas*, the Manganiyars or Langas, come regularly to the Pushkar Fair and smaller towns, attracting people with their rich and expressive repertoire of folk ballads.

During the Janmashtami festival (Aug–Sep) the Raslila, an enactment of the story of Lord Krishna *(see p34)*, is held in the Brajbhumi area of Brindavan and Mathura *(see p165)*. Local Ramlila's are staged all over North India during Dussehra (Oct–Nov) *(see p41)*. These folk productions, often loud and melodramatic, have a unique vivacity and charm.

Puppet Shows

Puppetry is a strong folk tradition practised by the Bhatt pastoral community in Rajasthan. String puppets, called *kathputlis,* play out heroic stories of popular folk and legendary characters. The romance of Dhola and Maru, royal lovers who were separated only a few weeks after they were betrothed but finally reunited, is one of the most popular puppet shows. The riveting performances of these travelling puppeteers is seen at every fair and festival.

Box office at a popular multiplex

Cinema

Cinema is still the country's most popular form of entertainment. Even the smallest town has a theatre screening the latest Hindi blockbuster. Jaipur's **Raj Mandir**, actually a theatre hall with a flamboyantly kitschy interior, also screens World Cup cricket matches. Indian films are a fantastic mix of action and romance, song and dance, shot in fabulous sets and locales. The films range from the crass to the brilliant.

Though art films have won many international awards, and directors such as Satyajit Ray are considered among the world's best, their films are rarely shown commercially. Nonetheless, a select audience continues to remain loyal to these films, lauding the directors' sensitive portrayal of incidents that more mainstream cinema may consider inconsequential. A visit to the local cinema will give you an insight into Indian culture and the most frequented form of popular entertainment.

Nightlife and Bars

Except for the five-star hotels, options for nightlife in Agra and Jaipur are limited. The luxury hotels all have their own bars where there is a good choice of both local and foreign liquors and the atmosphere is pleasant. A few other places in both cities are licensed to have bars. The choice of spirits is limited but the atmosphere is lively.

DIRECTORY

Performing Art Centres

Birla Auditorium
Statue Circle, Jaipur.
Tel (0141) 238 5224.

Jawahar Kala Kendra
Jawaharlal Nehru Marg, Jaipur.
Tel (0141) 270 6560.

Ram Niwas Bagh
Behind Central Museum, Jaipur.
Tel (0141) 256 5244.

Ravindra Manch
JN Marg, Jaipur.
Tel (0141) 261 9061.

Sur Sadan
Mahatma Gandhi Rd, Agra. **Tel** (0562) 285 4498.

Welcomgroup Rajputana Palace Sheraton
Palace Rd, Jaipur.
Tel (0141) 510 0100.

Cinemas

Big Cinema
Agra: TDI Mall, Phase 1, Taj Nagri Scheme, Agra.
Tel 936 810 3619.
Jaipur: B 6, Central Spine, Vidhyadhar Nagar.
Tel 931 410 6185.

Entertainment Paradise
Jawahar Circle, Jaipur.
Tel (0141) 512 7591.

Golcha Chandra Mahal
Near New Gate, Jaipur.
Tel (0141) 257 7011.

Inox
Crystal Palm Mall, C Scheme, Sardar Patel Marg, Jaipur.
Tel (0141) 511 7299.

Raj Mandir
C 16, Bhagwan Das Rd, Panch Batti, Jaipur.
Tel (0141) 237 4694.

Sanjay Talkies
Sanjay Place, Civil Court, Agra.
Tel (0562) 285 0384.

Shree
National Highway 2, Byepass Rd, Agra.
Tel (0562) 285 3737.

Space 1-2-3
City Plaza, Bani Park, Jaipur. **Tel** (0141) 220 8444.

Bars

Cheeta
Hotel Jaipur Ashok, Jaipur.
Tel (0141) 220 4491.

Polo Bar
Rambagh Palace, Bhawani Singh Rd, Jaipur.
Tel (0141) 238 5700.

Rajwada Library Bar
Rajvilas, Jaipur.
Tel (0141) 268 0101.

Rana Sanga Roof Top Bar
Mansingh Palace, Jaipur.
Tel (0141) 237 8771.

SPORTS AND OUTDOOR ACTIVITIES

Previously, only the traditional sports such as cricket and polo provided visitors with opportunities for participating in outdoor activities. But today, the tourism industry offers a vast diversity of choices for specialist holidays. For sports lovers, the main cities, especially Delhi and Jaipur, offer clubs and grounds for golf, tennis, swimming and riding. Those in search of adventure can explore the foothills of the Himalayas and the Aravallis by trekking or rock climbing, while the tumultous mountain streams above Rishikesh are ideal for white-water rafting and kayaking. A camel or horse safari is a good way to experience the haunting beauty of the Rajasthan desert, and wildlife enthusiasts can visit the national parks for tiger-spotting and birdwatching. For those wishing to delve deeper into the mystique of the region, there are centres for yoga and meditation, naturopathy and spiritual studies.

Spectator Sports

Cricket has emerged as the main national sport and, no matter where you travel, you will see men and boys playing cricket. India hosted the 2011 World Cup and won the tournament, an event that further fuelled the passion for the game and its players, who enjoy a celebrity status equal to film stars. Each year, several international teams come to India to play test and one-day matches in various cities.

The scenic Feroze Shah Kotla ground in Delhi is a major venue for the Indian Premier League which is based on similar lines as European football leagues, and has captured the imagination of the country's cricket enthusiasts. In Jaipur, the Sawai Mansingh Stadium is the main ground where the sport is played.

Advertisements for national and international matches appear well in advance in all the newspapers, and tickets (usually on sale ten days earlier), are in great demand, even though the more important matches are broadcast on the national network and sports channels.

Indian football is yet to reach international standards, and world-class matches are rarely held in the country. However, passions run high at the Ambedkar Stadium in Delhi where national tournaments are held, and a view from the stands can be a very enjoyable experience on a sunny winter afternoon.

A swimming tournament at the 2010 Commonwealth Games, New Delhi

Tennis and Swimming

In Delhi, the Lawn Tennis Association maintains some excellent tennis courts. So do some of the city's clubs and sports complexes. In Jaipur, the main tennis courts are at the **Jai Club**, just off Mirza Ismail (MI) Road. Both these cities are venues for the Davis Cup matches. With such great Indian tennis players as Mahesh Bhupathi, Leander Paes and Rohan Bopanna enjoying international acclaim, there is a heightened interest in the sport. However, because of the scarcity of public tennis courts they are often booked in advance and the best option for a quick game is at your own hotel's tennis court.

Come summer and all clubs, sports centres and five-star hotels in the region open their swimming pools. The most easily accessible to visitors are in the five-star hotels, usually with attached saunas and a gym. Non-residents can take temporary membership or pay a fee to use hotel pools.

The open-air Jawaharlal Nehru Stadium, New Delhi

Golf

All major cities have well-maintained golf courses. In Delhi, the oldest and most prestigious course is at the **Delhi Golf Club**, located next to The Oberoi Hotel. This 27-hole course, creatively developed around a cluster of beautiful medieval pavilions, hosts many international tournaments in the winter season. Military cantonments, both here and at Agra, have their own golf courses. Just outside Delhi, the **Classic Golf Resort** is publicized as a weekend getaway, but is open to golfers through the week. In Jaipur, the Rambagh Palace Hotel has its own golf course and offers golf sets on hire for residents to play on the premises. Most golf clubs offer temporary membership to visitors for a fee.

Teeing off at a scenic golf course, Jaipur

Riding

Both Delhi and the Jaipur area have excellent riding clubs which non-members may use for a nominal fee. The **Delhi Riding Club** has a stable full of well-groomed horses for hire. In Shekhawati, the heritage Dunlod Fort has a polo ground, organizes horse safaris and teaches equestrian skills.

Visitors enjoying a horse safari at the Dunlod Fort in Shekhawati, Rajasthan

Polo

Polo was once the preserve of royalty and the army, and the Jaipur maharajas used to personally lead their teams to tournaments abroad. Corporate sponsorship has now revived interest in the game, and a major attraction is the gaiety, pomp and glamour attached to it. Winter is the main polo season in Delhi and Jaipur. Most tournaments in Delhi are played at the polo grounds adjacent to the Race Course on Kamal Ataturk Road, and in Jaipur, matches are played at the **Rajasthan Polo Club** near the Rambagh Palace Hotel. Ramgarh and Dundlod are major polo centres, where the game is also taught. In March, visitors may see some traditional elephant polo at Jaipur's Chaugan Stadium.

Heli-tourism

Helicopter package trips are a new departure for the tourism industry in India. Apart from the transport by helicopter, they include lodging, meals and sight-seeing. Heli-getaways in the region, organized by **Deccan Aviation** for those who can afford it and are strapped for time, so far include Agra, Jaipur-Sariska, and Jaipur-Ranthambhore. From Delhi, **World Expeditions India** organizes heli-skiing in winter, and also cycling tours.

Jeep and Desert Safari

An adventurous way to see the countryside is by safari. For wildlife sanctuaries, jeep safaris are common, with camping along the way. Camel safaris, organized by travel agents from Jaipur, and by most heritage hotels, especially in Kishangarh *(see p219)*, Mandawa and Nawalgarh *(see p241)*, promise unexpected glimpses of desert life and a first-hand acquaintance with the ship of the desert. Prices vary, depending on the duration of the safari. Camping out in the desert is a romantic experience, especially at night around a camp-fire with your camel driver relating thrilling stories of desert lovers and villains. Elephant and horse safaris can also be organized for groups through private travel agents.

Children's Activities

Delhi offers much to amuse children, beginning with a sprawling Zoo. The **National Science Centre** and the **Nehru Planetarium** organize special shows for children on certain events, such as eclipses. The Rail Museum is also a great hit with children, and offers rides on a special toy train.

Experiencing desert life on a camel safari in Rajasthan

A man rock climbing in the hills of Rajasthan

Camping, Trekking and Rock Climbing

The Himalayan foothills above Rishikesh have ideal locations for camping, trekking and rock climbing. As most of Rajasthan's forts nestle in the craggy slopes of hillsides, they also offer excellent opportunities for rock climbing and exploring the neighbouring countryside. Just beyond South Delhi, near Sohna in Gurgaon, there are many attractive hiking trails. The best source of information on these activities is the **Indian Mountaineering Federation**, and private operators, such as Milestones and Outdoor Adventures *(see p235)*, who specialize in organizing treks. Most organizers can provide reliable guides, as well as campsite equipment such as tents and sleeping bags, though you may feel more comfortable taking your own things. The best time for this activity is in the summer months from April to June, and after the monsoon from October to early December, before the weather gets too cold.

Logo of a yoga centre in Rishikesh

Ecotourism

This relatively new concept in tourism, which combines various aspects of nature study along with participation in conservation activities, is steadily gaining ground in India. There are three main national parks in Rajasthan. Ranthambhore *(see pp228–9)* and Sariska *(see pp214–15)* are known for their tiger populations, while birdwatchers will find many exotic inhabitants at Bharatpur's Keoladeo Ghana *(see pp172–3)*. Tours can be arranged through Rajasthan Tourism. Near Delhi are smaller sanctuaries such as the Sultanpur Sanctuary *(see p120)*. The **World Wide Fund for Nature, India (WWF)**, with its headquarters in Delhi, has an active programme of activities, such as camps, film shows and seminars.

A yoga *asana*

Cultural Studies

Yoga and meditation are taught at ashrams found in most cities. In Delhi, at the **Sivananda Yoga Vedanta Nataraja Centre** there is a good programme all year round. The best centres are, however, found in Rishikesh, where some of the best gurus conduct courses of yoga and Hindu philosophy all year round, and an International Yoga Festival is held here every year *(see p45)*. Naturopathy and ayurveda, two Indian systems that rely on the healing powers of natural foods and herbs, are also practised and taught at many centres, such as the **Ayurveda Kendra Clinic**. In Delhi, the **Kairali Health Resort** specializes in ayurvedic oil massages. Pranic healing, a method that channels positive forces through the *chakras* or energy centres in the body, is taught at the **Aurobindo Ashram**. Those who are interested in Buddhist philosophy will find information on this area of study in Tibet House and at the **Tushita Mahayana Meditation Centre**. The **Vipassana Sadhana Sansthan** can provide details of courses in *vipassana*, an old and efficacious form of meditation, while astrology and palmistry are taught at the Bharatiya Vidya Bhavan. Triveni Kala Sangam *(see p80)* holds short courses in classical singing, dance and in painting. Crafts skills can be studied at the Crafts Museum. Some travel agencies have devised special interest tours on subjects such as architecture, traditional crafts and spiritualism, and can draw up itineraries and organize tours to suit individual choices. These agencies have government recognition and are members of international organizations. A "Gourmet Journey through India" is one such tour on the agenda of **Indo Asia Tours** who engage specialists as their consultants.

Trekking in the Himalayan foothills

River rafters relaxing on the banks of the Ganges

Kayaking and River Rafting

Just north of Rishikesh, a series of rapids on the Ganges as it rushes down the mountains make for excellent kayaking and river rafting *(see p149)* opportunities. A normal trip stretches over three days as participants are carefully introduced to the intensity of the rapids. The best time for rafting and kayaking is from September to April, when campsites are set up on the pristine beaches along the river both by the Uttar Pradesh State Government *(see p273)*, and professionally trained private groups, such as Outdoor Adventures *(see p235)* and **Himalayan River Runners**. All the required equipment – tents, rafts, life-saving jackets and helmets – is supplied, as well as meals.

Fishing

Fishing is permitted in many of the region's rivers and lakes. But you must obtain a licence to do so from the designated local authority on site. In Delhi, the Okhla Barrage, as well as the nearby Surajkund and Badkhal lakes, are popular with amateur anglers. Further north, where hill streams join the Chandrabhaga and the Ganges, particularly above Haridwar and Rishikesh, the rivers yield a good catch of the local variety of carp and other fish, though rarely trout.

Water Sports

Ramgarh lake *(see p201)* near Jaipur, where some events of the 1984 Asian Games were held, is being developed by Rajasthan Tourism as a venue for water sports with facilities for parasailing, water-skiing and wind surfing. Currently, you can hire rowing, pedal and motor boats for a ride on the lake. Also, in and around Delhi a number of man-made lakes have facilities for boating and water sports.

White-water rafting on the River Ganges

DIRECTORY

Sports

Classic Golf Resort
NH8 (to Gurgaon), Distt Gurgaon.
Tel (0124) 237 8849.

Delhi Golf Club
Zakir Hussain Marg, Delhi. **Map** 5 C4.
Tel (011) 2430 7100.
W delhigolfclub.org

Delhi Riding Club
Safdarjung Rd, Delhi.
Map 4 F5.
Tel (011) 2301 1891.

Jai Club
Mahaveer Marg, C Scheme, Jaipur.
Tel (0141) 237 2321/22.

Rajasthan Polo Club
Ambedkar Circle, Near Rambagh Palace, Jaipur.
Tel (0141) 222 7375.

Heli-Tourism

Deccan Aviation
G-11, Haus Khas Market, Delhi. **Tel** (011) 2652 0036.

Children's Activities

National Science Centre
Bhairon Marg, Pragati Maidan, Delhi. **Map** 6 D1.
Tel (011) 2337 1893.
W nscdelhi.org

Nehru Planetarium
Teen Murti House, Delhi.
Map 4 E3.
Tel (011) 2301 4504.

Camping and Trekking

Indian Mountaineering Federation
Benito Juarez Road, Delhi.
Tel (011) 2411 7935.
W indmount.org

Ecotourism

WWF India
172-B, Lodhi Estate, Delhi.
Map 5 A4.
Tel (011) 4150 4815.

Cultural Studies

Aurobindo Ashram
Off Aurobindo Marg, Delhi. **Tel** (011) 2656 7863.

Ayurveda Kendra Clinic
Rishikesh.
Tel (0135) 243 0626.

Indo Asia Tours
56, Insititutional Area, Sector 44, Gurgaon.
Tel (0124) 453 4500/600.

Kairali Health Resort
D 120, Andheria More, Mehrauli, Delhi.
Tel (011) 6566 4447.
W kairali.com

Sivananda Yoga Vedanta Nataraja Centre
A 41, Kailash Colony, Delhi.
Tel (011) 3206 9070.
W sivananda.org.in

Tushita Mahayana Meditation Centre
9, Padmini Enclave, Delhi.
Tel (011) 2651 3400.

Vipassana Sadhana Sansthan
Village Bhatti, opposite Radha Saomi Satsang, Chatterpur Temple Rd, Delhi.
Tel (011) 2645 2772.

River Rafting

Himalayan River Runners
101, Ashirvad Building, Green Park, Delhi.
Tel (011) 2685 2602.
W hrrindia.com

World Expeditions India
G-1, MG Bhavan, Madangir, Delhi.
Tel (011) 4164 9358.

SWAROVSKI
ēthos
ēthos
Samsonite
Boarding Gates
Microsoft
Just because traffic sto
business need not.

SURVIVAL GUIDE

PRACTICAL INFORMATION

India's most popular travel route, via the three cities of Delhi, Agra and Jaipur, receives the majority of the 5 million tourists who visit the country annually. Because of this, the range of transport, accommodation and information offered in these cities is among the best in India. The government-run Incredible India tourist department has a centrally located office in Delhi and many overseas branches. You can also get up-to-date visitor information at the local state tourist departments of Delhi, Rajasthan and Uttar Pradesh. There are innumerable travel agencies in these cities but it is wise to approach a reputable one when booking your accommodation, travel tickets and sightseeing tours. It is also sensible to plan and book in advance if you wish to make a visit in the winter, since this is the peak tourist season. The more remote areas are still not equipped to cater to the international traveller who may be used to better banking facilities or prefer to pay by credit card.

Visitors in local attire enjoying a rural festival in Rajasthan

When to Go

The finest weather for travelling in north India is from October to March. This coincides with an abundance of festivals and cultural events, especially from October to December *(see pp44–5)*. Though it can get quite cold at night during December and January, the days are crisp and sunny. The brief spring of February and March is beautiful, with the flowers in full bloom.

Before you travel it is worth thinking about the extremes of Indian weather. It is best to avoid the Indian summer, from April to June, when the region is unbearably hot, dry and dusty. The bad weather is compounded by frequent power cuts. From July to September it is monsoon season. The humidity accentuates the heat, making travel very uncomfortable. Climate and rainfall charts can be found on pages 42–5.

Visas and Passports

All visitors from outside India need a visa to enter the country. There are three types of tourist visa available from Indian Consular Offices around the world: the 15-day single/double entry visa, the 90-day, or the longer multiple entry visa for six months.

Getting a visa extension beyond 15 days is a complicated procedure. First, you must collect an extension form from the **Ministry of Home Affairs** office, then fill it in and submit it to a **Foreigners' Regional Registration Office** (FRRO), where it will be processed. Finally, you must go back to the Ministry of Home Affairs to receive the visa extension.

Note that if you intend to re-enter India on a multiple entry visa, you must allow a period of at least two months to elapse between visits or seek special dispensation from an Indian Embassy or High Commission for earlier admission into the country.

Customs Information

When entering India, visitors are allowed upto 950 ml of alcohol and 200 cigarettes duty-free. In case the value of an item exceeds the duty-free allowance, duty shall be calculated on the excess amount. If you are carrying more than US$10,000 in cash, you are expected to fill in the Currency Declaration Form at the airport, to be certified by a Customs official.

Antiques over a hundred years old and wildlife products, such as animal pelts, *shahtoosh* shawls or ivory cannot be taken out of the country. Contact the **Ministry of Environment & Forests** or the **Archaeological Survey of India** (ASI) for more details.

Brightly coloured blossoms adorning a Delhi roundabout

◀ Indira Gandhi International Airport, Delhi

The trafficking of narcotics and psychotropic substances is punishable by imprisonment.

Visa stamped on a tourist passport upon arrival

Embassies and Consulates

Most countries have diplomatic missions in Delhi, but none in Jaipur or Agra. Consular officials can reissue passports and help in case of theft, imprisonment, hospitalization or other such emergencies *(see pp278–9)*. Contact details for some embassies are listed on page 275.

Tourist Information

The **Incredible India** tourist offices offer insightful information on travel throughout India. The counter in the arrival hall of Delhi's Indira Gandhi International Airport is an ideal place to get practical help when first entering the country. However, for more reliable and detailed advice on Agra, Jaipur and Delhi go to the respective state tourism departments of **Uttar Pradesh**, **Rajasthan** and **Delhi** Tourism. The staff are helpful and can give plenty of tips on what to see and how to get around. They also offer an accommodation booking service. Tourist brochures and maps are usually distributed free of charge.

At popular sights, amateur guides swarm around travellers hoping to be hired. You should ignore them and look for English-speaking guides wearing a badge that certifies government tourist department approval. All tourist offices, travel agents and hotels can arrange a certified expert for you at a fixed hourly rate.

Admission Prices

Most museums, historical monuments and wildlife parks charge an entrance fee. This is often a modest amount, although admission to World Heritage Sites costs more. If you are carrying a camera or video camera you might have to pay an additional charge to use it. Most places of worship do not have any admission fee but usually have a donation box.

Opening Hours

All banks and government offices are closed on three national holidays: Republic Day (26 Jan), Independence Day (15 Aug) and Gandhi Jayanti (2 Oct) *(see p43)*. Markets are also closed on these days. Each year an up-to-date holiday list is issued by the Indian government, which includes all major religious festivals. Bear in mind that the dates for these festivals vary according to the lunar calendar. Keep an updated holiday list handy before planning your trip. Certain religious holidays are termed "restricted", so while sites may be open, most staff may be on leave.

Monuments and museums are generally open from 10am to 6pm, and are closed on Mondays and public holidays. Opening times for shops are usually from 10am to 7:30pm, while tourist and convenience stores remain open much later. Many malls are open on public holidays, offering most items at discounted prices. In Agra and Jaipur all markets are closed on Sundays, whereas in Delhi they shut on different days depending on the market.

Tourist bargaining with a vendor in a marketplace

Language

There are many regional languages spoken in India. In the northern region, both Hindi and English are used as official languages. In the cities, English is spoken by the majority of people, especially by those who deal with tourists – taxi drivers and guides – and in hotels, shops and offices. However, it is useful and appreciated if you know a few basic phrases in Hindi, the colloquial language of the region *(see p312)*. Road signs and numbers are written in both English and Hindi.

Sign for an auto-rickshaw stand, in both Hindi and English

Public Conveniences

It is best to use the facilities in hotels and restaurants. Most hotels will allow non-residents to use their toilets. Wayside toilets have poor hygiene and should be avoided. However, those known as *Sulabh Shauchalayas* (provided by the local council), are clean, easy to spot on main city roads and charge a nominal amount for use. They are of the Indian squatting variety and can be difficult to use if you are not used to them. It is a good idea to carry spare toilet paper as it may not be provided.

Travelling with Children

Child-minding services for travellers are rare, but children can accompany their parents to most places around India. Remember to protect children (and adults) against the fierce sun, and make sure they drink only mineral water. Most reputable restaurants have high-chairs available for kids as well.

Itmad-Ud-Daulah's Tomb, Agra

Travellers with Special Needs

Facilities for the disabled are still not well developed in public buildings and places of interest, as ramps or rails are seldom provided. However, airports and all main railway stations have available ramps and escalators, and porters to carry your luggage. Pavements are difficult to negotiate in a wheelchair as they are often bumpy. Only select hotels are equipped to suit the needs of the disabled traveller, although the staff will usually be helpful. It is advisable to check with the hotel for specific facilities before you make any bookings.

Student and Senior Travellers

In general, older people are accorded great respect in India. While most tourist attractions don't offer discounts for senior travellers, discounted fares are available for travel on Indian Railways. Visit a tourist information centre for more details *(see p273)*.

For students and young travellers, all three cities have branches of the **Youth Hostels Association of India** (YHAI). Though it is not necessary to be a member of the association to book a room, members do get priority and cheaper rates. In Delhi, the **Vishwa Yuvak Kendra** and **YMCA** provide institutional but comfortable accommodation. Apart from these hostels, plenty of other cheap options are available. Do not leave money and important documents in your room.

Gay and Lesbian Travellers

Homosexuality is still not widely accepted in India, although there is a burgeoning gay scene in the major metropolitan cities. Overt displays of public affection or provocative dress are frowned upon regardless of sexuality. For more information on the local gay and lesbian scene, visit www.gaydelhi.org.

Women Travellers

Women, both Indian and foreign, face a certain amount of unwanted attention from men in north India, even though "eve-teasing" is a punishable offence. When travelling alone, women can face problems – from being stared at, to more active harassment such as suggestive comments and unwanted body contact on buses and in other crowded places.

Such uncivilized behaviour is unacceptable, but unfortunately, it is still up to women to take certain precautions. Avoid wearing clothes that can be thought of as provocative in public places, though they can be safely worn indoors. Ignore men lounging at street corners, and if their attention gets offensive, swiftly walk away or head towards a member of the police force, if there is one nearby. Beware of men who try to draw you into a conversation. Threaten to call the police if they continue to do so. When hiring a car or a taxi, get the hotel to make the booking for you. Hitchhiking is not advisable under any circumstances. A confident attitude, common sense and wariness can help women travellers tackle problems that arise from travelling alone.

What to Take

Pack clothes that are suitable for the climatic conditions *(see p272)*. At the peak of winter you will require warm clothes – a jacket or a thick pullover, socks and warm trousers, especially during the early hours of the day and at night. For autumn and spring, pack light woollens and clothes in natural fibres that are easy to wash. In summer, only loose cotton clothes are comfortable. Indian-made, ready-to-wear outfits for men and women are available everywhere. Choose easy-to-remove footwear as you will have to take off your shoes while visiting places of worship.

A first-aid kit is a must *(see p280)*. It is advisable to carry some personal medication to avoid any health hazards, although pharmacies stock most things *(see p278)*. Bring an umbrella or a light raincoat, and a torch should be packed for unexpected and sometimes lengthy power cuts.

Time

In spite of its size, India has only one standard time. It is 5.5 hours ahead of Greenwich Mean Time (GMT), 4.5 hours

Visitors enjoying a camel ride at the Pushkar fair

behind Australian Eastern Standard Time, and 10.5 hours ahead of US Eastern Standard Time.

For all official work, the Western Gregorian calendar is used in India. This avoids the confusion of traditional calendars, that vary based on religions and regions. For example, at the Millennium, the official Indian calendar (Saka era), had reached only 1922, whereas the old Hindu calendar, which follows the Samvat era, reads 2057.

Electricity

The electrical current is 220–240 volts, 50 Hz. Supply is erratic during summer when power cuts can last for hours. Triple round-pin sockets are the norm but adaptors for other varieties, and transformers needed for some appliances, are available at large markets. Do bring along a power surge cable to protect your laptop against voltage fluctuations.

Conversions

The metric system is most commonly used in India.

Imperial to Metric
1 inch = 2.5 centimetres
1 foot = 30 centimetres
1 mile = 1.6 kilometres
1 ounce = 28 grams
1 pound = 454 grams
1 pint = 0.6 litres
1 gallon = 4.5 litres

Metric to Imperial
1 centimetre = 0.4 inches
1 metre = 3 feet 3 inches
1 kilometre = 0.6 miles
1 gram = 0.04 ounces
1 kilogram = 2.2 pounds
1 litre = 1.8 pints

Responsible Tourism

India's response to the concept of eco-tourism varies widely from state to state. Delhi has seen steady growth in environmental awareness. Several proposals have been introduced to reduce the level of pollution and rubbish. These measures include compressed natural gas (CNG)-propelled public transport *(see p286)* and banning the use of polythene bags – although some of these laws are not widely practiced. Separating garbage into recyclable, non-recyclables and biodegradable waste is also observed in the city.

In Agra and Jaipur, environmental consciousness is still in the latent stage, with little in the way of responsible tourism outside the national parks that surround Jaipur. In these nature reserves there are strict rules and regulations to uphold the parks natural beauty and habitats.

Tourists can help by disposing of their waste carefully and insist on eco-friendly vehicles and services from tour agencies. Visitors are discouraged from taking plastic bags and disposable containers into heritage areas. Tourists can also do their bit by using bags made of calico, or a similar reusable material, when shopping.

DIRECTORY

Visas and Passports

Foreigners' Regional Registration Office
Agra: 16 Idgah Colony.
Tel (0562) 236 7563.
Delhi: 8, East Block, RK Puram Sector I.
Tel (011) 2671 1443.
Jaipur: Police Headquarters, Behind Hawa Mahal.
Tel (0141) 261 8508.

Ministry of Home Affairs
North Block, Central Secretariat, Mansingh Rd, Delhi. **Map** 4 E2.
Tel (011) 2309 2011.
W mha.nic.in

Customs Information

Archaeological Survey of India
Janpath, Delhi. **Map** 5 A2.
Tel (011) 2301 3574.
W asi.nic.in

Ministry of Environment & Forests
Paryavaran Bhavan CGO Complex, Lodi Road, Delhi. **Map** 5 A5.
Tel (011) 2436 0605.
W moef.nic.in

Embassies and Consulates

Australia
Tel (011) 4139 9900.
W india.embassy. gov.au

Ireland
Tel (011) 4940 3200.
W irelandinindia.com

New Zealand
Tel (011) 4688 3170.
W nzembassy. com/india

United Kingdom
Tel (011) 2419 2100.
W ukinindia.fco.gov.uk

USA
Tel (011) 2419 8000.
W newdelhi. usembassy.gov

Tourist Information

Delhi Tourism
N 36, Middle Circle, Connaught Place.
Map I C5.
Tel (011) 2331 5322.
W delhitourism.nic.in

Incredible India
Agra: The Mall.
Tel (0562) 222 6378.
Delhi: 88, Janpath.
Map I C5.
Tel (011) 2332 0008.
Jaipur: State Hotel, Khasa Kothi.
Tel (0141) 237 2200.
W incredibleindia.org

Rajasthan Tourism
Delhi: Bikaner House, Shahjahan Rd. **Map** 5 B2.
Tel (011) 2338 9525.
Jaipur: TRC Govt Hostel, MI Road. **Tel** (0141) 511 0598.
W rajasthantourism. gov.in

Uttar Pradesh Tourism
Agra: 64 Taj Rd.
Tel (0562) 222 6431.
Delhi: Chandralok Building, 36 Janpath.
Map I C5.
Tel (011) 2371 1296.
W up-tourism.com

Student and Senior Travellers

Vishwa Yuvak Kendra
Agra: Sanjay Place, MG Rd.
Tel (0562) 285 4462.
Delhi: 1, Circular Rd, Teen Murti Marg, Chanakyapuri. **Map** 4 D3.
Tel (011) 2301 3631.
Jaipur: Bhagwan Das Rd.
Tel (0141) 274 0515.

YHAI
Agra: Youth Hostel Agra, Hotel Chanakya, Shamshabad Rd.
Tel (0562) 223 0959.
Delhi: International Youth Hostel, 5, Nyaya Marg, Chanakyapuri.
Tel (011) 2611 0250.
Jaipur: Youth Hostel Jaipur, D 81, Shiv Hira Path, C Scheme, Chomu House Circle.
Tel (0141) 236 1971.
W yhaindia.org

YMCA
Jai Singh Rd, Delhi.
Map 1B5.
Tel (011) 2374 6035.

Etiquette

Friendly and easy-going by nature, Indians consider hospitality intrinsic to their culture and religion. Guests are treated with immense courtesy, and people on the street will go out of their way to help you. If you need any guidance on issues regarding fares, rates or directions, feel free to ask around. Don't be afraid of haggling, bargaining is a normal practise in India. As there are diverse religions, castes and social hierarchies in the region, it is advisable to address everyone with respect without making allusions to their religious, ethnic or regional group. Public display of affection, like kissing, is frowned upon. Customs and rules of etiquette still follow traditional Indian norms, except in very Westernized sections of urban society.

Devotees with their heads covered in a place of worship

Greeting People

The most common form of Indian greeting is the *namaskar* or *namaste* (pronounced "namastey"), which is used when meeting or parting. The palms are pressed together, raised towards the face, and the head is bent slightly forward. Greetings and gestures may vary with religion or regional group. Muslims raise their right hand towards the forehead with the words *adaab* or *salaam alaikum* or simply *salaam*.

Namaskar, the traditional greeting

In north India, *"ji"* usually follows the name as a term of respect. On the first meeting, however, it is best to address someone formally with a Mr or Mrs or even Madam before their name. The use of first names is a sign of familiarity. The Western handshake is commonly used, though Indian women still prefer to greet visitors with a *namaskar*.

In many Indian families, it is a polite gesture to touch the feet of elders while greeting them.

As a mark of respect, elders are never addressed by their first names. However, a courteous greeting in any form will be acknowledged.

Personal questions about subjects that might otherwise sound intrusive, such as one's salary or relationship with one's in-laws, are usually not considered offensive in Indian society. Instead, it is often seen as a friendly gesture.

Body Language

Indians tend to shake their heads a lot while talking and what might seem to be a negative shake is actually a sign of agreement, especially the head wobble. They often talk loudly and gesticulate with their hands, which should not be misunderstood as a sign of aggression. Having lengthy conversations with friends and sometimes even strangers is part of the revered Indian culture.

Your head is considered to be the spiritual centre of your body. When an elder touches the head of a younger person it is seen as a form of blessing. Feet are considered to be the lowliest part of the body and shoes are treated as unclean. In most traditional Indian homes, you will be asked to remove them before you enter the house. At gatherings where the seating is on the floor, try to sit with your feet crossed and not stretched out before you. When food is offered to you, it should be accepted with your right hand.

A devotee bathing a linga in milk in a Shiva temple

Places of Worship

Every major religion of the world is practised in India. The three cities have several *gurudwaras*, temples, mosques, churches and, in Delhi, a synagogue, holding regular services. The etiquette differs in the places of worship of each religion but everywhere a simple decorum is expected. If in doubt about what you should do, it is best to observe those around you. It is courteous to ask for permission before photographing people or places of worship, but do not disturb people at their prayers by taking pictures or talking loudly. Clothes should be clean and unrevealing: women should ideally cover their heads, wear dresses that cover the upper arms and are at least mid-calf length, while men should avoid shorts. Shoes are taken off at the door and you should sit with your feet turned away from the idol or the holy book.

In Hindu temples, it is permissible to offer flowers and incense for worship. Apart from the central deity, the temples often have subsidiary shrines in other parts of the temple precincts. Even those in ruins are considered holy. Some Hindu temples do not welcome non-Hindus although this is rarely the case. However, if stopped at the door, do not take offence. In mosques and in *gurudwaras*, cover your head with a scarf, not a hat. You should avoid entering a mosque during prayers, and men should stay away from the women's enclosure.

Shoes left at the entrance of a religious temple

Suitable Dress

The Indian style of clothing is relatively modest and covers the body well. In small towns, women still prefer the traditional sari or the *salwar-kameez* and seldom wear Western outfits, though very young girls can be seen in skirts or dresses. Delhi has a more cosmopolitan attitude, and in the trendier parts of the city, jeans, short skirts and shorts are quite common. However, Indian men tend to stare at women, so be prepared for this, whatever you wear. Agra and Jaipur are relatively conservative cities, therefore, Western clothes might attract some unwanted attention.

Indians like to dress up for occasions. You can choose to experiment with traditional Indian clothing or wear anything that is smart and suits your

Traditional village women, veiling their faces with *ghunghats*

taste. Readymade clothes for both men and women are available in most markets at reasonable prices.

Bargaining

Bargaining is a part of life in India but do not fret over it. Firmly state what you would like to pay and walk away if the shopkeeper does not agree. Larger shops and malls usually have fixed price tags and advertise discounts if any.

Eating Indian-style

Though most Indian restaurants provide cutlery, Indian meals are often eaten with hands to facilitate the tearing of the chapati or bread and to scoop up rice and curry. It is considered impolite to use your left hand to eat. Many restaurants also provide finger bowls at the end of the meal.

Taxes and Tipping

There are no fixed norms for tipping, or *baksheesh*, as it is called. Most larger restaurants add a service charge so often there is no need to tip extra. In smaller eateries, the waiter would be pleased if you round up the bill as there usually is not a service charge.

Most upmarket hotels add a luxury tax of around 12.5 per cent onto the price of a room. Hotel staff, porters and most taxi drivers expect a tip of between 10 and 20. A few rupees given to the person who minds your shoes outside a place of worship will be happily accepted.

Smoking and Alcohol

Though cigarette kiosks abound and pavement sellers sell one cigarette at a time, smoking in Delhi is officially banned in public places. Some buildings have smoking areas within their premises.

Only certain restaurants are licensed to serve alcohol, and you are not allowed to drink in parks, buses or trains. Drinking near a place of worship is considered very offensive and can lead to arrest.

Beggars

Visitors can find beggars difficult to handle as they target foreigners and can be extremely persistent. Tourists who give money to one soon find themselves surrounded by a raucous throng demanding *baksheesh*. Be careful of being pickpocketed in the confusion. Beggars are found in the largest numbers around places of worship as they are more likely to be given alms there. But it is best not to encourage beggars and to walk on till they leave you alone. If necessary, complain to a nearby policeman or raise an alarm if in trouble.

If you do want to give charity directly, your hotel may have a donation box or the staff will be able to suggest a few charitable institutions.

The traditional Indian *thali* meal, eaten with the right hand, seated on the floor

Personal Security and Health

The three cities of Delhi, Agra and Jaipur are well equipped with efficient police forces and a number of good hospitals. As long as you take a few simple precautions, there is little need to worry. For example, do not get too friendly with strangers, protect your valuables and stay and eat in places that look clean and quality conscious. If you face a difficult situation, ask for help from a police person or file a report at the police station.

Policemen in uniform

Police

There are several different police forces in India and each fulfils a particular role. The two police forces tourists will most likely encounter are national police, who wear khaki uniforms, and traffic police, who are normally dressed in blue. Not all members of the police can speak English but most know at least a few words. The majority of officers are friendly and happy to help with directions. However, be aware that there is some corruption within the force, such as officers asking for money to file crime reports.

If you need to report a crime go to the nearest police station or your embassy *(see p275)*.

What to be Aware of

Travelling in the region is relatively safe for tourists. Since Delhi, Agra and Jaipur are major tourist centres, there are bound to be touts, beggars and pickpockets who target travellers. Take simple safety measures, such as wearing a money belt under your shirt to keep money and important documents in. Protect your camera and avoid wearing jewellery or carrying large amounts of cash. You can leave your valuables in the hotel safe but insist on a receipt. It is advisable to keep photocopies of your passport and credit cards in a separate place to the originals and also lock your luggage with a padlock, which can be bought at railway stations, during train journeys.

While shopping, make sure that shopkeepers create a bill and process your payment in front of you. Some shopkeepers lead tourists to believe that goods bought in India can be sold back home with a good profit margin. Unless you can judge a product's authenticity, do not invest your money on such dubious purchases.

In an Emergency

The national emergency number for police is 100, the fire brigade is 101, and for a hospital ambulance it is 102. Your embassy can also advise you in case of an emergency. If in need of immediate medical attention, your hotel's doctor-on-call can refer you to a private clinic. Otherwise, all public and most privately owned hospitals and clinics run a 24-hour service for casualty and emergency cases.

Lost and Stolen Property

If your passport or valuables have been stolen or lost, you must inform the nearest police station and file an FIR (first information report), but it is advisable to contact your embassy for advice about the correct procedure *(see p275)*.

There are railway police departments at major stations. If something is stolen on a train, continue to your destination and report it there. Bus stations in large cities may have a police post but it is more likely you will have to go to the nearest normal police station.

Hospitals and Pharmacies

Before you leave, check with **MASTA** (Medical Advisory Service for Travellers Abroad) in the UK for a health update for travellers to India. There are a number of well-equipped private hospitals and medical specialists in Delhi that offer excellent service. The renowned **All India Institute of Medical Sciences** (AIIMS), is a highly advanced hospital and a centre for research. Most of the embassies have a list of approved hospitals and clinics and the names of the best medical specialists and dental practitioners in town. The local **Indian Red Cross Society** is the safest option for blood transfusions.

Most big markets in Delhi, Agra and Jaipur have well-stocked pharmacies. The pharmacists are often able

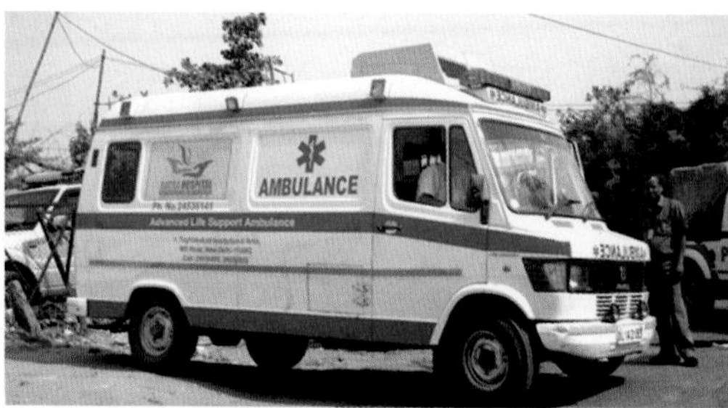

A hospital ambulance

to advise you on simple remedies. They also stock infant food, toiletries and sanitary items. If you are taking any special medication, carry the prescriptions with you or the packaging with the generic name; this will help if the brand is unfamiliar to the pharmacist. Most pharmacies are open between 9am and 7:30pm. Public hospitals such as AIIMS usually have round-the-clock pharmacies which are also open to non-patients. Ayurvedic medicine and holistic remedies are highly respected and widely available.

Travel and Health Insurance

It is important to take out a comprehensive insurance policy in advance of travelling to India. Make sure it covers any eventuality, including potential medical and legal expenses, lost luggage, theft, accidents and travel delays or cancellations. Adventure sports are not covered by standard travel policies so if you are planning to undertake any extreme sports while in India you will need to pay an additional premium to ensure you are protected. Insurance policies should come with a 24-hour emergency number.

Immunization Information

There are no official requirements for immunization unless you travel from Papua New Guinea or designated countries in Africa and South America, in which case to enter India you will need a valid vaccination certificate for yellow fever. Vaccination against tetanus, typhoid and Hepatitis A and B is recommended. Consult your doctor about taking a course of anti-malarial tablets, although north India is regarded as a low-risk area.

Legal Assistance

Legal problems are very rare for travellers, but if you do find yourself in a legal tangle, immediately contact your

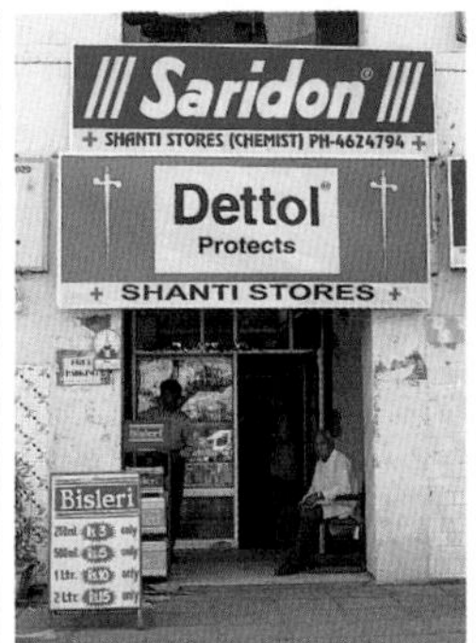

Pharmacy in a local market, stocking medication and toiletries

embassy *(see p275)*. Always keep a photocopy of your passport handy. Do not hand your travel papers over to anyone until your embassy has been informed. Some insurance policies also cover legal costs for certain emergencies such as accidents.

Narcotics

The image of India as a country that is tolerant of drug use is misleading, even though you often see sadhus puffing merrily on their *chillums*. Possession of all drugs, including hashish and heroin, is banned by law. Penalties for possession, use and trafficking of illegal substances are strictly enforced. Drug convictions lead to a minimum sentence of ten years without parole or remission. Make sure that you don't carry anything for strangers or check in their luggage at airports.

DIRECTORY

Emergency Numbers

Ambulance
Tel 102.

Fire Brigade
Tel 101.

Police
Tel 100.

Hospitals and Pharmacies

Agra
Parikh Nursing Home, MG Rd.
Tel (0562) 285 4781.

Delhi
All India Institute of Medical Sciences, Aurobindo Marg.
Tel (011) 2658 8700.

Escorts Heart Institute, Maulana Muhammad Ali Rd.
Tel (011) 2682 5000.

Indraprastha Apollo, Mathura Rd, NH2.
Tel (011) 2692 5858.

Max Medcentre, N-110, Panchsheel Park.
Tel (011) 2649 9866.

Jaipur
Sawai Man Singh Medical College, Sawai Ram Singh Rd.
Tel (0141) 256 0291.

Indian Red Cross Society
1, Red Cross Rd, opposite Parliament House, Delhi.
Map 4 F1.
Tel (011) 2371 6441.
W indianredcross.org

MASTA
London: **Tel** (020) 7291 9333.
W masta-travel-health.com

Pavement vendors peddling healing salves and ointments

Heat and Smog

Summer in north India is dry and extremely hot, and the monsoon months that follow are oppressively humid. It takes time to get acclimatized to this weather, so take things at a relaxed pace in the first few days. The best way to beat the heat is to drink plenty of fluids. Include a small amount of salt to your food to prevent dehydration. Shower often and avoid going out between noon and 4pm, which is the hottest part of the day. While walking, try to rest in the shade at regular intervals to avoid continuous exposure to high temperatures, which can cause heat stroke.

It is best to wear sunglasses and a wide-brimmed hat during the day as well as applying sun-screen every few hours to protect your skin. It is also advisable to wear light shoes and loose-fitting cottons that cover your arms and legs, in order to avoid sunburns. Covered shoes, socks and polyester clothing trap perspi-ration and can cause prickly heat and fungal infections. Prickly heat powder is available at most pharmacies *(see p278)*.

During winters, the city experiences smog. Asthmatic travellers are advised to carry their medication at all times to avoid problems.

A hand fan

First-aid Kit

While going on excursions or day trips, it is best to carry a basic first-aid kit. Include aspirin or painkillers for fevers, minor aches and pains, an antiseptic for cuts and bites, antifungal ointment, antihistamines for allergies and anti-diarrhoea tablets. Your first-aid kit should also contain water purification tablets, plasters, scissors, insect repellent, crepe bandages, lip balm, tweezers, a thermometer, some disposable syringes and any other personal medication. Most items are easily available at pharmacies in the cities.

Sugarcane and other juices sold on the street

Some effective herbal remedies for heat stroke and upset stomachs are readily available in pharmacies, but you should buy only brands recommended by a reliable practitioner or pharmacist medicine *(see pp278–9)*.

Minor Stomach Upsets

Diarrhoea is a common stomach disorder among travellers, usually caused by a change of diet, water and climate. Since Indian food is mostly hot and spicy, it can cause various digestive disorders. If stricken, it is best to eat boiled food without spices and drink boiled water that has been cooled, until the attack subsides. Most importantly, make sure that you drink plenty of liquids to replace your body fluids.

A good pharmacist can suggest an appropriate diarrhoea medication. In the case of a severe attack with symptoms such as exhaustion, nausea and cramps, it is best to consult a doctor. It is advis-able to immediately take oral rehydrating salts (ORS), which are commercially available under the popular Indian brand names of Electral or Electrobion. An effective homemade remedy of half a teaspoon of salt and three teaspoons of sugar mixed in boiled water which has been cooled, also helps to maintain the balance of body fluids.

Most visitors prefer sealed bottles of mineral water, although an increasing number of restaurants have effective filtered water dispensers. Most commonly known international brands of carbonated drinks are also widely available. Coconut water is a refreshing alternative to aerated drinks. Use your own judgement when eating from streetside food carts and *dhabas*. Opt for an eatery that seems popular with the local people as it is more likely to serve fresh and good quality food. Avoid raw salads, cut fruit and fresh juices at way-side eateries, at least until your stomach is accustomed to Indian food.

Cuts and Bites

Insect bites are a common problem during the rainy season. Many monuments also have huge beehives, so you should carry a good antiseptic ointment and an antihistamine in case of wasp and bee stings. Snake bites are rare, but if bitten, tie a tight crepe bandage above the knee or elbow joint of the affected limb and over the bite itself, keep it immobile and seek immediate medical help. Clean all cuts with an anti-septic solution and cover with a plaster or a light bandage.

Insect-borne Diseases

The summer and monsoon months are the seasons for malaria and the more serious cerebral malaria, though they can occur at any time of the year.

The symptoms of both include violent shivering followed by high fever and sweating, sometimes accompanied by headaches. A parasite carried in the saliva of the female *Anopheles* mosquito triggers the illness, and the incubation period can vary from a few days to several weeks. Another serious mosquito-borne disease is dengue fever, carried by the *Aëdes egypti* mosquito. The symptoms are similar to malaria and include rashes and severe pain in the joints and muscles. The dengue mosquito is more active during daytime, while the insects causing malaria are active between sunset and dawn.

If you are sleeping in a room without air-conditioning, keep the screened windows closed at all times. You can also ask the hotel for a mosquito repellent gadget, as well as a net over your bed. Avoid wearing dark clothing and strong perfumes as these tend to attract mosquitoes. If going outdoors in the evenings, you should wear clothes that completely cover your arms and legs, and rub mosquito repellent cream on exposed body parts.

If you experience symptoms of malaria or dengue fever, it is best to seek medical help immediately. For the latest information on malaria medication and whether to take a course of preventive antimalarial drugs, call a travel clinic or check the MASTA website *(see p279)* for information.

Mosquito repellent coil and cream

Food- and Water-borne Diseases

Visitors to India must guard themselves against several illnesses that can be contracted via water, including two types of severe intestinal infections, known as dysentery. The first, bacillary dysentery, accompanied by severe stomach pains, vomiting and fever, rarely lasts longer than a week. Amoebic dysentery has similar symptoms but takes a longer time to manifest itself in the human body. If not treated with a course of prescription drugs, this can later become a recurring, chronic ailment. The same is true of giardiasis, a type of chronic diarrhoea, caused by drinking contaminated water. Some forms of hepatitis, a serious liver ailment, such as hepatitis A and B, can be prevented with a vaccine. Symptoms of the illness include extreme fatigue, body aches, jaundice, fever and severe chills. The only treatment is to drink plenty of boiled water, rest and a strictly controlled diet.

If you are visiting a site ravaged by floods you must get yourself fully vaccinated against cholera at least one week before travelling there. Cholera is a serious disease that can be fatal unless the patient is rushed to a hospital for rehydration and medication.

Typhoid, which has a vaccine, is another gastro-intestinal disease transmitted through contaminated water or food. Early symptoms may seem like flu, but develop into high fever, leading to acute dehydration and weight loss. A doctor should be immediately consulted for the right antibiotics.

Since these are the most common ailments faced by travellers to India, it is best to remain hygiene conscious and eat only clean food and drink bottled mineral water throughout the course of your stay.

People- and Animal-borne Diseases

Awareness of sexually transmitted diseases such as HIV, which causes AIDS, is still low, therefore, screening at blood banks is unreliable. If you require a blood transfusion contact the trustworthy **Indian Red Cross Society** *(see p279)*.

Meningitis, a severe swelling of the membranes surrounding the spinal cord and brain, is accompanied by high fever and occasional seizures. It is transmitted by a bacterial or viral infection sometimes carried by rodents. Penicillin drugs are effective in combating it, but patients must be rushed to a hospital immediately.

If you are bitten by an animal, clean the wound with an antiseptic solution and seek medical help at once in order to avoid getting rabies or any other infection. The necessary anti-rabies treatment involves a course of injections. There is also a vaccination to prevent it. Vaccination against tetanus is essential before travelling. This potentially fatal infection is transmitted through open wounds that have been in contact with a bacteria found in soil and manure, and its symptoms include lock-jaw, stiff muscles and fatal convulsions. As a rule, if you badly cut yourself, you should clean the wound and go to a good doctor without delay.

Tuberculosis, commonly transmitted through coughing and close household contact with an infected person, is not a great risk for travellers.

Before an injection, buy your own disposable syringe, or insist that a new syringe and needle is unwrapped in front of you. Avoid shaves at dubious barber shops, and insist on a new razor blade. Any procedure using needles, such as tattooing and ear-piercing, is best avoided.

Shopkeepers display an array of delicious street foods

Banking and Currency

Agra, Delhi and Jaipur provide accessible banking facilities and money exchange services with English speaking staff at all counters. Delhi has a good selection of international banks that offer a range of services. Exchange facilities are available at major banks and hotels, travel agencies, Indira Gandhi International Airport and registered money changers. Unauthorized dealers and touts might offer enticing rates but they are illegal operators. Some shops will also give better value for money against purchases in major foreign currencies. Traveller's cheques are still a safe way to carry money, although people increasingly use debit and credit cards. Always keep small change for minor transactions.

Banks and Bureaux de Change

Banks across India offer such services as transferring money and exchanging currency as well as other banking transactions. Most national banks, including **ICICI** and **State Bank of India**, have several branches in Delhi, Agra and Jaipur.

American Express, offering money changing and banking facilities

Opening hours are 8am–2pm from Monday to Friday, and 8am–noon on Saturday, although hours can vary from bank to bank. Major banks branches remain open till 6pm. Banks are generally closed on public holidays *(see p43)* or occasionally in response to public protests or strikes. The State Bank of India's counter at Indira Gandhi International Airport, the **Central Bank of India** at Ashok Hotel *(see p235)* and other select branches of **Standard Chartered** in Delhi offer 24-hour banking services. The Ashok Hotel also offers 24-hour money exchange facilities.

Most hotels can exchange currency for resident guests, however banks offer the best rates. Visitors staying at government-owned hotels require a receipt to show that they have exchanged their money in a bank rather than through an unlicensed operator. The State Bank of India in Agra and the **Allahabad Bank** are well regarded for their low commission fees. Travel agents, such as Thomas Cook India *(see 291)*, can also exchange money at the official rates, but have higher service charges. Newspapers publish current exchange rates for major international currencies. The "black market" in India offers better rates than the official ones but it is safer to go to authorized dealers.

ATMs

All foreign and some local banks have 24-hour ATMs (automatic teller machines), that accept MasterCard, VISA, American Express and Diners Club cards. ATMs are easily found in cities and operate 24-hours. All instructions are displayed in English and cash is dispensed in rupees.

Debit and Credit Cards

International debit and credit cards such as **VISA**, **American Express**, **MasterCard** and **Diners Club** are accepted in many places including larger shops, hotels and restaurants. Look out for the credit card sticker on shop windows. Cards can also be used to book rail and air tickets. Some cards can be used to get a cash advance in rupees at many international banks. Debit and credit card

DIRECTORY

Banks

Allahabad Bank
Agra: Hotel Clarks Shiraz, 54, Taj Rd. **Tel** (0562) 222 6531.

Central Bank of India
Agra: 37/2/4, Sanjay Place.
Delhi: 3, Bahadurshah Jafar Road, New Delhi.
Tel 1800 200 1911.

ICICI
Agra: 5, Saket Colony, Shah Ganj. **Tel** (0512) 233 1042.
Delhi: 9A, Phelps Building, Inner Circle, Connaught Place. **Map** 1 C4.
Tel (011) 6757 4314.
Jaipur: Raj Bank Building, Sir Mirza Ismail Rd.
Tel (0141) 325 6145.

Standard Chartered
Delhi: 23, Barakhamba Rd, Narian Manzil, Connaught Place.
Map 2 D5.
Tel (011) 3940 1500.

State Bank of India
Agra: Chhipitola Complex, MG Rd.
Tel (0562) 226 2663.
Delhi: 11, Sansad Marg.
Map 1 B5.
Tel (011) 2340 7935.
Jaipur: Tilak Marg.
Tel (0141) 510 1547.

Debit and Credit Cards

American Express
Delhi: Hamilton House, Connaught Place.
Map 1 C4.
Tel 1800 22 2639.

Diners Club
Tel (44) 1244 47 0910.

MasterCard
Tel 000 800 100 1087.

Visa
Tel 000 800 100 1219.

Wiring Money

Citibank
Delhi: Shop No. 124, Jeevan Bharti Building, Connaught Place. **Map** 1 C5. **Tel** (011) 2336 6205.

HSBC
Delhi: Birla Towers, Ashoka Estate, Barakhamba Rd.
Map 2 D5.
Tel (011) 2371 9403.

related fraud is on the increase, so keep your cards safe and insist that receipt vouchers at shops are made out in front of you. If your debit or credit card gets stolen or lost, contact your bank to cancel the card.

Wiring Money

Indian banks with branches abroad and foreign banks that have offices in India, such as **HSBC**, **Citibank**, and **American Express**, can wire money from their various offices. Foreign banks usually have branches in Delhi, though not always in Jaipur or Agra.

Traveller's Cheques

Traveller's cheques in US dollars or pounds sterling are still popular in India. They are easy to cash, and can be exchanged at all banks and bureau de change counters. American Express in Delhi provides traveller's cheques in US dollars or pounds sterling. Some banks demand to see the original purchase receipt. Banks levy the lowest surcharge and therefore give the best value, but they always charge a small fee per cheque, so using large denomination cheques at a time is economical. Traveller's cheques give slightly better exchange rates than cash.

Currency

The unit of currency is the rupee (₹), divided into 100 paisas, although the latter no longer exists in practice. Among the coins, the most commonly used are the one, two, five and ten rupee coins. Currency notes range from ₹10 to ₹1,000.

Be careful with the ₹100 and ₹500 notes as these are quite similar in colour. Be wary of accepting torn or taped notes, as banks, restaurants and shops often refuse to accept or change them for you.

Bank Notes

All currency is minted by the Reserve Bank of India. The notes have either Mahatma Gandhi or the Ashoka lions on one side.

₹10 note

₹20 note

₹50 note

₹100 note

₹500 note

₹1,000 note

Coins

The following silver coins are in circulation, with variations of the ₹1 coin. All bear the national insignia.

₹1

₹2

₹5

₹10

Communications and Media

The post and telecommunications systems in India are reliable and relatively advanced. In addition to the government's postal network, several well-known international courier agencies have offices here. All the main hotels have business centres, and most markets have stalls where mobile SIM cards can be purchased and the Internet accessed. A wide range of newspapers and magazines are sold in Agra, Delhi and Jaipur. Most international newspapers and magazines are also available in bookshops across Delhi.

International and Local Telephone Calls

All hotels offer direct international calls (or subscriber dialling – ISD), but at inflated prices. With the popularity of mobile phones, ISD and subscriber trunk dialling (STD) telephone booths, once found in most markets, are declining. Those booths remaining can be used to make local and international calls at cheaper rates than offered at hotels. To find a telephone booth in a market, look for the ISD/STD sign above the shop door.

To make an international phone call you will need to dial the international access code (00), followed by the country code, the area code and the local number. Domestic long-distance calls are also made through STD. This service covers the majority of the country, including small villages. For mobile numbers, you will need to dial the domestic access code (0091), followed by the number. STD rates depend on the distance and time of the call. Calls made between 11pm and 6am are cheaper. Local calls can also be made from public STD telephones, costing ₹1 for every 3 minutes.

Mobile Phones

It is possible to use your home SIM card while visiting India, but the roaming charges are often exorbitant. Major local mobile networks include **Airtel**, **Tata Dokomo** and **Reliance**, and, the international firm **Vodafone** is also available in north India. To acquire a local SIM card, you must fill in a form (at the store you are purchasing it from), show your passport as identification and have the SIM officially registered with a local address before you can use it in India. There may be some roaming charges when moving between states within the country, but these are relatively negligible.

A regular post box

Internet

The Internet is widely available in Indian cities. Most hotels offer web access to guests, while an increasing number of establishments have Wi-Fi. Privately operated cyber cafés with modern facilities are ubiquitous in Delhi and can also be found in Agra and Jaipur. Libraries, such as the **American Library** in Delhi and those provided by the **British Council**, have computer facilities which can be used for emailing or browsing the Internet.

General Post Office or Gole Dak Khana, New Delhi

Postal Services

The national postal service, **India Post**, is efficient and reliable. Some of the services offered include general and registered post, *poste restante* and **Speed Post**. There is also a **Foreign Post Office** in Delhi that solely deals with international post. Fax services, though rare, are still available at the main post offices and at ISD/STD booths in all the three cities. Offices are open between 10am and 5pm Monday to Friday and on Saturdays until noon.

Run by the government, Speed Post is only available at a select number of post offices and provides courier facilities. If you wish to send a letter or parcel through a private international courier agency, there are many to choose from. **UPS**, **FedEx**, **DHL**, **Blazeflash Couriers**, **Desk To Desk Courier** and **Overnite Express** have a wide global and local network. Many shops may offer to send purchases by courier but, except for well-known shops and the government emporia, you will be doing so at your own risk. If in doubt, use a private courier agency and send the parcel yourself.

Useful Dialling Codes and Numbers

- To make an intercity call, dial the STD code of that city and the local number. For Delhi, dial 011; Agra, dial 0562; and for Jaipur, dial 0141.
- To make an international call (ISD), dial 00, the country code, area code and the local number.
- Country codes are: UK 44; France 33; USA & Canada 1; Australia 61; Ireland 353; New Zealand 64; South Africa 27; Japan 81
- Dial 1580 to book a trunk call (STD) in the country, and 1586 for international calls.
- For directory assistance dial 197 in Delhi, Agra and Jaipur.
- For a morning alarm, dial 116 in Delhi, Jaipur and Agra.

A streetside stall, selling newspapers and magazines

Addresses

The older sections of Indian cities are often a maze of lanes and alleyways. Some road signs can be confusing and hard to decipher, or sometimes there may not even be a street sign. If you are lost, a passerby should always be willing to help. Taxi and auto-rickshaw drivers are also happy to give directions.

Newer residential areas are divided into blocks. The block number usually appears with the house number, so B4/88 Safdarjung Enclave would be: house number 88 in the B4 block of Safdarjung Enclave colony.

Newspapers and Magazines

India has a wide variety of national English language newspapers. Leading papers like **The Times of India** and **Hindustan Times** make for lively reading with fierce political debates, humorous cartoons and good sports coverage. Weekly magazines, such as **India Today** and **Outlook**, provide excellent coverage of local and international news. Monthly magazines, such as **Delhi Diary** and **First City**, list films, restaurants, exhibitions and other events in Delhi. All newspapers and magazines mentioned above are also available in an online format.

The cities of Agra and Jaipur have their own local newspapers and magazines that give details of ongoing cultural programmes in both English and Hindi. For more English-language publications found in India, visit the **World-Newspapers** website.

Television and Radio

The state-run Doordarshan television network has programmes in English and major Indian regional languages. Since the arrival of satellite TV, the choice of programmes to watch has become much wider. Cable TV is available almost everywhere, including in hotel rooms, and features international channels such as the BBC World Service, CNN, Discovery, National Geographic and the Hong Kong-based Star TV network. Sports can be found on channels Star Sports and ESPN, while Channel V and MTV provide music entertainment.

India also has a wide radio network, with programmes both in English and local regional languages. Radio still provides the best way to get news and information, especially in rural areas. FM frequency channels are available in all cities and the popularity of digital radio channels is increasing.

DIRECTORY

Mobile Phones

Airtel
W **airtel.in**

Reliance
W **rcom.co.in**

Tata Dokomo
W **tatadocomo.com**

Vodafone
W **vodafone.in**

Internet

British Council
Tel (172) 274 5195.
W **britishcouncil.org/india.htm**

American Library
Tel (011) 2347 2000.
W **newdelhi.usembassy.gov/americanlibrary.html**

Postal Services

Blazeflash Couriers
Delhi: C 143, Phase I, Naraina Industrial Area.
Tel (011) 4297 4297, 98996 18482 (centralized number).
W **blazeflash.com**

DHL Courier Service
Delhi: 47–48, G5, Pragati House, Nehru Place.
Tel (011) 2643 0490.
W **dhl.co.in**

Desk to Desk Courier
Tel (011) 3300 4444.
W **dtdc.com**

FedEx Courier Service
Agra: **Tel** (0562) 2600 0015.
Delhi: **Tel** (011) 2386 0502.
Jaipur: **Tel** (0141) 606 4639.
W **fedex.com.in**

Foreign Post Office
Kotla Marg, Near ITO Delhi. **Map** 2 F4.
Tel (011) 2323 1281.

General Post Office
Agra: The Mall.
Tel (0562) 246 3886.
Delhi: Ashok Rd.
Map 4 F1.
Tel (011) 2336 4111.
Jaipur: Mirza Ismail Rd.
Tel (0141) 237 4000.

India Post
Agra: **Tel** (0562) 252 1863.
Delhi: **Tel** (011) 2332 4214.
Jaipur: **Tel** (0141) 401 1061.
W **overnitenet.com**
W **indiapost.gov.in**

Speed Post
W **speedpost.org.in**

UPS Courier Service
Agra: 19 & 20, Bhavana Tower, Sector 16, Mathura Rd.
Tel (0562) 645 6148.
Delhi: D 12/1, Okhla Industrial Area, Phase II.
Tel (011) 7172 6200.
Jaipur: E 51, Chittaranjan Marg, C Scheme.
Tel (0141) 511 3800.
W **UPS.com**

Newspapers and Magazines

Delhi Diary
W **delhidiary.in**

First City
W **firstcitydelhi.com**

Hindustan Times
W **hindustantimes.com**

India Today
W **indiatoday.intoday.in**

Outlook
W **outlookindia.com**

The Times of India
W **timesofindia.indiatimes.com**

World-Newspapers
W **world-newspapers.com/india**

TRAVEL INFORMATION

Most international visitors to India arrive by air. Road and rail links are also used for travel between India and her neighbouring countries such as Pakistan, Nepal and Bangladesh. Travelling within the country, and especially between the three cities of the Golden Triangle, is possible by air, train and road. The triangular distance between Agra, Jaipur and Delhi is less than 250 km (155 miles) and should only take a couple of hours by road or rail. The state-run Air India has the widest network of air routes. Private airlines including Indigo and Jet Airways cover many cities in this region. Indian Railways is one of the world's most widespread networks and travelling first class is a good way to see and explore the entire country. The long-distance luxury coach is another viable option. Whatever your mode of transport, you should be prepared for delays and unexpected detours that may test your patience.

Aircraft lined up at Indira Gandhi International Airport

Green Travel

Travel around Delhi, Agra and Jaipur is easy, convenient and cheaply priced. The public transport system is extensive, flexible and environmentally friendly. Visitors will find that they can reach almost any destination between and around the three cities by train or long-distance bus. Delhi's outstanding metro system also provides a fast, clean and eco-friendly way of getting around the city. Travellers who need to use hired cars can still minimize their individual carbon footprint by opting to share taxis with other passengers.

Within Delhi, the roads are well-maintained but can get congested, especially during peak hour traffic. The rising price of petrol and the prevalent pollution has led to the introduction of vehicles run on Compressed Natural Gas (CNG), which is more environment-friendly. All three-wheelers (auto-rickshaws) and yellow-top taxis painted with a green line use CNG-propelled engines. **Delhi Tourism** also runs a fleet of CNG buses that offer city tours.

Like in Delhi, many vehicles are fuelled by CNG in Agra and Jaipur. Another green travel option is to hire a bicycle at a local cycle shop. Jaipur is especially know for its many bike hire stalls. However, the weather can get hot and dusty, and only those who are fit and acclimatized to the climate should attempt cycling.

Arriving by Air

Most visitors travelling by air to India will arrive at Delhi's **Indira Gandhi International Airport** (IG), which serves both international and domestic flights.

Jaipur International Airport receives flights from local and Middle-Eastern operators, and **Agra Airport** (also known as Kheria Airport) runs a domestic service only. When travelling from abroad, to reach either city by air you must take a connecting flight from IG International Airport or one of India's other domestic airports.

India's national airline, **Air India**, along with many other major international airlines, such as **Air France**, **British Airways** and **Japan Airlines**, have regular flights to Delhi. Domestic companies such as **Jet Airways**, **IndiGo**, **JetLite**, **GoAir** and **SpiceJet** operate flights out of IG International Airport to Agra, Jaipur and other Indian cities.

All regional Indian airports have frequent scheduled departures to Delhi but few flights to Agra and Jaipur. Air India offers the largest choice of routes and the most frequent domestic services, but Jet Airways and SpiceJet also connect a wide network of cities within the country. IndiGo, JetLite and GoAir offer low-cost, no frills flights between the cities that make the Golden Triangle.

Indira Gandhi International Airport

Delhi's Indira Gandhi International Airport has two terminals in operation: Terminal 1 (T1) for domestic flights, and Terminal 3 (T3) for international and some domestic flights. The latter offers more facilities, with 24-hour currency exchange counters, left luggage services and an air-conditioned visitors' lounge. Travel agencies and hotel counters located in the arrivals area can help you organize your tour itinerary. T1 (domestic) is at Palam, 7 km (4 miles) from T3. If transferring to a domestic flight from an

Passengers in the airport lounge

international one (or vice versa), allow at least 15 minutes driving time to get between the two terminals. Internal airport coaches run hourly between the two terminals during peak hours and offer free transfers.

Tickets and Fares

Tickets can be booked directly through the airlines' websites or through reliable travel agents *(see p291)*. Air India and Jet Airways offer discount passes for multiple trips, although you should opt for this deal only if you are planning to travel extensively by air during your stay.

On Arrival

Immigration forms are handed out on the plane in advance of landing. Fill this out and hand it over at passport control.

When going through customs, the green channel is for passengers who do not have goods to declare, as listed in the Immigration Certificate. The Red Channel is for those with goods that attract customs duty, including money in excess of US $10,000. For more details regarding customs, see page 272.

Transport into Delhi

IG International Airport's Terminal 1 is 12 km (7 miles), and Terminal 3 is 19 km (12 miles) southwest of the city centre. The best way to reach Delhi is via the Airport Express metro line, which travels direct and takes only 25 minutes from T3. From T1 take a shared pre-paid taxi, which can be booked at a counter outside the arrivals hall, to Aerocity station where you can board the Airport Express.

Taxi rates are fixed – ₹500 from T3 and ₹350 from T1. Some hotels offer a free airport pick-up service. Whatever you use, the journey by road may take up to an hour.

Departure Tax

If you stay in India for more than 120 days from the date of issue of the visa, you need a tax clearance certificate to leave the country. Before travelling, you should apply in advance for the certificate to the Foreign Section in the **Income Tax Department**. This proves that you have financed your trip with your own foreign exchange and not by working in India. Keep all travel finance documentation after you leave.

A Departure Tax of ₹500 is levied, unless already included with your ticket. But if travelling to Pakistan, Nepal, Sri Lanka, Bhutan, Burma (Myanmar), Afghanistan or the Maldives, it is only ₹150.

DIRECTORY

Green Travel

Delhi Tourism
W delhitourim.nic.in

Arriving by Air

Agra Airport
Tel (056) 2240 0844.

Air India
Tel (011) 2462 2220.
W airindia.com

Air France
Tel 1800 180 0033.
W airfrance.com

British Airways
Tel (1800) 102 3592.
W britishairways.com

GoAir
W goair.in

IndiGo
W book.goindigo.in

IG International Airport
Tel (011) 2565 2420.
W newdelhiairport.in/

Jaipur International Airport
Tel (141) 255 0623.

Japan Airlines
W jal.co.jp/en

Jet Airways
W jetairways.com

JetLite
W jetliteindia.co.in

SpiceJet
W spicejet.com

Departure Tax

Income Tax Department
Delhi: Mayur Bhawan, Connaught Circus. **Map** 1 C4.
Tel (011) 2341 3317.

Airport	Information	Distance to City Centre	Average Journey Time
Delhi (Domestic) TI	(011) 2567 5121/26	12 km (7 miles)	Road: 30 minutes
Delhi (International) T3	(0124) 337 6000	19 km (12 miles)	Road: 50 minutes
Agra (only charters)	(0562) 240 0844	16 km (10 miles)	Road: 45 minutes
Jaipur (Sanganer)	(0141) 255 0623	13 km (7 miles)	Road: 30 minutes

Travelling by Train

Travelling through India by train is a truly unforgettable experience. It can be extremely relaxing and plenty of fun, or uncomfortable and hectic. But if you can spare the time, it is the best way of getting to know the Indian people and seeing the countryside. India has a well organized but busy railway network, so plan your train journey carefully and book your tickets well in advance – online is easiest. There are computerized ticket counters at stations and, for a commission, most travel agents can arrange tickets for you. The journey between Agra, Delhi and Jaipur takes only a few hours.

A modern diesel engine train

The Railway Network

The Indian railway network is divided by region, and the cities of Agra, Delhi and Jaipur are served by the **Northern Railway**. Delhi major railway stations are: **Old Delhi**, **New Delhi**, **Sarai Rohilla** and **Hazrat Nizamuddin**.

Taj Express and the Bhopal Shatabdi Express provide the fastest morning trains for Agra. With a journey time of less than 3 hours, these services make a day trip possible. Other speedy options to reach Agra include the Kerala Express, a morning service taking 1 hour and 15 minutes, and Tamil Nadu Express, departing at night with a journey time of 1 hour and 40 minutes.

The Ajmer Shatabdi Express and Jammu All Express are the fastest routes between Delhi and Jaipur, both taking less than 5 hours. Another train to Jaipur from Delhi is the Ashram Express, which takes 5 hours and 30 minutes.

Tickets and Fares

Be sure to buy your tickets in advance with reserved seat numbers noted on them. Your hotel travel counter or travel agent can arrange this for you. Avoid buying tickets from touts, as this is illegal and unreliable.

An **International Tourist Bureau**, on the first floor of New Delhi Station, is open Monday to Saturday, from 7:30am to 5pm, here you can purchase tickets, payable in US dollars or pounds sterling, backed by exchange certificates and get priority reservations. Tickets are refundable, subject to cancellation charges. Booking centres are also located at other railway stations.

Train timetable

Trains and Timetables

There are three kinds of trains: passenger, mail and express. It is best to take the express trains as they have fewer stops and offer better facilities and services. Avoid passenger trains as they stop at all stations, sometimes for long periods, and are always very crowded. The major cities are connected by air-conditioned "superfast" trains, including the Rajdhani and Shatabdi Express trains, which make minimal stops. Fares for these services include meals and the Rajdhani also provides its overnight passengers with bedding.

Most trains have a first and second class, chair-cars and two- and three-tiered sleeper coaches. Fares are higher for air-conditioned carriages. Sleeper coaches are a comfortable option on longer journeys and save useful daytime hours and hotel fares.

Railway timetables are listed in *Trains at a Glance*, a handy guide available at major railway stations or online at the **Indian Railways** website. Be aware that train times can change.

Discounts

If planning to travel extensively around India, the **Indrail Pass** is a good option, as it will save you hours of queueing time and, if you book in advance, reservation charges. It offers unlimited travel across the country, in either class, for 7 to 90 days. It can be bought in India or abroad, but must be paid for in foreign currency. Occasionally the pass may be more expensive than buying individual trip tickets, so work out what trips you want to make before purchasing. Also, ensure that you have a confirmed seat reservation for each journey by checking online or contacting the train station.

A crowded railway platform

Railway ticket booking centre at New Delhi Railway Station

Services

When at a station look for the licensed porters or *coolies* to assist you with your luggage. They wear red shirts and armbands with a metal tag bearing a licence number on it. Note the porter's number incase you lose sight of him in the chaos. Tariffs vary according to weight, although ₹40–75 per item is an acceptable rate – settle on a fee at the time of hiring your porter.

The **Rail Yatri Niwas** *(see The Railway Network)*, at New Delhi Station, offers very basic facilities, but is a convenient and safe night halt. Otherwise railway waiting rooms, most having proper beds, are the best place to spend the night if you are unable to go elsewhere. Go to the Upper Class Waiting Rooms. Left luggage facilities, called cloak-rooms, are offered at most stations. The quality of food and drinks at stations is good, both at the canteens and from platform vendors. Make sure that you carry a good supply of bottled mineral water to avoid any health hazards.

Porters in red, easy to recognize

On Board

Indians travel with a large amount of luggage and like making friends while travelling by train. So unless you bury yourself in a book, be prepared to spend time talking to fellow passengers. Try to get a window seat or the uppermost sleeper. Toilets are of the Indian and Western kind. Carry your own toilet paper, soap and towel.

DIRECTORY

The Railway Network

Agra Station
Civil Lines. **Tel** 36 4612.

Hazrat Nizamuddin Station
Harsha Road, Nizamuddin East. **Map** 6 E5. **Tel** (011) 2435 8753.

Jaipur Station
Railway Rd, Shanti Nagar, Hasanpura. **Tel** 131.

Old Delhi Station
Shyama Prasad Mukherji Marg. **Map** 2 D1. **Tel** 131.

New Delhi Station & Rail Yatri Niwas
Connaught Place. **Map** 1 C4. **Tel** 6663 3333.

Northern Railway
W nr.indianrailways.gov.in

Sarai Rohilla Station
Near Rohtak Rd, Sarai Rohilla, New Delhi.

Tickets and Fares

International Tourist Bureau
Map 1 C3. **Tel** (011) 2334 6804.

Trains and Timetables

Indian Railways
W indianrail.gov.in

Discounts

Indrail Pass
W indiarail.co.uk

The Royal Trains

Palace on Wheels
W palaceonwheels.net

Royal Rajasthan on Wheels
W royalrajasthanonwheels.com

The Royal Trains

Travel like the maharajas in the most luxurious trains in India – the **Palace on Wheels** and the **Royal Rajasthan on Wheels**. From September to April, the Palace on Wheels operates week-long tours through the finest sights of Rajasthan, covering Jaipur, Sawai Madhopur, Chittorgarh, Udaipur, Jaisalmer, Jodhpur, Bharatpur and Agra. The Royal Rajasthan on Wheels visits Khajuraho and Varanasi instead of Jaisalmer and Bharatpur. In opulent coaches, recreated to resemble the saloons of erstwhile royalty, you will be treated in royal fashion.

Insignia of the Jaipur State Railway

Royal service in the Palace on Wheels

Travelling Around by Bus

All major Indian cities are well connected by a large network of roads. The highways linking Delhi, Agra and Jaipur are among the busiest in North India. The advantage of travelling by long-distance buses, rather than by train, is that you have a wider choice of timetables and stops. Deluxe services operated by the state tourist departments are comfortable and keep to time. The Transport Ministry-owned buses that run throughout the day from city bus depots, though cheaper, can be crowded. Travel agencies and private tour operators have a wide choice of itineraries revolving around the three cities and their surrounding areas.

State government-run ticket counter for bus reservations

Buses for various destinations at the Inter-State Bus Terminus, Delhi

State Government-run Buses

State transport departments have a bus service around the Golden Triangle and the many other cities of India. The main bus station in Delhi is the **Maharana Pratap Inter State Bus Terminus** at Kashmiri Gate, where local and interstate bus services depart. It is a chaotic place, so arrive early to book your ticket. Then check at the enquiry counter to find the stand where your bus will depart from. Finally, be prepared for a lot of jostling as passengers rush to get to the best seats. Buses provided by **Rajasthan State Road Transport**, however, leave from Bikaner House, New Delhi. Coaches for Agra depart from **Sarai Kale Khan**, a relatively less crowded stop near Hazrat Nizamuddin railway station. The bus journey to Agra takes about 4 hours and almost 5 hours to Jaipur.

Regular interstate services depart from the **Idgah** bus stand in Agra, and from **Sindhi Camp** in Jaipur.

Delhi Tourism organizes a variety of innovative package tours

Department of Tourism-run Buses

Guided tours within the three cities are organized by the state tourism departments *(see p273)* as well as by the Indian government's **Ashok Tours & Travels**. Buses run by the various state tourism departments are the most reliable option; they are comfortable, clean and less crowded. These buses make fewer stops compared to the cheaper alternative of state government-run buses. There are overnight sleeper coaches to Agra and Jaipur from Delhi. Pick-up points are usually in city centres.

Uttar Pradesh Tourism Department buses collect tourists that have travelled from Delhi to Agra, via the Taj Express train service, from Agra City Station. After the day's tour of Agra, passengers are dropped back at the station well in time to catch the evening train to Delhi.

The best way to travel to Jaipur from Delhi by coach is via the Rajasthan Tourism Pink Line. It departs daily at 1:30pm from Bikaner House. It is advisable to buy tickets in advance, although you can buy your ticket on the day. There is a break midway in the 5-hour journey for refreshments. Returning to Delhi from Jaipur, state tourism buses leave from a stand outside Hotel Sheetal.

Package Tours

There are many wonderful sites to visit in and around Agra, Jaipur and Delhi that are within easy travelling distance. These include religious sites, places of historical interest and wildlife sanctuaries. Tour buses

An overcrowded local bus in Rajasthan

run by private operators and travel agencies have regular coach services departing from Delhi during the peak tourist season of October to March. It is feasible to have a day trip to Agra, however, if you want to visit Fatehpur Sikri and all of Agra's sites as well as go shopping, it would be wise to stop-over for the night. The same is true if you wish to take a one- or two-day trip to Jaipur.

If you have booked a short bus trip through a travel agent, a guided tour is usually included as is an overnight stay at a hotel. Luxurious coaches collect passengers from several pick-up points, usually designated hotels.

You can reserve a place on a short private tour through your hotel's reception desk or by visiting a travel agency.

State tourism departments and private tour companies, such as **TCI**, **Mercury Travels**, **Sita World Tours** and **Thomas Cook India**, offer a wide range of week or longer itineraries and extensive package holidays that make it possible to visit many of the region's best landmarks with ease. Most of these tours are by private coach.

Tourism offices and travel agents who specialize in adventure tours *(see p265)* offer excursion packages in smaller vehicles, including guides and accommodation.

Tickets and Reservations

Ordinary bus fares are slightly higher than passenger train tickets, however, deluxe bus fares are cheaper than first-class or air-conditioned train tariffs. It is important to consider what vehicle you will be travelling in before purchasing your ticket. Ordinary coaches are slow, uncomfortable and usually very crowded. In hot weather, an air-conditioned bus is essential for long-distance travel. Tickets and seat reservations for top-of-the-range buses can be booked in advance.

Clean and comfortable luxury tourist buses

DIRECTORY

State Government-run Buses

Idgah Bus Stop
Agra: Model Town, Idgah Colony.
Tel (0562) 242 0324.

Maharana Pratap Inter State Bus Terminus
Delhi: Kashmiri Gate, Mori Gate.
Tel (011) 296 0290.
W delhigovt.nic.in/newdelhi/dept/transport/tr6.asp

Rajasthan State Road Transport Bus Stop
Delhi: Bikaner House, Pandara Rd.
Map 5 B2. **Tel** (011) 2338 9525.
W indiatransit.com/public_transport/rajasthan_state_road.aspx

Sarai Kale Khan Bus Stop
Delhi: Mahatma Gandhi Rd.
Map 6 F5. **Tel** (011) 2463 8092.

Sindhi Camp Bus Stop
Jaipur: Near Station Rd.
Tel (1800) 200 0103.

Department of Tourism-run Buses

Ashok Tours & Travels
Delhi: Jeevan Vihar Building, 3rd Floor, Parliament St.
Map 1 B5. **Tel** (011) 2374 8165.
W attindiatourism.com

Uttar Pradesh Tourism Department
Tel (0522) 230 7037.
W up-tourism.com

Package Tours

Mercury Travels
Delhi: Jeevan Tara Building, Sansad Marg. **Map** 1 B5.
Tel (011) 2336 2008.
Agra: Hotel Clarks Shiraj, 54, Taj Rd. **Tel** (0562) 222 6531.
W mercury-india.com

Sita World Tours
Delhi: Tower B, Delta Square, Sector 25, MG Rd, Gurgaon.
Tel (0124) 470 3400.
W sitatours.com

TCI
Agra: Hotel Clarks Shiraz, 54, Taj Rd. **Tel** (0562) 222 6521.
Delhi: 520, Udyog Vihar Phase III, Gurgaon. **Tel** (0124) 612 0100.
Jaipur: 19 C, Gopal Bari, Ajmer Rd.
Tel (0141) 236 2075.
W tcindia.com

Thomas Cook India
Agra: Hotel Clarks Shiraz, 54, Taj Rd.
Tel (0562) 285 7777.
Delhi: M 32, M Block Market, Greater Kailash I. **Tel** (011) 4163 4521.
Jaipur: 19 C, Gopal Bari, Ajmer Rd. **Tel** (0141) 510 2344.
W thomascook.in

Travel by Road

Travelling by car is a comfortable and leisurely way to travel within and between the three cities, allowing you to move at your own pace and visit whatever sites you wish along the way. Hiring a chauffeur-driven car makes shopping and sightseeing much easier, as it relieves you of the stress of negotiating traffic and locating destinations. This is often cheaper than hiring a self-drive car. Vehicles can be hired from car rental companies, hotels and taxi stands.

What to Take

If you plan to drive yourself, make sure you bring your international driving licence. It is possible to get a temporary one from the **Automobile Association of Upper India** (AAUI) in Delhi, provided you have a valid driving licence from your own country. However, you may be required to take a driving test.

You should also have a good map or GPS system to help you navigate the often confusing road network. For more information on this see *Directions and Road Signs.*

Rules of the Road

Though there are established traffic rules, such as driving within your own lane and the discreet use of high-beam lights, traffic can be chaotic on Indian roads. All too frequently traffic lights do not function, and though major crossings should have police guiding oncoming vehicles, this is more often the exception than the rule. Bear in mind that there are numerous types of road users, from pedestrians to cyclists, bullock carts and buses. On highways, be wary of trucks that muscle in whenever possible.

There are also some unwritten rules that should be kept in mind. Note that flashing headlights indicates the driver is coming through, not giving you way to overtake. Few road users adhere to staying within their lane, and often illegally overtake from the left side without any warning. Driving through red lights is one of the biggest hazards and the cause of most accidents. Horns are used constantly, even in "No Horn" areas.

Directions and Road Signs

The placement of road signs is erratic and at times they are not in English. Road names have also changed, particularly in Delhi, from the old English names, to names of well-known Indian or international figures. Therefore it is important to carry up-to-date and clear maps for the areas you wish to travel.

Hand-cart prohibited

Bullock-cart prohibited

No horn please

Bicycle crossing

Good maps are available of Agra, Delhi and Jaipur as well as of some of north India's smaller cities and towns. It is best to buy any maps you need before you travel, but you can also purchase them when you arrive in India. If buying before you leave, **Stanfords** is always reliable for quality maps. For Delhi there is an excellent city map available from **Eicher**. Agra and Jaipur also have clear state tourism city maps which display all the major roads and sights. All maps are available in English.

If you are travelling by road between the three cities, it is advisable to acquire a road map of North India from the AAUI. The government **Survey of India** also has a good collection of detailed maps available at their office. These maps indicate lesser known places and various road categories. Road signs of food and bed symbols will inform you of approaching motels and eateries on the highway.

It may also be a good idea to buy a GPS system to help you navigate your way through the crowded streets and highways. **MapmyIndia** offers GPS systems that specialise in India's extensive road network.

Parking

Parking can be a serious problem in busy shopping centres and in the commercial complexes of the three cities. Most parking lots have been

A busy street in Delhi crammed with different modes of transport

redesigned to cope with the increased number of vehicles. Private firms are contracted by the state to ensure car safety and provide parking facilities for a fee of usually around ₹5–20, although sometimes you may have to pay more. You should keep your key but leave your car in neutral gear so that it can be moved back and forth. Make sure the attendant gives you a receipt and check that you pay no more than the amount written on it. In Delhi, Connaught Place and Nehru Place are among several areas that have a tiered and protected car park. The airport, malls and other public places also offer parking facilities in Delhi.

Petrol

Highways and main roads have petrol (gasoline) pumps at regular intervals, usually closer to a town. All fuel stations stock unleaded petrol in an effort to reduce air pollution. Some petrol stations in Delhi (such as **Inter Club** and **Queens Road Service Station**), Agra and Jaipur are open 24 hours along with several situated along highways.

Petrol stations located in cities often have toilets and a telephone booth that only allows local calls. Some service stations also have a shop attached.

Chauffeur-driven Car Hire

Unless you are physically prepared and mentally geared to cope with the driving conditions, you should rent a chauffeur-driven car. The drivers are familiar with Indian traffic rules and regulations, and you will not have to worry about finding somewhere to park either. Taxis with DLY or DLZ number plates can be hired through travel agents, hotels and some taxi stands. They have permits to travel beyond city limits. **Carzonrent** also offers chauffeur-driven cars as well as self-drive options. It is better to get a driver who is familiar with the city you plan to visit. If you are lucky, you may find yourself with a driver who could double up as a guide as well as an interpreter. Opting for a chauffeur-driven car is usually cheaper than hiring a self-drive car. Certain companies require foreign nationals to pay for the driver and car in foreign currency but most are willing to accept payment in rupees after negotiating a per km (0.6 miles) rate payable in cash. Car companies based in Delhi, Agra and Jaipur normally charge a fixed rate for a minimum of 4 hours or 40 km (25 miles), or up to 80 km (50 miles) for 8 hours. Rates differ according to the type of car and where you hire it from.

DLY and DLZ taxis which travel beyond the city limits

Self-drive Car Hire

Self-driving through the crowded and chaotic city streets of India, especially Delhi, is not recommended nor safe. However, if you are determined to drive yourself, there is a good choice of international and local car rental companies in Delhi. Among them, **Hertz** and **International Travel House** offer both self-driven and chauffeur-driven cars, which can be hired through travel counters at large hotels or from tourist offices. Rates are fixed on a daily rental and minimum kilometre basis, with each extra 1 km (0.6 mile) carrying an extra cost. Fuel and other running costs are extra and a security deposit is taken in advance, to be refunded only if there is no damage to the car when you return it.

DIRECTORY

What to Take

Automobile Association of Upper India
C 8, Qutub Institutional Centre, Delhi. **Tel** (011) 2685 2052.
W aaui.org

Directions and Road Maps

Eicher
W maps.eicherworld.com

Stanfords
Tel (020) 7836 1321.
W stanfords.co.uk

MapmyIndia
W mapmyindia.com

Survey of India
Tel (011) 2618 4388.
W surveyofindia.gov.in

Petrol

Inter Club
L1/15 Haus Khas, New Delhi.

Queens Road Service Station
Vasant Vihar, Delhi.

Car Hire

Carzonrent
E 4, Rani Jhansi Rd, Jhandewalan Extn, Delhi. **Tel** (011) 4308 3000.
W carzonrent.com

Hertz
43–44 Westend Green Farm House Rd, Mahipalpur, Delhi.
Tel (011) 4166 7242.
W hertz.com

International Travel House
Agra: **Tel** (0562) 403 0601.
Delhi: **Tel** (011) 4165 9466.
Jaipur. **Tel** (0141) 401 2020.
W travelhouseindia.com

Local Transport in the Cities

There are a variety of local transport options to choose from in Delhi, Jaipur and Agra, ranging from the Delhi Metro, buses and taxis to auto- and cycle-rickshaws. While the Delhi Metro is generally packed with passengers, it offers a faster way to travel, avoiding the busy streets above. The three cities are all notorious for their traffic jams. The narrow lanes in the older sections of these cities are best negotiated by the smallest vehicle possible – a cycle-rickshaw is often the smartest option. Though there is a wide choice of local transport, taxis are generally considered the most comfortable and stress-free way to travel. Most drivers can speak some English.

A CNG powered bus, driving in Delhi

Delhi Metro

Delhi's metro system provides an extensive and relatively cheap service. The network has six lines and an excellent Airport Express service, which provides a faster link between the airport and the city centre than making the journey by road. Delhi's metro network is complemented by a ring railway encircling the city centre, which provides connections with some of the outer boroughs.

Trains run daily from 6am to 11pm, at a frequency of about every 3 minutes in rush hour and every 12 minutes off-peak.

Tickets, in the forms of tokens, Tourist Cards or Smart Cards, are available to purchase from metro stations. A token is valid for a single trip, whereas Smart and Tourist Cards are refillable travelcards that allow multiple journeys.

Buses

Bus services in most Indian cities are never adequate for the large numbers who can only afford this cheap means of travel, and so buses are always crowded. You can buy tickets from a conductor once you have boarded the bus. However, if a bus is full, it will not stop, and so bus stops are usually crowded with waiting commuters who often jump onto the bus while it is still moving.

Delhi has an extremely complex bus network that is often too difficult for visitors to make sense of. Also, the city's bus drivers are notorious for their reckless driving. Even the so-called luxury buses move at a great speed.

If you insist on travelling by bus ask at your hotel or the nearest tourist information centre for advice.

Taxis

The black-and-yellow taxis in Delhi operate within the city limits. Cabs cruise the streets looking for customers, however it is safer to hire one from a taxi stand. There may be taxis waiting at large hotels. These vehicles are always well-maintained with the meters in good working order.

Another popular alternative are the various radio taxi companies such as Mega Cabs (www.megacabs.com) and Meru Cabs (www.merucabs.com), which can be booked by phone or online. Radio taxis do tend to be more expensive than regular cabs, but they are more reliable.

In Agra and Jaipur, taxis don't run by the meter but charge according to distance, a prefixed rate, or, if you want to hire the cab for a longer period, by the day. Your hotel or travel agent can tell you where to find reliable drivers and can give you estimates on what rates you should be paying. Many drivers have an agreement with certain shops who give them a commission if they bring customers willing to spend money, so you must be firm about where you want to go.

Auto-rickshaw, a cheaper travelling option

Auto-rickshaws

Auto-rickshaws are useful for travelling short distances or through crowded localities. The three-wheeled, black-and-yellow or green-and-yellow auto-rickshaws zigzag through the traffic. They offer a noisy, bumpy ride but are still a better

Different vehicles jostling in the streets of Jaipur

Cycle-rickshaws, convenient for covering short distances in inner city areas

option than buses and are cheaper than taxis. In Delhi, vehicles can carry up to three passengers but in smaller towns they are often jammed with people and luggage.

Cycle-rickshaws, Tongas and Tempos

The cycle-rickshaw is the most common mode of transport in small towns and congested older sections of Indian cities. A convenient means of covering short distances, these are most commonly seen in the walled city of Old Delhi. While empty cycle-rickshaws can be easily found and hired in Old Delhi and smaller towns, they are banned from Central Delhi. In Agra and Jaipur, cycle-rickshaws are also the most popular means of local transport.

In small towns, the creaky horse-drawn carriages called *tongas* and *ikkas* offer a leisurely ride. Tempos are wagons with the rear half fitted with seats. They are not very comfortable and set off only when all seats are occupied.

Fares and Meters

All auto-rickshaws and taxis in Delhi have meters but this is not the case in Agra and Jaipur, where fares should be negotiated in advance. In Delhi, you should insist on paying by the meter. Rates for metered taxis start at ₹20 for the fist km (0.6 miles) and then ₹11–13 for every km after that.

Auto-rickshaws charge ₹19 for the initial 2 km (1 mile) and then ₹6.50 for every subsequent km (0.6 miles). There is a 25 per cent surcharge for auto-rickshaws trips made between 11pm and 5am, and for taxi journeys between 10pm and 6am. As rates may change due to increases in fuel prices, it is sensible to use the up-to-date fare chart that auto and taxi drivers always carry to calculate the exact amount owning from the meter reading. Both day and night fares are given separately on either side of the rate chart. Be sure to check the correct column before you pay. There is also an extra charge of ₹7.50 for luggage.

Pre-paid taxi and auto-rickshaw booking booths stand outside railway stations and airports. You pay a fixed amount in advance according to the distance you wish to travel. Ask your hotel or travel agency about how much general rates cost. A receipt is given at the booth, that you must hand over to the driver at the end of your journey. It is not necessary to tip the drivers but any tips will be gladly accepted.

There is no set rate for a cycle-rickshaw ride but ₹5–15 is a fair price. Always negotiate beforehand as cycle-rickshaws tend to over charge tourists. A tip of ₹1–2 is sufficient.

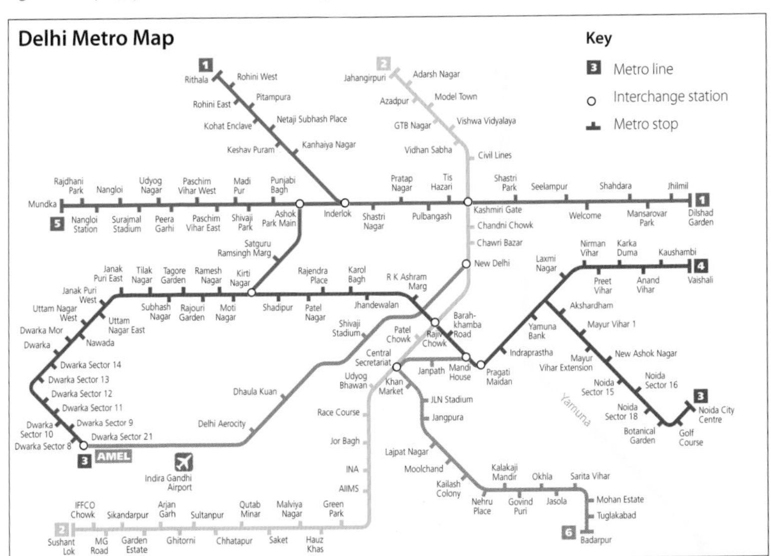

General Index

Page numbers in **bold** refer to main entries.

D

E

K

L

T

U

V

W

Y

Z

Acknowledgments

Dorling Kindersley would like to thank the following people whose contributions and assistance have made the preparation of this book possible.

Contributors

Anuradha Chaturvedi is a consultant on architectural conservation with the Indian National Trust for Art and Cultural Heritage (INTACH).

Dharmendar Kanwar is a well-known travel writer based in Jaipur. She has published several books on the architecture and culture of the region.

Partho Datta teaches Indian history at a college in Delhi University. He is interested in modern urban studies on which he has written several papers.

Premola Ghose is a gifted writer and illustrator of children's books. She is the Programme Officer at the India International Centre, New Delhi.

Ranjana Sengupta is a journalist and author of books on Ajanta and contemporary Indian society. She is currently writing a book on Delhi after 1947.

Subhadra Sengupta is a freelance journalist based in Delhi who writes on travel and tourism for several Indian newspapers and magazines.

Consultants

Ajai Shankar is a senior civil servant with the Government of India and is the Director-General of the Archaeological Survey of India (ASI).

Aman Nath has written extensively on the crafts and architecture of Rajasthan. He is involved in the restoration of heritage properties in this region.

Daljeet Kaur is the curator of the Indian miniature paintings section in the National Museum, New Delhi and has written several books and articles on this subject.

Ebba Koch has travelled extensively in the sub-continent and is an internationally acknowledged expert on the art and architecture of the Indo-Islamic and Mughal periods.

Giles Tillotson is Senior Lecturer in South Asian Art at SOAS (University of London), and the author of books on architecture in India during the Mughal, Rajput and British periods.

Jyotindra Jain is the founder-director of the Crafts Museum, New Delhi, and has authored several books on Indian crafts.

Kishore Singh is one of India's leading travel writers and is with the *Business Standard* in Delhi. He has written several books on Rajasthan.

Kumkum Roy is an Associate Professor of Ancient History at the Jawaharlal Nehru University, New Delhi. She writes for several prestigious academic journals.

Martand Singh is one of the country's best-known experts on textiles. He is based in Delhi and is a founding member of the Indian National Trust for Art and Cultural Heritage (INTACH).
Narayani Gupta is a Professor of Modern Indian History at Jamia Millia Islamia in New Delhi. Her book on the history of Delhi is widely regarded as an authoritative text.
RV Smith is a journalist who writes on the history and legends of Delhi. His column, "Quaint Corner", has been a regular feature in *The Statesman* for over 25 years.
Satish Grover heads the Department of Architecture at the School of Planning and Architecture, Delhi. He has written three seminal books on the history of Indian architecture.

Sunil Kumar is an Associate Professor in Medieval Indian History at Delhi University. He has a special interest in the Sultanate period and is currently writing a book on the subject.

Vijayan Kannampilly is a journalist and painter based in Delhi and has a special interest in Indian design and contemporary art.

Editorial and Design

Publisher Douglas Amrine
Editorial Director Vivien Crump
Art Director Gillian Allan
Senior Managing Editor Louise Bostock Lang
Production Marie Ingledew

Map Coordinator David Pugh.

Revisions & Relaunch Team

Ashwin Raju Adimari, Parnika Bagla, Shruti Bahl, Ipshita Barua, Imogen Corke, Dipika Dasgupta, Nick Edwards, Aditya Katyal, Jasneet Kaur, Sumita Khatwani, Kirit Kiran, Hayley Maher, Sushmita Malaviya, Kiran Mohan, Vandana Mohindra, Casper Morris, Preeti Morris, Nandini Mehta, Janice Erica Pariat, Lucy Richards, Ellen Root, Tara Sharma, Beverly Smart, Anna Streiffert, Avantika Sukhia, Priyanka Thakur, Stuti Tiwari, Deepika Verma, Tanveer Zaidi.

Cartography Assistance

Kishorchand Naorem, Shivanand.
Proof Reader Abha Kapoor.
Fact Checking Ranee Sahney
Indexer Bibhu Mohapatra.

Additional Contributors

Anirudh Goswami, Rani Kalra, Ira Pande, Ranee Sahaney.

Additional Illustrations

Aniket Vardhan, Arun P, Mugdha Sethi.

Additional Photography

Ashwin Raju Adimari, Idris Ahmed, Ipshita Barua, Benu Joshi, Rajnish Kashyap, Aditya Katyal, Mathew Kurien, Anand Naorem, Mugdha Sethi, Anal Shah.

DTP Designers

Shailesh Sharma, Jessica Subramanian,.

Special Assistance

Dorling Kindersley would like to thank all the regional and local tourist offices in Delhi, Agra and Jaipur for their valuable help. Particular thanks also to: Ajai Shankar, ASI, New Delhi; Dr Daljeet, National Museum, New Delhi; Malaynil Singh, TCI; Delhi School of Planning and Architecture; Siraj Qureshi and RVI Singh in Agra

Photography Permissions

Dorling Kindersley would like to thank the following for their kind permission to photograph their products: Preeti Paul. The publishers would also like to thank the following for permission to photograph at their establishments: Biotique, New Delhi; City Palace Museum, Jaipur; Crafts Museum, New Delhi; Gem Palace, Jaipur; Mathura Museum, Mathura; Maulana Abul Kalam Azad Arabic & Persian Research Institute, Tonk; The Next Shop, New Delhi; Ogaan, New Delhi.

Picture Credits

a = above; b = below/bottom; c = centre; f = far;
l = left; r = right; t = top.
The publishers are grateful to the following individuals, picture libraries and companies, for permission to reproduce their photographs:

Alamy Images: Danita Delimont/Walter Bibikow 195tr, dbimages 65tc, 270-271, Dinodia Photos 170tr, Alexei Fateev 14b,Stuart Forster 274tl, Anil Ghawana 242cl, Cris Haigh 285tl, imageBROKER 243br, Martin Lindsay 151b, Alan Moore 294ca; David Pearson 253br; Purepix 2-3, Jan Wlodarczyk 15cl.

Baluchi: 257tr. **B.R. British Library, London:** 47b.
Bobby Kohli: 58 & 59c, 59b, 60 & 61c, 61tr.
Dean K Brown: 82t.

Chopra Films: 213b.
Claridges: 233bl.

Corbis: Danny Lehman 12bl, epa/David Clifford 44cl, Frederic Soltan 185cra; Spaces Images / Bryan Mullennix 14tr. **Crafts Museum, New Delhi, Pankaj Shah:** 90tc, 91cr, 91bc, 91br.

Surya Deogun: 80br, 89cr, 100b, 105cr, 258bl, 265tr.
Diggi Palace: 256br. **DK Classic Asian Cook Book:** 248tc/crb. **DK Picture Library:** Rowan Greenwood Collection 11br. **DN Dube:** 56bl/b, 57cr, 79bc, 174tr, 175t, 176tr/c. **Dreamstime.com:** Antonella865 92; Boonsom 154tr; Jorg Hackemann 126; Milosk50 150; Dmitry Rukhlenko 102; Sergeychernov 15br.

Fotomedia Picture Library: 33tr, 56tc, 58clb, 59tr, 60cb, 109b, 124c (4 pics), 289bl; Aditya Arya: 289br; Akhil Bakshi: 25t, 26bcr, 32br/b, 33b, 36clb, 199b, 283t, 288t/b/bl; Amar Talwar: 64cl, 176b, 245clb, 263b, 290t; Amita Prashar Gupta: 260b; Ashim Ghosh: 25bl, 26bcl, 54b, 62cb, 177b, 272b, 274b, 277t, 295t; Ashish Chandola: 172b; Ashish Khokar: 277c, 291t; Ashok Dilwali: 154b, 174tl, 176tl; Ashok Kaul: 65tl, 219b; Bimla Verma: 24tl, 26t, 27cr, 53bl, 97b, 145bl, 167b, 262br/bcr; BN Khazanchi: 40c, 41br; BPS Walia: 147br, 264c; Christine Pemberton: 19c, 44cl; Dharmendar Kanwar: 260t; E Hanumantha Rao: 22tl/clb/bc, 215trc, 229cb/b; François Gautier: 25b; J Saha: 24b; Jatinder Singh: 24tr; Jitendra Singh: 26bc; Joanna van Gruisen: 22cra/b/bl, 23cra/bl, 52cb, 65ca, 214b, 228cl; M Balan: 37bcl, 173b; Manu Bahuguna: 43b, 75b, 95b, 236br, 267t; Marie D'Souza: 37cr, 184t, 263br; Mathew Titus: 27br; Mohit Satyanand: 268b; MS Oberoi: 26br, 248t; Nagaraja: 215t; Neeraj Mishra: 22cla; Nihal Mathur: 228tr; NP Singh: 36b, 188bl; NPS Jhalla: 262bc; NS Chawla: 31c; Pallava Bagla: 22tr, 23tl/tr/tc/trc, 42t, 214tl; Pankaj Sekhsaria: 173trc; Pradeep Das Gupta: 249tc; Pradeep Mandhani: 65t; Prakash Israni: 21tl, 26cl, 41b, 167tlc, 177bl, 268t; Prem Kapoor: 41c, 42b, 50t, 64tl, 64 & 65c, 65br; Raj Salhotra: 36cla; Ravi Kaimal: 21c; RK Wadhwa: 27cra; RS Chundawat: 22crb, 120b, 214tr, 215b; S Nayak: 172c; S Venugopal: 145c; Sanjay Saxena: 36cl, 149c, 189b; Sanjeev Saith: 141b, 269t/b; Sanjiv Misra: 45t; Shalini Saran: 24c, 32tr, 34cl, 36 & 37c, 41t, 42c, 50br, 53tl, 54 & 55c, 56br, 57br, 58br, 61tl, 67 77t/b, 111b, 118t,156tl, 157b, 177tl, 178b, 220tl; SK Panda: 23cla; Subhash Bhargava: 21b, 27ca, 40t/b, 43c/bl, 54cb, 58cla, 62t, 148b, 168t/cl/b, 169ca/b, 188t, 196c/bl, 204b, 229t, 232c, 248c, 262cr, 267c/b, 268tr; Sudhir Kasliwal: 52c, 191t/b/bl/cl, 199t, 262tr/trc; Tarun Chopra: 53br; Thakur Dalip Singh: 37bc; Toby Sinclair: 22br, 23crb/clb, 37bl, 214cb, 228tl/c/b, 229ca, 264b; TS Satyan: 23br, 80c, 145t, 201b, 232t, 246b (2pics), 249b; V Muthuraman: 245cb;

Frazer & Haws, New Delhi: 122c. **Fredrik & Laurence Arvidsson:** 18, 93t; Ganesh Saili: 105b.

Getty Images: AFP 35bc; Daniel Berehulak 266cr; India Today Group 266bl; JTB Photo 140; Lonely Planet Images 136-137; David Levenson 65crb; Mail Today 242br; Henry Wilson: 216t,236c.

Hotel Pushkar Palace: 236clb.
Idris Ahmed: 10tr, 173crb, 221tr, 258bl. **Indian Accent:** 252tr.
ITC Hotel Ltd. Welcomgroup: 232bl, 233c.

Kainoosh: 252bl.
Kaleva: 255tr.
Kamal Sahai: 49tr/cla, 51tl.
Rajnish Kashyap: 15tl.
Laxmi Vilas Palace: 237cr.

Lonely Planet Images: Andrew Bain 10br; Patrick Horton 122bl.
National Museum, New Delhi: 48t/cl/bl, 49b, 50c, 50cb, 50 & 51c, 51b, 54t, 55t/bl, 57tr, 76tl/tr/ca/cl/bl/br, 145br, 171b; JC Arora: 47t, 58bl, 59bl, 68b, 78tl/tr, 79t; RC Dutta Gupta: 33t, 48cla/clb/br, 48 & 49c, 49tlc/cl/cr, 50b, 51tr/cl, 52t/b, 56t, 58t, 78b, 79c/br. **National School of Drama: 35br. Neemrana Palace Hotels:** 52ca, 53tr, 234b, 243t.

Oberoi Amarvilas: 254tl.
The Oberoi Group of Hotels: 234t. **Otto Pfister:** 172t/bl, 173t/c, 215c, 264t.

P. Roy: 191cr/cb. **Peacock: John Eiberger 256tl. Photolibrary:** Gtw Gtw 194 cl; Imagebroker.net/Gtw Gtw 194br, 194cl. **Photoshot:** VWPics / Lucas Vallecillos 20. **Avinash Pasricha:** 32cla/clb, 32 & 33c, 124b, 286c, 287t.**Press Information**

Bureau: 62 & 63**c**, 63cr.

Radisson Blu Agra: 254br. **Rick's Bar**: 125tr. **Robert Harding Picture Library:** Gavin Hellier 182; John Wilson 193crb.
Satish Sharma: 26 & 27c, 27tl/tc/b, 38bl, 35tl.
Taj Hotels: 232cr, 235tr, 238br, 240tl, 241br, 250br, 251tr, 255br, 257bc.
The Imperial: 230-231, 239tr.
Teen Murti Memorial Library: 60bl/br, 61b, 62ca, 63tc/bl/br, 64cb. **Textile Art Society:** Benoy K Behl 37tc. **Theatre and Television Associates**: Tulsi: Hemant Mehta 263tl.
Courtesy of the Board of Trustees of the V & A Museum: 56cl/ca/cb.
www.nicopix.com / © Nicolas Chorier: 66-67

Works of art have been reproduced with the permission of the following copyright holders:
© National Gallery of Modern Art, New Delhi: 34 & 35 (all pictures except 34cl).

Special Assistance in Photography

Ajai Shankar, Director-General, Archaeological Survey of India, New Delhi; Aman Nath; Anjali Sen, Director, National Gallery of Modern Art, New Delhi; Aruna Dhir, The Oberoi Hotel, New Delhi; Dr Daljeet Kaur, National Museum, New Delhi; JC Grover, National Museum, New Delhi; Jyotindra Jain, Crafts Museum, New Delhi; OP Jain, Sanskriti Museum; Dr RD Chowdhouri, Director-General, National Museum, New Delhi.

Front endpaper: Left: Dreamstime.com: Milosk50 br; Getty Images: JTB Photo tr; Robert Harding Picture Library: Gavin Hellier cl.
Right: Idris Ahmed br; Dreamstime.com: Antonella865 tr, Dmitry Rukhlenko tc; DK Images: Ashwin Raju Adimari clb

Map cover – 4Corners: SIME/Marco Pavan.
Front Jacket and Spine – Alamy Images: Stock Connection Blue c. DK Images: Dinesh Khanna bl.

Every effort has been made to trace the copyright holders, and we apologize for any unintentional omissions. We would be pleased to insert the appropriate acknowledgments in all subsequent editions of this publication.

Further Reading

Architecture

Delhi and its Neighbourhood Sharma, Y.D., Archaeological Survey of India, Delhi 1982.

Delhi, the City of Monuments Dube, D.N. and Ramanathan, J., Timeless Books, New Delhi 1997.

Fatehpur Sikri Brand, M. and Lowry, G.D. (eds.), Marg Publications, Mumbai 1987.

Indian Architecture Brown, P., (2 vols), D.B. Taraporevala Sons & Co. Pvt. Ltd., Bombay 1964.

Mughal Architecture Koch, E., PRESTEL-Verlag, Munich 1991.

Mughal India Tillotson, G.H.R., Penguin, London 1991.

Sacred Architecture Pereira, J., Islamic Books & Books, New Delhi 1994.

Stones of Empire Morris, J., Oxford University Press, Oxford 1983.

Taj Mahal: The Illumined Tomb Begley, W.E., Aga Khan Program for Islamic Architecture, Massachussetts 1989.

The Architecture of India Grover, S., (2 vols), Vikas Publishing House Pvt. Ltd., New Delhi 1981.

The Forts of India Fass, V., Collins, London 1986.

The History of Architecture in India Tadgell, C., Phaidon, London 1990.

The Palaces of India Fass, V. and Maharaja of Baroda, Collins, London 1980.

The Penguin Guide to the Monuments of India (Vol 2) Davies, P., Viking, London 1989.

Culture and Crafts

A Second Paradise Patnaik, N., Sidgwick and Jackson Ltd., London, 1985.

Catalogue of the Crafts Museum New Delhi 1982.

Curry and Bugles Brennan, J., Penguin, London 1992.

Dance of the Peacock Bala Krishnan, U. and Kumar, M.S., India Book House, Mumbai 1999.

The Essence of Indian Art Goswamy, B. N., Mapin International, San Francisco 1986.

Hanklyn-Janklin Hankin, N., Banyan Books, Delhi 1992.

Indian Art Dehejia, V., Phaidon, London 1997.

Indian Painting Randhawa, M.S. and Galbraith, J.K., Vakils, Feffer & Simon Limited, Bombay 1982.

Masterpieces from the National Museum Collection Gupta, S.P., National Museum, New Delhi 1985.

Paradise as a Garden Moynihan, E.B., George Braziller Inc., New York 1979.

The Arts of India Birdwood, G.C.M., Nanda Book Service, Delhi 1997.

The Golden Calm Kaye, M.M. (ed.), Webb & Bower, Exeter 1980.

The Painted Walls of Shekhawati Nath, A. and Wacziarg F., Croom & Helm, London 1982.

The Splendour of Mathura Art and Museum Sharma, R.C., DK Printworld (P) Ltd., New Delhi 1994.

Fiction

A Passage to India Forster, E. M., Penguin, London 1924.

A Suitable Boy Seth, V., Viking, New Delhi 1993.

City of Djinns Dalrymple, W., Flamingo, London 1994.

The Raj Quartet Scott, P., Heinemann, London 1976.

Train to Pakistan Singh, K., Ravi Dayal Publisher, Delhi 1988.

History

A History of India (Vol 2), Spear, P., Penguin, London 1956.

A Princess Remembers Gayatri Devi, Rupa and Co., New Delhi 1995.

Annals and Antiquities of Rajasthan Tod, J., Oxford University Press, Oxford 1920.

Delhi Between Two Empires Gupta, N., Oxford University Press, Delhi 1981.

Delhi and its Monuments Spear, P., Gupta N. and Sykes, L., Oxford University Press, New Delhi 1994.

Freedom at Midnight Lapierre, D. and Collins, L., Vikas Publishing House Pvt. Ltd., Delhi 1976.

India Britannica Moorhouse, G., Paladin Books, London 1984.

Indian Mythology Ions, V., Paul Hamlyn, London 1967.

Jaipur Nath, A., India Book House, Mumbai 1993.

Lives of the Indian Princes Allen, C. and Dwivedi, S. London 1985.

Myths and Symbols in Indian Art and Civilization Zimmer, H., Harper and Brothers, New York 1962.

Symbols in Art and Religion Werner, K. (ed.), Motilal Banarsidass Publishers Pvt. Ltd., Delhi 1991.

The History of India Dodwell, H. H. (ed.), 6 vols, Cambridge University Press, Cambridge 1934.

The Great Moghuls Gascoigne, B., Dorset Press, London 1971.

The Wonder that was India Basham, A.L., Rupa and Co., New Delhi 1966.

Nature and Wildlife

Bharatpur: Bird Paradise Ewans, M., Lustre Press, New Delhi 1992.

Book of Indian Animals Prater, W., Bombay Natural History Society, Bombay 1948.

Book of Indian Birds Ali, S., Bombay Natural History Society, Bombay 1941.

The Garden of Life Patnaik, N., Doubleday, New York 1993.

In Danger Manfredi, P., Ranthambhore Foundation, New Delhi 1997.

Indian Wildlife Israel S. and Sinclair T. (eds.), APA Publications, Singapore 1989.

Nature Watch Singh, K. and Basu, S., Lustre Press, New Delhi 1990.

Birds of India Grewal, B., Local Colour, Hong Kong 2000.

Tigers: The Secret Life Thapar, V., Elm Tree Books, London 1989.

Glossary

Architecture

ashram: hermitage
bagh: garden
bangaldar: curved roof derived from Bengali hut *(see p32)*
baradari: pavilion with 12 pillars *(see p200)*
basti: settlement
charbagh: quadripartite garden *(see p33)*
dharamshala: charitable rest house for pilgrims
ghar: house, crypt *(see p118)*
gali: lane
jaali: carved lattice work on stone screens *(see p31)*
katra: side lane *(see p93)*
khirkee: window
kotla: a citadel or fortified area within a city
kund: pool, tank *(see p121)*
mahal: palace
mardana: men's quarters in a palace
maqbara: burial-palace, mausoleum, sepulchre *(see p146)*
masjid: mosque
mehmankhana: guesthouse
minar: freestanding tower
minaret: tower in mosque for calling the faithful to prayer
pol: gate *(see p192)*
toshakhana: state treasury *(see p194)*
zenana: women's quarters in a palace

Craft and Culture

bandhini: tie-and-dye *(see p90)*
dholak: drum *(see p101)*
Dhrupad: style of North Indian classical music *(see p34)*
ganjifa: set of playing cards *(see p145)*
gharana: school of classical music or dance *(see p34)*
ikat: tie-and-dye yarn woven in a pattern
katha: epic tale *(see p35)*
matka: earthenware pot
mela: fair, fête
patachitra: painted scroll with mythological tales *(see p145)*
phad: painted cloth scroll from Rajasthan *(see p53)*
pichhwai: cloth painting depicting Krishna lore
qawwali: style of devotional Sufi music *(see p34)*
raga: melodic structure with a fixed sequence of musical notes *(see p34)*
rasa: mood; essence *(see p35)*
shahtoosh: a fine shawl, now banned, that can pass through a ring. It is woven from the down of the endangered chiru antelope.
tala: rhythmic cycle of varying beats *(see p34)*
thal-posh: dish cover *(see p195)*

Dress

burqa: concealing cloak worn by some Muslim women
chador: ceremonial pall of cloth or flowers placed over a Muslim tomb *(see p86)*
dhoti: unstitched garment of Hindu men which covers the lower half of the body
gota: gold or silver frill
jootis: slippers *(see p190)*
khadi: hand-woven, hand-spun cloth popularized by Gandhi *(see pp62–3)*
lehenga: flounced skirt *(see p34)*
mukut: crown *(see p190)*
zari: gold thread

Religion

aarti: ritual of Hindu worship
ahimsa: non-violence
amrit: sacred nectar of the gods *(see p29)*
Balaji: one of Hanuman's many names in North India *(see p201)*
bhajan: devotional song *(see p32)*
Chishtiyas: followers of the 12th-century Sufi saint, Moinuddin Chishti *(see p86)*
dharma: duty, calling *(see p145)*
kalasha: urn *(see p119)*
lila: divine sport *(see p167)*
linga: phallic emblem of Lord Shiva *(see p90)*
madrasa: Islamic theological college
Mahabharata: famous Hindu epic *(see p145)*
namaaz: ritual prayers of Muslims
pir: Muslim saint *(see p86)*
puja: ritual prayer *(see p28)*
Ramayana: epic on the legend of Lord Rama
samadhi: memorial platform over site of cremation *(see p101)*
sati: practice of self-immolation by a widow on her husband's funeral pyre
Shaivite: followers of Shiva
tirthankara: Jain prophet
Upanishads: philosophical texts regarded as sacred scripture, dating to the later Vedic age *(see p26)*
Vaishnavite: followers of Vishnu
Vedas: texts codifying Aryan beliefs and principles, these were orally transmitted until transcribed into Sanskrit as the *Rig Veda, Sama Veda, Yajur Veda* and *Atharva Veda (see p26)*
yagna: vedic rite

Miscellaneous

badal: cloud *(see p186)*
bahi khatha: cloth bound account book *(see p190)*
charpoy: string cot
chowkidar: watchman
Doctrine of Lapse: this gave the British the right to take direct control of princely states that did not have an undisputed heir *(see p60)*
haat: open-air market
ikka: pony trap *(see p195)*
jheel: shallow lake
katar: two-sided blade
loo: hot westerly wind that blows over North India from April to June
machan: look-out post
mohur: Mughal gold coin
nawab: a Muslim prince
pachisi: a ludo-like dice game *(see p175)*
Raj: the period of British rule in India *(see pp60–61)*
Satyagraha: a form of moral protest started by Gandhi *(see pp62–3)*
thakur: Hindu chieftain

Road Map of Delhi, Agra & Jaipur